Mirror, Mirror:
Reflections of Self

11-15-2014

Carol,

To one of my favorite
people. I loved watching
you evolve.

Love

[signature]

Mirror, Mirror: Reflections of Self

365-Day Life Journal

Larry Robinson

Cover Design: Swati Patel
Cambridge, Massachusetts, USA
Edited By: Glen Doherty
Lowell, Massachusetts, USA

VagabondView Photography to the byline
- Stefanie Egan
Falmouth,, Massachusetts, USA

Library of Congress Control Number:		2014916944
ISBN:	Hardcover	978-1-4990-7358-4
	Softcover	978-1-4990-7359-1
	eBook	978-1-4990-7357-7

This book was printed in the United States of America.

Rev. date: 10/10/2014

To order additional copies of this book, contact:
Xlibris LLC
1-888-795-4274
www.Xlibris.com
Orders@Xlibris.com
552987

Megan Reiley
Marblehead, Massachusetts, USA

ACKNOWLEDGMENTS

The support I have received while writing *Mirror, Mirror* has been both inspirational and truly heartwarming. You all kept me writing on a daily basis with your wonderful feedback and your tireless support and understanding of how difficult some of the topics covered in *Mirror, Mirror* can be to navigate. I wish I could list every contributor that has commented on the daily posts, but that would be a book all in itself! There are, however, some of you who have committed to writing such great comments that I would like to take this opportunity to place you in this book. Thank you so much, Ti Na Agasshi, Mustafa Khan Charak, Beth Meola, Dorlene Walker, Nancy Asher, Mike Cutler, Mary Singleton, Pamela Jean Marie, John Carlos Balena, Johnny Mello, Jem Rose Mationg, Ronnie Orris Northrop, Marjorie Laderas Tiozon, Darlene Hornblower, Rick Staula, Coyote Karzarinoth, Monica Roychoudhury, Arlene Moran Verano, Mir Muzamil, Darwena Abendan, Jhe Espinosa Oebanda, Brandi Henson, Latoya Brand Parker, Redz Urquiola Vara, Deal Sally, Mir Muzamil, Cindi Beal Campbell, Rohi Dogra, Sincee Ferris, Shantelle Williams, Leo Prabhakar, Yonette Ince, Chris Lawlor, Kerri Lynn Wallace, Barbara Stackhouse, Tina Gonsalvez, David Rhodes, Jarey Dombuce, JoAnne Chisholm-Lake, and Brandon Boston, Robert Lawthorne, Matt Lawthorne (for all your sharing). There are so many, many more, so please forgive me if I failed to recognize you. And remember, *Mirror, Mirror* is for everyone, so you are *all* a part of this.

Also, in order to reach out and continue to include all *Mirror, Mirror's* wonderful friends, and now colleagues, from across the globe, it takes money. If it weren't for the following folks who believed in this project there would be no *Mirror, Mirror*. So from the bottom of my heart, I say, "Thank you!" to Baruch HaLevi, Rick Staula, David Rosenberg, Jay Tomasi, Carol Lena, David Juliano, Sandra Cavallo, Peggy Schrage, Sandra Gandsman (my sister), and Dana Gandsman (my niece), Brian Oppenhiem, Brian and Stephanie Benevento, Jordan Arbit, Laura Morton, Michelle Rosen, and Stephen Chambers. There are so many more who gave in order to help me reach as many folks as we could across the globe, and thanks to your efforts we have done just that! Just to give you an idea as to how successful we have been, I want you to know that as *Mirror, Mirror* goes to print we currently have over 150,000 folks from twenty-eight nations. It truly has become an international family. You all have made this happen!

Lastly, I want to acknowledge the person who has taught me the most in my life, my wife Joyce. Your honesty and integrity have humbled me at times. Your wisdom of life has given me so much "food for thought." Little did you know that you secretly wrote this with me. Love is everlasting!

Larry

INTRODUCTION

Mirror, Mirror: Reflections of Self—365-Day Life Journal is written for anyone who truly wants to understand their own behavior and feelings. The 365 single-day entries included in the following pages have an important message for each one of you. Although you will interpret them differently, they will be understood by all. You see, the truth is that we all feel the same. We all experience the same feelings and we all go through similar situations, no matter what culture, religion, or belief system we affiliate with.

This is your opportunity to really help yourself. Open each day with the appropriate date and read the daily entry. Take your time, and while you are reading make a conscious effort to allow yourself to focus on the particular aspects of each entry that relate to you and your life or the lives of family members and friends who you know and love. And if time permits, jot down some notes as you answer the questions or assignments asked in each entry. Since we are going to be together for a whole year, your notes will come in handy the deeper we get into your life change.

The point of *Mirror, Mirror* is to change all of our lives for the better. And if you follow the book faithfully for the entire year (you can skip a few, but just a few), you will see a definitive change in the way you see yourself, your life, and the lives of others. *Mirror, Mirror* is about positive change, so dare yourself to make that change!

This book is also fun. Do not take anything written as too serious, for it is meant to stimulate, not annihilate you. I do not really like the idea of self-help books. I would rather call this type of book a "help yourself" book. If you really want to change your life, then help yourself to the rich content that you will find within these pages. Even if you think that some of this doesn't apply to you, you'd better think twice, for while we all have different acts we are in the same play.

Since this book deals so much with the subject of personal change and growth, I have included for you "The Stages of Change" as a guide for your use.

The following steps will help you to see where you are in the process of change.

Denial: The First Stage of Change

When we are faced with looking at ourselves we tend to want to turn things around so that we can confidently find someone else to shoulder the blame for our bad behavior. "*You* made me act that way" is a typical statement we might make. Others, like "There is nothing wrong with *me*" or "It is not *my* fault," seem to pervade our thinking as well. Our defense systems rush to the front of our brains to prevent us from imperfection. If we let any knowledge in, then all our fears from childhood will be confirmed. We were not good enough!

Brain Awareness: The Second Stage of Change

After so many repetitions of the same behavior without any difference in our thinking, we begin to realize that something is off and maybe it isn't the other person. Something *is* beginning to happen. Our denial is beginning to weaken. Our repetitive behavior is not working the way it used to and there is a gnawing feeling inside of us that sends us the message that it is something that *we* are doing that is causing this pain. It becomes like a gut feeling that we cannot get away from. As we begin to analyze our own behavior, we begin to understand cause and effect. Now, in our minds things seem to become clearer. The way we are behaving can have a negative effect on our lives. Remember, this is all just beginning to become conscious to us.

Confusion: The Third Stage of Change

Now that we have accepted the fact that we were in denial and that we intellectually understand that we created the behavior we disliked, then what happens next? The old system of behaving doesn't seem to work any longer, yet we have nothing to replace this behavior with! We are now thrown into a state of confusion. We cannot move forward without the security of new behavior. What will happen? We retreat to our old behavior with a sense of defeat. Before we understood our actions we were often unhappy but ignorant to what caused this unhappiness. Now that we are aware of this unhappiness, we become stuck in a limbo of fear and anxiety as we cannot move forward. We do not know the answer to change.

Confusion is our hardest state to face. It causes us to flip-flop back and forth between stages 1 and 2 without mercy. We can numb ourselves with various addictions or habits to keep down the anxiety, but to no real avail!

Heart Awareness: The Fourth Stage of Change

What are we going to do? We feel so confused since nothing seems to go right for us, and while we do understand why, we keep up the repetition of negative behavior, but this doesn't appear to work either. Still, each time we go through a repetition with that knowledge of failure, something inside of us begins to understand. At a much deeper level than our intellect allows for, we begin to know what *will* work. We begin to feel differently, for now we can no longer fool ourselves with our distorted thinking. Our hearts can feel the truth! We are not just observing our behavior, we are feeling it! Do you know that feeling inside that tells you "I am beginning to understand"? The seeds of change are beginning to take hold!

Acceptance: The Fifth and Final Stage of Change

Now there is no question about what we are experiencing. We aren't even that tuned in anymore to the change. When we stop and look, we can see and feel what the other person is saying to us. It is usually other people who say, "Do you know that you do not yell anymore when I confront you?" We feel the acceptance in our heart and we now know that we can be in control of this behavior!

These are the "Stages of Change." There will be times in this process where we will regress, but our new behavior will prevail because we know that we are fighting our resistance. We can change!

You will also find illustrations, photography, sketches, cartoons, poems, and witty and wise comments from people all over the world. The talent is amazing and their efforts are so meaningful.

Mirror, Mirror needs to be used over and over again, for it is so easy for us to forget its lessons. It is the type of book that we will read as long as it takes to achieve the success that you want. I know I certainly grew a lot writing it.

—Larry

ABOUT THE AUTHOR

Larry Robinson is a renowned psychotherapist and life counselor with over thirty-five years of experience counseling children, families, adolescents, couples and relationships in the Greater Boston area. Larry holds a Master of Education in Counseling degree from Boston University and is a Clinically Certified Forensic Counselor and a certified divorce mediator. A native of the seaside community of Swampscott, Massachusetts, Larry's allegiance to his beloved North Shore brought him back to the region in 2004 after twenty-five years of private practice in metro-Boston. Larry is the founder of Mindful Thinking, a reality-based coaching and therapeutic practice that focuses on Change and living in the Now. Larry currently resides in Lynn, Massachusetts with his wife Joyce and their dogs Lola and Henry, and cat, Sweetie.

Stephanie Cavallo
Falmouth, Massachusetts, USA

"Our past does not predict our future. Yes, we can look back at our past, but let us not make the same stupid mistakes."

—John Carlo Balena, Philippines

JANUARY 1

Why can't we be content with who we are in life? Are we destined to remain stuck in the thinking that we are not good enough in our work and personal life? Do we give up too easily and then begin to think, "What's the use?" Where do you think your motivation is supposed to come from? We can wait and wait for it to show up, but it will not unless we produce it. It really isn't true that someone else can motivate us. Yes, we can be given the "motivation bug" by someone else, but it will quickly disappear if we do not run with it. This is about you and your life, and waiting for something to happen to propel you to your next level in life is wasting time. It actually becomes an exercise that is only a "mind game," and not one of action. So often we want to dwell in our past and we become fearful of our future because we do not have the strength to activate the present. The present is where our life *is*, not the past or future.

Are you mindful of your present? Do you see yourself clearly? If you were asked to describe yourself, how would you do it? If there are a lot of negatives, then you are really not describing you, but rather what your mind tells you is you. Remember that your mind can be your enemy without you even knowing it! If you listen to the ramblings inside your head, you will be frozen, either in the past or in creating a negative future for yourself. You are not alone in this futile place. Unfortunately, you have too much company. So how do you move forward with your life?

It is necessary for us to accept who we are and where we are in life. You might not like where you are, but wishing and hoping for a better life is just wishing and hoping! You cannot change if you do not accept where you are! So many of us detest the life we have, and because we have put such a negative spin on it, there is no way we can overcome that much negativity. We end up either defeated before we start change or so overwhelmed with where to begin that we do not start it at all!

New year, new effort! This effort can be yours if you truly want to change your life. Do not think for one minute that this is easy. No one ever told us that life was easy and that change was just a matter of the direction we took our life in. Change is a process, and motivation does not fall from the sky! It comes from being so sick and tired of the same patterns in life that we will either sink so low to the bottom that the only place we have to go is up, or we will get angry at the self that is holding us back! You are not your history! Get angry and decide that "I am going to defy the self that says I am not good enough! My motivation will come from being too easy on myself!"

It is too easy to beat oneself up. That is easy. The hard part is to stop! The first step is to defy your mind! Begin to climb the steps to success!

Assignment: List the issues that you want to work on this coming year. Be honest with yourself but do not be too hard on yourself either.

_____

_____

_____

_____

_____

_____

_____

_____

_____

_____

_____

January 2

We all look in the mirror, for there is no way to avoid it! What do you see when you look? Do you see a kind, loving person who appreciates life? Can you see your features and how beautiful they are? Smile. Do you see a happy person full of life and joy? Do you see your warmth and kindness? Don't we wish we saw this every time we saw a reflection of ourselves? Unfortunately, we do not!

Do you know that your looks do not change every day? So how can you like what you see on Monday and hate what you see on Wednesday? How long have you been doing this to yourself? And oh, do not think that men escape this torture, because many men see in themselves the same things women see. Are we people who judge ourselves by how we look rather than who we are inside? Look in the mirror right now. What do you see?

Can we get past the outside of ourselves and see the inside? That is what determines what we will see in the mirror. Oftentimes our body image appears to take on our inside self, and the inside self is about our emotional beauty. You do not have to be one of the select beauties on the outside to have a beautiful inside.

So what determines the inside beauty and who we are? It's when we feel love and compassion for our fellowman; when we stop the endless judging of other people; when we stop talking behind people's backs and stop lying. This helps determine how we see ourselves. There is some part of us that cannot fake when we look in the mirror, and maybe that's our true self that doesn't allow us to hide.

When someone with an eating disorder looks in the mirror they see too much weight, even though they are either bone thin or just the right weight. Why? Because they carry so much negativity that they cannot see clearly.

Assignment: Test yourself. Do something kind for the next couple of days and check yourself out. You will begin to see the beauty inside you, and that will reflect in the mirror that controls your life. Beauty is only skin deep, but real beauty is a light that is always shining!

LARRY ROBINSON

JANUARY 3

Are we victims of this life? Do we feel like we have been singled out to deal with the pain while others get away scot-free? Or are we just doomed? How often do we think that life is unfair and we have been given the boot when it comes to being successful?

These are questions that so many of us ask ourselves, but this is a side of ourselves we'd rather not expose. It is like when we are in a bad relationship and it ends. We would rather stay in it than be alone. Of course we are going to pretend everything is fine, but inside we again feel like the victim. We could have ended it, but waiting caused us to be in pain. How about the promotion we got passed over on or the school we got rejected from? We see ourselves as victims of society and of other people, and we feel like everyone makes it but us!

No, no, no! We are not victims, but we do have a negative attitude about life, and we either hide it inside or we spread our negativity all over the place. How are we ever going to get through this piece of our life journey?

This is only about you, not the rest of the world. Who have you been? Are you brave enough to admit how you have seen yourself and your future? It is so hard to be honest, but today you can use *Mirror, Mirror* to begin a new day by admitting who we have been and what we can do in order to rise above the junk we think about ourselves. You are only who you make yourself be!

Think about your attitude, for you wake up to it every day. Look around your room and your house. Is it messy? This is how you see yourself first thing in the morning. Is this is a great way to start your day, in a mess? You can and will do better!

Today you can begin to clean up your life. Why are you still so pissed that you are blaming someone else? Get over that one! *You* are in charge of your own life!

Assignment: List in order the things about your life that have made it difficult for other people to communicate with you. Are you defensive, shutdown emotionally? Think hard about this one!

LARRY ROBINSON

JANUARY 4

Are you truly an honest person? Do you tell other people the truth at all times when you are asked questions you know will be confrontational? Do you believe that you can get away with it by rationalizing that you do not want to hurt anyone's feelings? Do you believe that you are honest with your friends and family, or are you the type of person who is either causing conflict or avoiding it? What happens when you get caught in an omission or lie? How do you explain your behavior?

We are all guilty of omissions and little lies at times. They suck up our positive energy and leave us emotionally drained.

Do you exaggerate a story in order to impress others, or can you be truly honest about who you are? Sometimes we are so afraid that we will not be cared about that we invent a different person, only to be called a fraud when we are found not to be telling the truth. Why does our false self emerge to screw up potential relationships?

If you do not start off honest, how do you know whether you will be believed or not later on in the relationship? Placing doubt in someone is truly the most uncomfortable feeling for both people. The person you try and impress will love you but will not necessarily trust you.

You, the person who has invented the false self, well, this cannot be your first time, so the pattern is already there for you and it does not just disappear because you want it to! Take time to really know the other person and allow for them to know you. Life cannot transform itself into your dream just because you want it to. Start to be honest with those around you and understand that even though family and friends will still love you, you need to be able to handle the consequences when you are truthful with them.

Honesty doesn't grow on trees, it happens when we are children. And depending upon what we observe in our home, well, that will determine how truthful we are, first to ourselves and then to others.

Question: In what ways have you been dishonest with yourself? How has that affected your relationships with others?

January 5

Where is your heart today? Did you wake up and feel its warmth, or did you go to bed cold and angry? How often do you shut your heart down in order to not feel its pain? There is no way to avoid "heart pain" unless you pick up an addiction. Alcohol, drugs, sex, and food—they just cover the pain for short bursts, but then it returns. That is how we become addicts.

God, what a hard time we give ourselves trying to avoid pain. The things we set up to avoid the pain cause pain all in themselves, and so we are packing pain onto pain. Great! It is so easy for us to become addicts. We don't realize that when we are kids and we have heart pain we pick up addictions before we are even thirteen. We think we are *cool,* but our hearts know differently. When we believe in our minds that we are forgotten, blamed, or made fun of, our mind turns against us and says, "Drown those feelings and do not care anymore."

You have to face the heart pain; that's all there is to it! Heart pain is something we grow from when we identify what it really is. Relationships cause heart pain in that they break our hearts, but we have to look at who we choose and why it is always someone who will step on our heart.

This is not new! Remember, our hearts got stepped on when we were children. It is all we know. Stop and look inside yourself before you repeat this dynamic again. If it is a parent who does this to us and continually makes us feel like we're not good enough, it's a safe bet they will always do this! It is you who goes back for more pain.

You cannot change another person; you can only change your reaction to them! Tonight maybe you will go to bed with a warm heart because you finally took care of you! Stay away from poison; it kills!

Question: What traumatic event in your life caused your heart to feel pain? Did you grow from it or are you still obsessing about the what-ifs?

LARRY ROBINSON

JANUARY 6

What does courage mean to you? Are you someone who believes they have it? Do you see yourself as a courageous person or doing courageous things in life? Try to remember the most courageous act you've done. How old were you when the event or deed occurred?

Have you been courageous since? Courage is only up to you to define in your life.

So many of us think that being courageous means running into a burning house to save someone, or stopping a robbery. Some might say these people are courageous, but they are more than that, they are heroes, and we are not talking about that. No, we are talking about the kind of courage you have. Do you let others do your dirty work for you? Are you someone who would rather avoid a conflict than face one? Do you think about confronting your parents, spouse, partner, or boss and becoming a "want to want to" person? That person takes no action, they only think about the deed. Sometimes we spend so much time talking about it in our heads or "bleeding" to our friends about it that we actually believe we have dealt with the issue.

Do you hide from confrontations or agree with someone because you really don't have the courage to stand up for yourself? Ask yourself why. Do you tell yourself you're lazy? Well, lazy is only a block to protect us from courage.

How do you obtain courage? Well, it isn't something you can buy!

It is something that is inside of you, and it is called "self-esteem." So many people wonder why they feel bad about themselves, but if they'd stop and look again they would realize that they have the chance to work on it. And saying how you feel is not the problem here! Dealing with the consequences is.

We are afraid of others' reactions. If they are people who love you, they will listen. You might not like their reaction, but if the relationship has meaning you will both get over it. And as far as confronting someone you don't know? Well, why would you really care about what someone you don't really like thinks about you? This is all left over from childhood—"like me, like me"—enough! If you do not take risks in your life, then this is going to be as good as it gets! You might surprise yourself and break out of the half-empty you!

Assignment: List some of the things that you could do to make you a better person in life. Do not worry about whether you can fulfill this now or not. The idea is to start thinking this way. Do you see yourself as a person with courage?

_____

_____

_____

_____

_____

_____

_____

_____

_____

_____

_____

_____

LARRY ROBINSON

JANUARY 7

Half empty? Half full? How do you really *see* life? Are you one of those people who put on a good face to the world while inside you feel horrible and hopeless? How many secrets do you keep so that people will think that you have it together? But *you* know what you really feel.

We do not learn this behavior as adults. We learn it way back in our childhood when we have no defenses to fight others' negativity. We learn through our parents' low self-esteem that they cannot see us as better. Believe it: some parents don't even want you to do better than they have, for that just points out their failures. Have you ever heard the saying "I want you to do better than I did in life"? *Bull!* What they're saying is they want you to do well in life and succeed, but not *be better*!

Be different from them and watch for the part of you that is most like their worst personality trait. Women have their mothers as role models, and men have their fathers. You cannot have a parent of the opposite sex as your role model no matter how close you are to them. Genetics interferes.

Half full! So often we do not look at what we have accomplished, but rather at what we have not done. How do you expect to see life in a positive way if you are stuck in the negativity of what hasn't happened? There is not one of us who is a complete failure. You have to take the time to look closely at what you have been capable of accomplishing and then build on it! It does not matter how small it is, it still counts!

This is where you start, and the first thing you need to look at is your bedroom. Is it a horrible mess or is it clean? How you get up in the morning will sometimes depend on your surroundings. Clean is clean, dirty is dirty. Your negative mind is very attached to dirty.

Assignment: Sit down and make a list of all the things you have done well and those that you still need to do. Do not worry about how many things are on your list. Just begin to chart out what you can do. If you try to do too much at once you will likely give up, so make it one goal at a time and start with the easiest!

LARRY ROBINSON

JANUARY 8

Are you an "escape artist" or a person who stands up and starts a fight over the slightest incident that hurts your feelings? Do you ever find yourself "spacing out" while in a discussion or even a heated argument that feels like it is ripping you apart? How old is this issue in your life? My hunch is that it goes way back into your childhood and that you did this with your parents when you were being yelled at.

It's almost as if you found a "wormhole" into an alternate universe where you could just about hear what they were lecturing you about or yelling at you over, but you were in your world where there was peace and quiet. You could fantasize anything in that world, and often when you were asked if you were listening you could repeat word for word what they said. What great manipulation!

Now, perhaps you are the "heated up" person who jumps into fights as if you are trying to win a world title. Every little thing gets your body heated up. Do you find yourself sweating a lot or crying at the drop of a hat? This tells us that you are full of anger, and that anger can sometimes come out of your body very quickly. Anger is a "fire" feeling, and because water puts out fire, what are tears made out of? That's right, water! And the same goes for sweating. The anger just cannot be contained! But this does not stop the fight. It just gives you an added advantage. It isn't even as if you can stop the anger from coming. Do you remember standing in front of a screaming parent and crying? Why were you crying? It wasn't because you were so sorry over the "crime" you didn't commit, it was because you were outraged at being reprimanded or punished when you did not feel you were guilty!

Neither of these forms of behavior work. One leaves you always holding the bag while the other leaves you impossible to deal with.

Keeping yourself present and not going into your "defense mode" is the idea. And how do you keep yourself present in these dangerous circumstances? Breathe! Yes, that's right, take a deep breath and allow yourself to be present so that you have a voice in the dispute. We all know when we screw up, so taking responsibility isn't a sin. And listening to someone else's feelings will not kill you. You are still a good person, just one with bad behavior!

Question: How well do you deal with your anger? Explain!

_____

_____

_____

_____

_____

_____

_____

_____

_____

_____

_____

_____

LARRY ROBINSON

January 9

I t is that tiny little feeling inside of us that starts to warn us that it is beginning to happen. It starts out as a queasy (uncomfortable) feeling in our stomach that begins to grow as we start our day. Perhaps you have it right now. It does not like to be interrupted and has set up camp inside of you.

This is *anxiety* and it has come to mess with you! It shows no mercy and it does not pick and choose who it attacks! It attacks all of us at one time or another, and some of us live with it as if it were our roommate—a roommate, mind you, that has no immediate intentions of moving out!

This is anxiety and it can screw us up for life if we do not get in control of it. Sometimes we do know what causes it, while other times we have no clue as to why it is there. It can come in waves or in little tiny bubbles inside of us. Anxiety has no friends except fear and anger, and we often do not even get to what it really is that is scaring us, for it is overpowering!

We need to spend more time on this issue, for it has consumed our minds at times, often leaving us feeling sick and unable to function. It is the one issue that is the most difficult for us to overcome. In fact, just trying to overcome it can often cause more anxiety. What then is the solution to this menace inside of us?

We must be willing to explore what is going on in our lives at the time we begin to recognize its ugly existence. We cannot let it rule us, for if it takes over our day is ruined and we hide from life. "Hiding from life," now that's an interesting thought. Is that really what this is all about? When we hide from our issues they begin to cook inside us. Anxiety is a "hot" feeling, not a cold one. We begin to cook our issues, and the end result is nothing but a big juicy bowl of anxiety!

This is our beginning lesson in learning to fight back and win over it. Tomorrow we begin to define the different kinds of anxiety and where they come from. Let us take this very important issue and tell it to get lost once and for all!

Assignment: List in order of intensity things that make you anxious.

LARRY ROBINSON

January 10

There are so many different ways in which we experience anxiety that it would be impossible to describe all of them. And the reason for this is that anxiety is really unique to each one of us. But there are certain generalized types that we can all identify with.

The first type of anxiety is that which is related to the unknown. We can focus on what is to come in our future and that causes us to be afraid in the present. Many times, when we become anxious about the future, we are "predicting" a negative outcome. The what-ifs overcome us and we begin to fantasize worst-case scenarios in our heads. And the more negative scenes we create, the more anxious we become! We create a self-defeating attitude, and now we are frozen by our anxiety. Any sense of reason is wiped out and we fall victim to anxiety's power.

There is another type of anxiety that we do not like to identify. It is the type that comes with telling a lie. We are basically good and honest people, but there are times when we do not want others to find out something about us that we feel ashamed of. We cover this shame with a lie. Now we have "double anxiety" because we fear both the exposure of the lie and the underlying reason that we lied in the first place. One way that we protect ourselves is to cause a fight or argument to keep the attention away from the lie. This type of anxiety eats at our soul, for we are deliberately being deceptive. The only relief we get is by exposing ourselves to the truth!

Fear of failure is another form of anxiety that can actually predict doom. We become so obsessed with doing things "right" that we end up doing it wrong! How many times have you talked yourself into believing that you are stupid and then freeze when confronted with the task at hand? Humiliation always winds up being the end result.

Assignment: Take some time and make a list naming the ways in which you become anxious. The more aware we become of the instances in which we know we experience anxiety, the more likely we are to understand the other types of anxiety we experience that do not yet have the label "anxiety" attached to them in our minds. And remember, if someone tells you they do not experience anxiety, then they are not looking at their own truth!

_____

_____

_____

_____

_____

_____

_____

_____

_____

_____

_____

_____

_____

_____

January 11

Are you a selfish person? Are you the type of person who is always reminding others about what you have done for your family, friends, or even strangers on the street? Do you consider yourself someone who puts others before him/her and does not feel taken advantage of? Do you see yourself as doing "God's work" and are humble about it, or do you have to let people know that you are doing it for "him"?

Are there truly selfless people in this world, or do we all have something that we believe we are doing in order to get some sort of salvation in return?

This is a very difficult topic, and *Mirror, Mirror* does not want to offend anyone who truly believes this, but we all have sin. If we didn't, we would not be able to exist in this world, for there is no such thing as perfection.

Perfection is something that someone laid on us early in our childhood. If a child is perfect, that means he/she would have to have perfect parents. Don't think so. Perfection is God or whatever your faith determines, but that is not us! We are all flawed, and if you meet people along the way of your life journey who profess to be perfect, run fast, for they are deceiving you! Name one perfect person you know!

We all need to strive for perfection, but if we achieved being that perfect person in this life we would be sitting at God's right-hand side. We are all made human, and who has the right to demand perfection from us? Not even God does that. He accepts us for who we are and loves us equally. And if you don't believe in God, that's fine, you still have the same issue as the rest of us.

There is no perfection. How many of us felt like such a disappointment to our parents because we were not perfect? Were they? Live by your own standard, and do not try to live by anyone else's or you will fail! We are who we are, and there is nothing that says that we cannot do better, but those people who have a "better than thou" attitude are selfish, for they decided to become our judges. We have a hard enough time with our own judgments, let alone those of others.

If you truly accept yourself and believe that you are doing your very best, then you have received your salvation here on earth. You know who you are!

Assignment: Make a list of the imperfections about your life that can drive you crazy.

_____

_____

_____

_____

_____

_____

_____

_____

_____

_____

_____

_____

_____

LARRY ROBINSON

January 12

Do you apologize for everything even if it isn't your fault? Are you always feeling like you have to take care of everyone while you never ask anyone for help? Are you the one in the family who gets burdened with your parents, with your siblings always knowing that you will take care of everything while they do nothing? Don't you want to scream at the world to let you be when your phone keeps ringing, and there are always people dropping in without prior notice? And no matter what you need at the time, you drop everything for someone else? *This is sick!*

Once again, you are the victim of your own life. You look and feel worn out, but you wait for someone, anyone to notice. And when finally asked if you're okay, you say, "Oh yes! I'm fine."

Ask yourself, "Why do I do this? Why is my head filled with complaints while I'm smiling on the outside?" You have the "martyr syndrome." Who else in your family has it? Look at your father or mother and see which one of them you followed. Are you repeating their life and you don't even know it? Would the world fall apart if you started to take care of yourself? *Doubt it!*

But who would you be if you let go of this role? It is time to reidentify yourself and want more out of your life. If you think this is selfish, then look around you. There are certainly other people who can give but who also still have the ability to look out for themselves. You have to be willing to delegate responsibilities and give up your role as the only one who can do it! You don't even know if others resent you over this.

You see, there is no "fix" to this mindset, just an ability in yourself to either accept who you are and quit the complaining or begin to take charge of your own life and decide what you can do or no longer want to do.

Remember that you are in control of your own behavior!

Question: How would you see yourself if you didn't need to be in control all of the time? Does being in control of others or situations make you feel like a stronger person?

LARRY ROBINSON

January 13

Why don't we let go of the past? We seem to hold on to it as if it is our punishment in life. So many of us are always going "back there" and blaming either ourselves or others for the misery we've experienced. "If only . . ." is our daily prayer and we cannot seem to get past that, or do we really want to?

What would happen if we decided to learn from our past instead of continuing to live it over and over again? We would have to stop and really understand that the only true victims in life are those who have been seriously injured, raped, robbed, or murdered. Many of the rest of us have become victims of our own fear. How many of us hold on to past bad relationships because we fear being hurt again. We then begin to measure everyone else to that person, who by the way, was no "day at the beach" when it came to respecting us.

Are we afraid to grow? Do we even know where to begin? It is not as hard as we think, but in order to change we must leave our "I want to change" behind. That is a theory, not *action*. Wanting something means taking charge! If you cannot do this on your own and need coaching, then just don't sit there and wait for someone to show up. Find that coach!

We have given ourselves enough excuses. What are we waiting for, "snow in the summer"?

Question: What is it that you would truly like to change about you and the way you live your life?

LARRY ROBINSON

JANUARY 14

What causes us to be isolated and lonely? We say that we want friends and a relationship with someone, but we remain waiting as if it's supposed to drop out of the sky and automatically bring us what we need. Sadly, this is *not* the case. So why are you, at your age, still waiting and looking for that feeling of "wow!" Is this only in your fantasy? Or do you *really* believe that if you sit by yourself most of the time you'll somehow be "blessed" with your dream?

Dreams do not just happen. We *make* them real! And every one of us has the ability to make a dream of ours come true, just as long as it's one that is based in reality. Now, maybe we are afraid to face reality because it then becomes "work" and we are forced to put ourselves "out there" and run the risk of facing rejection. But so what? If someone doesn't want us, it's really only our ego that feels rejection, and that's because we've convinced ourselves that we normally don't put our feelings on the line so quickly. But that's fine, we can get over that. And it's okay, too, to be tentative, just as long as you understand that no one is going to come falling out of the sky to you at this point in life. You have to put yourself out there!

And if you have just read this and are saying, "Bull! Who would want to be my partner or friend?" then start by talking yourself through your own bull. When you see how many excuses you've made for yourself, you'll begin to see that it's your own stubbornness that has caused you to still be sitting and waiting.

Question: List the excuses you make for yourself about why things go wrong for you.

_____

_____

_____

LARRY ROBINSON

JANUARY 15

A re you always struggling with who you are and who you want to be? Are you truly satisfied with yourself and your career and your relationships? Do you fantasize about what it would be like if you weren't poor or stuck in a rut or even frozen, with the prospect of changing your life? Are you a "wannabe" rather than a "doer," and "well done is better than well said" is *not* your motto? Well, is it?

Why are you holding yourself back from your life? Do you think you are not capable of doing more and doing better for yourself? Are you too comfortable with your complaints about life to change it? Are you part of a family system that did not work on improvement and stayed attached to a system that kept them wanting more, but were never able to achieve more?

Well, it's time to look at where you are and why you are still there. You stopped believing that you could do more. Do not look back at any school failures, for they do not really represent who you are today! Who knew what education meant if it was not really stressed at home, or if, on the other hand, it was stressed too much and you rebelled by screwing up. We do that at times because we are angry and afraid, afraid that we cannot do better. Bull!

You are as smart as you want to be, and do not let anyone take that away from you. If you are content with your life, then there is no reason to read on. But I doubt it. Who can be content with not being able to better themselves or provide adequately for their family?

You are really the only one who is holding yourself back. Get away from those people in your life who are always being negative about where they are in life and do nothing about it. Get away from family members who believe that you cannot do better than they did. Remove your negative voice and replace it with a desire to do better, and begin to think in terms of where you are in the present and where you want to be in the future.

This is your life! You have one shot at it! Do not waste it by dwelling on terms like "if only" and "I could have, should have, would have," because those are only excuses for you. And do not let finances stop you either, for where there is enough will there is a way. Now or never!

Question: What are the issues that you, personally, dwell on?

_____

_____

_____

_____

_____

_____

_____

_____

_____

_____

_____

_____

_____

_____

LARRY ROBINSON

Looking in the Mirror

By Aaron Alcoreza Riego
Candelaria, Quezon, Philippines

Looking in the mirror
Staring at your reflection
Afraid to go outside the door
For you have not finished getting ready.

Examining every line and wrinkle
Complaining: "Why don't I have dimples?"
Comparing yourself to others
I am not good enough, they're always better.

Lack of self-confidence
Wanting to feel better
All your life, you were criticized
No worth, no price.

Why let anyone do you wrong?
Dominate you,
Why let anger
Put you in danger?

Stop comparing yourself to others
For there always will be a person who is better
Compare yourself to who you were in the past
And see if you improve and are better than before

As you stare at your reflection
Be Positive. Accept every rejection.
For it will not just bring you peace,
It will strengthen you. Your confidence will increase.

As you look in the mirror
Let everything be clearer
Stop focusing on what you cannot do
And believe that God has a better plan for you!

January 16

How do you define living a "moral life"? Do you believe that you live up to who you say you are and follow your belief system? Do you have a strong belief system, or do you sometimes feel like you are all over the place in your beliefs? Do you believe one thing one day and then another day something else, or are you a rigid person who cannot accept others who view life differently?

We want to believe that we can accept everyone, but do we? Do we hide inside ourselves with prejudices because for the life of us we cannot tolerate or understand how others can be the way they are? Do we judge before we understand and then cannot let go of our judgments?

How did we become so small-minded when as children we basically did not discriminate until someone made fun of another who looked different or spoke differently or was not "cool"? In order to feel accepted we "followed the leader" and shunned someone whom we had nothing against just to be part of a bigger picture.

Does this way of behaving go along with your moral belief system? Are you a hypocrite when it comes to loving somebody by acting one way yet feeling another? Do you believe that we all have these prejudices, or are they just the ideas put into us by our parents or the surroundings that we grew up in?

It is so important in this world to begin to understand that people are not just good or bad, but *different* from one another.

How did your parents see life? Are you similar to them, or have you rejected everything they stood for and gone in the opposite direction? Do you judge their belief systems as negative and yours today as better? So much of who we become is a reaction to who our parents were. Have we done what they did and judged their beliefs as wrong rather than try to understand what they were taught? Can we even answer this question?

In your life journey, you need to define *you*, not through your past, but from what you need to uncover from it today. This is your journey!

Assignment: List some of the roadblocks that you let stay in your life that get in the way of progressing on your journey.

LARRY ROBINSON

January 17

Would you consider yourself a grateful person? Do you look at your life and what you have been given and feel thankful for whatever it is? Are you always looking at other people's images and wish you were them or have whatever they have? If this is the case, then do you think you are grateful?

So often nothing seems enough for us and we are always lamenting about what we do not have. We look at our family or our spouse and believe that they could make so much more of themselves, and how much prouder we'd be of them if they did. Of course you do realize that this thinking is really about us, not them.

Do we give off a vibe to our children that they need to be better? Do we teach them about gratefulness or are they envious of others too and always want more? Monkey see, monkey do, you know! And this is what they have learned from our dissatisfaction with life. You are responsible for how they view life! Yes, it is you who are! They might see others with more, but it is your responsibility to show them what gratitude is really about. And if you do not possess it, then there's no way you can convey it to them.

Take today and look around you. What do you see? Are you "whole" and together as a family? Can you pay your bills and put food on the table? Do you all have your health? If you do not have some of these things, then look even closer. You can overcome almost any obstacle by becoming a stronger family, and you achieve this through understanding that you are so much more than you believe you are. And when you are grateful for what you have, you can achieve even more! Appreciate what you have before you start wishing for more!

Assignment: Whether you are single or married, with or without children, list the things you say you are truly grateful for.

JANUARY 18

Do you believe that your partner or spouse should be talking to someone else about his/her feelings about your relationship? Are you afraid you will look insecure and possessive if you confront the situation? Are you trying to read his/her e-mail or look at their text messages or phone calls hoping that you won't find anything but knowing that you will (and by the way, there is no other reason for you to do so if that wasn't the case)? Do you fear that even if they had a friendship with that person before you met them that it would be a threat to your relationship? Better yet, do you think your spouse should maintain any relationships with the opposite or same sex after you are in a committed relationship or marriage?

These are questions that stir up such strong opinions in us that sometimes we cannot discuss the issue without it ending up in an argument. To be truly honest, there is no easy solution. If you are really secure in your relationship, then what is the worry? If it is a new relationship, then you have not yet built enough trust to see your partner talking to another male/female about your relationship. This is where you really have to think about your own feelings, because they can determine what you will and won't tolerate in the relationship.

If you do not talk about this issue together before you make that commitment, then you are asking for trouble! Many folks do not sit down and talk about these feelings, and they often end up either having frequent fights or splitting up because of unwanted—many times, unwarranted—jealousies and fears.

In the beginning we are so eager to feel loved and wanted that we will agree to things we do not have time to think about, and because we don't we usually end up looking so insecure that it turns the other person off. Both men and women are equally affected by this issue, and do not let anyone tell you differently.

Sometimes it's easier to act like we aren't bothered as a way of avoiding the conversation. If you are getting into a relationship, or even if you are in one now, talk about this issue before you end up regretting you didn't.

LARRY ROBINSON

Question: How would you begin this conversation regarding information about your relationship shared with others?

_____

_____

_____

_____

_____

_____

_____

_____

_____

_____

_____

_____

_____

_____

_____

_____

JANUARY 19

What has happened to the word "respect"? Does it mean the same thing it did fifty years ago? Why has that word become obsolete in our lives? When do we regain that feeling for one another in our families, relationships, schools, work, or children? Are we just products of our society and accepting of the fact that there is no respect? Are we to just carry on as if the word no longer exists?

We first have to start with ourselves and get to start seeing who we are. Ask yourself this question, "Do I respect who I am, and are my behaviors in life worthy of respect?" If we can answer yes to that question, then do we give that respect to others or do we feel that they do not live up to the standard we have set for respect?

If you do not respect yourself, then how can you know what the word feels like? It would just be some theory we were following without any real meaning attached to it. You are the only real judge of your behavior, and inside you there is this little voice that will tell you the truth about the word "respect." Listen to it and learn from that little voice! This is called your "higher self" and it is your gut feeling. It does not betray us, we betray it! How many times have you heard it and then ignored the message? Were you right? It is truly doubtful, for when we go against it trouble usually follows.

Today is the day to decide that you will overcome your negativity and start to change your disrespectful behavior into respect for yourself.

Question: Do you think you can muster up the courage to make that change? What don't you respect about yourself?

_____

_____

_____

_____

LARRY ROBINSON

JANUARY 20

Why can't you *stay* in the present? When an issue arises in the present, we are often thrown back into the past and to old hurts, angers, and resentments. It's as if we rush back there to validate all the pain from years and years ago that never went away! The ability to live in the moment disappears and we feel like nothing has ever changed in our lives. The thought of any future that could be filled with joy and contentment is gone, and we no longer even want to think about the future!

If this is the case, we're missing the present! We cannot be there for anyone, and our lives are pretty much stuck. The past invades the present and wipes out the future. Heaven help us if we have children, because then we're not teaching them how to get rid of pain. And how can they if we cannot? If we give them a dim view of what lies ahead, then why would they want to plan their own futures? Do you realize how negative this is? I'll bet you don't even realize you do this.

In the present there is most certainly pain at times, but there is also love! If we fail to let in the pain, then we have no choice but to keep out the love!

Assignment: Take today and try to just stay in the present! Keep yourself from drifting into the past and see what this brings to your life. A most beautiful healing will begin to take place!

LARRY ROBINSON

_____

_____

_____

_____

_____

_____

_____

_____

_____

_____

_____

_____

_____

_____

_____

_____

_____

_____

_____

JANUARY 21

A re you afraid to take risks even though you know in your heart that it is the right move? Are you stuck in a kind of limbo because you fear the future and what it might bring? Does everything you do have to be a 100 percent certainty before you make a move? If it is, then you are truly paralyzed! You are the type of person who is afraid of the unknown, and change is something you dream about but never fulfill. How sad it is to watch others move ahead while you sit enviously watching them. For you, "well said" is much better than "well done," and you need to choose the security of where you are, even if you hate it! And you probably do!

Who told you that you are better off staying where you are because you "know the routine"? Who told you that you would stumble and fall if you took a risk and followed your heart? Remember, your mind is always giving you negative feedback. When has it ever said, "Yes, go ahead and get out of this place that you've been in all your life"? Never! And because of that you have become so complacently afraid to move ahead and take on your real journey in life that you're no longer even bothered by your inability to move ahead. Yet another "well said" is better than a "well done!"

How fast has your life flown by with you still in the same job, the same town, and the same lousy relationship without you having done anything about it? And there are no longer any psychological problems stopping you. It is just you. You are the problem!

Apply for a new position and then find the place you really want to live. Work on your relationship, and if it still turns out the same, leave it! You need to do something before your life's journey ends!

Question: What things you have not done yet in your life do you want to accomplish on your journey?

LARRY ROBINSON

_____

_____

_____

_____

_____

_____

_____

_____

_____

_____

_____

_____

_____

_____

_____

_____

_____

_____

_____

_____

JANUARY 22

Why is it important for me to always be right in an argument? Why don't I ever give the other person the chance to disagree with me before I tell them they're wrong? Sometimes I even know I'm not right, but I insist on keeping to my illogical stance just to be right! How often have I made the other person feel stupid or ashamed of their opinion?

Somewhere deep down inside of me there's a feeling that if I'm wrong it will then trigger some of the messages I heard as a child, like "you will never be smart enough" or "you are stupid" or "only a moron would . . ." The list goes on and on. I've kept these thoughts buried deep inside me, and when I'm challenged about the "right" answer I rush in with my answer, sometimes before the other person has even finished their sentence!

I pronounce, "You are wrong," which is generally followed up by the other person saying, "Why can't you let me finish my sentence?" I am way too caught up in my past. It is almost as if I am still eight years old again and my parents are reprimanding me for being wrong. The child within me will not let the truth come out.

You can be wrong, but no one will despise you for telling the truth. In fact, respect comes from telling the truth, not from being right. Think of all the times you knew your parents were wrong and how you didn't respect them over how they made you feel. Why would you want to make someone else feel the same way you did as a child?

Question: If you could make one criticism go away from the past, what would it be?

_____

_____

_____

_____

JANUARY 23

D o you pay attention when people are talking to you? Do you have people in your life who tell you they are listening to you and who can repeat word for word what you have said, but who you know did not hear anything you had to say? Are you capable of sitting across from someone and by simply looking intently while they're speaking have them actually believe you are "engaged" in their conversation, despite the fact that you are a million miles away? Did you do this in school? Did you make the teacher believe you were present when you were not paying attention at all? Do you think this is ADD, or is it really something else?

Today, *Mirror, Mirror* is declaring a "pay attention day," during which we all will try to listen to whatever is coming our way. You are the one to determine whether you pay attention or not, or if those around you pay attention to you.

If you are speaking, why aren't you being listened to? Do you talk too much over simple common issues in your house? Do you get sidetracked and go off on "tangents," resulting in you losing contact with others? Most likely it is how you are presenting your conversation. Too many words without periods at the end of sentences can lose people rather quickly, especially children.

Take your time and really pay attention to what you are saying and who your audience is. If you have brought the current issue up more than a few times and now find yourself bringing it up again, you are not being listened to. You need to find a different approach. It might be that you need to stop and stand there for a few seconds and look at who it is you are talking to square in the eyes in order to gain their attention.

If you find that it's you who is wandering off, then maybe you need to tell the other person that you are having trouble listening to them. You can do this without insulting them. Just remember to be sensitive about how they might feel. Remember, it is not what we say as much as it is how we say it. Too many times we unknowingly begin arguments based on how we say things, and that's the result of us not paying attention to our delivery.

LARRY ROBINSON

Wouldn't it be wonderful if we really learned the art of communication? We would truly begin to be appreciated, and we'd also appreciate others because we'd be paying attention.

Question: How often do you not listen at work or at home when you are being told how to do something, and are then afraid to ask again later for fear of looking stupid?

_____

_____

_____

_____

_____

_____

_____

_____

_____

_____

_____

_____

_____

January 24

How do you get up in the morning? Are you anxious, groggy, disconnected, and full of complaints, like "I didn't sleep at all last night because of you snoring, and it's your responsibility to do something about it," or "the kids are still in our bed, and it's your responsibility to do something about it"? These are *so* common. Do you yell at your children to get out of bed?

What a great way to start your day, rushing to make breakfast, making the kids' lunches, and then making your own as you grab a cup of coffee while screaming at the kids to get in the car. If this is how you start your day and you say that it's all because you're just not a "morning person," then you are just giving yourself an excuse. Evidently, you are still wrapped up in yourself and cannot see the consequences on your spouse and your children. Well, this has to stop, because all of you are beginning your mornings on a negative tone.

Now, how do we stop this? To many of you this will sound ridiculous, but a family prayer in the morning can bring you all together. Just get yourself up ten minutes early and then wake up your child without yelling. Get together in the family room and join hands and say any kind of morning prayer you like. If you believe in God, then mention his name, and let the children lead the prayer if they wish to. If God is not part of your life, then welcome in the day.

There is enough pain in this world already without you adding to it. Now prove this right by following this suggestion. Start your day with love and not chaos!

Assignment: Whether you are single or married, with or without children, develop a way of starting your day with joy.

_____

_____

_____

January 25

Are you afraid of intimacy? Do you feel at times that you are too cold inside? How many times have you wanted to reach out to someone special and either just touch them or tell them "I love you" without having been prompted to do so, but found a coldness inside of you that prevented you from sharing the warmth you so wanted to give?

You have no problem being intimate with people you are not that close to or people you hardly even know, but you find it difficult with those you profess to love! Why does this happen? Are you a "detached" person? What kind of feedback do your loved ones give? Do they say you can be "cold as an iceberg"? Do people stop attempting to be intimate with you? Yes, you can have sex, you may even relish it, but you just cannot connect in that loving place. You are not making love!

This is not something you can blame on your partner, even though you try to find reasons for your detachment. You may say, "I don't feel the same way," or "I'm not as attracted as I used to be," or "the sex was terrible!" It's never, "What is wrong with me?" Can you finally admit that intimacy scares you and you cannot let anyone that close to you? You fear the feeling of being vulnerable and you cannot tolerate the feeling of rejection. You never initiate sex anymore because you feel like "What if my partner pushes me away?"

Ending denial is the first step toward recovery. Being able to admit that you are the problem allows you to go deeper inside and look more closely at yourself.

Question: Ask yourself who left you either emotionally or physically as a child. Are you still mourning their loss?

_____

_____

_____

LARRY ROBINSON

January 26

Are you an "attention seeker"? Do you need to "lead the band" wherever you go? Are you someone who can't help reaching for the center of groups and need to lead and control? Are you someone who needs control all the time? Can you allow others to make decisions for you without putting down their decisions? Do others gravitate toward you because you always seem to be the person who knows the most, holds the most interesting conversations, and is constantly joking around in such a sarcastic tone that no one knows whether you're serious or not?

Why are we seeking this, mostly trivial, attention when we are out in the world? What is our drive to "ham it up" with people so they remember us, even though we usually fail to even recognize them when we see them out and about? Are we the "hams" of the world?

Can we look back into our past and see a ham in school? Were we always trying to get attention from teachers and friends back then? Most likely we were the class clown or the kid in school whom everyone knew. It was so important for us to be liked that it mattered not how we got there! Do we really like people that much, or are we just trying to get everyone to want us? Maybe some of us didn't feel wanted at home and we made up for it in school and just never stopped seeking that attention.

There are so many ways we can seek attention as adults, including some that benefit others too, but we are always the first priority. And we can often offer our assistance, because in our eyes the best reward for us is someone saying, "I don't know how I could have done this without you!" But that only lasts for a short time before we feel the need to have to move on to another situation. We cannot say no. We *live* for that attention, and the sad thing is that there is never enough! We suck the attention we need out of others, and sadly, some of us do not even realize we do this! We believe that giving, doing, entertaining, and controlling is just who we are!

Question: In what ways do you seek attention that can turn others away from you?

January 27

D o you understand what the word *restraint* means? How many times has it come up in your life and you felt it in your gut (we will call it your "higher self") and missed that feeling completely with rationalizations about why you shouldn't listen to it? Do you set these outrageous "goals" for yourself knowing that the chance of you restraining yourself enough to complete them is next to impossible? Do you know what this means in your life, or do you really not want to know? This is going to be one of the harder issues you will have to deal with in your life. This is about addiction and self-control.

Another word for restraint is *self-control*. Whether it be alcohol, drugs, sex, gambling, food, or even tiny addictions, such as candy, cheese—these all require self-control. No one can give it to us; we have to really want it. We do not like to deny ourselves anything!

"Denial," which, by the way, is not that river in Egypt, is not our enemy but rather our saving grace. Without seeing denial as something positive, we have no restraint. We tell ourselves it will be "tomorrow." "Yes, I will start that tomorrow!" How many of us have said that not knowing when "tomorrow" will happen? We like to think that we will.

Have you known people who believe that the way to stop smoking is to smoke a whole pack of cigarettes in the matter of an hour? The thinking being that if they overdo it they will lose forever the urge to smoke. But no, they only end up losing that desire for perhaps a day.

We will talk a lot about addiction, but to start off the first two words we will deal with are "restraint" and "denial." As addicts, we suffer not while we indulge, but through the sheer emptiness afterward.

It is time for us all to work on this. We *can* and *will* get healthy!

Assignment: List your addictions in order of the most to the least power they hold in your life.

LARRY ROBINSON

January 28

D o we get disappointed by others very easily in our life? Do we set our expectations too high for others to reach? Or are we always the "giver," and when we dare ask for something we are turned away? This does happen in life, so don't go blaming yourself too much for others, especially when you hardly ever ask.

Does your spouse disregard your needs and you make it okay because you are afraid to "upset the applecart" of your relationship? Do you feel that you are destined to always be the giver, and that no one takes you seriously when you actually ask for something? Well, why would you think that giving has a "return to sender" label attached to it?

We give because we have a giant hole inside of us and we constantly need to fill it with thinking that others really value what we give. Do you believe that, or are you kidding yourself because inside you are really saying, "I did this for them, and now what do I get in return?" *Altruism*, which is the act of truly giving unselfishly while expecting nothing in return, is something that we can do once in a while, but to do it continually would put us in line for sainthood, and I doubt that will happen. Now I might be wrong, but how many saints do you know?

There needs to be a balance in life with everything, including giving and taking. We need to stop trying to fill a hole that we cannot fill by any means because it is our "damage" in life. To begin the recovery process is painful, for what is going to fill that hole? Well, how about a person who has a better sense of self, one who now asks for what he/she needs instead of forever being the giver who has so many resentments that at some point they're either bound to explode or become physically sick?

Growing up is painful, but that is what "growing pains" are. They are the pains that come with letting go of the old mechanisms that temporally make us feel better. We need to break the cycle of finding ourselves back in the same spot in which we started, because the hole just gets bigger and bigger as we get older!

Assignment: What does your *cycle* look like to you? Can you explain it?

LARRY ROBINSON

January 29

Do you know the type of person who is always giving advice to you or others when they are not asked for it? Do they seem to get either angry or dejected when you refuse their help? Are you told that if you don't listen to them you should not complain about your situation to them anymore? Does it feel like they believe they are always right and perceive you as a "whiny" person if you don't follow their advice?

These folks are not really concerned about your wellbeing, they just want you to not complain or vent. They are not interested in truly being there for you, because they cannot tolerate your issues. They only appear to want to help, and life is really all about them!

How many times have you listened to them go on and on about something? How many days have you spent listening to them? And why did you do that? Well, maybe you would have felt guilty telling them enough is enough, or maybe you just truly cared. In either case, these people are not your friends, and telling them anything about your life only puts you at risk of either being talked down to or lectured about why your issue came about in the first place!

Question: It is time to take control of your life and figure out if you need to talk about something in the first place. And if you decide that you do, then who can be trusted as a caring friend who understands that you need to talk and why? No one can fix us but ourselves!

_____

_____

_____

_____

January 30

Have you ever been bullied? Have you been a bully yourself and didn't realize it until someone called you on it? Do you still get bullied by your loved ones and do not know how to fight back? Do you really think that just because you are an adult you will not be bullied again?

Let's look at what a bully is and where they come from. A bully is someone who is in love with power. They often do not have any at home, so they tend to find those who do not fight back to ultimately torture and humiliate. This humiliation gives them a sense of satisfaction. A bully is like an addict addicted to anger. It does not take much to set him/her off, especially when they have been bullied at home by loved ones. It is almost like a chain reaction, and unfortunately the person on the other end of the bullying allows the bully to achieve his/her desired response, which is fear!

Bullies see themselves as strong and fearless. Their anger is their source of power, but it is also their weakness, for they are nobody without their anger! There are so many people who cannot let go of their anger for this very reason. Bullies have been told most of their lives that they are not good enough, and so they attempt to prove to themselves through the use of power that they are not lacking in other areas, usually social skills or academics. Their anger makes them seek out our fear!

Bullies usually come from homes where there is either too much discipline or not enough. They are left to wander about on their own with no real supervision and no curfews. They feel unattended to and neglected, but they cannot show weakness or fear, despite the fact that those two are ever present in their lives. Remember, their anger eats up our fear!

Question: Bullies do not know what to do with words, only actions. Are you still being bullied even as an adult? Are you still bullying others? Look at yourself and decide!

LARRY ROBINSON

_____

_____

_____

_____

_____

_____

_____

_____

_____

_____

_____

_____

_____

_____

_____

_____

_____

_____

_____

JANUARY 31

We are *Mirror, Mirror* and we are working on mindfulness. And how do we define *mindfulness*? It is the awareness that appears through our ability to pay attention on purpose and to be in the present rather than stuck in the past or thinking ahead to the future. Mindfulness does not have judgment attached to it, and it takes into account all the aspects of life that we take for granted or ignore. It does not listen to the *dribble* our brain produces, because that is our downfall. Mindfulness passes that part of our brain and redirects us to the present moment. The present moment is what is going on in our minds or how we are feeling.

Do you think we actually pay attention to things as they really are rather than what we want them to be? Mindfulness talks a lot about how we see things as opposed to what they really are, and mindfulness helps us on our journey to understand that we can create chaos in our lives by how we see ourselves rather than who we really are.

The opposite of mindfulness is "rumination." When our "racing minds" keep going over and over something in hopes of a positive outcome, rumination prevents that positive outcome from taking place. How many of us ruminate about the past and can never seem to stop it? Ruminating can cause major anxiety and depression. It feels awful to move from depression to anxiety and to constantly keep exchanging them. It freezes our ability to move through certain important issues in our life and can retard our emotional growth. Without any release from this horror show, we can turn on ourselves and think we, or even others, are the cause of this nightmare, when in fact it is out of our control!

So which are you, a ruminator or a mindful person? Do not kid yourself, mindfulness is equally as hard to find as rumination is to lose, but what are our choices? Do not give yourself a choice, but instead make a commitment to yourself. If you are the ruminator, then tell yourself that you will not only choose, but also fight to be mindful. Take an issue you have, make it a small one, and see if you can be mindful of it. And this means to step back and look at how you feel about it and what your mind does with it.

Here's an example of mindfulness: Jack wakes up feeling irritated at his wife. The coffee is bad this morning and she just keeps rambling on about something he couldn't care less about. Jack's mind tells him, "She just never seems to 'get it' that I don't like to talk in the morning." He plays this out over and over in his mind. "Shut up, woman!" his mind keeps telling him.

Now, let's look at how Jack can be mindful about what he thinks and feels. Yesterday, Jack went to the doctor and was told that he had prostate cancer. He was devastated, but he was afraid to tell his wife. When he woke up in the morning and acted so edgy and mean, he stepped back and realized that he was taking his fear out on her because he was afraid she would not be able to handle it. When he finally opened up his heart to her and told her what was going on, she was right there by his side. Jack suffered, and the damage he could have continued to do to his relationship was real! Being mindful of the moment allowed him to see what was happening.

Assignment: Begin to look at how you can negatively act toward others and see if you can relate it to a greater, more painful issue going on in your life.

_____

_____

_____

_____

_____

_____

_____

_____

_____

_____

"Fear is the eroding thread of whatever type of life we have."

—Darlene Hornblower, Lynn, Massachusetts, USA

Jem Rose P. Maitlong, Bacolod City, Negros Occidental, Philippines

FEBRUARY 1

D o you feel respected in life? Do you feel that others respect you and see you as an honest, decent person? If you know there are things you do, whether you're a "secret addict," talk behind people's backs, or just *fudge* things a little at work, do you really respect yourself? Maybe it's that little secret voice inside you called your "mind" that says nasty things about others or yourself!

We are the only ones who really know ourselves, and we are the only ones who can better the "me" in this world. Sometimes we even feel entitled to our inner negative voice and we feel that we're better than others, but our true attitude is one of caring and giving. Wouldn't you rather not give than be false about how you give?

These are all things that cause us to disrespect ourselves, and so why should we believe that others respect us? How we see ourselves in this world determines how we believe others see us. No one is perfect, that we all have realized, but being responsible for who you are and being able to tell the truth, those make you a genuine person. People respect genuine so much more than they do fake.

Today, start to become that genuine person!

Assignment: Test yourself and see if you can go through your day without telling a lie or talking behind someone's back. I bet you think it's easy! Well, try it and see!

LARRY ROBINSON

FEBRUARY 2

Friendships! They seem to come and go in our lives. We change friends these days like we change clothes. One day we are best friends, and the next we hardly acknowledge each other. We spill our guts out to our "new best friend" and feel like we finally met someone who really "gets" who we are, and they do the same with us. It's as if we never really had a friend until we met them. We speak to them every day or talk to them on our long car rides home from work, and the time just flies! Where has this person been all my life?

We feel so excited to share with this special person, but after a few months something seems wrong and we don't speak as much, and then suddenly the other person isn't as *available* as they used to be. Our conversations take on a shorter, colder tone, and when we hang up the phone we feel a distance.

But we really *know* this person, and we rationalize that they are going through a stressful time and that's why they seem so removed. Now we are leaving phone or text messages for them and it feels like it takes forever for them to get back to us. And when they do, there is always an excuse for why they aren't available. We can no longer explain away why they are getting us off the phone so fast.

We begin to feel insecure and start wondering what we did to create such shortness from our "best friend." And when we casually bring up their unavailability, they say it is nonsense!

Ah, but we begin to feel something "old" inside, and that is the feeling of being passed over. We learn that our BFF is seeing someone else and spending large amounts of time with that person. We never hear from them again, and when we see them they pretend not to see us. What happened? Well, we did it again!

We rushed into a friendship without slowly getting to know that person. We shared judgments of others with our friend and they seemed to agree. What we did not look at is how this person handled their previous friends. We didn't realize that we were one of a hundred people who got blown off by this person, and now our privacy is being shared with someone else, just as their last friend's privacy was shared with us.

We get so excited that we fail to realize that trust takes time and energy put into each other. Rushing a friendship is like trying to run before you walk. Take your time! Friendships are to be forever, so what is the rush? How many times have you told yourself this and ended up in the dumpster?

A true friendship takes years to develop, and they don't go away!

Question: Are you a true friend or do you change friends often? Did you ever hear the term *fair-weather* friend? This is when we have no one to do anything with and we call someone we do not really like but want some company. Are you one?

_____

_____

_____

_____

_____

_____

_____

_____

_____

_____

_____

_____

LARRY ROBINSON

FEBRUARY 3

The "dark side," how often have you been aware that it has risen in you and you cannot control it? When it takes over, all the goodness seems to drain out of you and it seems as if a demon has taken its place. Anything that makes us steal happiness from others through our negativity and crashed hopes for our children is our "dark side."

How many times have you warned your children that they'd better behave during an upcoming trip when they've already *been* behaving? All we can see is black. And this is not about anyone except us.

Where does this come from? It comes out of our own disappointments that we either swallow or repress. It may take a day or two before it surfaces, but it comes with a fury. Once this demon is out, it takes a complete cycle of rage, anger, guilt, and shame for it to go back down under. But what damage does it cause during its cycle?

Believe it, you are not seen as angelic! When this is happening, the best that you can do is to try to trust those around you when they tell you you're being mean or selfish. They won't say it right away, because it takes some time for them to realize that you are not being nice. But when they do tell you, listen to them! No one has any reason to tell you a lie about your behavior.

What is the matter, are you afraid to see the truth?

Question: What is it that you are afraid to see about yourself that makes you anxious about your life?

_____

_____

_____

_____

_____

LARRY ROBINSON

FEBRUARY 4

Do you ever feel *scapegoated* for something that you didn't do or know that you did? Have you ever been blamed for someone else's bad mood and then treated as if you committed a major crime? Do you often wake up in a good mood and are then brought down by everyone around you who cannot accept that you are feeling okay?

Not everyone wakes up in a bad mood. Some of us look forward to getting up and starting our day. True, not many of us, but could that be because we are conditioned to be crabby, irritable people who cannot tolerate our dispositions? Sure, maybe some of it is just to counter the ugliness of other people, but we can be sincere in our efforts to start our day in a positive mood. How often do you feel shot down by the people that you care about?

Do you remember what it was like in your own household waking up? For some of us, there was no complaining or lying in bed until we got dragged out, almost as if there was a game going on. No, we had no-nonsense parents, and if you misbehaved, well, you knew what the consequences were. How were your parents in the morning? If they were grouchy, I bet you didn't feed it, but instead stayed quiet until you left the house. Which person in your family wakes up positive only to be attacked until they are in a bad mood too?

Have you ever done something by accident, say, like get up in the middle of the night and wake up your spouse or partner and then face their wrath the next morning? I bet you never even knew you did that. All you get is lectured by a grump who blames you for something you didn't do on purpose!

Here we actually have two issues bundled together: being scapegoated and waking up in a positive mood in the morning. You and your spouse need to talk about where each of you came from as children so you can begin to change your own living situation.

We often have no idea of what the other person's experiences were growing up. Maybe they were the scapegoats and now they are just reacting to their past. Perhaps you are just forcing that good mood in your house because in your house no one ever smiled at each other in the morning. Children should be included in this talk, for they are just as vulnerable and responsible as you are with their own moods.

If you feel scapegoated for something that you didn't do, neither dismiss the other person's feeling nor defend yourself. Listen to what they are saying to you and do not react as if they are wrong. Be willing to say "I am sorry" if you can understand what they are saying. If you didn't know you were guilty of something, do not respond with hostility. Respond with empathy. Also, do not take responsibility for something you didn't do just to block any confrontation.

You are not anyone's whipping block, and you need to learn to stand up for you!

Question: Are you the type of person who takes on too much responsibility for other people's actions?

_____

_____

_____

_____

_____

_____

_____

_____

_____

_____

FEBRUARY 5

Is there such a concept as "unconditional love"? What do we expect from our spouses and children when it comes to this? Remember the old saying, "We love you no matter what"? Is it true or false?

Most of the time this statement is not true. Parents have some harsh expectations about who we are supposed to be, just as both people in a relationship generally also have high expectations about who each other should be. And sometimes they are so far beyond who we are, and sometimes our demands are so great that it is like, "Love me no matter what I say to you and no matter how I hurt you."

We can say such mean things to one another and be so selfish. How are we supposed to find this concept of unconditional love? This is the foundation of the *work* of a relationship. In order to feel that warm, loving feeling in your heart, you must look at your own behavior and stop focusing on the other person's. It is their responsibility to look at themselves. When two people are fighting there is no indication of loving unconditionally. We can actually hate the other person at that point in time, but that is all part of the process. We must destroy the loving feelings to continually find them again. That is what fighting does.

If each of you can look inside yourself and truly ask, "Do I like who I am in this fight?" (and never has anyone come out and answered yes to this question) then you *can* be responsible for your own actions. Both people do this, and guess what? They find unconditional love again!

We might be doing this over and over again in our relationship, but after a while we stop wanting to leave and know, instead, that we will resolve our fight.

Unconditional love is the result of working on a relationship!

Question: How do you define unconditional love? Do you actually believe in it?

LARRY ROBINSON

February 6

Is being self-centered an issue you face? Perhaps you don't even realize you are taking up everyone else's time and space with you! Do you need attention all of the time? Does being at the center make you feel better about yourself, or is it just a temporary fix? Why is it so hard to let someone else speak or even be at the center for a while? Are you too needy and jealous to allow that to happen?

So many of us just need it and don't know why we are so focused on being liked and wanted. Were you that kid in school who never raised your hand? Or were you the one who not only waved their hand, but who shouted out the answer too?

Why are we this way? We do not become this way as adults. Unfortunately, like most of our issues, it starts in early childhood. A lot of times our view of reality as children was that we didn't get enough attention at home, so we made up for it at school. For some, it didn't matter whether it was positive attention or negative attention, attention was attention! We saw ourselves as either not smart enough, good-looking enough, or funny enough, and this wounded us terribly. How we made up for it was to try to be at the center wherever we went!

Do you remember feeling that your brothers or sisters were always (in your mind) better than you? How much did you resent them for this? Remember that as children we have a difficult time truly seeing reality, so our impressions can often be wrong. Even if we were right, that was when we were young and that does not have to rule us today.

We must remember that the "neglected child" is still alive in us and controlling that need to be wanted. As adults it does the opposite and it pushes people away.

Assignment: For three days remain pleasant, but as a listener rather than a talker, and see how people respond to you. You might begin to see that attention is not about what you get, but what you give.

LARRY ROBINSON

February 7

"Racing minds," they torture us and they are relentless in crowding our lives with repetition after repetition. At times, this in itself becomes an addiction, because we "predict" what will happen, knowing all day that at some point it is going to start. It takes us away from family and work, and it usually causes us to lose sleep. Yes, we are among the tortured, and only those close to us know our pain, but they do not understand it. There are even some who don't want to.

It is up to us to resolve this. Ask yourself how long this has been going on in your life, and understand that we cannot rid ourselves of it easily. How many of us are really dedicated to becoming stronger folks? This is all about you, so if you are thinking that this is the fault of bad parenting, bad relationships, or a fear of life, forget it! No one makes us act a certain way. This is caused by damage we experienced long ago. I know you suffer—believe me, it takes one to know one, so I am fully empathetic to the pain but not the blame!

Let us do a little "child development" so we can begin to understand the nature of this damage. Remember, this is not about blame, but it also does not excuse negligent responsibility. All children experience trauma at some point in life, usually before the age of five. This trauma is either how they saw life or it might have actually been true. It does not matter at this point which it is, because from this trauma comes the damage.

Here is a story that will give you an example of the trauma. Once there was a little boy who was riding his new bike for the first time without training wheels. He was with his friends in the neighborhood and they had these little fake firecrackers that they were scaring little girls with. One of the girls went and told his mother. Now, his mother was a very miserable, mean, unhappy person. She came out of her house, down the stairs, said nothing, and smacked the little boy across the face so hard that he flew off his bike, breaking the pedal in the process. She then, in front of all his friends, did the "I am going to pull your arm out of its socket and make sure your bum hits every stair," and threw him on his bed. She then said, "You wait until your father comes home!"

Now, he was not as scared as he was angry, really angry! And so to impress upon his father how evil and bad his mother was, he rubbed the spot where his mother slapped him all day. It ended up looking like a big round, ugly burn. He scratched layers of skin off. He just couldn't wait until his daddy got home so that Daddy could beat up his mother! As soon as his father walked through the door, his mother yelled at him, "You spank him, right now!" And he did! That was it!

From that moment on this little boy knew that he was never going to be loved and that no one would ever stand up for him. You see, he loved his dad so very much, and now there was emptiness. His life became a horror show. His mind began to race so constantly that he could not pay attention in school, and he eventually got himself deeper in trouble throughout his growing years. He never slept, for his mind had taken control, and all the anger he had would come into his mind and his obsession would begin.

Assignment: Go back in your life and find your trauma! If you think you cannot remember your childhood, then perhaps it is blocked because of pain. You can find it! Just listen to your mind and what it tells you about yourself. You didn't invent these thoughts, someone planted them in your head and you still carry them. Today, no one but you create your pain.

_____

_____

_____

_____

_____

_____

LARRY ROBINSON

_____

_____

_____

_____

_____

_____

_____

_____

_____

_____

_____

_____

_____

_____

_____

_____

_____

_____

_____

_____

_____

February 8

Do people take you for granted? Are you the type of person who never says no to anyone and then you feel taken advantage of? Inside of you, is there a monster creeping around who wants to devour everyone who makes you feel like their "bitch" without even thanking you for your efforts?

Yes, you are that person who would pick someone up at the airport at 3:00 a.m. and you don't even know the person that well. You hide at times when a number pops up on your caller ID because you just know you'll be used again, but you still can't stop yourself from answering it.

Do you blame all these feelings on others and walk around with a negative outlook toward life on the inside? Well, stop, look, and listen! This is about you, not them!

Who told you that you had to say yes to everyone? Who whispers in your ear that if you do not do as you're told no one will like you? Listen carefully to the messages your mind sends out, and you will see that this has been your behavior for as long as you can remember. Your need to be needed has overtaken your life and now you are trapped.

Stop for a minute and begin to understand that a part of this racing mind is merely a cover-up for your anger toward these people in your life who are taking advantage of you. You are too afraid to say no, fearing they will not want you in their life if you do not do as they ask. If that's the case, then they were never your friends to begin with! Why would you even want that person in your life? What benefit do you really get?

It is time to begin to understand how your mind works. This is a "racing of the mind" issue, and until you decide that you are someone who can learn to say, "No, I am sorry, I cannot do that," then you will never stop your mind. This is example number one of why our minds take control. It is because we haven't!

Assignment: List all of the situations in which you did not say no.

FEBRUARY 9

Are you the type of person who holds on to resentment? After repeating the same situations with people, these resentments will turn into grudges, and they rarely go away. They grow deeper and deeper inside of us, while helping our mind focus on our anger toward another.

You can have nothing to do with a specific person and then suddenly see them and the grudge pops right back up and takes control of your mind. Our peaceful self instantly turns into the angry, mean-speaking person. We can resolve resentments, which are typically minor issues that we can eventually dismiss. But a reminder: holding on to them will erupt into grudges.

Are you a vengeful person? Does that deep hurt from that grudge turn into "wishful thinking" that something bad will happen to that person, even if this is your spouse or partner? How awful we really feel if this comes up. Do we take it to the point of silence or having no contact with that person? Do we avoid their calls and sometimes even talk behind their backs about how awful they've been?

Do they really know what they did to you, or is this just a secret you love holding on to? This is part of the racing mind. Remember, the racing mind is not about just one piece of your life, it is about your whole life!

How honest can you be with yourself? You know how sometimes we can be so stubborn that we refuse to let go of the grudge? Well, you had better believe that it will enter your mind and that you will not be able to let go it. Now, additional issues can take control of your mind, and perhaps cause you to have trouble concentrating and sleeping, but do not let your mind get away with this!

You will ask for answers. First of: "change" has different levels that it goes through. It is not an event in our life. It is a process. Nothing happens overnight, but we can become stronger by identifying what it is in our mind that remains unresolved.

LARRY ROBINSON

Sometimes, by approaching the situation we find that maybe, just maybe, we were too sensitive and did not understand the other person to begin with.

Assignment: List the grudges that you have been holding on to in order of importance.

_____

_____

_____

_____

_____

_____

_____

_____

_____

_____

_____

_____

_____

February 10

So it is finally over and you cannot and will not let go! You still want that horrible relationship no matter what, because after all, isn't it better than nothing? You have heard so many lies that if you were called a different name right now you might answer to it! The pain and hurting does not stop, and you feel as if your heart has been ripped out of you and you will never get over the pain. You would take back the lies and deceit in a second just to not be alone.

You tell yourself differently, that even though you loved this person with all your heart you really wanted "out" so many times. Were these just idle threats that you wouldn't follow through on because you believed the lies? You knew they were lies, but you still turned your back just to feel wanted.

Why on earth would you want to be with someone who didn't want to be with you? Is it because you could not handle the rejection? It is way too scary for you to think of yourself as alone again.

For younger folks, it feels like life is done at age twenty. *Twenty* and life is done! You will meet someone else. The most important thing we can remember is that if we met this loser, we can probably meet another loser. We are not very smart when it comes to looking at the other person. How many times have you met the same person?

If you are in this situation, it is most likely not the first time. Too eager to be wanted can be very dangerous for you. Think, do you need this person or do you want this person? If you need a loser, well, enjoy the ride. But if you wanted this jerk, him *or* her, then it doesn't take much not to want them.

Who told you that you were not entitled to a good relationship? And if you are following after your parents, take a good look now before you end up just like them!

Question: Have you learned from your bad relationships how to be better in the next one?

LARRY ROBINSON

February 11

How many of us have heard "Today is the first day of the rest of your life" and then said, "Yeah right"? How could today be "that day" when we cannot get out of our own way? We are supposed to change because we are in a bad place in life, and now today we're going to change it? Who takes into account that we suffer?

Is it that easy to just stop suffering because we are supposed to? No one knows how we suffer, the rejection we feel, the abandonment we experience, and the losses we have had. Who can tell us what we are supposed to do? If you really want to stop your pain, and if you really want to change your life, then it is you who makes that decision.

Do you think you cannot change, or are you so used to this way of life that change seems out of the question? Do you know that children hate change, and that anything that takes them out of their "circle of comfort" makes life painful until they adjust to it? So many of us are still that child who is afraid to stop suffering because we are unsure of what will take its place. At least suffering is familiar, and it requires no new knowledge on our part. So that's it, we are afraid of the unknown.

But why can't we view the unknown as something exciting and challenging, as opposed to still looking through the eyes of that child inside of us who views it as scary and dark? What are we going to find in the unknown, the bogeyman? Maybe that's it; maybe we are afraid of our own nightmares and believe that if we leave things alone then what we know is better than the unknown.

We are wrong if that is the case. Letting go of fear and pain from our past opens up so many opportunities to the future. The pain of the past is not the same as "no pain, no gain!" Growing pains are all about letting go of the past and entering into the present so we can find out what it is that we need. If you are afraid of that pain, then you will always stay in the past.

Let it go! Think in terms of what your dreams are so that you can begin to achieve them rather than feed them to the bogeyman!

Question: Have you been afraid of the unknown? Why?

LARRY ROBINSON

February 12

Are we selfish? Do we automatically tell someone no before they have even finished their sentence after we ask them a question? Are we always thinking we're right no matter whether we know the subject matter or not? Do we engage in fighting when someone disagrees with what we say? Haven't you been in the situation where after you're asked your opinion on something the first thing you hear are the words "No, that's not right," or "Oh no, that won't look good," and you haven't even finished your sentence? Is it possible that you do this and aren't even aware of it? Do you have people saying behind your back that they're afraid to ask you anything because you don't listen?

We are all guilty of this at some time or another in our lives. Again, this is not a new issue. We create this in childhood because we want to be noticed. It was a defensive part of who we were, and we have never let it go.

And who were we trying to please? Yes, you guessed it right, it was our parents. And we must remember that, for some of you, you could never please them! Might it be that this was their fault and something based on their own limitations?

It really doesn't matter any longer, because we picked up the ball and ran with it, and now we are that person! And we do not have the patience to listen before we need to jump in with, "No, you're wrong!" When we recognize this piece of ourselves, then we can fix it. No one wants to be viewed as a know-it-all, and no one wants people to shy away from them due to annoyance.

Today, take the time to listen. Even children can be right and teach us something!

Question: Are you one of these people who say no too fast? Be honest with yourself!

LARRY ROBINSON

February 13

Are you a disciplined person? Do you envy those who can complete tasks while yours always go unfinished? Do you start projects with the best intentions and end up with a giant mess? Are you the type of person who always takes on too much and then ends up feeling overwhelmed and cannot finish any of it? Do you wonder why you live in chaos and can never find anything?

Well, welcome to the group of us who are "part-time people." What is meant by "part-time people" is that half of the time we have the right intentions, but the rest of the time we tend to give up on the enormous tasks we have undertaken.

Are you disciplined enough to always show up at work on time and your desk is so organized that you can always find what you need? Or are you always searching for something that you have inadvertently misplaced? Perhaps you grew up in a house that was so organized that if you left something out of place it was discarded and it didn't matter what it was! Maybe you grew up in a house that was always chaotic and messy, and you just got used to living without any discipline.

Often, children who had no true parenting were forced to make decisions for themselves at an early age, and often they made poor ones that resulted in big trouble. The consequence of that needs to be that as an adult you discipline yourself to stop making those bad decisions. Without discipline, we do not develop inner discipline, which is the ability to make *good* decisions and follow through with them.

This is much harder to learn as adults, but do not think that you cannot change it. You have to want to develop new ways of dealing with your life. Do not tell mindful thinking that you can't or you are too old to change your ways.

When you decide that you want order in your life, you can develop discipline!

Assignment: List the issues/items in your life that remain unorganized and begin to create a plan to organize them.

LARRY ROBINSON

Christina Alvarado Ulate Heredia, Costa Rica

FEBRUARY 14

Are you a "fighter" in a relationship? Do you ever take the time to listen to what the other person is actually saying before you jump in and turn it around and make it about the other person? Can they ever get a word in without you saying that the fight is their fault? Maybe they were not looking for a fight but just needed to tell you how they were feeling, and you *assumed* that you were going to be blamed for something you know you didn't do! And maybe you are just carrying around a storehouse of guilt and anger toward the other person and it all just comes pouring out.

Does either of us ever listen completely to the other person before it gets so out of hand that we don't even know what the real issue is? Do we try to hurt each other because we are hurt ourselves? This pain that we carry around is the failure of our "dream person" to be there for us. We get so anxious and depressed because they are not who we want them to be! We wonder what the hell we are doing with this person who cannot satisfy our *fantasy* of who we wanted them to be. Does this mean that we don't need to face ourselves in a relationship but only criticize the other?

This need that we all have to be in our "fantasy relationship" is really a way of filling in emptiness that most of us experience. Do you know that when we are thinking of what it would be like to be with someone who shares the same values and ideas about life as we do, well, that's a crock! That just means that we do not have to change, that we are perfect and that they are a disappointment. But who are we? We are incapable of looking at ourselves and cannot see beyond our disappointment to what the other person is feeling!

Let us face the fact that we are all damaged and that we need to listen and learn about ourselves from what the other person is saying and that they need to do the same. The "perfect relationship" is a fairy tale, and reality, although it can suck, is where our hearts lie buried. Get your shovel out and start digging before you are alone again!

Question: Do you fantasize about being in a new relationship rather than dealing with the one you are in?

LARRY ROBINSON

February 15

Can you be depended on? When you are asked to do something for someone else, do you say "Of course" and then wait until the last minute before doing it? Or do you have to be reminded that you said yes? Are you the kind of friend who promises to be there, yet when the time comes you don't want to or cannot handle the situation?

These are real situations that happen to real people, so it is time to start being honest with ourselves. We all want to be liked and respected, and the word "no" is hard for most of us, but it is our downfall when we cannot keep promises. This issue is one of the harder ones, for it leads to the "racing mind syndrome," and also to addictive behaviors.

Our sense of self from when we were children depended upon how others saw us. Now that we are adults, are we still trying to please others by giving of ourselves and not really wanting to or just not being able to find the time in our own lives to be "there" for someone else? This becomes part of our shame, for most of us know that we don't want to be attending to someone else's issues when we can't even figure out our own.

How many times does the phone ring and that caller ID shouts at you "If you pick it up you are going to lie"? Do we answer it anyway? Think about how many times this has happened to you, and then think about whether you like what you see in the mirror. Are you losing sleep at night because your mind keeps telling you you're bad, or even worse, you reach for a glass of wine or beer to wash away your lie?

Mirror, Mirror will try to tie in a lot of things that will help you to see the things we do that truly make us feel bad about ourselves.

Question: What do you think makes you feel bad about yourself?

LARRY ROBINSON

February 16

Can you make a decision with another person? Are you someone who is truly open to another person's ideas, or do you "fake it" because you do not want to be viewed as negative or argumentative? Maybe I should ask if you're an argumentative person when it comes to going someplace or deciding on a color of a room or picking a piece of furniture. We all want our opinion to matter, but how far will we go to have it chosen?

Making decisions with others at home or at work is a very difficult task. How many times have you experienced someone interrupting you with an automatic no before you even get your thought out? Doesn't it just infuriate you when this happens? But what do you do about it? Are you that person who simply just cannot tolerate listening while someone else is sharing their opinion? We have to be right! Ask yourself: "Why is this so important to me?" Say it out loud and I guarantee you will hear some anger or desperation in your voice.

Have you always experienced being wrong? Have you ever been listened to? Does your sense of self-esteem depend on you being right? This is usually the case. We have been disregarded either at work or at home, so we demand attention in what our choice is. At home we might go along with our spouse to avoid conflict, but might we be a bull at work? Maybe it could be the opposite.

Why can't we just state our opinion and say, "I disagree," and let it stand? If others override you, then you can either stand your ground or let them know what it feels like to always be told no. That's not easy, but it's much easier on you in earning the right to have your own opinion.

Assignment: List the situations in which you always relinquish your opinions to others.

LARRY ROBINSON

February 17

Do you believe that you let go of anger? How far back does your mind take you until someone triggers that hotspot in you? I thought I let go of all my past angers, but I still get crippled by my wounds from the past. My seemingly laid-back self takes on a whole new identity and a cascade of anger rushes to the front of my brain and it burns! I do not think that I was ever really able to let go. I believe that this is *my* damage, as it is all of ours. And the goal is not perfection, not to wipe out all the anger, as many of us would like to do, but instead to realize that I have damage in me!

My only ability is to face that part of myself, and to understand how during the times that I am in that place and carrying around all that pain my life is anything but normal. Oh, I pretend that I'm cool and I try to move forward, but just the attempt at blocking my anger prevents me from "living" in the present!

Are you the type of person who "spaces out" but who can also look like you're listening? This is your anger coming up. Some people might think you're a "space shot," but you know the truth. There are no space shots in life. We are just angry.

Are you the type of person who tears up and cries at the drop of a hat? This hot feeling inside is your anger, a fire that your tears you out. Allow yourself to face you and you will feel a cool relief.

Assignment: Identify the ways in which you deal with your anger.

_____

_____

_____

_____

_____

LARRY ROBINSON

FEBRUARY 18

W hy do I want you to be someone else? So many times I have thought that if only you were kinder, prettier, and better looking; if only you were richer or more successful; if only you didn't work so much; if only you weren't so anxious all the time; if only, if only, if only! But who then would I be?

Do I rely on you to bolster my self-esteem? Do I think that if you had any or all of the above qualities that it would make me a better person? If that were true, then wouldn't I have found the right person? Oh my, how misguided I am, for it is not up to you to make me a better person! And yet I walk around feeling like my image would improve if you were all those things. I could pump up my chest and feel like I was better than others, but deep down inside I know I would be lying to myself! You do not determine who I am, only I do!

It is my work in life to become all those things I want you to be. It is my responsibility to accept myself and you, and to appreciate what we are, who you are, and who I am. I know this work is mine alone! And never let me put you down because of something I want you to be. I am with you because I fell in love with you, not to make me better, but to make me see all your good qualities.

Assignment: Today I will tell you how much I love you and how much your love means to me! If I do not have a significant other, I will tell the person who means the most to me why I value them so much.

_____

_____

_____

_____

_____

LARRY ROBINSON

February 19

We all know parents, siblings, and friends who look at the glass as half empty rather than half full. We try to brighten their day, but to no avail. They are determined to see life as a series of mishaps and dramas rather than appreciate what they have.

How many of us have folks in our lives who constantly complain and talk about their woes? And what do we do? We generally try to lighten their load. So how many of us have succeeded in undoing all these years of negativity? Do we do this for them, or do we do it because we can no longer stand listening to their dramas?

Have there been instances when you've actually put the phone down while they're talking, only to find that when you pick it up again they were still talking as if they thought you'd been listening all along? We cannot change anyone, and to try to be angry or confront the other person on this issue is only going to cause both you and the other person pain.

People who are negative have spent their entire lives feeling neglected, and the more you try to hush them, the more their negativity rises. Stop fighting the battle and understand that when you do not accept them for who they are you are merely helping them repeat their negative cycle of "No one listens to me!" You do not have to spend countless hours on the phone with them, but just acknowledge their pain and then say you have to go. If you give them unlimited time, without dictating a time limit, they will take advantage of you.

Remember, they are like this because they've always felt unloved. It is not necessary to "fix" them, but to help them understand that they are the only ones who can fix themselves. And maybe, just maybe, if you stop fixing, then they will reduce their dramas!

Question: Is your life filled with negative people? Why do you let them into your life?

LARRY ROBINSON

FEBRUARY 20

Are you a reliable person? Do you think your family and friends can count on you to be there for them, be it a small incident or a major crisis? Do you view yourself as someone who is really there for others? Is it at all possible that you've tricked yourself into believing that your kindness extends toward the rest of the world first and yourself second? Truly, how many of us are really *that* selfless?

Aren't there times in your life when you have resented others because you have done so much and gotten nothing in return? How often have you asked for a helping hand and gotten no true response? Well, you have set yourself up for this behavior because you do too much and then expect the same in return! And how many saints are there living out there now? How many martyrs do you think it would take for the rest of the world to start seeing beyond its own issues?

Remember, we do not give without expectations! So many of you will disagree, but if you take the time to be totally honest with yourself you will know the answer. And you do not have to tell anyone but yourself the truth.

Now, it is not that we shouldn't give. Of course we need to do that, but we should give only when we feel it is right to give and not just to impress others or to hold people hostage as a result of our giving. If you are doing that, then you are, honestly, not a reliable person. "Reliable" goes beyond the task at hand. It goes to our true feelings that we are doing the right thing for the right reasons! And if you can say that is the case for you, then you are truly a rare human being. We all have to face our own reality sometime!

Question: Are you the type of person who gives too much and has expectations of receiving in return? If so, how?

LARRY ROBINSON

February 21

Who taught you that you need to control every single aspect of the lives of everyone who is near and dear to you? Why is it so important that you act as "overseer" to your spouse and your children? Do you always have negative comments to make over their choices? Is it absolutely imperative that you approve everything lest you become "hell on wheels"?

This issue hits both men and women, and a lot of it depends on who you marry or have a relationship with. You find very few totally controlling people together. There just isn't enough real chemistry for the both of you. But if you sit back and pay close attention, you'll find that the person who has "no control" is constantly complaining to friends and family about you, while at the same time you are doing likewise, complaining that you always have to be the one to take control and make all the decisions.

This is a problem for us, because the real truth is that the person constantly taking control really wants control, while the opposite is true for the one feeling controlled. They want to follow! Yes, we can continue to complain about it, but try reversing the roles. See how that works! Until you admit that you like this situation because you're too afraid to make decisions, and the other person admits that they are afraid of relinquishing control to someone else, the complaints will just keep on coming!

Assignment: Step back and see who you are, and then talk to your partner about switching roles for a week. And include a stipulation that neither of you can complain about the other! You might see a change in the whole family or relationship, one that allows for respect to be earned. Children need to see that while their parents can screw up, they can recover too!

Question: If you are still a single person, have you been known to be controlling in a relationship? Can you explain this? If you are in a relationship, how controlling do you get?

LARRY ROBINSON

FEBRUARY 22

Do you "dream the impossible dream," only to wake up to an ugly reality? Do you aspire to be better than you are and never succeed at it? Are you the type of person who creates wormholes to alternate universes and lives happily ever after in your own world, while continuing to disappoint yourself in this one? If so, then you are "hiding," and maybe you do not even want anyone to know that you're living like that.

I bet your image is fine and you appear to be content with your life, while on the inside you are crying and feeling very empty. You are afraid of what others will think about what your dream is. "You're nuts!" will echo in your head, causing you to think that no one will have any faith in you. And why? Because this is not your first daydream!

No, you are the type of person who lives through them. "Well said is better than well done" has been your approach in life, and now you have been exposed as a "dreamer." Well, do you really think that you cannot fulfill your dreams? If so, how sad, because you are going to regret your life, and who wants that feeling?

It is never too late to begin to fulfill a dream. Who told you that? Is it because your parents accepted their lot in life and you have modeled yourself after them? God, what fools we are if we accept their fate as our own. And do not tell yourself that you don't know where to begin, because we can always find a way if we really believe we can succeed!

Start with today and not yesterday, because you had no hope then. And remember, that if we do not have hope for tomorrow we will remain "stuck" today, and on and on and on it will go. This life is way too short to be the procrastinator everyone seems to view you as. Do you remember hearing, "He/she has so much potential; it will be a shame if they don't do something with it"?

Question: What is your one most important dream that you believed you would never fulfill? Have you given up on yourself?

LARRY ROBINSON

FEBRUARY 23

Do you understand what freedom is? Every other reality in our lives is determined by nature. Our hearts beat, our eyes see, our ears hear—and these are all organs that function on their own and without choice—but the nature of freedom is very different. *Freedom* is the possibility of us having choices in our life to choose to change one thing to another. We can choose to shut ourselves up, to withdraw from life, or to make our life better. We have these choices! We can deny our growth or we can enhance it! Now, you might say, "I have no choices, my life has been determined," but that is wrong. We all have that possibility, but we very rarely look at change as the freedom to choose! How many of us do not feel that way or have never even looked at life in such a way that allows for us to become something more than we were at any given moment?

Are we products of our parents' way of looking at life? Are we just another generation stuck in the past in the exact same way our parents were? When do we decide that we want the freedom to have a better life? Do you think that it is impossible, or are you afraid to change the norms in your life that you cling to because you fear the challenge of change?

Freedom gives us that ability, so if you feel stuck, then you are not actively trying to figure a way out of your painful situation. There is no one who does not have the freedom to make the most out of their life! There is only our fear that it will not work, so we start to believe that that there are no choices in life. We think this is our "lot" in life, and that it will not change! So tell me, why do you think that you do not have this freedom?

Freedom can also be the choice to remain just as you are. You have a job that you hate, a relationship that gives you no satisfaction and can even be abusive, but your parents didn't do any better, so why should you? And do you love with freedom, or do you think that you "should" love? Take for example the parent who has always rejected you and who abused you and put you down. Do you truly love that parent, or do you just think you have to? What if you realized that after years of trying to get approval from them that they were not lovable, and that you wasted most of your life trying to love an unlovable person? You had the freedom to choose not to try anymore, but you always thought there was something wrong with you and not them! Surprise, surprise, it wasn't you!

Now is the time to examine your life and decide if you ever really felt free or if you were just following what you believed were your failures in life because you thought you never had the freedom to do anything different.

Question: If you were to exercise your freedom today, what is the one thing about yourself that you would change?

_____

_____

_____

_____

_____

_____

_____

_____

_____

_____

_____

_____

LARRY ROBINSON

FEBRUARY 24

D o we all tell lies? Whether they are small "white" ones or huge "black" ones, do we all lie? Sometimes we do not believe that what we tell people *is* a lie, such as when we're approached by a friend or a family member who asks us, "How are you?" and we answer, "Fine," even though we might be in emotional or physical pain. Is this a lie, or are you just omitting the truth? You might say, "Well, I don't want that person to know my business," but to say, "Fine," is a stretch of your own imagination. What could you say that wouldn't be a lie in that particular situation?

Another white lie we're always telling is when the phone rings and it's someone we don't feel like talking to at the moment. We might look at the caller ID and say to our child, "Answer it and tell them I'm too busy right now," and we do this without flinching! But at the same time we insist that our children tell us the truth! Some great role models we are!

What happens when we tell a black lie? Remember, a white lie is so little it does not hurt anyone (at least, we like to think that), but these black ones, they are even more dangerous. They not only hurt, but are sometimes hard to forgive too. Do we all tell black lies? Well, you have to be the judge of that.

A black lie is a true distortion of the truth. We may be asked why we didn't pay the rent and we might respond that, "The company didn't give out the checks yet," but the real truth might be that we gambled it away or bought drugs or drank it away. Of course we hide all this until we eventually get caught and then we show extreme remorse, but we usually just go back and do the same thing all over again. And how many times have you suspected that an affair was going on, and when you asked you got a reply like, "Are you crazy? Why would you think that?" Of course you'd "accidentally" scrolled through that person's text messages and found some pretty damning evidence on it, but what do you do? Do you hold on to the evidence because you don't want to be labeled a "snooping" partner, or do you tell the truth?

Assignment: We all could come up with examples of these two types of lies, or even about exaggerating the truth to make it sound much more painful or dramatic. Here is a test for you: go for one day without telling a lie. And if you think it's easy, well, get ready to fail multiple times, because if you're paying close attention, you will automatically know when you're telling a lie. Oh, and good luck, because if you're really honest with yourself, you'll most likely find yourself telling one within the first hour!

February 25

Are you an independent person? Do you think on your own, or are you influenced by others? When you believe in something, do you stick to your ground or do you waver like a flag in the wind? How easily persuaded are you when it comes to changing your views? And this does not pertain to how stubborn you are, but instead how truly convinced you are that you are correct in your line of thinking. Are you an independent thinker?

Where does independent thinking come from? Did we emerge from the womb independent and did our parents often say, "You always wanted your own way, no matter how hard we tried to convince you," or "It was always your way or the highway"? The answer is no, we did not come out that way. We came out without any thought at all about whose way it was supposed to be, but we did realize at some point that we were either "overparented" or "underparented."

Overparenting gave us no room to explore or to breathe, and we were restricted at each milestone in our developmental years. Our reaction to that was we were afraid to voice an opinion out of fear of reprimand, and we remain that way today. On the flipside, underparenting gave us so much freedom that we made all our own decisions to the point where we became resistant to the opinions of others. And many times we stayed glued to our opinions regardless of whether they were right or wrong! If we thought it was right, it was right! You see, when you're a child and there's no one in your life to challenge your way of thinking, then you develop always thinking that your way is the right way!

These two ways of thinking really mess us up. They do not allow us to have interesting, challenging conversations or decision-making possibilities with our spouses or partners. We either agree on everything and secretly hate the choices being made, or we dominate every conversation or decision-making discussion with our ideas and cannot listen to others.

It is time to take stock of this so that you either gain an identity or tone your current identity down. No one can actually live like this forever. It's way too hard!

Question: Are you one of these types of people, or are you with someone who is either of these?

_____

_____

_____

_____

_____

_____

_____

_____

_____

_____

_____

_____

_____

_____

LARRY ROBINSON

February 26

How do you deal with failure? Are you the type of person who won't even approach something new if you believe that you won't do it perfectly? Were you the type of child in school who acted up just to avoid looking like you could not do the classwork? Are you the same at work in that you won't volunteer for a new project for fear of failure? This means you are stuck in life doing only repetitive work that is easiest for you. How sad that we cannot advance in life for fear of failure.

Failure does give us a chance to do it right, but it may be necessary to analyze every aspect of the work we have done just so we can see where we went astray and so we don't repeat the same errors. Why is this such a difficult task for us? Are we only a "one shot" person who goes into hiding when we know something new is coming up, because we're still holding on to our past failures?

Every failure needs to stimulate our need for power and growth. Who gave us the message that we cannot succeed? If we do not try one more time, then how would we ever know if we may have gotten it right the next time we tried? Each failure needs to bring on more determination to succeed, and this goes for both work and relationships. There is no ending point! There is only the desire to get it right!

Who told us that failure is our "fate"? Would we rather stay in "failure mode" all of our life, or know at the end of our life that we never gave up the struggle to succeed? Success determines what we have learned from our past mistakes. It is an accumulation of all of our knowledge up to this point. Why would we give up this struggle and end up back where we started? Come on, we can do much better than this! Just get those damn voices out of your head that have predicted failure and fight for success!

Question: Who in your life never gave you the credit you deserved for your accomplishments? Are you still looking for validation?

LARRY ROBINSON

FEBRUARY 27

Are we stubborn to the point where we would sacrifice our relationship to prove our point? Even when confronted with the truth, do we still hold on to our belief system even though we know the other person is right? Could we do this with everyone in our life, including our children, knowing that we are in the wrong? Why are we so stuck in this place that doesn't allow us to show vulnerability to others, especially people we love?

Are we relationship wreckers who are out to prove that no one can be with us unless they totally accept our truths and do not challenge us or put forth their own beliefs? Is it often the case where we decide what we are going to deal with and what is and is not "baloney" coming from the other person? Only we decide the path of the relationship, and it does not matter what we say or do to harm others in order to prove our point. In fact, if we screw up, we don't view it as a big deal, but God forbid the other person says or does something we don't like. All hell breaks loose!

Are we beyond stubborn and entering into a "dark zone" that has no escape exit? Are we becoming more screwed up by our inability to let go and move on to a more connected and better place? It can be very frightening to feel such vulnerability, but is that the underlying cause for our stubbornness? Are we so damaged from our past that it is too frightening to think we could be wrong? And what's worse is that for some of us being wrong equals not being loved.

How much pressure has there been in growing up and "getting it right"? Were your parents *ever* wrong? Did you ever hear them say "I'm sorry"? I wager that if you look back you very rarely heard them say that, especially as a child. If we put it all together, then maybe we can see that being wrong is just being wrong, and it does not make us less lovable. In some cases it can make us more lovable, because we show the human, vulnerable side of ourselves.

Question: Are you the type of person who can say "sorry" *and* really mean it?

LARRY ROBINSON

FEBRUARY 28

Mind, body, and spirit—we have heard these words countless times and listened over and over to those who think they know what they're talking about as if we were stupid. How many folks do you know who profess to believe in these three parts of us, but who only "talk the talk" and never "walk the walk"? This topic is difficult to understand, and even more difficult to follow.

You are not ignorant if you do not understand what they are talking about. How many times have you nodded your head to someone preaching about how "enlightened" they are while you were thinking to yourself, "Bull, you were out partying last night and your body sure didn't look *enlightened* when you were passed out on the floor"?

As we have talked about, there is a harmony in life, and what harmony really relates to is what we call a "balance." If you are not in balance with your *self,* then you are out of harmony with life. It is the same for all three, mind, body, and spirit. If, let us say, you are really feeling troubled and your mind is full of anger, sadness, depression, or hate, then it produces stress. And unless the stress is unraveled and done away with, it will find the weakest part of your body. Once it does that it will really settle in and have itself a ball, and I mean a full-fledged party without the slightest concern for you.

Now your mind has thrown your body "out of sync," and you will either get sick or you might want to medicate yourself with "home remedies" until you achieve your ultimate goal, which is to feel nothing! But your body will still suffer. And when your body suffers, so does your heart, for we feel nothing for our spirit. And spirit does not necessarily mean *God.* It can mean our own compassion and understanding and kindness toward the world. So when all three are dysfunctional, we fall into those dark, lonely, hopeless places, and all we feel is despair.

The long and short of this is that if you take care of your body, your mind feels better. If you take care of your mind, your body feels better. Consequently, if you take care of both your mind *and* body, then your spirit feels better. They all work in harmony with one another.

We can resolve a lot of our own negativity by following this guideline. And we feel so much more powerful and "enlightened" when we are in charge of our own lives.

Question: Of mind, body, and spirit, which is the hardest for you to focus on? Why?

_____

_____

_____

_____

_____

_____

_____

_____

_____

_____

_____

_____

_____

LARRY ROBINSON

"The relationship we have with ourselves has a lot to do with how we interact with others on a daily basis. When the time is taken to look within and you get to know the good and bad of who you are, then it is easier to live a focused, centered and positive life because you understand that the one constant is *you!*"

—Latoya Brand Parker, Rancho Cucamonga, California, USA

Dustin Hornblower, Lynn, Massachusetts, USA

MARCH 1

D o you know people who just complain and who every time you speak to them have something negative to say? You want so much to like them and you try to, but they continue to turn you off. It is so frustrating when we talk to a friend or even a parent and all we hear about is how awful they feel, how sick they are, and what bad things are happening in their lives. It is especially bad when it is a parent and they start in immediately when you talk to them and they just go on and on. You might even put down your phone for a spell, and when you pick it back up they are still talking!

It makes you so disgusted that they almost never ask about your family, and if they do they interrupt you when you start to speak and just start complaining all over again! And when they're finished, they say, "So how are you, dear?" At that point all you can muster up is, "Fine," and the conversation ends.

This is your problem, not theirs! You have not figured out a way to deal with them, and they kind of know it! When people go on and on about themselves, they are lonely people who have no idea how to listen to others. They have been this way all their lives, and it is a deep damage that keeps them from giving.

Assignment: Figure out ways to cut the conversation short. Listen and have empathy, but cut it short! They stay on the phone because there is no response from your side. It does not take much to give them a little, but do it without distress.

LARRY ROBINSON

MARCH 2

Do you know people or spouses who say no before you even finish your sentence? Is the word "no" a part of your relationship? Do you use it as a staple for your everyday language, or do others among your family and friends use it equally as much?

How frustrating it is for us to hear that word as adults from someone who is supposedly our equal. Sometimes you just don't want to even *suggest anything* because you know "no" will be the immediate answer. Don't you wonder what magic the other person possesses that they can read your mind before you finish your own thought? "Honey, do you think that we can—" "No" is the interrupting word that flies in your face.

As children we can do this a lot because we anticipate having to do something we don't want to do, but we are no longer in that position. Nope, we are not children!

Aren't we (both males and females) entitled to being heard? How rude we are to each other when this happens, and this does become the role model that our children pick up. No one person can tell another person that what they feel or think is wrong. In order to respect one another, we need to listen and not think we are always right, or that we run the show in our family. We all know that we do this, and don't think that it doesn't create resentments and grudges, especially when said in front of friends and family.

Question: What is your biggest fear in saying no? Do you understand that without that ability you are forever at the world's mercy?

MARCH 3

Do you know the difference between envy and jealousy? Do you think they are the same thing, or can you feel that they are not the same?

When we envy someone, we do not want to be them, but we want to have what they have. Envy is not a negative feeling, because it has its roots in "desire." Sometimes it makes us want to achieve more, and gives us the motivation to do so. When you see that friends are buying their first car or even a new home, envy can give us that push that says, "I can achieve those things also!" You can achieve when your motivation is there.

On the other hand, jealousy is a very difficult feeling, for it causes us to feel as if we want to take away something or someone from another person and own it for ourselves. The hardest issue that a lot of us face with jealousy is when it comes to relationships. Remember when there was someone you secretly liked and your close friend ended up going out with that person? How painful was that, and how did you end up feeling about your friend? Every time we saw those two people together we got that pain in our heart, and unfortunately we ended up having ugly feelings. Life would be so much easier if jealousy didn't exist.

There is also the jealousy that siblings feel toward each other. There is that wicked feeling inside when we think that a parent favors our brother or sister over us. We end up disliking that sibling because we see how fake they are. This fuels *our jealousy* because we think, "Why can't Mom or Dad see what is really going on?"

Jealousy can freeze us, and all we feel like doing is either be mean or feel sorry for ourselves. It is time to get over it! These kinds of feelings keep us children, and today we can still have the same feelings we had when we were young. We cannot change the past, just as we cannot change another person. We can only change our reaction! Holding on to such negative feelings harms our life so much.

You do not need what you think the other person has or you would have had it yourself. Well done is better than well said, so stop wishing and start looking inside yourself. Look closely and you'll see what you are capable of!

LARRY ROBINSON

Question: Are you the type of person that compares yourself to everyone else and ends up feeling "less than"? Or perhaps you end up feeling more superior to others. In any case, neither is productive.

_____

_____

_____

_____

_____

_____

_____

_____

_____

_____

_____

_____

_____

_____

March 4

Do you have emotional pain? Do you hold on to it as if it wasn't there and no one can tell you are suffering? Do you put a smile on your face and when asked if you are okay just always say, "Fine"?

You know you are not fine, but you refuse to admit to the pain. There is usually a smile on your face to disguise the ugly, dark feelings. Maybe you are the type of person who just shuts down and says nothing and has a look of indifference. You cannot break out of this frozen prison that you have created. You don't even let your best friend know how much pain you have.

Are you hyper-sensitive to everything and everyone, so much so that you walk around waiting for the next wound to open inside? Can you be whistling a happy tune for a while and at some point from the smallest disagreement comes a flood of dark, mean feelings, feelings you had no idea were even there?

This is not normal! Now, it's true that no one really knows what "normal" actually is, but this isn't it! We only hurt ourselves, and the damage that those outbursts can cause really does hurt others, especially children who witness these tirades. They do not know who you are or trust that this will not happen again.

We are meant to learn about ourselves from emotional pain, not others. If we block emotional pain we do not grow up. This is the same pain we have always carried around, and any feelings that you still have from childhood are childish! They do not represent the you of today!

Again, it is time to step back and tell yourself that you will deal with this pain, and if not, then you cannot blame anyone else for it. Do it now before you are stuck there for a lifetime!

Question: Are you afraid to let go of this pain? It has been such a part of your life. Facing it will help you let it go. Are you addicted to it?

LARRY ROBINSON

MARCH 5

Why don't we really forgive someone we love? How often have you thought that you had forgiven them for an issue you had and down the road in a fight your anger bursts open again? There it is, the same issue rearing its ugly head once again. Why did you go back there and stir that ugly pot another time? Did we really forgive or did we only *want* to forgive, and in the end there was so much resentment there that even though we thought it went away it didn't?

Is this our fault? Did the other person do so much damage to us that it is their fault, or is it something that we just cannot seem to get through? In that moment, we cannot feel our love for that other person, nor can we remember that we had forgiveness. Are we so hurt that we cannot see in front of ourselves anymore? The answer is: No!

We have not dealt with who we were in the situation, and we still want to put all the responsibility for our pain on the other person. When we are in pain over another issue and we begin to fight, that other pain in our subconscious rushes to the surface and we scream out, "And how could you have done that to me?" It could have been six months ago, and yet it hurts more now than the immediate issue.

We seem to forget that we are responsible for our own choices, and because we are we can be filled with so much guilt that it overwhelms us and we cannot look inside. We must decide today that we will truly look at the choices we have made in the past and not place all the responsibility on others. Facing who we were and why we made the choice to stay in a relationship when we were hurt or did not agree with our partner is not their fault, but our own fear of being alone.

We stayed for our own reasons, and that is the truth!

Question: Have you made the right choice to stay in your relationship or are you afraid to leave?

LARRY ROBINSON

March 6

D o you fool everyone, even yourself, about how you feel about being in the world? Do you pretend to be funny, sweet, obliging, and caring, yet inside you feel isolated and alone? Are you someone who is covering up your fear of decision-making, socializing, and pushing ahead at work by self-medicating in order to do these things? Do you tell people half-truths about where you are in life while you are screaming inside to be left alone? This is not because you want it, but because you have never gotten over your fear of being part of something since you were a child.

Do you remember times in school when you felt invisible, as if no one even recognized your existence? Or did you cover for yourself by acting stupid or making fun of yourself just to be noticed? How much has changed for you today?

It is so terribly lonely to be invisible, especially when you hate yourself for being a coward! The feeling does not even go away when you are grown, because the same behavior is still there and only now you feel hopeless. Over and over it races through your mind, saying, "Why doesn't anyone talk to me?" But have you ever stopped and thought that maybe, just maybe, it might be you?

Do you really believe you are shy, or is that just an attitude you took on once you went to school? Was your attitude that it really didn't matter if no one spoke to you anyway?

Sometimes we give off an attitude of not caring. Have you ever seen a child shaking in a corner because he/she is not recognized? I doubt it! "I don't need you because I am better than you" becomes our thought process, and that begins our journey of hatred and jealousy. Those feelings haunt us, and they only get more sophisticated as we grow older.

I imagine you are stuck and will not do anything about it. You can tell yourself, "I don't know what to do," but that is bull! It takes the same strength you needed as a child when you approached someone trying to make friends, and I mean real friends, not fake ones. Do you really think other people are supposed to approach you? You need to think about what it is you give off that says to other people, "I have something to offer!"

Assignment: List your positive attributes. Do you believe that you have something special to offer other people, or do you see yourself as boring?

_____

_____

_____

_____

_____

_____

_____

_____

_____

_____

_____

_____

_____

_____

_____

_____

MARCH 7

Do you wear your feelings on your sleeve? Can everyone tell that you are "emotionally distressed," or do you try to hide your pain by shutting down and keeping a somewhat "fake" smile going so no one notices you? How do you deal with your hurt inside? In an attempt to numb your pain, do you tell so many people about it that by the time you're finished you are so emotionally exhausted that you feel nothing? Do you talk about it so much that it begins to feel like a tale you are telling rather than heartache you are experiencing?

Are you a person who deals with his/her pain by self-medicating it with "booze and sex and rock and roll" until you feel empty? Do you really think these methods help you through the pain, or simply block it up? How are we supposed to deal with this horrible empty feeling that makes us feel like we are craving something, even though we have no idea what it is?

Any way we look at this, the answer is that we want attention. Who doesn't want people to feel compassion and see that we are the victim of someone's cruelty, or that we've suffered the loss of a parent or friend? We need as much support as it will take, but do we tend to carry on too much about how we feel, or are we really feeling at all? Many of us tend to condition ourselves to hide the real feelings while *projecting* ones that we think the world wants to see. Do we ever get the chance to feel genuine about our feelings?

To experience this true feeling we must look at the reality of our feelings. We have to be honest with ourselves. Many of you will challenge me on what constitutes real feelings, and you might even be angry that I would challenge the death of a relationship or person or loss of a job, but it is so important for you to know what you are really mourning and what you really want from others, because otherwise they cannot help fix you.

You must look inside you and be honest with who you are in these situations. This will help you see that perhaps the relationship was too painful for the both of you or that the person you lost was suffering or needed to move on. Maybe they were just too hard to love. You will grow through this.

LARRY ROBINSON

Question: What ways or methods do you use to avoid your emotional pain?

_____

_____

_____

_____

_____

_____

_____

_____

_____

_____

_____

_____

_____

_____

_____

_____

_____

MARCH 8

Why do we punish one another? When is enough, enough? Oftentimes we hold on to our silence in order to make the person who has hurt us suffer, and yes, the word "suffer" does enter into your mind but not your heart. We think that if we stay silent or act cold or mean, then those who have abused our trust will learn a lesson. We think that as long as we continue to inflict our pain on them they will learn that they are bad, selfish, and deceitful, and that we will not be hurt again.

Wrong! You see, it does not matter what they did, they most likely did not set out to hurt us to begin with. They screwed up in some way that either broke our trust or damaged our faith in them, but now you are deliberately setting out to harm them, using the rationale that "what is good for the goose is good for the gander." And that's not necessarily true. We did not have time to evaluate the situation, we only reacted to it. And if we had had more time to control the emotions that have welled up inside us, we'd be more capable of handling the situation without inflicting punishment.

Is this too much to ask? Perhaps if we tried holding our tongues and made an effort to really listen, then maybe we would begin to understand the other person's actions. And this applies to our children also, especially when we say things to hurt them after they have disappointed us. Remember, some things we say cannot be taken back!

If someone breaks our trust, don't we really want to know why? If someone acts negatively toward us, don't we really want to understand them?

Question: Ask yourself who you are punishing today. What form does it take?

LARRY ROBINSON

MARCH 9

Why do we suffer so much? Why is it that one moment we can experience life's joys, and the next such deep pain? We get so confused as to why this goes on, but for many of us there is a reason for this, and we bury it deep in our subconscious.

We cannot view joy as something that balances out our pain. No one experiences the void of joy in their life, just as no one experiences a lack of pain. We have somehow become addicted to our "past thinking" that paints us either as a victim or "not deserving" of happiness. We view joy as just a fleeting moment followed by a return of the pain.

Deep inside of us we have wounds from childhood, wounds we have buried so deeply that we react automatically to stressful situations and equate them with pain. Stress is a part of our life, just as it's a part of a child's life, and yet we do not explain stress as something we all go through but as something we try to avoid. Do we teach our children what stress really is, or do we "identify" it as their pain? If we make the identification, then we experience their pain as part of our own.

When you can separate yourself from their pain, that's when you are really there for them. We reduce their suffering by normalizing stress as part of life. This will work if you do it for yourself as well. You can be the victim of your past or the hero of your present! It is up to you to see the difference!

Question: Whether you have children or not, are you a victim of your past? How and why?

_____

_____

_____

_____

LARRY ROBINSON

March 10

A re you someone who is always reminding others about how much you do? Do you know people who are constantly talking about what they do for others or their families? How annoying is this for you? Do you get calls from folks who ask you how you are and before you can even answer the question they start talking about themselves, either complaining about their day or venting about what their spouse does not do and how they carry the bulk of the family chores or finances?

I'll bet there have been times when you've placed your phone down only to find that when you put it back to your ear they are still talking! Do you ever think you could be doing this to other people? Do you ever stop to think about the person on the other end when you are in this mode? After all, they never stop and think about you when they're doing it!

We are either too afraid to stop or don't want to be selfish, but when we hang up the phone we are often angry because it's usually them who says, "I have to go," and they cut you short. Or how about when they get another call while you're talking and tell you they've got to go, and you know it's not an important call and you haven't even said two words?

If we do not gently confront people who do this, then they're probably not aware and it's our fault for not saying anything to them. If they get insulted, then they really weren't a friend to begin with. And if someone doesn't tell us, then the same goes. We all need to learn to speak up and listen. We all need to feel heard!

Question: Who is it in your life that appears to always be talking about themselves? Have you had enough of this? Why can't you confront them?

LARRY ROBINSON

MARCH 11

Do you think too much? Are you the type of person who needs to analyze everything so you can find a "rational" answer but skip over how you feel? Do you think your feelings would influence your thoughts? Have you been accused of being too rational or too emotional? It does work both ways for men and women. How did it come about that you couldn't put together a single mindful thought (keeping your thoughts that will validate your feelings) and because of it you became "too cold" or "too hot" with your emotions?

We need to remember that an emotion is not a "feeling," but rather an unconscious reaction to a feeling. If I am angry, I might scream at you, but screaming is not a feeling, but moreover a reaction to being angry.

So many of us are reactionary people! Even the rational person who is constantly thinking about why they did something that is disapproved of is covering their feelings with thoughts. You might be the type of person who is impossible to disagree with because you always have a rational answer to every confrontation. Yes, something may make sense, but it makes the other person crazy because you dismiss their feelings as out of control. Well, guess what? You pushed them there! It was that rational self of yours that showed no feelings during the conversation or confrontation.

Do you always end up walking away from these discussions wondering why you even bothered? Has your partner, parent, boss, or even child held you hostage to your emotions while they analyzed why you behaved a certain way?

Question: How are you going to handle this now that you can identify which one you are? The "analyzer" or the "emotional mess," which one do you think has a harder time in life?

_____

_____

_____

LARRY ROBINSON

MARCH 12

W hy do so many of us have difficulty maintaining healthy relationships? Why do we always seem to end up in the same battles even though we promise ourselves that we will not go there? We especially promise our partners or family members that we will not erupt, but we always do, and we humiliate ourselves by saying horribly mean things to our partners. What is set off so quickly in us that we do not even hear what the other person has said when many times it's merely a question they're asking rather than a statement about us? A good example is when our partner says, "Sue, could you take my cleaning in today," but we hear it as an order: "Sue, take my cleaning in today." And this works both ways in a relationship. We do this to each other!

Are we that fragile that we cannot listen to our spouse, child, or parent? And this can happen any place we are, even at work, where most of the time it is essential that we hold it in for threat of losing our job. There are so many ways in which we feel put upon and angry at the other person, for we are always feeling misunderstood or at fault for what we are presumed to have done. After so many of these episodes, we either give up on the relationship or we settle into such low self-esteem that we automatically think that everything is always our fault. So how do we begin to change this and learn to communicate?

These are very difficult situations for us to handle, for we have to change something about ourselves rather than try to change the other person. Why do we rush into unfair judgments when we are faced with criticism or even perceived criticism? At this point, *Mirror, Mirror* does not think it is that important to answer the "why" of the question, because there could be a vast number of reasons and they only have to do with you. The more important answer we are looking for lies in whether we are actually hearing the other person or really listening to them!

Assignment: Just "hearing" sends our minds back in time and dredges up old ghosts who tell us we are not good enough, while "listening" allows us to step back for a moment and ask whether the criticism may be valid. When faced with this situation, take a deep breath and count

LARRY ROBINSON

to ten slowly. This may sound silly, but when some of us get heated too quickly we spew out our defensiveness. And since anger is hot, we explode! Taking some time to breathe allows our bodies to cool down, resulting in clearer and more rational moments.

Another way of avoiding these fights where we build up resentments and grudges is to set aside ten minutes every other day (every day would be ideal, but sometimes not possible) and check in with each other. This gives us the chance to really talk. And if someone doesn't take the opportunity to open themselves to their feelings, well, then at least you put it out there! Remember, we can all do better at developing healthy relationships if we commit to changing and improving ourselves.

_____

_____

_____

_____

_____

_____

_____

_____

_____

_____

_____

_____

_____

MARCH 13

A re you someone who is still looking for your parents' approval? Did you have a healthy relationship with them when you were a child? Do you know what the word "attachment" means? "Attachment" is an ongoing relationship between parent and child that provides experience, discipline, and positive childcare. It provides consistency of caregiving over time and your parents' sensitivity to your individual needs. Healthy attachment knows when and *how* far to allow a child to be free and then brings the child back in, providing safety and healthy boundaries. But what happens when there is an unhealthy attachment between parent and child? Do you think you fit into the category of healthy attachment or unhealthy?

Did you ever feel abandoned by your parents when you were a child? This could be both imagined and real, because it is about a child's feelings. Often we have parents who are very inconsistent in their ability to be there when a child needs them; i.e., to be fed, changed, picked up and held, or to be played with. And when there is inconsistency in this there is damage done to the child. This can make us either too needy or too independent.

Sometimes we'll see a child cling to a parent and have to be pried off them, while other times we'll see a child who does not want to be picked up by not only the parent, but anyone at all. They squirm in the laps of their parents until they force them to put them down. And often the parent will reject either type of behavior. But if we do not fix this problem in childhood, we will see it reappear in our adult relationships. We can tend to be very needy and smothering in our adult relationships, or we might be cold and untouchable.

Either dynamic is unhealthy, and to make matters worse, we can hand it down to our children. We either hold on to our children too closely in reaction to our parents' rejection of us (real or imagined), or we give them too much freedom, which ultimately makes them feel abandoned. Generation after generation can experience this, and it is time to stop!

Look closely at how you act in a relationship. Now is the time for us to realize that no one can fix us when it comes to our insecurities.

LARRY ROBINSON

We have to be the heroes of our own lives. And understand that it is never too late to become more independent and less needy, and on the reverse, more able to depend on others and less stubbornly independent.

Question: Can you describe who you are in a relationship? What are some of your positive and negative characteristics?

_____

_____

_____

_____

_____

_____

_____

_____

_____

_____

_____

_____

_____

MARCH 14

Are you filled with doubt most of the time? I do not mean fear that cripples you, but doubt that makes you question everything you and anyone else does. No matter how hard you try, you cannot refrain from questioning the validity of your own thoughts or the feelings of others. No matter what you try, it rambles around in your mind like a tumbleweed that is picking up more questions along the way. You tend not to listen once doubt gets into your mind, and you become an "inquisitor" with a full line of interrogations. You make yourself a painful person to be around, for you cannot just be happy for the other person, and you make it your business to be the devil's advocate. How does it feel when you are interrogated?

Make a mental note of the term "Doubting Thomas" and remember it, for it will follow you around your entire life if you do not begin to understand that it prevents people from wanting to confide in you or ask your opinion. Maybe now you understand why you may be left out of certain conversations. It is because your doubts become so annoying that people avoid you when there is a problem, or even happy news, for that matter.

So ask yourself, "Have I always behaved like this?" I don't think so! We become this way because we have been interrogated ourselves when we were children. There wasn't anything that didn't become a huge drama when we were kids because of our parents' negativity. "Why would you be elected class treasurer?" "Why didn't the teacher recognize you as a class leader?" "Why aren't you 'most popular'?" "What's wrong with your brain that it doesn't function like the other kids'?" "You are not being very smart right now!" How often did you hear something like these negative questions and comments growing up?

It is not uncommon for a child to grow up confused about right and wrong, so naturally they bring it along into their adult lives. And again, everything we talk about now is "mindfulness," where you stay in the present and recognize when you drift into the past. And keep your negativity away from others too, for they have enough of their own and certainly do not need yours! I'm sure that as far as you are concerned you could fill a book with your doubts.

Now, begin to understand that life has its risks attached to it and if we do not take chances we stay stuck in our lives. You can stop the doubt by being mindful when it happens.

Assignment: List all of your fears that prevent you from moving forward in your life. What are you afraid of?

_____

_____

_____

_____

_____

_____

_____

_____

_____

_____

_____

_____

_____

_____

_____

_____

"Even when we lack praise in our childhood, we still have many chances to move forward. Finding praise from others is not always necessary. What really matters is appreciating how productive you are now compared to before and that *praise* is just a bonus."

—Marjorie Laduas Tiozan, Philippines

Christina Alvarado, Ulote, Costa Rica

March 15

Are you your own worst enemy? Are you always out to sabotage yourself and cannot stop once you've started? Do you always put yourself down or belittle your actions when you look at yourself, constantly picking yourself apart though there is no real reason to? Are there never-ending cycles you go through where you start off investing yourself in something you're excited about only to see your enthusiasm fade right in front of you? Does it look like you never finish anything? Are you the first to say something negative about yourself when you are with other people? Do people start to shy away from you after a while because they can no longer tolerate your self-putdowns? You have a problem that has not changed since childhood and it is preventing you from achieving your own happiness!

As children it is necessary for us to find coping mechanisms in order to get through our childhood. Often we take the path we believe is easiest for us and which reflects the real or perceived messages we receive from our surroundings. Since no one can tell us how we are feeling, it is left up to us to determine what we believe to be true. Now, most likely it is not true, but we build a life based on these misinterpretations.

If you are overweight as a child you make fun of yourself before anyone else can, or if you do not do well in school you may call yourself stupid. Look to see what you did to your self-esteem as a child. At times we become the "problem child" as a way of validating our negative view of ourselves and give off the vibe that we do not care, but the reality is that we are in constant pain! We are our own worst critic and our greatest deceiver. We invest ourselves in trying to prove our low self-worth, and this creates a shield that we use for protection. We do this along the lines of, "If I say something bad about myself first, it won't hurt as much if someone else says something about me later!"

Inside of you there is this child who cannot see their goodness and value. Every time you decide that you want a better life, a voice in your head decides that you do not deserve happiness! This is not you, but rather the child in you who could never let go of feeling bad.

As an adult, it is your responsibility to catch that child in his/her negativity about you. Let the past rest, and approach life as a person who has gone to battle with you and won! If you have the same negativity you did as a child, then you have not left your childhood and are keeping it alive and well inside you. And what a shame that you will not feel success until you take control of that voice inside!

Question: What does your inner voice say to you? How has it stopped you from growing up? Does it whisper bad things to you?

_____

_____

_____

_____

_____

_____

_____

_____

_____

_____

_____

_____

_____

MARCH 16

Do you carry resentments around with you? Are you easily *triggered* by a statement you hear or a picture you see that brings back your resentments? Are you unaware that you even have resentments, but you get bad feelings that come out of nowhere and your mood changes? What is resentment to start with, and why is it so powerful over us? Will we never have that peace of mind we so desperately need but cannot seem to reach? What is the difference between "resentment" and a "grudge"?

Resentments come from issues we usually have with another person that we have not confronted. This person has so deeply wounded us that we feel unforgiving. The resentment stays deep inside of us and grows uglier the longer we hold on to it. Sometimes we even get off on them as we twist them around in our head and we think up all these bad things about the other person. We create dramatic scenes in our minds that torture the other person or put them in humiliating situations. And we can run into them with a smile on our face but with evil in our hearts. Our hearts are "frozen" toward these folks, and we do not want them to know what is really going on.

We are afraid of that confrontation and we try to keep the resentment hidden as if it is our secret. When the resentment gets so big inside of us that we are unable to contain it, we usually end up exploding, and often over something that has very little meaning. We have no choice at the time and we let it out, and we catch the other person completely off guard with the depth of our anger. Our secret is out! Do you realize how many times resentment can be a misunderstanding, and yet we have been wasting away in unhealthy anger that has no meaning whatsoever except in our own "fragile" mind?

A grudge goes much deeper into our mind and causes us to "exile" a person from our life. We cannot tolerate seeing them or even hearing their name. It is so deeply rooted that not even their death can make it go away. Sometimes we can hold on to the grudge for years even after a person dies! It can be with family, friends, and even ex-spouses with whom we have deep, unresolved issues. With grudges, we will never find that peace of mind; in fact, we often do not even realize we are holding our grudge until it is too late. We spend so much of our life secretly hating. It is very sad.

In AA there are steps aimed at helping people with their recovery. Step 4 is "Made a searching and fearless moral inventory of ourselves," and it is truly valuable for this work in getting rid of resentments. This is a very difficult task, for it asks us to look into ourselves to see what role we played in these resentments we carry around.

In most cases we will be able to see truthfully the role we played with certain people we did not want to deal with. It is important to start in childhood because ignored and unresolved resentments do not go away; they just go "undercover" as we age. So make your list, and it is sometimes important to talk to someone else about the list because it brings the resentments to life.

And lest we forget, *forgiveness* is a fine way of letting go of our resentments. You do not have to forget that you were hurt by someone, but with forgiveness you begin to let go of your pain. Remember, this is about your pain, not the other person's. Do not worry about them. You will work this out for yourself, and it is not about protecting others from your hurt.

Do you forgive yourself for things that you have done to others? If you haven't, then you can forgive yourself for those things. You see, you must want to rid yourself of this burden in order for this to be effective. If you cannot confront someone in person, then write two letters to them. The first is called "The letter I never sent," and in this letter you want to let them have it good with everything you have inside you. This is to relieve yourself of painful feelings. Then write the letter you will send, and speak from your heart about the disconnection you feel and tell them that you want to mend broken fences. Remember, this is not about their answer as much as it is about your feelings. Some people will probably not be able to handle them, but the point is to rid ourselves of the load we carry. This is not selfish. What is selfish is not letting someone know how you feel while pretending everything is all right!

There is no single answer to these issues, but there is a direction that we need to head in, and that is toward the letting go process. If you think you cannot let go no matter what you do, then there is a part of you that simply doesn't want to. Chalk that up to your stubbornness and not to your hurt. Look closely at you!

Assignment: Write down a list of resentments, no matter how small, in order to first see what you have been dragging around in your life. This is vital in letting go.

_____

_____

_____

_____

_____

_____

_____

_____

_____

_____

_____

_____

_____

_____

_____

_____

_____

_____

MARCH 17

B rothers and sisters, our siblings, sometimes we cannot live with them and sometimes we need them more than we even know. What happens when there is a distance between you and your siblings and you cannot or will not heal it? How do we let them back into our lives and how do we mend these broken bridges? Have we burned that bridge completely, or is it not too late to repair it? Why is it always so difficult to deal with this issue? Is it our pride, or is it that we have always felt misinterpreted by them?

Resentment toward our siblings starts in childhood, when we either had to accept that they were coming into our lives or we into theirs. The difficult part is when we do not get enough nurturing and then suddenly another child is on the way. Either we become best friends with that brother or sister, or we become secret and silent enemies. But is that friendship truly real when we see them get something we do not and they see the same with us? Do we sometimes not want to listen to them because they take up all the space in a conversation? Is it that by the time they've finished their long-winded monologue and finally ask, "How are you?" all we can muster is, "Fine," and then the conversation or visit is over?

Do you feel that resentment? Can you feel it right now after reading this? If so, let it come up and maybe we can finally deal with some truths that have been hidden. How long has it been in there while you've continued to deny anything was wrong?

It is also important to understand the order in which you were born. Each position has its own issues attached to it. If you are the firstborn and you do not get at least two and a half or three years of single attention from your parents, you may run into a competitive relationship with the next-born child. We need the individual attention to secure ourselves before we can accept any new sibling. Sometimes children are born so fast that they do not have the chance to find that security and end up being pushed back on the chain of children, where they end up fighting everyone for attention.

The firstborn is the "experimental child," for if the parents have had no experience raising a child, then the first becomes a "practice child."

We often get inconsistencies in our parenting, and that can cause one parent to be pitted against the other in how to raise children. And if one parent is too hard and the other easy, this can make it so the child remains unafraid of the parents and in control of them. And when the next child comes along it can become very difficult for the first to manage.

If the first child is a girl, they many times become "mommy's little helper" and are often left later to care for other children if mom becomes overwhelmed by her attempt to mother more than one child at a time. If a boy is born first, he is held up as either a good example or a bad one to follow. This will add to the child's resentment, for they often see others get away with things they couldn't. This also happens with girls, but not as much because they are generally relegated to "caretaker."

Now, if you are the middle child, you basically have two options. You can be the best child or the worst child. The *best* child shows mom and dad how great they are and does everything they're asked to do and sometimes even more, especially if they are competing for attention with the oldest. The second child can be the "tattletale" in order to show the parents that they are the best child. They can continue this with every other child that is born and even into adulthood!

The "worst" second or middle child will be out of control and a real troublemaker who is constantly seeking negative attention from parents both at home and in school. They listen to no one and can be oppositional children who are always looking for fights with other children or even adults. They can be bullies to other siblings and children in general. If they do not get the nurturing they need, watch out!

The "baby" of the family either gets too much or too little. Too much means they are spoiled and get away with everything the others didn't, and they never get in trouble. They are held in contempt by the others because different sets of rules develop for older and younger, and they know it! They play out the "victim" and are always running to the parents because they are being teased by the others, which is often not the case.

The youngest who gets too little often results from older parents who are worn out from parenting. They can leave this child to be raised by other siblings and allow them to make their own decisions, because as parents they are just not available. They are often needy adults, either wanting too much from their spouse or unavailable emotionally.

This is just a small list of order in normal-sized families, but in larger families "splits" can be created where basically the same issues play out. What generally happens is that the very oldest and very youngest get very different parenting.

Question: Which one are you and what has been your experience as that sibling?

_____

_____

_____

_____

_____

_____

_____

_____

_____

_____

_____

_____

_____

LARRY ROBINSON

March 18

Have we lost sight of what "family" really means? Do we feel that we are a family unit or individuals who are all very separate but living together almost like roommates? Do we rush around every morning and feel hassled by our spouses, partners, or children? What is the most important thing you do for them each morning? Are you really a family, or do you even question it? You can be a single parent or not even have children and yet still be a family to each other. Who runs the show at your house?

If you are parenting children, do you realize that both you and your partner must act as a united front to your children in order for them to thrive as a unit? When one parent is too easy and another too hard, children are neutralized, and because they fear neither parent, they tend to get out of control very quickly. If you are a single parent, your work can be either harder or less difficult, depending on whether or not you can maintain a consistency with the children. Children should not make decisions for themselves when they are three, but many end up doing just that because parents feel it is easier to give in than it is to be consistent. This is such a Western problem, and I assume that at some point it will become a world problem as children will eventually devour us through their electronics.

There is no way we can realistically keep electronics from children, but how many of you feel like you're fighting a losing battle with objects because they are no longer children that you recognize? If you fail to be consistent, remember this: medicating your child because you think something must be wrong with them is way out of bounds! It is not their problem that they do not listen! After all, why would they if there is no structure in their lives? But who then is responsible? And how many children respond only if you are yelling at them? They cannot hear softly spoken words any longer and they now only respond to yelling!

Okay, so let's make today "National Get It Right Day" with our children and even our spouses. We will begin with consistency, and we will go in fully expecting that they will all rebel against us. But we are going to be as fearless as warriors going into battle, and with one main goal, that of succeeding in making it a better world for them! We asked for children, and now that we have them, who is going to get them through the harshness of their childhood?

Assignment: Do something today that is positive for your children, spouse, or partner.

_____

_____

_____

_____

_____

_____

_____

_____

_____

_____

_____

_____

March 19

Do you feel disappointed by the people in your life? Do you feel that at first you really trusted someone and then it was as if you never knew who they were because you felt betrayed by them? They never respected your business, and before you knew it people would come up to you and ask you personal questions that only the person you told knew. Did you feel that now you had to keep everything locked up inside because there was no trusting anyone? Is it possible that you unconsciously knew your problems would not be held by the other person and that you were unknowingly using them to tell others something very personal about yourself? Or maybe it is you who cannot keep someone else's private issues to yourself!

Why do people tell something that binds them to a secret when we ourselves might have trouble keeping quiet? Isn't it normal for people to gossip and spread the word about someone else's problems? We might not like that idea, but so many people have trouble keeping quiet over explosive news. What kind of position do we put others in due to our own fear of exposure, or better yet, our own inability to tell others? If we didn't want anyone to know, then why did we tell someone in the first place? Now, you might say there was a need to vent out our troubles to someone in order to relieve some of our pain, but this is basically not a great idea, for oftentimes after venting, even though we may temporally feel as if a burden has been lifted from shoulders, we still have not confronted the person we needed to! We played it out with our confidant instead! We may feel better, but the issue remains unresolved. We have unloaded on someone else and now they have to carry around those ugly feelings until they get the opportunity to vent to someone else! Do you think that the secret is safe?

What if you are not reliable in keeping someone else's private feelings to yourself? How often have you blurted out something you knew about a person you were discussing and exposed information that was supposed to be secret? We do not help anyone by forcing them to expose their feelings because we cannot keep things under lock and key. Perhaps we have never been able to keep others' secrets. Maybe we should let someone know what our truth is so they at least know the risk they're taking before they tell us something. Honesty, in this case, is really the way of preserving friendships and relationships. It is no fault of your own if keeping secrets is too hard for you. The real fault is not telling the truth about it!

Secrets are not secrets if you deal with your own issues and do not put the burden of knowledge on someone else. Learn to deal with your own stuff without involving someone else. And let others know that you are not one for keeping secrets. It saves a lot of pain in the end!

Question: Who do you vent to when you are in trouble? Has it helped you?

_____

_____

_____

_____

_____

_____

_____

_____

_____

_____

_____

_____

LARRY ROBINSON

MARCH 20

D o you know what a "gut reaction" is? Have you ever had one? A gut reaction is a feeling in the pit of your stomach that alerts you to some truth that you need to listen to. It tells us whether something is good or bad for us. Here is an example: "One day, driving his shiny new car into the city, John had difficulty finding a parking spot. He circled the block around his office building umpteen times until a legitimate spot finally opened up. As John was stepping out of his car, a tiny voice whispered in his ear, "Do not park here, you cannot see your car from your office window!" But being who he is, he paid no attention to it and instead just felt relieved to find the spot. At the end of his day he walked up and down the street looking for his car. John was sure it was where he thought it was. Wrong! It had been stolen!" And that is an example of a gut reaction *ignored!*

Have you ever had a gut reaction toward someone you thought was "the" person for you? Remember that tingling feeling in the pit of your stomach that said, "You have entered the 'I am going to get *crushed*' zone"? You knew what your gut had said to you, but the charge you got from that person was so great that you ignored your intuition and went with the "electricity." Well, that shock was to come back and bite you, for the pain was about to begin.

Rather than go toward someone that was normal, you chose the guy/gal who would emotionally tease you, abuse you, cheat on you, and never be able to make a commitment to you! The little quirks (that were not so little after all) you figured you could change later. And the only thing that changed was you heart, for it was broken!

We do not listen to our gut because we are lazy, bored, or looking for excitement and doing the "right thing" just doesn't cut it. Let's face it, you have low self-esteem. Why would you choose all the negatives over someone who could provide you with security, safety, stability, and consistency, the core components of a healthy relationship?

It is time to get out of these messy relationships that go nowhere. You must go back and validate that gut feeling from the first time you met this person. You need to see that you are drawn into the intrigue of this person who is unavailable to you. Want better for yourself, and stop being afraid of the word "forever"!

Question: Have you had gut reactions before that you didn't listen to and you still regret? What were they and do they still creep up on you?

_____

_____

_____

_____

_____

_____

_____

_____

_____

_____

_____

_____

March 21

A re you someone who gets defeated very easily? If things do not go as you planned, do you junk the plan and give yourself an excuse as to why you don't want to do it anymore? Are you really just afraid of failure and therefore always hiding from your own truth? Do you start off a project with a gung-ho attitude and end up feeling disgusted with yourself because you failed to finish it? Did you quit as soon as the going got tough, and you either made up some lame excuse about why you didn't finish or you carefully planned an argument and stomped away? You are the one who knows the truth. Do you think that this can be a recipe for defeat for everything you do?

Do you remember in school when you didn't know something, and rather than feel stupid you might have caused some trouble and been reprimanded by the teacher? This became an easy way to not feel humiliated and for not knowing the right answers. You might have grown up thinking you were stupid and that you really had no future, but the real issue is that you failed to study and when you got something wrong you quit on yourself!

Do you know that you have a great deal of potential and that no one, including you, knows it? Do you ever tell yourself that you are not smart? This is often the first indication that you will not be able to finish tasks. If you start out with a negative, then you will most likely follow up with negatives. This is your setup for defeat and you don't really even know it. It might even be worse if you did! Why even bother with it? All this conditioning from your past emerges into the present to repeat the same pattern, and then, exhausted and defeated, you fail again!

Let's fix this one. It has been your "evil twin" for too long. First of all, you are always shortchanging yourself. Maybe that child from your past couldn't concentrate or was subjected to horrible incidents at home that made it impossible to focus. Perhaps you were responsible for other siblings and were too wiped out to study your own lessons. Just think of all the "junk" that went on and you will see that it would have taken a miracle for you to pay attention and complete assignments.

You are not that child anymore! Stop thinking like him/her and realize that as an adult you are much wiser than a teenager! There is nothing that positive energy cannot accomplish! Now, you might say, "Well, how do I get from negative to positive?" You do it by reminding yourself that you are not in that bad situation any longer, and you then start looking at what you have accomplished! Perhaps you have become a fantastic cook or a great auto mechanic, and it took brains to become those things. You minimize your accomplishments, for that is what you do, but in reality you have accomplished things you give yourself no credit for.

Give yourself credit! No one in your life can give you credit until you take away the stigma that you have placed on yourself!

Question: Why do you think it has been so hard for you to give yourself credit in your life?

_____

_____

_____

_____

_____

_____

_____

_____

_____

_____

LARRY ROBINSON

MARCH 22

Have you lost your credibility with people? Have your actions ever turned others away and getting back into their lives has been difficult or impossible for you? Do you turn situations around and put the blame on others when you need to take responsibility for your own behavior? How often do you create drama and then deny you had anything to do with it? These are not uncommon issues in our lives, but the resolution just depends on whether you are willing to take responsibility for your part or not. What situations in your life are unfinished or have been discarded because you have been unwilling to look at you?

Making amends is not an easy task, and often we are looking for some reward or praise, perhaps we took the lead and tried to fix broken bridges with folks we have cared about. In fact, sometimes we cannot see beyond ourselves. It has been way too important for us to be right rather than sorry, even if "right" is in our eyes only!

How did we get this hard and stubborn? How many people have we left behind because we needed to be right and did not care about their feelings? Is your life having fewer and fewer people in it? Your credibility does not depend on whether you were right or wrong in a situation, but on whether you can be responsible for your part in a dispute that took part between two people. Remember the old phrase "It takes two to tango." There are very few situations in which it is only one person's fault. And the idea here is not to get the other person to see that you are being honest simply so that they should follow after you. Your credibility does not depend on someone else!

We make amends because we need to do this for ourselves. That is the major reason. Our hearts need to feel light in order to be free. When we "stew" in anger over something we contributed to, our hearts are heavy. And the longer this goes on, the more difficult it becomes to say, "I am sorry for my part." Can you even say "I am sorry"? How difficult has this phrase been for you? Remember, when you take control of your life you are free! When you own up to your own responsibilities you begin to recover that credibility that you need in order to like yourself.

Assignment: Make a list of the people or situations that you need to make amends to. Do not allow yourself to reinvest in the who is right or wrong of the situation.

_____

_____

_____

_____

_____

_____

_____

_____

_____

_____

_____

_____

_____

_____

MARCH 23

Are you afraid to make decisions for your life? Do you wish that someone would come by and take control of your decision-making process so that you don't have to worry about what is right or wrong for your life? Let someone else do it! Do you hate it when someone asks your opinion in front of a large group and you subsequently stumble through your answer? Are you someone who says they are really shy, but in reality you do not like to hear yourself speak? This is also part of making decisions about what you believe in.

Do you remember back in school there were those kids who constantly raised their hands and would even blurt the answers out, and who were not afraid of speaking up? In fact, they stole the show. Well, where were *you* in your class? I'll bet you were not the one waving their hand all over the place, but rather the one trying not to be noticed! "Please don't call on me. I do not want to be humiliated. I do not know the answer!" And how many times did someone else give an answer that you already knew but couldn't decide if it was right or not? Sometimes you might even have been pushed to the point of causing some kind of trouble in class so as not to have to answer questions. It is better to be called a problem than stupid! How sad were you at that time in your life? And to make matters worse, nothing has changed for you since you were in school! You still doubt yourself!

This inability to make decisions does not come from school, but it does get played out there. You might have been the type of child who was always corrected by parents or other siblings. You hated to be corrected all the time, so you just shut down. You tried not to care, but you were so angry that no one valued what you thought. Trying to take the attitude of "who cares!" was all you were left with, and what a shame that was! You are not stupid! You were just never given the chance to feel good about your opinion, and unfortunately, today you still live by others' opinions.

It is less important to be right than it is to be heard! You do not learn if you don't speak out. You are lost in the shadows and will accept being less than others in exchange for your silence. It is time to say, "Enough!"

Make this your first declaration, "I will learn that my decisions are about how I see things and not how others see them! I am no longer going to hide my opinions. Why did I think that everyone else was smarter than me?"

Assignment: Stand in front of a mirror and smile at this person who now has a voice, and tell him/her that you will be right there to guide them along. Be heard! Make decisions!

_____

_____

_____

_____

_____

_____

_____

_____

_____

_____

_____

_____

MARCH 24

Why do we withhold things or situations from our loved ones? Is it that we are so used to keeping secrets, or is there a greater issue behind this? Do we like this way of dealing with things: "What they don't know won't hurt them"? This is a very popular statement we make in order to rationalize why we keep quiet about certain behaviors we have. But are we really sneaky?

Many times we meet people in our lives who are the exact opposite of who we are. They would never take risks or behave the way we would. That is just the way it is. Can you imagine meeting someone the exact same as you? It would have a great deal of difficulty working. We all need checks and balances in relationships so that they have a certain amount of balance attached to them. Sometimes, though, we do not want our behavior to be judged. If our spouse or partner is our opposite, then there is a likelihood that they will not accept something that we want or need to do for ourselves. We rationalize our behavior and decide that not telling them is not lying to them or withholding from them, but it is instead "our business." And we promise ourselves that if they ask, then we will tell them what we're doing. This generally creates a dispute between the two of you, and your chances of winning are very slim!

Why slim? Because despite the fact that there is a difference between withholding and lying, albeit a very small one, your partner or spouse usually cannot see it at all. To them, withholding is a form of lying, and that is all they see. They also do not see that they may judge you for the choice you made, and that feeling judged has been a big part of your life. Do you think you have been judged because you have always been a "withholder" ever since childhood? Did your parents always judge your behavior, to the point where you thought that by withholding you could maybe get away with something without a fight or punishment? This behavior might not just be with your partner or spouse, but very old in your history!

You are responsible for this! Do not go blaming this on your partner or spouse, for they did not withhold. Maybe the judgments come from not being upfront rather than the behavior or choices you made. You are an adult, and you may do whatever you feel is right for you, but to withhold information is poor communication. This is your issue, so get ready to face the consequences for not being upfront! Why did you think you would get away with it?

Question: What have you been withholding from someone you care about? Has it been eating away at you? Do you run from this situation by avoiding the other person?

_____

_____

_____

_____

_____

_____

_____

_____

_____

_____

_____

_____

MARCH 25

Where is your physical and emotional positive energy? Do you realize that it has been missing? Dragging yourself out of bed and dreading your day starts you off with negativity, so how hard is it to recover from this ill feeling inside yourself? Do you really recognize how "disabled" this makes you? There is no chance for you to achieve success in life when you are fighting the healthier side of you on a daily basis. Guess who is winning?

"Energy" is what allows us to pass from one stage to another in life. It takes motivation in order to grow, and that won't happen when you are at war and taking the side of yourself that is determined to lose. This is not conscious, but sitting just beneath your mind where it can control you the most. Negative energy is really no energy at all. It fights what is right and good about us and leaves us disabled until we get it. We are in control of our lives; it is not the other way around.

Positive energy is movement and growth. When we feel it, there is no other feeling like it. We can believe we are capable of doing just about anything. The catch is to know that we have its polar opposite, negative energy, whispering in our ear, "You can't and don't even try!" You are not your negative energy. What makes you believe that you are? Maybe it has been there all your life, but that does not mean that the positive is not equally as powerful. It just depends on how you want to approach your life.

We have all been given the ability to balance our lives. If you find yourself leaning way too much toward the negative, recognize it and then step back and see what it is that is producing such defeat. Now is the time to be a warrior and go to battle with your defeated self. And the only way you can accomplish this is to understand that you have both inside of you, positive and negative energy. Every action has a reaction! Well, maybe it is necessary to check out why you have so much negativity. If you think negatively, you get no action. If you think positively, you'll have no more negative reactions!

Question: Ask yourself: is negative energy different from negative thinking? How would that look to you in your life?

_____

_____

_____

_____

_____

_____

_____

_____

_____

_____

_____

_____

_____

_____

LARRY ROBINSON

March 26

What about doubt? Doubt can be "dis-ease" all in itself. It invades our minds like an enemy attacking everything we do. Are you a victim of this, or are you a person who instigates it in others? And it really does not matter, for either way you experience doubt, whether you provoke someone else or it is done to you.

"Oh, I think that what I said was right or maybe it wasn't, but I needed to voice my opinion. But was it too much?" "I know what the boss said was wrong, but who am I to speak up?" On and on we go until we can no longer tell the difference between right and wrong. We are exhausted from challenging ourselves over and over again about the choices we make. There is no end to this and it becomes another habit/addiction in our lives. And what if you have negative thinking *and* doubt going on at the same time? Do you think you can have one without the other?

Doubt is insecurity about whether we are right or wrong. We all experience it at one time or another, but when it becomes *obsessive* and it invades all of our time, then it becomes a huge problem. We stop taking chances and we stay where it is safe and secure. It can be that by living in doubt it takes no effort to get into doubt, while it's a heck of a lot of struggle to get out of it. Are you willing to get yourself out of it, or are you so stuck that you would rather stay in this life sentence of never feeling secure with a response to life?

There are some things in life that are so old that it is useless to pick them apart in an effort to find the answer. What is important is that you recognize its existence in you! The answer is in the present. You are not your history. The last part of the word, his*tory*, is just what it is, and it is your story! Change the present by taking chances! Who really cares about right and wrong? Your feelings can never be wrong; they just sometimes do not fit a particular situation. And who is it that is holding you hostage to right and wrong, because that is the development of doubt!

Question: Is being right all the time a cause of you doubting your decisions? Remember, if we have to be right, then decisions would be harder.

_____

_____

_____

_____

_____

_____

_____

_____

_____

_____

_____

_____

_____

LARRY ROBINSON

MARCH 27

Negative, negative, negative thinking! It consumes our minds. Do you remember a time in your life when you thought, "Wow, I cannot wait for tomorrow!" When did you last say that? What do you think negative thinking does to your life or to those around you? Are you truly tired of this thinking or do you "want to want to" change?

Changing negative thinking is a difficult task, but if you sincerely want this to stop then you have to make a pledge to yourself that you will work on this every day. It takes every day to change something you dislike about yourself. And that will seem overwhelming to you, but look at it this way: you can't really get to the heart of your negative thinking without it being difficult.

We just do not like the consequences of that thinking, so let's turn it around. Each time you start thinking negatively, switch it to something positive! An example might be, "I hate my job and it bores me to death. I do not want to get up and go to work today!" Turn this around and say, "This job is not forever, and to lose it because I hate it will set me back in life. At least it is helping me to survive!" It is just a little twist, but the results are so much better. Remember that nothing stays the same in life whether we want it to or not!

Negative thinking can be both addictive and a habit at the same time. If we have been conditioned to think this way over the years, then we have to recondition ourselves to think in a positive manner. This is not to say that we can always switch it around, but once you begin to do this it gets easier to get to the positive side. Learn to be patient with yourself. If you were my client I would tell you, "Stop, look, and listen to yourself," because this is what everyone else hears! And why would you think that people would truly want to be around your negative thinking? The truth hurts, but if you are always looking for a way out of dealing with yourself then the negative thinking will again consume you!

Question: Are you someone who is addicted to negative thinking? Or in other words, whenever something goes wrong in your life, do you run to your negative thinking and stay there? Write down some of the negative thinking you can get into.

_____

_____

_____

_____

_____

_____

_____

_____

_____

_____

_____

_____

_____

March 28

How do we measure success in our relationship when we have never felt it to be what we wanted in the first place? Are we always holding the relationship up to some expectations that do not come close to who the other person is? How did we get it so wrong? Or is it that we were so "in love" that we could not see the real person?

We do see the real person. None of us is so blind that we suddenly discover one day who the other person really is and declare, "Oh my god, who did I marry? I had no idea this person did blah, blah, blah . . ." We knew, but we really didn't want to know for whatever reasons we had. We still wanted this person, and without dealing with the issues we had a pretty good idea were already there. We can all become so laid back and easy-going when we really want something. Do we neglect what we need from someone else only to discover later that it is almost too late to expect we will get it? Are we always going to feel that something is missing from our lives as long as we stay in this relationship? And have we actually brought children into this world without dealing with any of the issues we felt were there? How selfish were we?

We do not realize the extent of the damage we will do when children are involved. Remember, you can always meet someone new and find whatever happiness you think someone new will provide, but your children only get one family, one mother, and one father, and you "think" they will adjust? Well, if you came from divorce, did *you* adjust? No one really does, for no matter how bad a husband and wife get, all the children know is Mom and Dad! Split it up and it will cause them to be screwed up. Why wouldn't they get caught up in your dissatisfaction?

You "fell in love" with this person and it still exists somewhere inside of you. You are so angry and resentful that you didn't get what you wanted, but did you get what you needed? There is a big difference between the two in that one is about "survival" and one is about "desire." The both of you have to decide that you are a family and that you will get through this part of your journey *together*! There are no couples who cannot work out their differences unless there is severe abuse involved.

Need your family intact, want to heal! Find out where your spouse/partner is with the relationship. You might discover that they have been feeling the same way. That is a beginning! Understand where each other has been. Do not wait any longer or you will make decisions based upon the trap you feel you're in rather than the reality of what both of you have neglected.

Question: Have you given up on your relationship without really trying? What do you need to do in order to make this better? Did you ever try counseling?

_____

_____

_____

_____

_____

_____

_____

_____

_____

_____

_____

_____

MARCH 29

Why don't you take time for yourself? Are you always complaining about how tired you are and yet you refuse to stop? Why are you so hard on yourself and ultimately on others because you cannot slow down? This is no one else's fault, not even your own, for if you do not see the damage to yourself or others with your attitude, then you cannot be responsible for the outcome. Once you know, *you know*, and it will no longer be possible to put your life on someone else and blame them for your unhappiness. We can find fault with anyone when we set our minds to it. If you are into being the victim or the martyr, then nothing will stop you from holding yourself "higher" and letting people know what you have accomplished.

Don't you hate it when you hear someone talk about their life and all the "wows" that go along with it? Do you understand that sometimes this can become you without you even really knowing it? We can get so invested in being the one who carries the ball all the time in the relationship or the household that it becomes painfully difficult to give it up. But what would your life be like without this label of *the one* attached to you? Would it be too boring, or would there not be enough positive feedback about what you are responsible for? Let's face it. For you, giving up control is like being damned if you do and damned if you don't, because having to do everything has been your role most of your life. It didn't suddenly fall onto your head! You know how to take charge because you have been doing it forever. You know how much your parents depended on you, and now you have just moved it into your relationships. You are responsible for your own life!

If you understand this, do not be angry at anyone, including yourself! It is time to face this issue right in the eye and no longer let it take control of you. You see, you have believed that you are not worth very much, and this, at least, is a way of proving you wrong! There just isn't enough that you can take on that will satisfy your need to be recognized. No matter how much you do, it will never be enough for you.

The first step in recovery is always accepting what is. The second step is to let someone else know what has been going on. Now, maybe you feel safer talking to a friend, as opposed to your partner or spouse, but in any case let someone know! The third step is to "understand you." You have done a lot of good, and now is not the time to get ticked off at yourself or others for allowing this to go on. You have a voice, so use it! Let go of the control and let someone else help, no matter how hard this might be! After all, what is your choice?

Question: Can you really see how much you take on? How has it affected your life?

_____

_____

_____

_____

_____

_____

_____

_____

_____

_____

_____

_____

March 30

Why are we so hard on ourselves? It never stops, does it? Do we obsess over and over again about what we did wrong or how bad we sounded? Do we dwell on whether we were right in our interpretation of a situation? It never ceases!

We come across to other people as really apologetic and remorseful *before* they even question whether we are right or wrong. No, it doesn't matter to us. We are so invested in our self-destructive thinking. We go over and over our part or story in a situation, and no matter how we size it up we are the bad one. It always comes down to it being our fault!

Where does this "stinking thinking" come from? How old is it in your life? Have you ever not had its presence in your life? This is old thinking, and it starts at a very early age. We realize at some point that we cannot please our parents. No matter how hard we try, we cannot please them. Well, we are not children anymore, so why hold on to all this negativity?

It is time to start a new approach. The old one is boring and we have played it out so many times that we are actually numb to it. If you think like a child, you will be treated like one! Remember the old saying "It takes two to tango," which means it is never really just one person's fault. It is time to grow up, and that means letting go of any issues that you have been carrying since childhood. You are automatically conditioning yourself to think the same way over and over again.

Once you realize this your change can begin. We need to accept who we are in order to make significant changes to our way of thinking. At some deeper level you do know that what you did is either right or wrong. In essence, we all do, we just do not like to think about it. We jump to take responsibility because it is easier than defending our position. Now, don't you feel foolish taking responsibility for something you did not do?

Question: Are you afraid of change? What have you been holding on to in order to avoid changing?

LARRY ROBINSON

March 31

Why do we give up on ourselves so quickly and easily? As soon as we sense that defeat might be in the air, we start to negate all the good we have done and we settle into low self-esteem. Is that a comfortable place for us, or are we very insecure about our own value?

Have we always allowed others to determine our self-worth? No matter how much we work at feeling more powerful in life, it is sucked right out of us by the smallest piece of negative feedback. We are a train wreck waiting to happen! It takes so little to throw us back into feeling hopeless about ourselves. Why do we allow others to determine who *we* are?

We have no true value of ourselves. It is a sad story for so many of us that those around us are given permission, and by us, to judge our value. We welcome it! And trying to defend yourself becomes virtually useless, because if you quit on yourself, then that becomes who you are, no matter what kind of feedback you might receive.

You have no sense of commitment to yourself! It is time to understand that we are not our history in life. It is what it is, and we are always given the opportunity to be successful. You need to ask yourself, "Am I a quitter?" You already know the answer if you have gotten this far with this entry. Well, what do you intend on doing about this? Or are you just going to let this negativity continue to rule your life?

Assignment: Take one small step in your life that will show you that you can be successful. The first step might be to stop looking for everyone else to approve of your attempts at becoming successful and start believing in yourself. You are the master of your own destiny, and you need to lead your own way into the "arena of success" by committing yourself to following through on what you set out to do! It does not matter how long it takes you to achieve something, it only matters that you do it!

LARRY ROBINSON

Eric Krouss, Marblehead, Massachusetts, USA

April 1

Would you turn your own child in to the police for selling drugs, or would you just pretend it didn't exist and ignore the situation? You don't have to have a child to answer this question. It is probably one of the hardest decisions that a parent or relative can be forced to make.

Here's a scenario: Let's say that it is your nephew or cousin, and this child is a brilliant kid who rose up out of poverty to receive a scholarship from one of the finest Catholic prep schools around. You know he is in his last year of school and has already skipped three out of the last four days. Remember, this is a real scenario and the kid has a real chance to attend college and free himself from the trappings of his childhood.

Both his parents are recovering addicts and they see their child as a kid who never gave them problems until recently when he fell in love with a girl who pulls his strings and controls him like a puppet. Her parents think their relationship is "sweet," and do not see any harm in the two kids using certain drugs.

Now, is the problem drug addiction because he uses every day and supplies his girlfriend, or is it "love addiction" because they fight daily and only using stops the fighting? They are never far from each other, and he gets out of control because she is always either trying to make him jealous or breaking up with him. He, in turn, goes out with other girls to make her want him back.

Does this sound familiar? Now, there are various ways to deal with this problem. Remember that he is a star pupil, but he refuses to follow any rules at this point. He doesn't even come home at night anymore. He makes all his own decisions, and as of late, they are all bad!

The parents have done so much to help this child, so what do they do now? The dad wants to throw him out, while the mom still wants to save him. The only real alternative they have now is to go to the police!

Question: How would you deal with this situation if this was your child? Let's see if you can come up with solutions to help this family. You be the expert and counselor in this case. Some of us will face a similar situation at some point. Some may have already! Do you save or let go?

April 2

What qualifies as a "good" parent? Are there rules for parents to follow that create a healthier home for their children? How many households are out of control and chaotic every morning? To be sure, you are exhausted and frustrated within the first hour, and hiding out and relaxing for the rest of the day would be like paradise, but that's not going to happen!

So what happened to your control over these kids? How do they always seem to get the best of you, and why do they always seem to win? Or do they win? If you are angry and fed up, how do they go off to school? Do you have a great day when you've had a fight with your spouse in the morning? Do you forget about it and rush into your work, or do you fume about it all day? Well, children do the same thing, only they are forced to sit still and pay attention for eight straight hours every day! Could you do that?

Maybe it is time to teach them lessons they can handle. Do not pick out their clothes unless they are wearing PJs to school. They need to learn what to wear. Now, it is fine for them to ask you if they look okay, but do not judge them! We all hate to be judged. Let them find out for themselves if they look all right. You know the other kids will let them know, so let them learn from their peers, not you.

Do not force them to eat! Give them an apple or a banana and some nuts and let them be! Maybe they'll get hungry in school and that's when they'll learn about eating properly in the morning.

If they won't get in the car, let them walk! If a child is over the age of nine and the school is half a mile away, let them walk! Take off with the other kids in the car. A day or two of being tardy is going to be about them, not you. So relax, and do not worry that other parents are going to think you're a bad parent. They're having as much trouble as you are!

Teaching your children is not an easy task, but doing everything for them is only going to create little spoiled monsters who will grow up incapable of taking care of themselves. And good luck having adult children living with you who are there only because you thought more

LARRY ROBINSON

about how others were perceiving you when you were supposed to be teaching them how to take care of themselves.

Assignment: List the ways that your children make you crazy and have them come up with consequences for negative behaviors. Make them part of the solution.

_____

_____

_____

_____

_____

_____

_____

_____

_____

_____

_____

_____

_____

_____

APRIL 3

What kind of world have you created for yourself? And we're not talking about the larger, disturbed world, but rather the small, private world you live in day to day. Are you really happy or content with it, or are you always wishing that you had someone else, were someplace else, or did some other job? Is your day filled with anxiety or anger and sometimes even fear that tomorrow will be worse than today?

These are not uncommon thoughts, but they are usually our secrets. We don't tell these damaging thoughts to the people we're close to, but sometimes when we're filled with them they come pouring out of us without any prior warning. And when they come, it is an explosion of unhappiness blasted at our partners, spouses, and family members. Remember, you can say you are sorry, but you cannot always take back what you've said. Why have you built up such a torrent of negativity?

Our fear guides us to this. Our mind tells us to get that other person because they do not understand us, but do we understand them? Is life all about your fantasy dictating the way things should be or is it a shared fantasy? I doubt it!

We are all selfish when it comes to how we want life to be. Even if you believe you are the most compliant person on earth, you still have your own feelings about how life should be. Have you ever checked out if you are a person who will initially agree but then find a way to sabotage a plan?

Assignment: Describe how you want your life to be and then compare it to what it really is. How far away are you from the truth?

_____

_____

_____

_____

APRIL 4

Are you the punished one in a relationship or do you punish your partner when they do something you cannot stand? The punished one is usually the passive-aggressive partner who always has some excuse, or even a real reason, for why they did something that went against their partner's way of seeing things. They are the excuse-mongers!

The "punishers" are the *parent* of the relationship, and they decide what your punishment will be. That might range from something like shaming you to withholding money or even love. They act stern and mean, while the punished one ends up righteous, full of excuses, or humiliated. This is the dynamic that the two of you have arranged in your relationship.

Now, where does this come from? If you look into your parents' relationships I am sure you will see carbon copies of the two. For all of you who say, "My parents were loving people and were the best parents; I had a wonderful childhood," well, you missed seeing the dynamics and lived in your own little world. All parents have their own dynamics, just as you do in your relationships, and that is true even if you raised yourself because they were not available.

We all pick up the issues that our role models have (a woman is not a role for a man and a man is not a role model for a woman). So maybe there are some "emotion genetics" or just "nurture issues" that we absorb from them, but you have to look at them as people, not as "mommy" and "daddy." No one can actually say they aren't part their mother or father, and that even goes for those of us who have sworn we would never be like them! Now, we may do the exact opposite, but that will still come out the same way. The parent who smothered you, well, that might make you into the parent who is way too liberal. And there are so many variations, but the end result is the same. Truth is, we are so much of our parents, and the only way we rid ourselves of their damage is to recognize it in ourselves!

It is time to learn to accept our partner or spouse and to confront the issues in this dynamic of punished and punisher. We have to know ourselves and stop ourselves or this damage can ruin relationships. And

LARRY ROBINSON

so you ask, "How?" Well, you learn to know yourself, that's how! And learn to see your behavior in action!

Question: Which role do you end up in a relationship, punished or punisher, and why?

_____

_____

_____

_____

_____

_____

_____

_____

_____

_____

_____

_____

_____

_____

_____

April 5

Why does our anxiety ruin everything for us? Why can't we approach something new without freaking out and turning things into a nuclear war? How many of us suffer from this horrible affliction? Do we always worry about things to come like the "ghost of the future to come," or are we stuck in the "ghosts of the past"? Why is it that when we look around us everyone seems to be having fun, while our mind is running a marathon and we cannot even seem to get past the first mile without breaking down? This is a serious disease for us, and so many people just do not take it seriously, choosing instead to cling to outdated thinking that says we're just supposed to let it go and move on!

How many times have we not understood what our spouse, parent, or child is going through before we throw our hands up and make them feel like there really is something wrong with them? Anxiety is a cancer for some of us, and it eats away at every fiber of our body. With cancer today there are no cures, but "treatments" that can help it stay dormant. But what do those of us who suffer from anxiety have? Typically, just addictive drugs that either make us like zombies or give us a false sense of security that enables the world to judge us as incapable of dealing with life! Do we really feel compassion for those who suffer from extreme anxiety, or do we pass it off as a "quirky" mood that our loved ones get into? Do we see them as "downers" whom we'd rather not share anything good or bad with because they're prone to turning it into their own issue? Or do we really see the pain they are suffering?

How cruel are we, and how cruel do they get when anxiety rears its ugly head? It is easy for some to judge anxiety as only a moment in time that has no purpose, but some of us actually live our lives in and out of it. Now, do we purposely set out to feel this way, or is it our mind that can immediately take over, causing us to feel out of control?

Our problem is that we do not tell people, "I feel anxious today." Instead, we act it out and find, a great deal of the time, something stupid to focus on as opposed to dealing with the disease we have. Until we see this as a real disease, whether we are the ones afflicted with it or the ones who have to tolerate it, we are not going to be connected in life

LARRY ROBINSON

the way we had hoped. No one will want to be around us, or we will isolate our close friends and loved ones and make them feel damaged.

Let us declare today a day in which we either accept someone's anxiety and not torture them with it, or try and see our own anxiety as only a passing moment. It will go away!

Question: How impatient are you about dealing with another person's anxiety? Does it trigger your own?

_____

_____

_____

_____

_____

_____

_____

_____

_____

_____

_____

_____

_____

April 6

What do you see when you look in the mirror? Does it change all the time? Can you really say to yourself, "Wow, I look pretty good today!" and the next day hate your looks? Do you think that your looks change overnight and that you are on a never-ending trail of looking good and looking bad?

What causes this to happen? Our looks do not change on a daily basis, but our feelings can! Looking in the mirror is a clue as to how we are feeling on almost a daily basis, and it can be so painful that we want to break the mirror or chop off our hair. That's how bad it can get. And by the way, this happens to both men and women. Yes, women tend to get called out on it more often while men tend to stay more silent on the matter, but our feelings often determine how we see ourselves.

When we are not carrying around negative feelings, we see ourselves looking fine. We primp (continually fix ourselves) and give ourselves positive reinforcement like "Yes, I like the way I look this morning," but when we are carrying around anger, frustrations, sadness, and mean feelings, well, we cannot expect to see our real looks. In this case, what you are going to see is a reflection of yourself that is dominated by those negative feelings. We start to pick ourselves apart, saying, "This doesn't look good; god, I hate my hair," and it goes on and on. So in other words, yesterday we looked fine while today we are totally ugly!

Know this life lesson: we see either our positive or negative self in the mirror. It can be our greatest supporter or worst enemy. The only one who knows what is going on is the person in the mirror! Use the mirror to give you clues that something might be going on inside that can be determining how you see yourself. It is the best indicator of how you are truly feeling about yourself. Look in the mirror today and ask yourself, "What do I see?"

Question: Do you see a different-looking person each time you look in the mirror? Do you understand that the mirror shows you how you appear to yourself. Often it shows our feelings more than our looks. How do you see you today?

LARRY ROBINSON

APRIL 7

D o you know the difference between being a lonely person and being alone? Can you be alone *and* lonely at the same time? How much of your life have you thought you were a loner when in reality you were really lonely? These look like they are interchangeable conditions, but are they really?

First, let's look at what each term means. A "loner" is a person who does not truly want others to get that close to them. They may know a great number of people, but those who really know them are few and far between. They are very secretive folks who do not want others messing in their business. They can spend a lot of time alone and do not need to be entertained by others. They have a darker side that they tend to keep hidden, and they prefer it to remain that way. A loner isn't someone who rejects people, but rather rejects the intimacy that people would like to give and get back from them. Some loners are quite popular and like it that way, but they keep you at arm's length when it comes to their personal lives. Some never invite you into their homes, and many loners are actually only children who learned to entertain themselves without siblings around. These are some of the characteristics of loners. Can you add more?

Now, what about "lonely"? Who are these people and what are their stories? Lonely people have always been lonely. They consider themselves shy and fearful of others. They stood alone in the schoolyard looking as if they didn't care about playing with others, but on the inside they were hateful and judgmental due to their jealousy. They can tend to be standoffish or silent in groups, and they normally wait for others to speak to them first. They can also be folks who, once you do speak to them, belong to you because they will chat your head off, often without caring whether or not you are even listening. They have superficial friendships and do not really develop intimate relationships either. They cry to themselves at night about how lonely they feel, but there is something about them that is bothersome. They can entertain a crowd and move from group to group just as the loner can, except these people hate doing it because it makes them feel even lonelier. And they can

LARRY ROBINSON

often reject others because they are always finding fault with people, and yet they will still complain about being lonely. A lonely person hates to be with themselves. And why? Well, there are a lot of feelings about self-worth that come up when they are by themselves.

Question: Can you be truly honest with yourself? Can you decide which one of these you are?

_____

_____

_____

_____

_____

_____

_____

_____

_____

_____

_____

_____

_____

_____

April 8

W here does hopelessness come from? Are we conditioned to feel it at an early age, or does it come from some traumatic childhood event that causes our "inner attitude" to feel this way? No one is there for us, no one has our back, and no one loves us unconditionally—these are some of the thoughts that race through our young minds before the age of six. Every child feels either a false sense of reality or a real crisis in life that transforms the happy child into the moping, depressed child. And parents often cannot understand what has happened, for they cannot get into the mind of the young child to help them see what was real. It's a no-win situation for both parent and child. Do you understand how this works? Can you identify your trauma that created the reality you have lived with most of your life?

Today, as an adult, you are feeling stuck due to you repeating the same patterns you did as a child, and you often feel burned out from the rambling thoughts of hopelessness in your mind. But let's look at this. Let's say that what you thought was a real situation in life, one which you blamed yourself for, was not actually what you thought it was. Let's say mom and dad got divorced when you were a child, and inside your mind you thought it was because they argued over you a lot. Maybe there were times when you actually wished that one of them would just go away, and then it actually happened and you couldn't tell anyone what you'd wished for! You were left feeling that your little mind was so powerful that it actually had the power to split them up! Right!

Do you see now how you might have developed negative and hopeless feelings due to the power you thought you had? And what if you wished something bad on another relative or family member because you were angry at them and then that happened too? Again, that powerful little mind took over and began to form a self-hatred that you could not stop! All of this is from your childhood!

Now, are you still believing this as an adult? Do you hate who you are and cannot let go of the negativity and hopelessness? Look back into your past and begin to piece together the circumstances of your life. Start to see your parents as human rather than all powerful! Can they still determine your self-worth? Look to see which one really let hopelessness become a way of living. You took it on, and now it is your responsibility to let it go! Remember, they were not gods and you were not perfect. Your view of yourself came from how they lived their life. And this is not about blaming them, but rather understanding that they did not have it as together as you thought they did or maybe even think they do today!

Get up off that bandwagon of self-hatred and begin to see the reality you could not see as a child!

Question: Do you still rely on your parents' approval before you make decisions for your life?

_____

_____

_____

_____

_____

_____

_____

_____

_____

_____

_____

_____

APRIL 9

Today we go into the spirit of this journey of our life and ask why. "Why am I here and what is my purpose?" Have you ever thought that there is a purpose to your life that is more than just being born, living your life, and then dying? Yes, everyone gets sick and everyone gets old, and we all die, but what about in between our birth and death? What do you believe you are to get from this life? Believe me, it travels so fast. Do you remember when summer seemed so long that you secretly wished school would start? Now, just blink a few times and it is yesterday's summer! Are you someone who believes that your life is preplanned, or is life dictated simply by chance?

Remember, this is your journey and *Mirror, Mirror* is hoping that you will find a purpose to your life through questioning how it has been so far. And if you've been stuck, then why? If you have been repeating the same negative pattern in life, then you will continue to repeat it until you find the resolution to it. It is a struggle, but who told you it would be easy?

If you are taking the time to read this, is it by your own choice or were you destined to read it? If you do not see your life as a journey, then *what* is it? Does it just stay a big mess until it is over? Some of you will talk about God and his path, and that is great. But we all have different beliefs about where we go after this life and this part of our journey, that life is not over after we die but continues on to the next part of its journey. None of us can tell each other we are wrong in our beliefs. Let's face it, we just don't know. But there is something that most of us can decide is true, and that is that we have a shot right now to find that purpose and to fulfill our destiny!

Look back into your past. Have you changed? Do you see a difference from then to now? And if you don't, why haven't you questioned you? Are you a "pity-myself" person? Only those who are extremely honest with themselves will answer that correctly. And if you are, then you know why you are not growing!

You see, a journey can have no end, and that means we are given the chance again and again to find our destiny. And it does not matter

LARRY ROBINSON

if you are thirteen or eighty! Remember, it starts at birth, and where does it end?

Question: Have you seen your life as a journey? Have there been times when you wanted to give up?

_____

_____

_____

_____

_____

_____

_____

_____

_____

_____

_____

_____

_____

_____

APRIL 10

Do you keep secrets from those you know and love? Are you someone who has to present "two selves," one that is really working on yourself and another that is working against you? Are you a secret addict and no one knows you are a secret drinker, eater, smoker, drug user, or sex and love addict? Could it be, in fact, that not even you believe this other side of you exists? It is so difficult to always sneak around, especially when the world sees you as totally different. How much pain do you suffer when you are in this place? Whom can you talk to that will offer you support?

Most people would tell you that you have to come "clean" with your spouse, partner, or family. You know you cannot live this way forever, but still you cannot seem to let go of the darker side of you that is constantly hiding or lying about where you were or what you were doing. Lying in order to hide can often morph into lying just for the sake of lying, and this is not you, which is what you tell yourself all the time. But who is it then?

This is the child inside of you who grew up in a chaotic home and who was always dealing with parents who were angry with each other or who just shut down toward everyone because of their unhappiness. You took on so much of the unhappiness and blamed yourself, for this is what children do when they cannot read life's negative situations.

Sometimes the secrets you keep actually do feel good, because it's almost as if you're getting away with something, and in a way, getting even with those whom you've felt betrayed by. When conflict arises in your family you can turn to some addiction that will numb you and take away any real or perceived pain you have. So why should you give this up?

You have not been real in life. You are fooling the world and isolating yourself at the same time. How lonely is it, and when do you think you will get caught? Remember, we never truly get away with anything! It is time to straighten out this part of your journey. Secrets are dangerous. And aside from harming others, they also harm you!

LARRY ROBINSON

Assignment: In what ways have you been a fake person in life? Explain!

_____

_____

_____

_____

_____

_____

_____

_____

_____

_____

_____

_____

_____

_____

_____

_____

APRIL 11

D o you ever feel that your heart gets "cold"? Are you confused about why this happens? Are there times when you think that you are going to bed in a good place and then wake up on the "wrong side of the bed" and honestly have no idea how you got there? Your behavior toward your family is cold and shut off, and it does not take much to send you over the edge. Before you know it you sound bitter and disappointed, and no one can approach you. You do not ask to be this way, but is it not familiar to you? Isn't this behavior part of the story that you carry around inside, the one you have continued to repeat over the course of your life?

"Coldhearted," that is how you are viewed and that is how you feel. It is almost as if you cannot let any consistent goodness into your life. In your mind, nothing good ever stays, so why bank on it? Growing up there was always either turmoil or violence, both emotional and physical. Screaming and vulgarity were never far away.

Are you repeating your story as your parents did, or do you think you can change this mindset that is like a revolving door in your life, in one side and out the other? You are protecting your heart from those who love you, and you do not seem as if you can ever truly let someone in. And why should you when love is only pain? That was proven to you over and over again in childhood. Maybe you came from a background that was really sweet on the outside while silent and cold on the inside. As a child you didn't exactly know what was wrong, but there certainly wasn't any sense of being loved going around. Both your parents seemed coldhearted, stern, and unloving, but to the rest of the world they were kind and loving! You must have thought there was something wrong with you, for everyone else thought they were great, even your friends!

You are not your story! As we have said too, you are not your mind! You are someone who has not given your life a chance to let go of the pain from the past. Take a good look at what your behavior has been and how detached and edgy you are today. And look only at today! Do not hide in your past! Get to a mirror and look closely into the eyes of the person who is standing there. What do you see? If all you see is someone who is bad, then you are not seeing clearly. You are seeing only the child from your past. Tell that child to get lost, and that you have had enough of him/her! They have damaged you enough. You have to be willing to see who you thought you were in the past and also who you are today! There is a difference, and it is up to you to find it. Do you really think you have anything to lose?

Question: Do you think that you are your history, or do you believe you can start right now to change it to a positive sense of self?

April 12

D o you feel alone in the world? And does it frighten you that there's a possibility that no one will ever come by and "sweep you off your feet"? You have been waiting for such a long time, and despite the fact many people have been interested in you, you still feel that maybe, just maybe, there is someone who is better than the one you just let go. This is your pattern. You want so much to be wanted that when you achieve that goal with another person, you just don't want them anymore. The consequences of this pattern are loneliness and being alone.

You didn't start out this way, so how did this need to be wanted and ultimately rejecting anyone who really wants you happen? Once again, it is important to be your own historian and to look into your past when you were a child. If you were from a large family and your parents were just tired out from just surviving, you might have felt rejected by them because your older siblings seemed to get so much more. Therefore, your goal became always wanting to be wanted. The problem was that there was just never enough of that feeling for you to be satisfied, so you sabotaged each relationship in order to move on to the next.

Perhaps you came from a background where the main focus was alcohol and there was no parenting to speak of. You had to make decisions for your own survival at a very early age, and there was just no one you could trust to be there for you. And it has continued to this day, that feeling that no one had your back and loneliness was all you had. You have conditioned your mind to play back all the negatives from the past so that when someone dares to want you now it takes little effort to push them away because you view them as just another person who could disappoint you.

Why do you want to accept loneliness? "Oh, I don't need anyone. I can be alone!" Maybe that's true, but can you be that fragile that you cannot tolerate the disappointments we all go through in relationships? You are so protected that you would settle for being alone rather than hurt or angry. These are normal feelings, yet for you they appear to be ones that you cannot tolerate. It might just be time to take notice that life is passing you by and that you are still either waiting for the "right"

LARRY ROBINSON

person or too afraid to be vulnerable to someone else. Do you really think you were meant to be alone? Why you?

Question: Are you locked into loneliness as a way of living your life? If so, how does it appear to you?

_____

_____

_____

_____

_____

_____

_____

_____

_____

_____

_____

_____

_____

APRIL 13

D o you understand how we become depressed? Does depression run in your family? Were there generations of your people who were depressed? How often have family members told you, "Oh well, Aunt Sally has depression and so did her sister. It runs in our family"? Do you often tell yourself that you are not depressed, and yet you cannot rid yourself of this heavy feeling inside that leads you to be unmotivated and tired all the time? Do you feel shut down, and even though you have that empty feeling inside you still feel heavy? Do you sleep too much or too little? Do you eat too much or have no appetite? Are you constantly experiencing mood swings, where one moment you feel like you're on top of the world while the next you feel useless and unworthy? Do you really lack motivation? If you experience more than three of these symptoms of depression, then you are depressed!

There are many different types of depression. Today we are going to deal with depression caused by how we conduct our lives. When we are passive and do not stand up for what we believe in but want to be accepted so badly that we go along with the crowd, we swallow our feelings. Swallowed feelings have no place to go but back inside of us. And when these feelings sit inside of us and we cannot let go of them, gradually they turn into depressed feelings. In other words, feelings that are pushed back down inside of us are *depressed*, and therefore create depression.

How often do you depress your feelings and unknowingly end up depressed? Well, now you know how that develops! It is so difficult after a while to bring the majority of them back up when some of them are so old and now part of our subconscious. Depression can be hereditary, but is the way your family deals with feelings hereditary too?

Every time you do not deal with how you feel about situations or people, you can almost bet on the fact that you will feel depressed later. It does not hit us right away hard, for we are too busy either trying not to react or struggling to agree with something we really don't believe in. We just want to be liked.

Question: What have you been willing to put up with in order to be liked?

LARRY ROBINSON

April 14

Today it is not a matter of whether or not you are self-destructive, for everyone is to some extent, but how much of your life is based on you *neglecting* it. Therefore, "how self-destructive are you?" is the question we start off with today. Do you believe that you are self-destructive, or is that only for people who have hardcore addictions or are mentally ill or deeply depressed?

If you do see yourself as a self-destructive person, at what level would you put yourself? There are those who knowingly get into toxic relationships believing fully that they can "save" the other person, but usually all they really do is get lost in someone else's mess. There are those who see only perfection in life and so no one, not even themselves, can live up to their high expectations. They punish themselves and others for the lack of perfection.

There are the "I am going to save the world" people who put everything and everybody before themselves but internally feel unloved and neglected. There are people who are always "sick" and need constant attention, yet cannot rise up to take care of themselves. It is almost as if they need the reassurance that they are loved by being the focus of others. And there are the people who say they need nothing, just as there are "victims" in life who appear to be selfless but who are actually self-focused and who need to remind folks constantly about what they have done!

If you fit any of these categories, then welcome to the club of self-destructive people! Maybe you can think of other situations that are self-destructive in your life now that you have the chance to think about it. How long does this continue for you? Are you following in someone's footsteps and don't even recognize it? We can become conditioned to this way of life without really knowing it.

This can be corrected! Do not think that every issue is etched in stone and that we are stuck with it. The first step is to recognize and label what you do that is self-destructive. Make a list of those things that drive you crazy about yourself. See how long each has been there and then commit to wanting change! If you cannot commit to change, then you will stay exactly where you are and nothing will get better.

LARRY ROBINSON

You must see your weaknesses and not run from them. Begin to step back from yourself so that you can better understand yourself. It is no easy task, but this is your life's journey and no one said that changing things would be easy.

Next, you need to get rid of "How does the world see me?" For in the long run no one really cares because they're in the same place and struggling just as you are. Who do you want to be, that is the real question! Within reason, you can be anyone you want to be. We are only stuck in our minds. And remember, your *mind* is not your friend but only a voice inside of your head! Try to go to your heart and see that you are different from the way you are acting. The goal is to put heart and action together!

Question: How often have you listened to your mind and you got in trouble?

_____

_____

_____

_____

_____

_____

_____

_____

_____

_____

_____

_____

D'Arave Willmore, Fullbrook, California, USA

"We must never be afraid to fail at things in life. If we are always afraid to fail, then we will never push ourselves and know what our true potential could be. Never let the fear of accomplishing something hold you back; and if you happened to fail, well, at least you tried."

—Chris Lawlor, Lynn, Massachusetts, USA

April 15

How well do you handle rejection? Do you believe that your world has fallen apart when someone you have been with tells you, "It is over," or that you did not get a job or were refused a loan? These are all pieces of rejection and they are in your life for a reason. Do you really think that things just occur by chance, or do you think there is something more to it? If we all could handle rejection with a simple "oh well" and leave it at that, then the world would be a much easier place to live in. But this is not the case, and for the vast majority of us rejection is like having an operation without being put under!

Rejection has such a sharp pain attached to it that we feel as if we will never recover from it or ever be the same again. Neither men nor women handle it any better than the other. Pain hits us in different ways, but the bottom line is that it is pain! Emotional pain can be more difficult to deal with than physical pain. We at least know that with physical pain, in most cases, we will recover and heal. With emotional pain it feels as if it can go on forever. Your heart can feel like it's been torn out of your chest! Can you imagine having open-heart surgery while you are awake? So the majority of you know what rejection feels like.

Do you know that rejection is something to grow from? You might think that you will not recover, but from what? Is it the pain that comes with being in a relationship that you perhaps fantasized about leaving anyway? Is it because the other person has beaten you to it and now your heart feels like it's broken? At least now you can validate that you are capable of being rejected. And we need to listen to what the other person has to say about what it was that drove them away. Someone pointing out our needy or demanding or controlling behavior is *vital* to our recovery! Maybe we thought we were getting away with something. We all get caught in the end!

Perhaps we were with someone who cheated on us and we took them back but could never get over it. And when they split from us we begged them to come back, only to have the same thing happen again. What does this say about us? Are we weak and have no self-esteem?

Learn from this rejection rather than wallow in it. What is meant to be is meant to be, but you will emerge from it having improved! And do not make this person, job, or whatever the rejection is bigger than life! Say goodbye to bad behaviors and do not think you will be alone. Just remember, you met this one and many before them, so you will meet someone again! Let's make sure this time that we really want the person or position, rather than just wanting them to want us!

Question: How do you deal with rejection? In what ways do you hide from it?

_____

_____

_____

_____

_____

_____

_____

_____

_____

_____

_____

_____

_____

_____

APRIL 16

Where is it? When do you think it disappeared? Are you the type of person who gives your all in a relationship to the point where eventually your own sense of identity disappears? Have you started to live your life only to please the other person and have forgotten that you were once a "real person" also? You have let this happen, and now it might be too late to regain a sense of yourself. In order to regain *you*, it is necessary to defy the self that needs to be so loved and so wanted by someone else. You readily gave up your sense of self to be in a relationship that by now you probably do not even want!

What do you do? Most likely you are afraid that if you come out you will totally turn off the other person. They might even say to you, "Where is that sweet person who was at my beck and call?" Well, you know exactly where you are, you are in a struggle to regain a sense of you and you do not know where to begin!

The first step in regaining yourself is to understand that *you* did this. You became who the other person wanted you to be, and in the process lost you! Did you really have a strong sense of yourself before this relationship, or have you always been a "chameleon" who can change their color to fit someone else's? It has always been so easy for you to be who everyone else needs you to be.

Remember back in high school, didn't you always go along with the crowd? Some of us even became bullies because we wanted so badly to be with the popular kids. We would do anything for that acceptance. Well, what has changed today? Let's face it, you have spent your whole life being who you thought others wanted you to be, and what did it get you other than heartburn and heartache?

You need to gradually begin to voice an opinion. Pick something easy, like dinner, and instead of saying "It doesn't matter" when you are asked where you want to eat, make it matter! Speak up! This will start to condition you to have opinions, so that when the bigger ones come along you aren't frozen any longer with fear about saying how you feel. Practice in front of a mirror, or better yet, rehearse with a friend who will challenge you to hold your opinion tight! You (and all of us together) are going to make this the year of change and growth.

Question: How far back does pleasing others go for you? Are you lonely because you never seem to need anything and no one knows it?

_____

_____

_____

_____

_____

_____

_____

_____

_____

_____

_____

_____

_____

_____

LARRY ROBINSON

April 17

D o you dwell on your past? Is it difficult for you to move past old hurts and resentments, or do you linger there, building up new negative feelings against people who might not even still be alive today? Can you deal with the word "forgiveness," or is forgiveness the biggest issue that you choose not to face? Let's face it. You can be "no day at the beach" when it comes to letting go of past hurts. Have you ever looked really closely at what was happening between you and someone else that made it so difficult to forgive, or is *forgiveness* really even the issue? Perhaps you "like" holding on to negative thinking. In some instances it is called "stinking thinking."

Stinking thinking, it swallows you up and leaves you truly handicapped in your relationships with others. How many people have you shunned or let go of because they "hurt" you? If this is a constant in your life, then you must be angry and lonely at the same time. This combination of feelings is a dangerous mix, and one that does not just disappear overnight! It takes a lot of work to begin to understand how damaging this really is.

Some people have lost their entire families over not being able to let go of the past. Think about siblings you have resented because you saw them as the "good" child who got everything while you were the "bad" child who got nothing. Did you really blame your siblings for the way that they had to cope with their childhood? Did you always think it was about you, when others in your family suffered as well but in a different way? Each child strives to be valued and wanted by their parents. Take a good look at how each member of your family dealt with this issue. Do you ever think that if you had had better reactionary skills that you might have taken their role as opposed to the one you took on?

It is time to look at your past resentments, grudges, and hurt feelings. Make a list of those people you have alienated from your life. Did you really need to push them out, or are you just a hypersensitive person who is wounded so quickly that your response mechanism is to either shut them out or shut yourself down? Remember, this is your journey in life and you only get one time around! What kind of damage are you ending up with? Do you dwell on your past?

Question: Who do you regret kicking out of your life and why?

_____

_____

_____

_____

_____

_____

_____

_____

_____

_____

_____

_____

_____

_____

LARRY ROBINSON

April 18

When are you going to stop all the negative thinking and realize that this is not a new issue, and that it is just a very stubborn one that refuses to go away? Let us call this your "habit." You automatically send yourself there when you are faced with adversity and/or pain. Sometimes it doesn't even take a major crisis to send you into "flight mode." There just is no fight in you. Have you always run away from conflict or adverse situations? Face it, this is the way you have always operated in life, and change looks to be almost impossible.

This, once again, is your negative self fighting against any chance of being healthy. Isn't it strange that you do not have to think twice about retreating into yourself and pretending that nothing is off, or thinking that if you just let it pass then you will be all right? No, that is not how it works! The more you rush into ignoring things or reverting to negative thinking, the worse the situation becomes. We are not meant to hide. If that was the case, we would all be stuck in the same hole. Fortunately, many of us refuse to be defeated! More often than not we are afraid we will fail at something even before we attempt to tackle it. Conditioned to be the person who could not achieve or who had so much potential but screwed around, no one took us seriously! We didn't even take ourselves seriously. Not until now!

Living out someone else's nightmare about who we are is way too easy. Today we are fighters! We will not stand back and let you determine who we are! We have stayed in that position way too long. We have lived the way we think others have seen us, and now we are angry, angry enough to see the foolishness of our ways. You cannot encourage our negativity because it makes you feel better. No longer will we stand for you making yourself feel better at our expense!

Just by stating this we are getting stronger and we are even more determined than ever to succeed in the world. We can be who we believe we are and we do not need permission from you to become it! This negativity has played itself out once too often in our lives. Goodbye, negativity, I am leaving you behind!

Do not ask the "how" in life. The recognition that this is who you are is the first step in your recovery!

Question: Who is the major contributor in your life besides yourself that is always being negative toward you?

_____

_____

_____

_____

_____

_____

_____

_____

_____

_____

_____

_____

_____

April 19

D o you make promises you cannot keep? Are you volunteering to do something you really do not want to do but are hiding this fact? Do you end up disappointing people and all you can try to do is defend yourself? Why did you make the offer in the first place? There are times when we know we will not do what we have committed to do but still are the first one to jump in and take over. We can become a constant disappointment to those around us, especially children, when we fail to honor our commitments. We not only disappoint ourselves, but also the damage done to others is great.

Where does this come from? Are we "role modeling" after a parent who disappointed us? No, this issue is not one that we can blame on our past, because this is who we have become in the present. Sometimes we try too hard to interpret our past in order to explain away behavior, and it can become our crutch that we lean on when we get caught. No, this issue is ours and it will not get any better until we confront the truth. We can be too afraid to look at the truth and therefore shift the responsibility around and make others responsible for our lack of follow through! We make it too easy to place blame and rationalize it as someone else's fault. "I only did it because you wanted me to and I was in over my head." Have you ever thought or said that before?

There is only one way to fix this. You need to understand your own limitations and not feel disappointed if you do not offer to do something that you do not think you can either follow through on or be successful with. You are not less than if you know yourself. If the goal is to be there for others, then be there! Do not let your pride or your ego get in the way of your honesty. You save yourself and those around you much more than you know when you tell the truth. Promising without follow through is a lie!

Question: List three times in the recent past that you have promised something you did not follow through on. What are your feelings about yourself when this occurs?

LARRY ROBINSON

April 20

Do you ever think you are two different people inside and that some of the time you feel like *this is me,* while other times you negate that very self you praised just a short time ago? Do you think this is called a "split personality," or could you have definite issues with saying what you think is the right answer as opposed to voicing your own true opinion?

This is a topic you will run into over and over again in your life until you decide that your "true voice" is the most important one. You will find it here throughout these pages, for it is one of the most important issues you will face: real vs. image. Don't you sometimes feel like, "Will the real me please stand up!"

Challenge yourself as to why you need everyone's approval before you commit to a voice of your own. Remember, this is about your life journey. No one is on this trip except you, and when you speak up it needs to be without blame or hatred or anger coming from your voice. Speak from your heart, which is all forgiving, and not from your mind, which seeks to avenge feeling injured. Speaking up is not about destroying someone else, but solely about freeing yourself!

Too often we think that speaking up means that we have to pull someone else down. If you take this approach you will find yourself no better off than you were before you voiced your feelings or opinion. Do not "follow the crowd" in slandering someone else as a way of fitting in, but speak your truth as your way of being heard. Listen to your heart! Do not allow your mind to deceive you!

Question: What prevents you from speaking out about how you really feel in negative situations? What are you afraid of?

_____

_____

_____

LARRY ROBINSON

April 21

D o you ever think you are crazy? No, not the type of crazy that says you are mentally ill, but rather the type that refers to someone who may feel stupid, unworthy, and unlovable. This is the worst kind of feedback we can give ourselves.

When we look at ourselves in this negative light and we keep repeating the same patterns as if we are on a merry-go-round, why wouldn't we become dizzy and disoriented? We never seem to get off this ride. In fact, at times we even begin to see this as "normal."

Are we crazy for wanting to believe in something that everyone else sees as ridiculous? Are we that far gone that we cannot figure out what is good for us and what is poison? No, we are not out of our minds, we are just so lonely or frustrated or scared that we place all of our hopes in one basket. When this occurs we will always be disappointed.

It is so important to remove these negative labels that we place on ourselves and begin to see that we are wishing for a miracle when we believe that someone will come by and make us feel better about ourselves. There is no one on this earth who can be greater than ourselves! We are the only ones who can increase our self-worth. Why would you think that someone else can boost your sense of self when you cannot do it? Can't you see that if you do not feel good about yourself then no one else can make you feel better? How would you feel better if you do not like you? You would stay in doubt and negativity and eventually ruin any positive feedback you receive. When this happens, then you can call yourself crazy, for you will keep repeating this pattern throughout your entire life. It is time to wake up and smell the coffee! Deal with you!

Assignment: List your negative labels and place next to each one a positive way to look at them one by one. Remember, there is not just one negative!

LARRY ROBINSON

APRIL 22

We hate talking about them. We deny that we have them, but we all have experienced them! And what are they? Mood swings! Before cancer was really understood back in the 1970s, people "whispered" about the disease as if it was the dirty disease. Now we have mood swings, and we whisper about each other having bipolar disorder.

Bipolar disorder is a chemical imbalance within the brain that causes us to go from one emotion to another, either in a matter of minutes or sometimes weeks. We have a warning sign that tells us that we are acting manic, and we do not sleep and we can stay up for days until we literally explode with crazy ideas and fantasies. We eventually crash into a dark depression.

Stress is the major factor that triggers this disorder, but mood swings are not necessarily the result of a bipolar disorder. No, they come from our inability to express our displeasure or anger over something that can be huge for us or even something trivial. Understand that when we hold back our true feelings around certain situations we are creating a time bomb within us. Each time that we hold things in the fuse gets shorter and shorter on that bomb until we eventually explode!

This is not bipolar disorder. This is about not being able to swallow our feelings any longer. Do not let anyone tell you that you are crazy or that you need medication or that you are out of control. You are simply fed up and have not learned how to deal with your negative feelings. Spouses or partners can use your explosive self against you. Well, take responsibility for the explosion but not for your feelings! It's interesting, isn't it, that when you finally open up your true feelings you are labeled as crazy?

Question: Are you someone who has mood swings? Do you understand when they are coming by paying attention to clues that your mind throws at you or are you taken by surprise?

LARRY ROBINSON

APRIL 23

Do we really ever totally forgive someone for wrongdoings against us? Whether you are in a relationship with a life partner, a spouse, or a friend, does the pain ever really go away when you get hurt?

It isn't that you want to hold on to the hurt, but how often have you believed that you have forgiven someone only to have the pain pop right back up the minute they do something, even a small thing, that ticks you off? Suddenly you are dealing with the initial pain all over again. And this can happen years down the road, and it isn't planned, and yet you to rage against the other person once again!

There is something so deep rooted in this pain that we cannot, for the life of us, let it go. It is a primal pain of rejection and abandonment, and it does not matter whether it was a right or wrong situation that originally brought it up. It hurts just as much now as it did then. We had been wounded in our past, and it still stings today.

This is our problem, not the other person's. They have made their amends to us, and yet we still hold on to the pain. It is almost as if we need this pain as a reminder of our low self-esteem. You see, we never truly let go of the original anger and pain, and that wasn't created in the fight we just had. It is old and needy pain and it stinks! And as soon as we get a whiff of it we lash out with our rage.

What is the solution to this? We must own our own pain! Nothing that anyone does to us is not forgivable. But is the person we are having the fight with the one who truly needs our forgiveness? Look at this issue very closely and you will see your own history right in front of you. And remember, it is better to own your pain than it is to dump it onto someone else who does not know why your rage continues!

Question: Do you consider yourself a forgiving person? Do you hold on to resentments? What has been the longest resentment you have held on to?

LARRY ROBINSON

APRIL 24

Are you afraid of the dark? Did you fear it as a child and often needed to check out your bedroom to make sure there was no "bogeyman" under your bed? When the lights went out at night, did your heart start to pound and fear just crept into your heart and mind? There was nothing you could do to stop it and you became a prisoner of your own mind. No one really understood that you knew something was lurking in the shadows, and no matter how much you tried to tell your parents that you were being invaded, they did not listen!

What is the "bogeyman" and how do we rid ourselves of it today? For so many of us, we never truly got rid of this demon on our back. For children, the bogeyman is really just all the negative and angry feelings they cannot process. They do not have the insight to understand that they have unresolved feelings and that the bogeyman is simply formed out of those feelings. This is why it is so scary to a child. As adults, we no longer call it the bogeyman, but we still cannot sleep and our minds race at the thought of the next day. The demon then becomes our fears and the damaging thoughts that invade our minds.

The dark is an ally to negativity. Have we really grown up or are we still stuck with not being capable of dealing with these bad thoughts about life? It is time to put the bogeyman to rest and drive him from your mind for good. You see, he is just your creation from unresolved feelings. Once you face yourself, these feelings of paranoia begin to disappear and we take on a lighter load.

There is no one in life without a bogeyman. It is time to grow up and face the feelings that have been there since you first brought the bogeyman home. He has no value now! Why keep him around? Tell yourself, "I can face anything!"

Question: Are you still afraid of the bogeyman? What issues have been chasing you since you were a child?

LARRY ROBINSON

APRIL 25

Are you truly a "giving" person? Do you even know what "giving" means? So many of us give only in order to receive. If we could just be honest with ourselves, then we could admit that. There is nothing wrong with wanting to be given to. But if that is all we are about, then we are being selfish, because there is a motive in our giving. There is a neediness inside of us that seems to never get filled.

Are we empty? Is that what not being able to truly give means? Or are we stuck in our childhood looking for validation of who we are? There is an empty piece that does come out when a situation arises in which it is appropriate for us to give. No, we are not selfish; we are desperate. We want so much to be recognized that we have based our entire self-esteem on what we are given!

Remember back to the holidays when you were a child. For some there were never enough presents or the "right" present. We measured our value on what we received! So here is the dilemma: we need to be given to in order to prove our worth, and yet there are not enough things that we can receive to fill us up. We are always feeling not good enough!

It is necessary to remember that this was who we were in our childhood. Children receive, adults give. Where are you now? Be honest with yourself. Are you still waiting to see what you are given? If that is so, you are missing the finest times in your life, the time of giving! The warmth that you are missing will not be found unless you begin to understand that you no longer need to be given to. If you did not get it in childhood, you do not need it as an adult! This is the time when your ability to give can grow. The feeling that you get from giving becomes so much greater than being given to! Only in adulthood can we truly understand this.

Question: Are you a giver or someone who wants to be given to? After deciding which one you are, describe that person.

LARRY ROBINSON

APRIL 26

D o you dream about the future as a way of dealing with the present? Is the present hard on you and just a repetition of your past experiences? Do you think you are someone who avoids dealing with your present situation by creating a "fantasy future" that is pain free? If this is you, then life has already begun to pass you by.

Why do we either rush to the future or sink into our past when we have a crisis in the present? We do not know how to do anything different to stop the turmoil from entering into our lives. We become childlike and are either frozen in our tracks or helpless in our mind. When our mind takes over, it tells us we cannot help ourselves and we even give ourselves permission to "medicate" our problems. Take a good look at how you deal with issues that create pain in your life! Are you someone who turns to addictive behaviors to stop your pain?

We all have something that we are addicted to. It is extremely hard not to want to run from the major stresses that enter into our lives, and this is certainly not a new topic for us. It is our reality, though, and it is essential that we learn how to handle this.

The first position you must take is to understand that running away from your issues is the problem! The issues themselves can be used as tools that we need in order to resolve our conflicts. It is a fact that life presents us with certain issues that will continue to repeat themselves until we find a resolution to them. Repetition without resolution is dangerous, for each time that we do not deal with something it will come up again, and often the resulting situation will be more complicated than it was the time before.

Here is a good example: Jake forgets to pay bills all the time. He is extremely fortunate in that he makes the deadline for his phone bill right before it is about to be shut off. He does not care about the late fee, for as long as he pays the bill he is fine. Each month the same thing happens, except that last month he was out of town and he missed his deadline. This time he had to pay the entire phone bill off before his phone was turned back on. Not only was he embarrassed, but he also had to ask friends for help.

Do not run away from yourself! Take the time to be honest about how you deal with things and then commit yourself to changing it! The "how do I do it" is tied to accepting your behavior and taking control of your issues one at a time!

Assignment: List ways in which you can stop running away from your negative self.

_____

_____

_____

_____

_____

_____

_____

_____

_____

_____

_____

LARRY ROBINSON

APRIL 27

Do you see yourself as always seeking attention? Do you walk into a room and immediately look to see who is looking at you? Is it almost impossible for you to walk past a mirror or a store window without checking yourself out? You are your own worst enemy!

You do not change every time you look into the mirror! Your looks remain the same but how you see yourself can change all the time! One minute you can think you look great while the next you can hate the way you look, and you are constantly picking at your face, combing your hair, or changing clothes. And this is both a male *and* female thing, because insecurity has no gender preference. The attention you need has to live up to your expectations or else it will never be good enough. The only problem is that there is not enough attention in this world to satisfy the hunger inside of you!

You are the only one who can give yourself value. Perhaps you look for it everywhere you go. But think about it, there never seems to be enough or it lasts only for moments and then you are back looking for it again. Let's face it, you do not like yourself but your expectations are that everyone else should! Does that make sense to you? If you do not like yourself, then why would you believe anyone else does? Any compliment you heard you would twist in your mind to mean that you were either good enough or you'd take it as an insult.

Give yourself a break and realize that you do not want to deal with you. It is much easier for you to keep repeating the same dynamic over and over again than it is for you to face what you're thinking. You see, your thinking is messed up. The negativity you hold on to and the judgments you make eat away at the core of your existence. How can you feel you look good or accept positive attention when you can be hateful, jealous, and mean inside? You can change this thinking by being aware of your own negativity. Try it and see!

Assignment: Test yourself to see if you can only look in the mirror two times a day. Difficult, isn't it? Looking on the outside stops our ability to really see what life issues we are dealing with. Can you see more than your image?

_____

_____

_____

_____

_____

_____

_____

_____

_____

_____

_____

_____

_____

LARRY ROBINSON

APRIL 28

S elf-pity! Are you someone who suffers from this "disease of the mind"? Yes, it *is* a disease, and it makes us so unapproachable and actually so turned off to ourselves. We hide behind the feelings of being victimized by the world in general. It causes our strength to dwindle down to powerlessness and we are then paralyzed to help ourselves. In fact, we do not help ourselves, for we believe we cannot. This is the damage that self-pity does.

Where do we develop this monster of an issue? It starts in our childhood, where we believe that we are targeted by everyone and that we do not fit in. There has to be an answer somewhere that we're ignoring. If we were able to find it we might not fall into such despair. And "despair" is the key word here because it is a byproduct of self-pity. You cannot feel self-pity without experiencing despair. Being picked on at school, feeling as if our parents always blame us for some wrongdoing even if we didn't do it, these are some of the thoughts that come out of self-pity.

Self-pity has no gender to it. Both men and women alike experience this crippling issue, and yet we hate to admit it. Who wants to think of themselves as someone who feels sorry for themselves? Sometimes we hide the fact from others, but it does not go away! It eats at us like a cancer, and yet we are sometimes helpless in finding a solution to it.

Fight back! Yes, you have to fight back against believing that you cannot get yourself out of this "stinking thinking"! There really is no such thing as self-pity, for it is something that our mind makes up when we do not want to deal with our issues or a problem that is plaguing us. We want someone else to take care of this for us! We must stop ourselves from the pity that we try to evoke from others. We know what we are doing, and we must stop it! The "how" comes from the acceptance of the self-pity itself, and once we really see it we are then capable of stopping it from taking over. You are in control, for if you created the feeling then you can destroy it too! Get it now before you slip into self-loathing again!

Question: Is there a repetition to your stinking thinking? If so, what is it and how long have you thought this way?

_____

_____

_____

_____

_____

_____

_____

_____

_____

_____

_____

_____

_____

_____

APRIL 29

We have all heard in one form or another the phrase "inner happiness." It covers every religion and belief system in the world, and yet do we really understand it or even know what it is? What if my life is screwed up, can I still have inner happiness?

To truly have inner happiness, we need to be able to tell ourselves the truth about who we are. That does not mean that we have to beat ourselves up or puff our chests out. It means embracing an honesty that we never truly see. It is how we really see ourselves in the world. When we can reach that place, we can begin the work on inner happiness. You do not have to have your life completely resolved to achieve it. So many of us think so negatively about ourselves in the world. We have no idea that there is deep inside of us a light of goodness and tranquility that we rarely get to.

Do you ever see your light of goodness? It is a feeling that can overcome us when we do something to help others. Sometimes, even though it seems strange, we can well up with tears when watching a commercial on TV. We ask, "How is it I'm crying over a man walking his dog with his son at his side?" This is a picture of happiness and a place that sometimes we fear we will never get to. Just the fact that we could feel this and that it did touch us tells us that there is that light of goodness that leads us to inner happiness inside of us.

You see, inner happiness is not a constant for anyone, but instead something we strive to obtain. We all are capable of reaching that place. How long we stay there depends on how long we remain negative. If we overcome the negativity we can find the inner happiness again. Again, again, and once again, true inner happiness is in you! When you remove the negativity it will light your path!

Question: Why do you not believe in your own inner happiness? Do you only see the negative in your life? List three positives about yourself.

LARRY ROBINSON

April 30

Stop it! Stop it, stop it! Do you tell yourself this enough times when you are confronted with things about yourself that you dislike? Do you continue to follow this screwed-up issue without paying attention to your inner self? Yes, we do have an inner self! This is the self that fights the part of your mind that is always giving you bad advice. This inner self allows you to decide if what you are doing is right or wrong.

How often are you confronted with your mind fighting against you? Most of us fight a lifelong struggle with not giving in to what our mind tells us to do. It is the darker side of us, and it is relentless in its constant whispering into our ears, "Do it. Why not? Who cares?" Can we really fight off this beast that constantly criticizes us? Is the first sound we often hear when we wake up a little voice that says, "Why bother?" There is not one of us out there that has not been plagued by this.

Fighting off these awful sounds in our heads is the next phase of our journey. Enough is enough, right? Some of you will say, "This is easier said than done," and you are right, but that does not mean that we give up on ourselves. It means that we fight our demons even harder, for they want to enter our space and build a fortress inside of us that prevents anything positive from getting in! Well, too bad!

People need to have support, and that is what we will give! We will support your struggle, and all of us can be there. We are the same, even though we come from different cultures and religions and backgrounds. We are the same! Pain is pain! If anyone says that theirs is worse than yours, just say, "No, it is not! It is just different!" No one can tell another that their pain is not real or less than someone else's. Until we live someone else's life we cannot say this. Today we stand together and say, "Stop it!"

Assignment: List all the issues that cause you pain, and determine that you are going to face them one at a time, starting today!

LARRY ROBINSON

"If someone is jumping from relationship to relationship, or is in a long-term dysfunctional, unfulfilling relationship, chances are they have not experienced a true one with themselves in a long time—if ever. Being willing to settle or seek happiness from a partner becomes the only pattern they know. The sad thing is this can go on for years and years, even a lifetime, if the pattern is never broken. The only way to make change is to get to know yourself again without any influence and get back in touch with your true self. Try and remember the things you used to do on your own that brought happiness and confidence, and start doing them again independently. Slowly you will start to recover yourself and life will start to show you what was meant for you all along."

—Johnny Mello, Springfield, Massachusetts, USA

Isabella Walsh, Limerick, Ireland

MAY 1

It is so important to see our life as a journey, one that continues for eternity. None of us knows if there is a God or not, and none of us knows whether our soul continues after we finish our work here. Some believe in "dead is dead," and that it *is* the end. For them, this serves as their truth and they do not need to believe in a "higher being," but for others, faith in God takes us to the next part of the journey.

We need to look at death as just another part of life. And when we grieve for someone, we forget that their journey continues and so does ours. They were put in our lives to learn, and we in theirs. Remember that when we grieve for our loss and what they meant to us. Be at peace, knowing that they have finished this part of their journey and have now moved on to the next phase.

If we can truly believe that this is not the end but only a part of life, then we can be less afraid about what awaits us. Remember, they are no longer suffering this world and are now beyond it.

Faith teaches us to never doubt that we will partake in our journey until we are called "home," just as our loved ones were. We have to remember that we all get sick, we all get old, and we all die. This is the cycle of life. *Old* is not a matter of numbers, but a matter of *wisdom*. Some are new souls, some are middle souls, and some are old souls. Which do you think you are?

Question: Are you someone who has faith? Is it strong, or do you stop believing when something goes wrong?

_____

_____

_____

_____

MAY 2

Do you have difficulty with people who are always complaining that they are sick? They cannot find a diagnosis, and we begin to believe that they are "drama queens" who always have a sad story about their health. Well, guess what, the majority of them *do* have an illness! We cannot see it and doctors think it is a mystery or put them through batteries of tests only to find nothing, but they are sick! This is called psychosomatic illness: "psycho," meaning "mind," and "somatic," meaning "body." This is caused by stress.

Stress is anything that enters into our heads and renders us unable to rid ourselves of it. When it begins to "race" in our minds, it will very often find a true weakness in our body and rent space there. This is real! We rush to doctors with our lists of ailments and we are put through the batteries of tests, but to no avail, because nothing pops up to explain why we feel this way. Hasn't this happened to you? I know that I have experienced this before. And it is so painful to realize that people think you are faking, to the point where after a while you cannot even talk about it without someone rolling their eyes.

We need to be able to look at what things might be happening in our lives that we are not dealing with. I am positive you will find something! Remember, it does not have to be a major crisis, because those are right in front of us and we usually have no trouble dealing with those. This is something that has hurt us, and rather than deal with it we bring whatever it is into our body. And this causes illness.

If we develop patience with others, then perhaps we can find it in ourselves, and then, rather than rush to a doctor, we can begin a healing process by identifying the stress and begin dealing with it. I promise you, you will be on the road to recovery.

Question: What are some of the stress factors that you believe cause illness in you? Think carefully, for it is important to identify them to keep healthy.

LARRY ROBINSON

May 3

Can you face your own mortality? Remember when we were children and we had absolutely no concept of what death even meant? We thought we would live forever! Now, as some of us head into the last quarter of our lives, we are faced with this daunting question: can I accept that I will, or am, getting older? That I will get sick and that I will die? This is true for everyone, and yet it can be so frightening!

If you have no faith, then maybe you feel you are just born, live your life, and then just disappear without any sense of your life journey continuing. This is fine for some of you, but not for the rest of us, because we feel there *is* a "higher power" and that we will rejoin this "energy" when we move on. We believe that in the next life we are taught the lessons we did not learn in *this* life. Is that so frightening?

Do you believe that you will be judged for your deeds here? If this was the case, then your god is not so compassionate, or it could be that your belief takes you back to childhood when sin was sin. It probably isn't true that we will suffer in hell for what we didn't accomplish, but rewarded instead for what we did do!

If you believe that death is the end of your journey, then maybe it is for you. But for those of us who believe that death is only a part of our journey, well, we have a lot in store for the future! Remember, we are here until we are called back to right our wrongs and learn what is God-given in us. And this is not meant to be "preachy," but rather to help those of you who are sick and afraid of dying. Only you can make that peace with yourself and find your own truth!

Question: What is your view on the afterlife? Do you believe in one?

_____

_____

_____

LARRY ROBINSON

May 4

D o you have difficulty sleeping? Are you one of those people who toss and turn and keep checking your clock to see how much time you have slept? Do you wake up in the morning feeling as if you've been run over by a truck and wondering how you will survive the day? Have you been this way since you were a child and just never thought about it too much until you became an adult and it became a bigger problem? Has it affected your ability to concentrate at work or to be able to complete household chores? If any of this pertains to you, then it is most likely that you have a sleep disorder. But remember, most likely there are other things that can keep us awake at night, such as eating at night. Do you know that feeling of being famished right after we eat dinner or right before we go to bed? Do you wake up in the middle of the night and sneak downstairs, even if you live alone, to find something to eat? And isn't it amazing how we actually try to hide from ourselves by sneaking?

Are you shut down or grumpy in the morning and rationalize it by repeating to yourself that you're just not a morning person, despite knowing full well that the reason for this is lack of sleep? Do others avoid you in the morning because they are afraid you will snap their heads off, and it doesn't bother you that they feel this way? Do you tell yourself you are like this because you cannot help it?

There are a multitude of issues that may be going on. First off, check any medications you may be taking to see if weight gain is listed as a possible side effect. This might explain why you are eating late at night and can't seem to satisfy your appetite. Second, do you snore very loudly? Is your partner always pushing you to roll over, or in many cases leaving the bed? If you live alone, do you ever wake yourself up with a choking sound? You may be better off telling your doctor about this and not just dismissing it as just who you are. This could be a serious condition called sleep apnea, and it needs to be addressed immediately because it can lead to heart attacks or strokes.

There are also psychological reasons for your inability to sleep, such as resentments toward your partner or spouse who is sleeping next to you. Unfinished issues can keep the mind racing and the tiniest noise

LARRY ROBINSON

can wake you up, and then you begin the "mind torture" where your mind has now taken over and you are its victim. Nothing can get you back to sleep now.

The feeling of sexual rejection by either partner or the worry over the relationship lasting doesn't help, even though when you wake up you put that fake smile back on your face. But you do not want the other person to see your insecurities. You need help! These issues do not just disappear! And have you ever wondered if all of these issues might be intertwined?

Maybe today is a good day to start taking a good look instead of brushing them all away!

Assignment: Describe what your sleeping pattern is and what issues come through your mind that have prevented you from a good night's sleep.

_____

_____

_____

_____

_____

_____

_____

_____

_____

_____

_____

MAY 5

How do we deal with pain? Whether it is emotional or physical pain, it is still pain and it kills our spirit in life. It is an energy sucker and it has no boundaries, takes no hostages, and is out to destroy us! We are at its mercy and we so easily submit to it. How often do you experience this debilitating pain in your life? Why can't you fight it off and not surrender to its evilness? And yes, it is evil, for it stirs up in us horrible thoughts that can, in some cases, have deadly consequences.

Looking at physical pain, do you think it is worse than emotional pain? With physical pain we have a great audience that sees us as victims of a horrible, painful disease, and compassion and sympathy rush at us. We go to doctors and have surgery. And whether we recover or not, we will not be looked at as pathetic. Some of us take on pain as our badge of courage, putting up a great front and never showing our fear or anguish. We might feel as if we are dying, and that may or may not be the case, but we try to keep our physical pain all locked up in an effort to show the world how brave we are. We become victims of the attention we get rather than the strong fighters we could be. We need to embrace the pain and realize that we can withstand a lot more than we believe. The brain is the control center for pain. Go with the flow of your pain and do not fight it. Tension and the stress that follows create more pain. Breathe and take deep breaths and allow those breaths to wash out as much pain as possible. Your pain will not go away, but it will lessen!

And what about emotional pain and the tortured mind that refuses to let up? That tortured mind's demanding and damaging thoughts continuously play out loss, over and over again, and it does not hear our cries of desperation for relief. No matter how hard we try we cannot seem to let go of those feelings of abandonment or rejection. How horrible this is! We blame ourselves, we blame everyone else, and sometimes we even feel suicidal because we cannot handle this retching emotional distress. It tears up our hearts and we cannot control our mind. If we could stop the pain in our heart, we would be so much better off! But it is not our heart that is in pain, it is the mind playing its dirty little tricks on us, convincing us in the process that our hearts

LARRY ROBINSON

are broken! Since when did we know that this relationship was doomed and now suddenly we cannot handle it?

As for the pain of loss from death, well yes, we grieve for what we have lost and it creates great emotional pain. And maybe we'll never get over it, but we can work on allowing it to slow down inside us to the point where it becomes a pinprick rather than a knife wound.

So breathe! Breathe through this pain also, and you will see that our breath is our true companion through pain.

Question: Which do you suffer the most from, emotional or physical pain? Do you see a connection to both in your life?

_____

_____

_____

_____

_____

_____

_____

_____

_____

_____

_____

_____

May 6

Why do you believe that we lie at times? Where does lying originate? Do you believe that people start lying when they are adults or are its origins in our childhood? What is the difference between a white lie and a black lie? Or is there a difference? It can become a serious problem in our lives if we cannot be believed or cannot believe someone else. And how do we develop positive relationships if they involve lying?

When we were children and we lied, many times our parents would call this a "fib," which won't necessarily qualify as a lie but will meet with mild disapproval from our parents. But when does the child cross that line and end up telling lies? When there are no consequences to fibbing, the child almost has permission to continue to lie, for there is nothing to be afraid of or to be ashamed by. And if we had parents who told us to lie for them, such as, "Tell them I am not home," then they were teaching us to lie. And why wouldn't we pass this on?

It seems ridiculous to think that the simple little lie can create a bigger lie. If we do not feel acceptable, then why would telling the truth be something we would opt for? And what if no one ever bothered to catch us at lying? What would we believe about ourselves? It seems that we wouldn't understand the extent of the damage we'd be doing to ourselves and others.

Sometimes we have to make the decision to not tell someone the truth. When the truth is more damaging than keeping our mouths shut, then we have to take into consideration who the other person is and whether they can benefit from the truth or not. This is a real problem, for what is our ethical responsibility? It is up to each individual to decide what crosses their own morality when it comes to telling or omitting the truth

Assignment: Can you think of situations in which you would not tell someone the truth because you'd know it would be too difficult for them to hear? What about to protect yourself from feeling humiliated?

LARRY ROBINSON

MAY 7

Can you truly love someone and not respect them? Have you been, or are you still, in this type of situation and believe that you have the ability to fix what you do not respect so that you can be free of anger toward the other person? It is anger that you feel, but if you expose the anger, what will the other person do? Will they blow up at you and make you feel guilty that you have confronted them? Or will they threaten to leave you? For some of us it is better to keep the repetition going in our lives than deal with the consequences of our confrontations.

Why do we think that we can love without this respect that is so crucial to a genuine relationship? How much does it take to start feeling as if the intimacy is not real? The word that needs to stand out in our mind here is real, for we kid ourselves when we get involved with someone whom we think we can mold into who we want them to be. But it is not going to happen, no matter how much we put up with and no matter how much love we give to this other person. We cannot change another person; we can only change our reaction to them!

If we get involved in this type of relationship and seem to repeat ourselves many times over with similar relationships, then it is not about the other person. At that point it is all about us! You see, we are codependent! A codependent person makes themselves secondary in all their relationships, hoping that by giving so much they will be loved in return. No way! We end up always feeling taken advantage of, and then our cycle of anger and guilt begins all over again. It is as if we are stuck in quicksand, and sink deeper and deeper into despair.

Breaking this cycle is the work we need to begin. Low self-esteem keeps us spinning, but which came first, the chicken or the egg? Do we need to feel loved or do we look to give love? These are the answers we need to find!

Question: Do you believe that as much love as you give you should get back? Why?

LARRY ROBINSON

MAY 8

D o we hunger for approval? Are we always doing what we believe
is right in order to get that approval? Are we a "supposed to"
person—supposed to be obedient, supposed to be happy, supposed to
be strong and brave, supposed to put ourselves second to others? If these
traits describe some of us, then we can call ourselves passive-aggressive.
How are we so nice to some and yet end up hurting others? It is time
to take a look at this!

What passive-aggressive people do not know is how to be real. They
are always creating a personality that will please others, and it is like
wearing a different colored robe for different folks. They can be what
they believe they should be to gain acceptance, for in their minds they
are the "ultimate doers" and "sacrificers" in life. They bypass the things
they cannot tolerate and are the happy people, always with a smile
and always with the kindest words to say, even in the most horrible
of situations. They do not recognize it on the outside. They are those
people who come up to a grieving person and say, "Don't worry, dear,
you will move on and start your life anew." Isn't that just what someone
needs to hear in a time of grief? The passive-aggressive only predicts
what they think is right and not what they truly feel because they are
detached from negative feelings. PAs are not aware of their anger, but
can certainly act it out at times.

This is the "aggressive" side of the passive-aggressive, but they do
not see it in themselves. Inside, their minds are extremely negative about
life and people, for they do not want to accept these feelings. At times,
when wanting to be of help, the PA will say inappropriate things to
other people under the guise of helping, such as, "I wanted you to know
that Laura told me she doesn't like you, and I was hoping the two of
you can mend your broken relationship!" Well, the other person didn't
even know that Laura was upset with her, but the passive-aggressive had
always internally disliked this woman, and so instead of acknowledging
those feelings, she detached from them, causing grief in the process.

Passive-aggressive people can be the ultimate "givers," and most of
the time it is from their hearts, but there is also a tendency to manipulate

people in order to create an alternate reality in which they are the most beloved people. It is very difficult to recognize this in oneself, but it is also important to create a true reality, one in which we can grow from our mistakes. Do you screw up? Do you want the world to see you as this person? Can we really stop for a minute and look at this and see how it exists in us?"

Question: Can you describe what being mindful means to you? Are you living in the moment or always thinking about your negative past or fearful of the future?

_____

_____

_____

_____

_____

_____

_____

_____

_____

_____

_____

_____

May 9

Do you believe what your mind tells you about your life and the people in it? Do you always listen to your mind, or is there something inside of you that tells you to stay clear of its messages? Everyone has a story about their life. Everyone! So if someone tells you they do not, then that is their story; they are empty inside! As children, we form our life story around the messages we get from our parents and other adults around us. It is created in our minds and it can be rock solid. So if you have the same story you had as a child, then you have not grown!

Can you accept the fact that there is a story that you have been playing out for most of your life but that you are not your story? You are so much more, but in order to become more you have to be willing to give up what you believed to be the truth and what you have carried throughout your life journey. This will go against everything you believed in that was connected to your life. This is no easy task, but if you want to see what you are truly capable of, then you must learn how to let go of the story you have created about you!

Do you realize that you have always lived out of the past and been afraid of the future? You do not know how to live in the moment of your life in order to experience the now! When folks are always in either the past or the future, this doesn't mean that they aren't playing out their story, but you will find that if you keep repeating your issues and pushing them to the forefront, your future will be no different from your past. And how defeating is that! No, your mind is just a compilation of all the pain you have experienced. It whispers to you that you will screw up or fail just as you did in the past! What a complete rip off your mind has become in your life!

Assignment: Take a moment and find a quiet place and allow yourself to sit for as long as you can. When your mind starts to tell you, "You are being foolish; you have things to do," stop yourself and just sit a little longer. Each time a thought comes into your head count to ten.

Try this exercise, and eventually you will be able to sit for ten to fifteen minutes totally free of your mind!

_____

_____

_____

_____

_____

_____

_____

_____

_____

_____

_____

_____

_____

_____

_____

_____

MAY 10

Happy Mother's Day, Mom! Today is the day that we honor you for who you have been as a mother. We ask ourselves, has she been a kind, loving, compassionate mother when we have been suffering? Or has there always been a "but" after her soothing words? Has she needed you as her ear when she is hurting, but as soon as she feels better she is ready to hang up? Has she told you that as a child you were no day at the beach when you complained to her about mothering? Has she used you as her surrogate mother, father, husband, priest, or counselor?

Do you always feel like hanging up or not answering the phone when she appears on your caller ID? Is she always "there" for you? Does she love to be with her grandchildren, and does she offer to give you a break when you are at your wits' end with parenting? Does she put herself second for *you,* or does she always come "first" no matter what is happening in your life?

Some of these questions are true for all of us, and we try, as parents, not to repeat her life. But we also take from her what we believe she does, or did, the best she could. Today is Mother's Day, and if she is still here with you, give her this day. If she has left this earth, then honor her for bringing you into this world, because your life is so much better than hers ever was. Happy Mother's Day, Mom!

Question: How would you describe your relationship with your mother? If she has passed, are you holding on to guilt or anger about your relationship with her?

_____

_____

_____

_____

May 11

Can we truly love and live with someone who is our exact opposite? How did we fall in love with someone who defies all our ways of looking at life and still feel love for that person? If you are one of those people who have done this, have you been happy? Or has everything been a struggle to find some sort of balance in your relationship? Are you always agreeing to disagree and winding up in one big fight after another, even though you did not expect this to happen? Maybe you need to answer the question: why didn't you know that there would be fighting if you were the exact opposites?

We usually cannot live with someone who is exactly like we are. There is no challenge whatsoever and boredom generally creeps in. The person like ourselves just agrees with everything we say because they feel the same way. We all think this would be the perfect relationship, but that person will portray issues that are just like our own, and that does not make for good partners. If we are not able to resolve these ourselves, then how can we expect our partner, who has the same issues, to be better than us and have the answers to these issues?

If you look carefully right now at your partner or spouse, or even your choices from the past, you will see they are your opposite! You might be someone who is a time fanatic, while your partner never shows up on time. Perhaps you are a night person and your partner is someone who likes to go to bed early. Does this make for strange bedfellows? I imagine that you could name tons of issues that you did not even think were issues until you got together with this person.

Why are you trying to get your own way in the relationship? Neither one of you is wrong in your approach; you just have not worked out the compromise. And you will not as long as you are judging the other's ways as right or wrong! "Different" is what the label says, and only after you validate how each other sees an issue can you then look for an answer in a combination of the two. If you cannot reach that agreement, then ask yourself if being right is so important that it is worth continuing to fight over. Is it worth the ending of the relationship? And you can't say you're shocked at the disagreements because you knew they were there

LARRY ROBINSON

all along! Learn to be honest with your feelings, for it is only then that you can expect the same from the other person!

Question: Are you someone who has to be right in a relationship or do you always give in and then build a resentment that your feelings do not count? Well, who knows how you feel if you hold things in?

_____

_____

_____

_____

_____

_____

_____

_____

_____

_____

_____

_____

_____

MAY 12

C an you admit when you have been wrong and hurt someone with your words? Do you often try to shift the blame onto the other person or give an excuse for why you acted the way you did as if that gives you permission to be mean? Why do we become mean to others, especially people we love? It takes a lot of courage to look at yourself and without needing help from the other person admit that you were being harsh or mean.

Sometimes it feels as though it just shoots out of our mouths without any thought about the damage it will do to others. We become so wrapped up in ourselves that we fail to see what we're actually doing! And we can do this with children as much as we can do it with spouses or partners.

Did one of your parents say horrific things to the other when they had a fight? Are you just repeating an abusive cycle, and I do mean *abusive*, for that is what it is without us even knowing it. Don't you feel that as children we sometimes inhale the air our folks exhale and suddenly find ourselves so much like them? How else did we mimic their behavior—the exact behavior, by the way—that we swore we would never repeat!

Which parent can you identify with? And are your words repetitions of their nasty intentions? Are you really remorseful afterward or do you just pretend to be? The venom you spewed felt too good for you to genuinely apologize to the other person, and isn't this sad?

How many of you are courageous enough to take responsibility for this behavior and not be afraid to tarnish your image? The first step in recovery from the "addiction to meanness" is to own yourself in it! If you bypass your responsibility with an excuse for why you were like this, then you will do it over and over again. This is not about the "whys" but the action of meanness. It does not matter why!

There are a million reasons for losing it but only one conclusion: a part of us likes it! Yes, it is a purge, as if we were throwing up, and the aftereffect is surprisingly calm. The fever has passed and we return to our "normal" self. But the objects of our meanness, do they ever recover?

You have to know who you are and what your damage is in order to stop this acting out. You have to breathe deeply and catch the "inflamed" you from coming out. Surprise yourself and begin this journey toward recovery—and oh, by the by, you are not alone out there!

Question: What nasty behaviors did you inherit from your mother and father? Can you identify them?

_____

_____

_____

_____

_____

_____

_____

_____

_____

_____

_____

_____

_____

MAY 13

How much do you worry? Is worrying about things that have not happened yet always invading your mind? No matter how much you tell yourself there is nothing to worry about, you cannot find relief from the obsessing that goes on in your mind. People can tend to avoid you when you are in this frenzy of worry, for it makes no difference how they approach you. You cannot let go of it! It is almost as if the "stinking thinking" that takes over your mind is your way of not dealing with other issues. The wall around worry at times becomes so high that you are locked in and feel as if you will never get out.

And what will stop the worry? Nothing! Nothing will stop it until you decide to look beyond it to what the real issue might be. Your mind has the capability of creating worry as a way of not dealing with your true feelings. Yes, you say that the worry is real, but if you are worrying about something that has not happened yet, what do you get from it? It can take over your mind and consume all your thoughts and still it has accomplished nothing except divert your attention away from some other unfinished business you have not attended to. Did you ever think that worry was a defense against being angry?

For some people, the feeling of being angry is just too much for them to cope with. They have swallowed their anger, and instead of getting depressed they bypass that feeling and jump right into worry or anxiety. Anxiety then becomes the major feeling they have toward everything that could be troublesome or have even the potential to become a problem, even if it's years away!

The anxiety (worry) is so powerful at times that it causes us to not want to eat or be able to sleep. It is on our minds before we sleep *and* when we wake up! Anxiety can become a body sensation too. It can cause us to feel like we are "climbing out of our skin," and we pace or get up every few minutes because our mind just cannot focus. But if we were to really focus, we'd see that the anxiety is really just anger that has now rooted itself inside our body. Go for a long enough period of time without dealing with it and suddenly you'll find yourself in a

LARRY ROBINSON

full-blown anxiety attack that can make you feel as if you're having a heart attack or even dying!

Not all anxiety is anger, but all anger can become anxiety or worry if we do not learn how to deal with it. Now is the time to face your feelings!

Question: Do you spend most of your time worrying about the future? Can you determine whether it has hurt how you see your present?

_____

_____

_____

_____

_____

_____

_____

_____

_____

_____

_____

_____

_____

MAY 14

Do you have anxiety attacks? These are those devastating episodes when you cannot stop your mind from racing and your heart rate goes up and you cannot sleep. Your mind goes over and over the same issues until you are mentally, physically, and emotionally exhausted. No matter how hard you try, you cannot stop this noise inside your head! One might say that anxiety is a "killer," but at best it is a reaction to something that we do not want to face! The anxiety does not leave us until we either resolve it or continually medicate it. This is our reality.

When you do not deal with the anxiety, it goes undercover and out of nowhere we experience a panic attack. Panic attacks do not deal with a racing mind as much as they deal with something buried so deeply inside of us that we have no idea what is going on! All we know is that we either feel like we are having a heart attack or become physically and emotionally unable to function. We sweat, palpitate, feel shortness of breath, and mimic many of the signs of a heart attack. Remember, it comes out of nowhere, and usually after a trip to the emergency room we calm down. And this is usually so debilitating that we need some sort of medical support after it dies down.

What do we do? Well, we "medicate" the initial problem, but in addition to the medication initially stabilizing us it also prevents us from really discovering what it is that is really going on. We are looking for the easy way out, but the "hurricane" we have created is very powerful due to the fact that we have allowed our defense mechanisms to totally take over! We feel hopeless and like we are a lost cause!

Anxiety is, nine times out of ten, unresolved feelings within you. Those feelings are usually based upon how much anger you swallow. When anger is swallowed it has no place to go but back onto you. If you are angry at your spouse/partner and you do not confront it, you will assuredly create some anxiety inside and not recognize where it comes from. The more you recognize the consequences of your inability to confront others, the more you will understand your anxiety. Anger unresolved is deadly! And the more anger you hold on to, the deadlier the anxiety feels. Do something now and stop being so afraid of confrontation, unless of course you would rather deal with the anxiety and panic attacks!

Assignment: Describe an anxiety attack or a panic attack that you have had. How long did it last and how did you remove it?

_____

_____

_____

_____

_____

_____

_____

_____

_____

_____

_____

_____

_____

_____

Photo by Julian Edelstein
Marblehead, Massachusetts, USA

"Sometimes it is difficult to let go of the past especially when it hurts. . . . but if we never let go of the past we never move forward."

—Adsesuyi Babatope, Amassoma, Nigeria

MAY 15

Do you believe there is more to your life than what has been presented to you? Is this it, or is there more after we die? This question is probably one of the more important ones that we find difficult to answer, and yet so much of how we live our lives depends on the answer to this question. For so many of us the disappointments we continually encounter can warp our thinking to believe that this life is it and that there is nothing beyond except nothing.

What is life like for us without faith? Faith is very different from belief in that it is something that no one can take away from us and no one can manipulate us into disbelieving. We all want proof that there is life after death and that God or a higher power exists; however, we will not get that while we are still on this earth. No, it is only your belief system that can guide you through this life and into the next. If there is nothing to believe in, then why are we basically moral people who are living our lives as if we might have to answer to someone?

Where does that thought or feeling come from? Is it the religion of our parents or is there something deeper inside of us that call us to be accountable for our actions in life? Some of us have rejected the religion of our ancestors but still have this innate fear that we are being judged by something much more powerful than ourselves. Without this belief we are in turmoil. We have no true direction. We are born, we live our lives, and then we die. *Kaput!* This is all that it is about. How empty does that make us, and does it mean that we can do anything we darn well please without any repercussions? What meaning then does that give to your life? And what do you pass on to your children if you have no faith? Anything that happens is just life, and that is that. "Don't worry, be happy," that is the song that we want to sing!

Question: What has happened to your faith? Or did you ever really have it? Can you distinguish between faith and hope? Which seems stronger to you?

LARRY ROBINSON

MAY 16

Why do we have to be so mean to one another when we disagree? The amount of pain we cause is so much more potent than the issue we disagree on. Is it truly because we need to get our own way? Or is there some deeper meaning that comes out of the nasty things we say to each other? Once that button is pushed in either person, watch out! This is when we really need to be in touch with our feelings; otherwise, the meanness will continue. And none of us can say we didn't realize we were being mean, because we are not ignorant of what we feel in the moment. It is almost as if we feel entitled to say hurtful things because the other person crossed a line that opened the door to mean!

There definitely is the possibility that we are experiencing something very old when we are rejected or criticized or put down. The rage that shoots out is as hot as when we discovered the pain for the first time. We are so outraged that we cannot contain ourselves! If you think that by holding things in you are doing something better, then you are mistaken! The silent rage is deafening! Can't you hear it? Nope, probably not, for you are too caught up in it to be able to listen. Oh, you hear it, but your words have little meaning to what is actually going on. You are lost in some time warp that is still filled with pain!

For those of us who think we had the perfect childhood, well, we cannot see our past very clearly. Now, there are people who will say they have no or very few memories of their past. But perhaps these are people who do not want to remember their past, either because it just was too painful or they were so neglected emotionally that they think, "Why go back into something that I do not want to remember?"

How often, when asked something, do you give the answer "I don't know"? We rarely accept this phrase when children say it, so why do we accept it in ourselves? Next time, instead of saying, "I do not know," try saying, "I do not want to know!" Often the words come out so quickly that we have not given ourselves a second to think about what is actually going on. Do not despair, for you are definitely not alone, but you do not want to join any more clubs that give us permission to ignore our meanness and "acting out" behavior. I think there is already a waiting list to get in!

Assignment and question: Make a list of all the people you have been mean to. If the list has more than two people on it, then you have some work to do! Are you still carrying baggage from your past that is spilling over into your present?

_____

_____

_____

_____

_____

_____

_____

_____

_____

_____

_____

_____

_____

_____

MAY 17

D o you think we value father as much as we do mother? Do we place *mother* in a higher category and see her as the most important person in our lives as we develop? Remember that mother is a biological component of us, while father is a psychological factor in our lives. For the first two years, father is really secondary to mother (we come from our mothers, not fathers).

Who do we run to when we are hurt or want soothing? Yes, there are the exceptional fathers out there who have the ability to nurture, yet we still want to be cared for by mother. Do you think there is something to a child's instinct actually knowing the relationship with its mother from the womb?

What if mother is cold and unavailable? We still want her despite the fact that we most likely have already chased this person away because they cannot tolerate closeness. This is not your fault as a child, and too many of us think that we must have done something to make mother not want us. Wrong! Have you ever thought that mother is unlovable? Try loving someone who is unlovable and you will end up asking yourself, "What's wrong with me?"

We turn to father when we have mothers who are almost impossible to love. Most often, the father in this situation knows who mother is and tries to compensate for her aloofness and coldness, but the damage is already well on its way to being done. We do need the love of a mother.

Society is changing and there are different types of families now. It will take quite awhile and probably many generations before we readjust our society to these different family systems. We will then begin to determine that perhaps "love is love" and "nurturing is nurturing," and that *gender* no longer matters. But until that happens, mother looks like she is the most important person in our young lives!

Question: Which parent was most important to you? What did you learn from them? What did the other parent contribute to your life, both good and bad?

LARRY ROBINSON

MAY 18

Why do you think that we blame others for our misfortunes in life? We all do it, so there is no use denying it! Even if on the outside we appear to take all responsibility for our screwups, we still tend to think: "Well, if he/she just left things alone, I would be fine." Haven't you heard that echo around in your head before?

We do not like to look at our failures, no one does. It is much easier to blame others or the situation or the bad luck we ran into than it is to take the responsibility ourselves. Is this another area of perfection in life or are we just not capable of looking at ourselves? Blame is so damaging. Haven't you been blamed before for something that you didn't do? Often, our friends will blame us for the advice we gave them, when honestly, we just simply gave our advice. If they followed it, is that our fault?

How many relationships have been lost due to blame? Blame also comes with different types of anger. There is the "stewing" anger that develops as if we put it in a slow cooker and let it simmer all day. We are so cooked at the end of it. There is the "lash-out" anger that directly accuses and then punishes the other person for their part in our bad choices or decisions. There is also the "swallowed" anger, where the other person usually has no idea that we are even angry at them, but we tend to ignore or reject them without them knowing why! What a mess blame can be!

Take responsibility for yourself, because in the long run it is so much easier than placing it where it doesn't belong. You alienate yourself from life when you defend your mishaps by placing and attaching blame. It is time to stand up and be responsible for your own actions. There is no "how" in this, just a desire to feel stronger and less defensive in life!

Question: Have you always blamed others for your misfortunes? Think about this before answering!

LARRY ROBINSON

MAY 19

How are you dealing with conflict in your life today? Are you someone who stands strong in the face of it? Or do you run away and feel the need to either hide or pretend that it is not there? Do you end up feeling weak and miserable, or are you just relieved that you do not have to deal with it? Face it: you hate yourself either way you look at it. You are a "conflict avoider" and have always been one.

Did you receive lectures and get put down as a child and had to stand there and take it from one or both of your parents because they were frustrated with their lives? You were their punching bag, weren't you? Now is the time to ask yourself, "Have I continued to act as a punching bag for other people all my life? Am I destined to either stand there or take it, or do I need to run away?" Maybe you're thinking, "This is how I have operated all my life, why should I change when others will still see me the way they want to and not for who I am!"

It's your journey! This is not about how others see you, but about how you see yourself! You do not see yourself as strong, so why should anyone really listen to someone who "whispers"? I cannot hear you! That's right, no one can if you are always ducking the punches and not standing up for you! Did you think someone else would do this work for you? I doubt that will happen, for we cannot change anyone except ourselves.

Wake up! Perhaps you have been sleeping for a very long time, but your life is rushing by you and no one else is going to take responsibility for who you are. This is your time to take correct action. Make a list of all the things you run from and all the people who are attached to those issues. How long is your list? Start to talk to yourself about what the truth is and listen to yourself speak these vital words. The more familiar these words are, the more capable you will become in addressing these issues. Remember, at this point in your life you will not be able to determine whether there is a habit going on or if it is, in fact, real fear.

Question: Do you want to be seen as someone who is too weak to stand up for themselves or just lazy? Make that list stated in the above paragraph.

LARRY ROBINSON

MAY 20

Do you live in chaos? Can you ever clear your mind enough so that you can follow through on something that you need or want to do? Are you always rushing from point A to point B and forgetting that there is life in between the two? Do you get so disgusted with the chaotic life you live that at times you give in to it totally and become immobile? Does life take on a darker edge when you feel overwhelmed by your inability to stop the chaos? This is a serious problem for you, and you are so caught up in it that you actually think it just might be normal.

Look back in your life. Has there always been a chaotic feeling attached to it? Do you feel at times like you're detached from everyone else because your chaos is taking over and preventing your peace of mind? Are you so conditioned with chaos that you just can't seem to do without it? You are a "chaos junkie" and you do not know how to live without it! How are others in your life affected by your chaotic tendencies? Often we are so unaware of our behavior that we do not see the damage it does to others in our lives. This is so important, especially when you have children. They need the stability of structure, while all you can offer is a potential recovery from you!

Slow your life down! Do not think that you have to take on everything in your world at one time. When you slow down, your ability to make decisions gets easier, for there is not the normal despair around you. When you slow down, you explain yourself better and you become more tuned into other people's feelings. When we are in that chaotic mode we cannot see what someone else is trying to say. It is all about us. Our chaos rules and we are slaves to it. This is a sign that you are getting too self-centered with your chaos and can no longer see the damage it does to others. Get some feedback about your approach to others. See if there is something that you can change about yourself that will slow down your need to get things right all the time. Just learning how to breathe when you are in stressful situations can slow down your chaos. One breath in, one breath out! Slow, slower, slowest!

Assignment: List the ways in which your own life becomes chaotic. Do you see this as normal or have you given up trying to find different ways to slow the chaos down?

_____

_____

_____

_____

_____

_____

_____

_____

_____

_____

_____

_____

_____

_____

_____

LARRY ROBINSON

"We want to be right all the time because that is one thing
we feel is under our power. We feel the need to be right because
we are helpless in many other aspects of our life. The problem lies in
not how stubborn our views our but that we are so powerless."

Tom Xu, Brooklyn New York, USA

Isabella Walsh, Limerick, Ireland

MAY 21

D o you pay attention to your inner voice? You know that little voice inside your head that whispers to you about what you should think rather than what you are thinking in the moment. Is it constantly talking?

How right has this voice been for you? When situations arise, do you hear it tell you not to believe what you are feeling or thinking? Does it make you question your feelings and thoughts until you are totally confused and have strayed from where you originally were with the situation? Do you think this is a friendly or unfriendly voice?

Perhaps we will believe that this voice is really our subconscious speaking to us, but we must remember that this is the area in which all our negative, doubting, angry feelings and thoughts reside. Our subconscious is our "disbelieving self," and it can be very dangerous. Do you listen to it?

Do not be fooled by it! Take a moment and look at the situation that you are in, and then listen to what your voice is saying. Is it disagreeing with how you feel?

Remember, your feelings are "heart centered" not mind related, and this is your negative mind trying to trick you into believing something that is not real! How many times have you said to yourself, "I should have followed my intuition and not listened to my mind"? We have all been guilty of this. Until we realize that we have the answers that we're looking for in our heart, we will let our inner voice rule!

You are smarter than that voice. It relies on you to keep listening to it and changing your mind. Do not be fooled by it! Listen closely and you will know what this means!

Question: What has your inner voice always whispered to you about you and your life? Has it been a positive influence or a negative factor?

MAY 22

This is a topic that needs to be repeated throughout our lives until we get it. So many of us still do not understand that we are the masters of our own destiny. Do you know when it is time to let go of "toxic" relationships? Are you the type of person who cannot understand that when things are over they really are over? You are hanging on to your fantasy of who you wanted that person to be rather than seeing the reality of who they are. How much pain can you take before it becomes unbearable?

You have been in this situation before, haven't you? You do know what heartache feels like, so why are you back in this position again? Didn't you learn anything from your last broken heart? We are stubborn and we do not want anyone to say no to us. Do we really want this person, or are we hung up on the fact that they didn't want us? Rejection is extremely hard to accept. We were not good enough, that is the message we received. We no longer have the courage to let go of this poison.

Now we are addicted to removing the rejection. We will call, follow, interrupt, and stalk this person until they see what real value we possess. We have lost our sense of shame and we don't even care anymore. All we want is to have this person want us again. But did they really want us to begin with? If they did, then why did they reject us in the end?

It is time to stop being a mess over someone, who if you took the time to really look closely, you don't even like. Why would you like someone who doesn't like you? Make a list of all the things that you believed were good about this person, and then make a list about all that was wrong. If the good outweighs the bad, then you are in trouble. You do not want to see reality, only your version of it. You are in love with someone who does not exist! Relationships do not end when people are happy. If one person is and one isn't, then the relationship does not stand a chance of continuing. Both people need to want the relationship to grow. If there is only one who wants it, it is time to leave!

LARRY ROBINSON

Question: In what way can you at this time in your life become master of your own destiny? What does that entail and how would you go about getting that control that has been so lacking in your life?

_____

_____

_____

_____

_____

_____

_____

_____

_____

_____

_____

_____

_____

_____

_____

_____

_____

MAY 23

D o you have the need to be dramatic? Do you feel that you are not interesting enough unless there is some crisis in your life? Do you always present your life as if it is in turmoil and that you are the victim? This is extremely difficult to look at for it requires an ability to be honest with yourself. And you can't just pretend to get it, you have to have the sincerity you'll need to change it! Do you really think people are attracted to drama? If that was the case, what would be the benefit for them?

So often we do not know how to be loved for who we are but for what we do. If it wasn't recognized and celebrated during our childhood, then we still have a hard time identifying our value. So many of you will say, "There he goes, blaming our childhood again," but it is not about blame, this is about understanding ourselves. We just didn't become dramatic at age thirty. This is something that we bring with us from our childhood and into our adult life.

How many of us know people like this? We probably know too many, but the question is can we admit it in ourselves? Until we are ready to acknowledge that this is an issue for us then we cannot move forward. We will go after bad relationships and lousy jobs that are unfulfilling, and we will have friendships that will make us feel used. This is all because drama entails negativity and hopelessness. There are times when drama is able to make us look like we can handle anything, but there is a steep price to pay for it! Either people think that we are so brave that we can handle anything or they'll think we are a complete mess! Only "saviors" will be able to take care of us.

Maybe this is what the drama and victimization is all about, that we just need to feel cared for. We can see our lives as meaningless unless there is a drama we can be saved from. We can also put on our superhero's cape and fly to our own rescue. This will show our value. We can make it like we can take care of any situation and therefore we are filled with value. We are the wanted person. How fake have we become? How sad for us!

LARRY ROBINSON

Assignment: Make a list of all the things that you are not truthful about that you make dramatic issues in your life.

_____

_____

_____

_____

_____

_____

_____

_____

_____

_____

_____

_____

_____

_____

_____

_____

MAY 24

Are you someone who has been lied to over and over again by someone you love? Do you want to believe them even though your support system tells you you're nuts? Why do you continue to place your trust in them when they continually break your heart? Are you just a foolish person who cannot see beyond your own need to be loved and who disregards all the warning signs that say you are being lied to once again? You are not foolish! You are not addicted to punishment. You are, instead, a scared person.

Why scared? Because you do not want to believe that someone you could love so much doesn't really love you. What an awful feeling to want so much to be loved by a liar. If this person was who you wanted them to be then there would be no problem to begin with. Have you ever walked away from a conversation and felt, "Was I really being told the truth?" If you have to ask yourself that question, then most likely you were being lied to! We know the truth! It is a feeling that is deep inside of us, and when the truth is violated an uneasy feeling in our stomach tells us, "Danger!" Of course we don't listen, and that's because our need to be loved becomes even greater when doubting the truth. We cannot believe that someone we love does not love us the same way.

What way is that? It is called "overkill," and it can feed the liar to continue to lie. We want so much to believe them that we rationalize their behavior. We make excuse after excuse for them because we do not want to let go of that need to be loved. It is almost as if we really do not care about them but only for what we need from them. Remember, we never meet anyone in life who is better or worse than we are. So wouldn't it be fitting that the person who needs to be loved so much meets the person who lies about everything and who is constantly challenging the meaning of love? How can we say, "I love you, but I do not *like* you"? How do you really love someone you do not like?

You need to accept reality. You do know what that is, but maybe you do not want to deal with it! Is the act of you continuously trying to take this person back into your life about you or them? Where is your self-esteem? Or does that even play a role in your decision to accept or reject

LARRY ROBINSON

the liar in your life? Perhaps you need to look and see if you have intimacy problems and that dealing with the pain of lies is keeping you from letting someone else into your life. It is always easier to look the other way until the lie hits you in the face, that way you can once again play the wounded victim as opposed to staying strong enough to say, "I am done!"

Question: Do you understand what your reality is? What is real and what is fantasy in your life? This question is so important to answer honestly!

_____

_____

_____

_____

_____

_____

_____

_____

_____

_____

_____

_____

_____

_____

May 25

A re you someone who needs to show people how much you love them? Do you want or need hugs and kisses a lot, and at times make people feel uncomfortable because they do not know how to respond to you? Do you often not know how you are coming across to others? Do you know that you are being viewed as needy?

Perhaps this is not you but you know someone like this. They/ you are folks who smother other people with love. Oftentimes it is impossible for us to wait for someone to approach us with affection and our need to give overwhelms others to such a degree that we are avoided at times, and yes, we do feel the avoidance! We end up rationalizing other people's behavior as opposed to our own.

Here is a good example: Joan went to visit her daughter and grandchildren for the holidays. She bought so much for everyone that it made even her grandchildren uncomfortable. They could only say thank you so many times before it just seemed empty. As for Joan, she got so disappointed that she became distant and depressed. Her efforts to give her family a great holiday went sour. Each time someone opened a present she jumped up to hug and kiss them, only to feel rejected by their lukewarm responses.

What happens to people like Joan in life? Is she always going to feel the need to smother others with love, affection, gifts, or whatever it takes for her to be thanked and noticed? Will she always feel that no one appreciates how much she loves them and wants to give to them? If she continues to make her need to be recognized for what she gives stronger than the actual giving, then she is doomed to feel unappreciated and rejected. There are not enough "thank yous" for Joan in life. Her constant need to be accepted and loved is always challenged by her giving too much. Joan will never feel loved enough!

Many of us share similarities with Joan in that if we went back into her childhood we would find that Joan thought she wasn't good enough to be loved for who she was. Her parents made demands that she felt she never could live up to. It didn't even have to do with what her reality was, for she was just that type of sensitive child who always felt she needed to be more than expected. Perhaps she was competitive with other siblings and always felt the need to outdo everyone else.

If you have this trait inside of you, stop and think about what the expectations were for you! You are no longer that child who needs to feel *overloved* in order to measure your self-worth. If this is the case you will never feel truly loved. There will always be that insecurity inside you forcing you to give more and you will always end up feeling unappreciated.

You are not measured by what you give materially or physically, but by the way your heart responds to others. The measure of a person's worth is not determined by their ability to give the most, but by the way that they can love. Love does not have a price tag on it, just as it doesn't have expectations about what we should receive. When we give love from our heart we are enough, and we do not need the reassurance from others. We instinctively know!

Question: Do you know what your heart feels as opposed to what your mind tells you? Do you give because you think you should or does your heart tell you it is the *right* thing to do?

_____

_____

_____

_____

_____

_____

_____

_____

_____

MAY 26

Do you feel desperate about your life going by so quickly? Do you remember when you were in grade school and how the summer felt like it was going on forever, and how you secretly wished that school would just hurry up and start? Let's face it, we got bored! Things are no longer that way today. With everything that goes on in the world and with the rush of various technologies and the fact that we are getting older, it seems as if time is just flying by. I once heard that when you feel as if yesterday was the summer and tomorrow will be fall, time really is speeding up and taking us closer to death. If this is the case, then what are we waiting for to kick-start our lives? Remember, it is not as if we have eternity to get it together! How much do you dream and how much do you deal with your reality?

Being a dreamer, it is almost as if you "want to want to" do more with your life but that it is still all a "mind creation" as opposed to an action! This cannot be the first time that we have dealt with this issue, because most of us do dream and it is often what actually holds us back. It is as if we have to have the dream perfect in order to actually begin to live it. Are we afraid to go after what we want for our lives, or are we so out of whack with reality and our expectations are so high that we cannot possibly meet them? You are that daydreamer, aren't you?

You sit inside your head and have the most elaborate thoughts about what you are going to do with your life but then you go no further. Do you not believe that you can be any more than you already are?

When we age we have the opportunity to look back on our life to see if we gave it the best shot possible. Did you? You might think that you are young enough to wait awhile, but *do* not be foolish, because time does not stand still! If time moves forward and you do not, you will be left behind. This is not what your life is supposed to be. Do you get this? You are so much more than you think you are. Do not let your past control your future. You must live in the present and live it to the best of your ability so that you can begin to shape your future. Too often we get stuck with stinking thinking about our lives and it freezes us with low self-esteem. This makes our past become our present and

LARRY ROBINSON

then ultimately our future. You will ask, "What is the answer to this?" Set a goal for the present and fulfill it! Stop the past dead in its tracks and chase it away! You are not your past. Your past is what you have experienced but it is not you! *Now* is the time in your life, not yesterday and not tomorrow!

Question: Are you someone who dwells in the past a lot? If so, what have you learned about yourself from going there?

_____

_____

_____

_____

_____

_____

_____

_____

_____

_____

_____

_____

_____

_____

_____

MAY 27

Do you have self-doubt? Is this something that has been part of you for your whole life? Do you understand where this comes from and why you sit with it rather than try to work it out for yourself? Did you know that there is a difference between self-doubt and worry? We might say that worry is a byproduct of self-doubt, but does self-doubt come from worry? As self-doubting persons, there are times when we just give in to it and do not worry. We have already determined that we do not know how to do something, and therefore we do not attempt to do it.

When we were children we relied on our environment to give us feedback on who we are. If the feedback is positive and reassuring, then the likelihood that we will be positive and not self-doubting is fairly secure. If we get negative feedback and we are always being told that we are wrong or can always do much better, then we can be assured that we will end up doubting our opinions and our attempts to try new things or enter into new situations.

If we just have worry over doing something, that does not necessarily mean that we won't do it, whereas with self-doubt the anxiety that it creates will most often stop us completely. We end up feeling safe because we will not have to feel wrong, but in the process we create more low self-esteem because we didn't attempt to do it. This is the between a rock and a hard place situation. It definitely freezes us and creates a standstill in our lives.

We are the only ones to determine what we feel and what we truly are capable of doing. We have listened to other people all our lives, and anything that they said that had negativity to it we believed. Like sheep being herded toward a slaughter, we cut ourselves down in order to please others or to feed someone else's ego.

It is time to stop this behavior before our life becomes one of no meaning. It is never too late to find meaning. The first step is to understand that the self-doubt is the child inside of us that heard bad stuff about him/herself. We listen to our enemy, our mind, which continually feeds us negative thoughts about ourselves. As an adult you

LARRY ROBINSON

can begin to distinguish the difference between child thoughts and adult ones. Remember, adults need to teach children to be positive.

Question: Are you someone who worries a lot or are consumed by self-doubt? How does this worry or doubt affect your life?

_____

_____

_____

_____

_____

_____

_____

_____

_____

_____

_____

_____

_____

_____

MAY 28

Are you familiar with this statement? "I thought everything was going along fine until I realized that you were making plans without me. It always seemed that you were annoyed with me over almost nothing at all. I get it. I get it. I am just like all the others. When you're done, you're done, and I am just collateral damage in your life."

Why do we not see who we are getting involved with? Or is it just that we did not listen to what the other person was saying about their life? Maybe they exaggerated, or maybe we have poor listening skills and only listen to what we want to. We bypass all the negatives and just look lovingly at the other person because we want to be wanted by them. We cannot remember what they said to us when we first met because we were ready to agree with anything just to feel wanted.

How often have you jumped into a new relationship because that need is so great? What happens when the need to be wanted is so much greater than who it is that wants us? This relationship will fail. It has no strong foundation to build upon, just shaky stilts that will collapse under the weight of bad communication and ego boosts. An "ego boost" is when someone feels bad about themselves and wants someone else to want them. This raises our self-esteem, but is rather empty.

This is your life, your journey! How much time do you waste in relationships that you really are not invested in? "It is better than nothing," you tell yourself, but is that really the case? Face it, we sometimes do not even like the person but we tell ourselves that we will fix or change anything we find unacceptable. Our minds are telling us, "Okay, let's find our security first and then we will pay attention to the other person. Right now just eat up the attention and the feeling of being wanted."

Are we being selfish, or is this just another part of being desperate to be part of something? It is a selfishness that we cannot really identify. At some level we do know we're being selfish, but we quickly put it into the back of our mind in order to receive this most-needed attention. It festers in our subconscious.

We let people suffer because we cannot pull ourselves away from choosing second best when we already know that we do not have the

LARRY ROBINSON

kind of feelings we should have to be in an intimate relationship. Accept it and you will at least not be able to tolerate hurting someone for a longer period of time. There is something about knowledge that makes it harder to fake feelings. The lesson we need to learn here isn't about ending bad relationships. No, the lesson is about not getting into them in the first place! We all know!

Question: Do you see yourself as someone who needs a lot of attention? Do you ever take the time to take into consideration who you are getting it from?

_____

_____

_____

_____

_____

_____

_____

_____

_____

_____

_____

_____

_____

MAY 29

Why is it that when we are hurt we run to tell everyone our business? Is it not possible to keep things within the confines of our own life rather than spill it into others' lives? How many times have you talked negatively about your spouse or partner to your friends when you've been hurt or angered by them in order to get the exact support you feel you need? In fact, some of your closest friends are finally relieved that you're done with someone who is always making you feel bad. It also becomes a big relief for them, as they now believe you will be a better person. By not being involved with someone who it seems is almost always putting you down and creating havoc with your self-esteem, you can go back to being the friend they've missed!

Once you receive this mountain of support you feel great! It becomes pleasurable to hear how people really felt about this person who was not very "engaging" with your friends and who treated you with disrespect, but how are you really feeling inside? There is something missing and you are really feeling it! You are alone and no longer attached to someone else. This empty feeling is driving you crazy and you cannot really tell the people who are helping you through this hard time that you are beginning to miss the other person. God forbid you expose your vulnerability to others about this relationship you have just convinced them was horrible for you. What are you supposed to do with these feelings now that you have sliced up the other person in front of your closest confidants?

You know you have been guilty of this before. You want so much to make up with this other person, and in fact, many times you do. But what is the cost of your foolery? Remember, when you make up with this other person your friends are left with all your pain and anger toward them. They do not have the opportunity to make up with your spouse or partner. They only know what has been done to you, and not the good things, only the bad. Now you risk alienating everyone because you could not keep your mouth closed until there was a resolution between the two of you. People would much rather like to hear about how you resolved things, as opposed to the pain you allowed yourself to suffer.

LARRY ROBINSON

You now risk losing this solid support system, while it is likely you'll run into the same problems with your spouse or partner that you had before. And who do you go to now? You need to stop trying to get support from the whole world when you are hurt. You must learn to face each other with the truth. And if one or the other of you cannot hear the truth, then what are you doing in this relationship?

Question: Are you someone who works out your issues with your spouse or partner with others and leave them with your anger when you resolve the issue you had? Remember, they do not get a chance to make up with the other person.

MAY 30

D o you drive yourself crazy? Do you often have too many things going on in your head at the same time and do not know how to sort it all out in order to feel a sense of accomplishment? Are you always thinking that you will finish things tomorrow, when in fact there is a little voice inside of you telling you that's not likely to happen? Are there some mornings that you just want to hide in bed?

You are not alone and you are not crazy! You just want to do it right, whatever "right" is. There are no bad intentions in your disorganization, only your inability to organize yourself. You have become so good at overwhelming yourself that you might be able to add this to the list of habits you have developed over the years. Sometimes it feels as if we are on this merry-go-round and that getting off of it seems impossible! It's almost as if you no longer believe you are even capable of doing it differently. If you give yourself permission to screw up, then you will!

There are probably so many things that you give up on in your life, why not include organization and completion? Add these two to your list of things you cannot do in life. We need to get rid of words and terms such as "cannot," "should have," "would have," "could have," and "have to." These words are our enemies! They strangle our voices into believing that we are hopeless, and when that happens the voice becomes negative and silent. We "cannot" breathe. Now, to fix this!

You have most likely always set yourself up to fail. Taking on too much over and over again tells you something about yourself. You know, to some extent, that this pattern has always existed, but you do nothing about it! It is so much easier to tell yourself that you, "should have," "would have," "could have" done it better. If you continue to tell yourself these things, then you know at some level that you are hiding the fact that you might just not want to do it differently.

Assignment: Start with being honest with you! Now, think about what your next step would be. Do not get defeated, for there are no wrong answers.

LARRY ROBINSON

MAY 31

How do we let go of past relationships? Do we really even want to? We say that we do, but we talk about it endlessly to our friends and family, and that does no good. At first it feels right; the other person did us wrong, so then why isn't that enough?

After the initial "I hate him/her moments," we are faced with the bitter truth that we were rejected. Someone did not want us. We become consumed with trying to figure out what we did wrong, and every little thing that we ever did that the other person complained about becomes THE reason. We spend endless days obsessing over what we did wrong only to come right back to the beginning and feel lost and empty. WE WERE REJECTED!

Of course we were extremely happy in this relationship. For us there never were any problems. RIGHT! No, we were engulfed in problems, and either we tried to hide them with being super nice to the other person or we were relentless in trying to "talk" and still nothing changed. We need to face the fact that we were miserable.

It does matter who rejects who first. At least we think it does. How often have you thought "I want out!" and when the other person ends the relationship we are devastated. No longer do we want out; we want back in!

We need to face the fact that the relationship needed a ton of work on it, and neither person was inclined to do the work. Of course we might say we wanted to, but when it came down to it, we did not walk away from it when no work was done. We kept repeating the same fights over and over again. We felt horrible.

It takes courage to end a relationship, or to accept the fact that someone else had already taken our place (if we have proof that there was someone else; if there was, why would we want the other person anyway!). We do not start a relationship only to end it. There is too much pain when a relationship does not grow. Someone has to end it if two people cannot or won't go any farther. Remember, rejection when we are miserable in a relationship is not about lost love but about our ego and pride. It does not matter who goes first. As much as we want to blame the other person, we need to look at ourselves and be responsible for WHO WE ARE!

Question: Are you always the one to end a relationship or have you been rejected before?

_____

_____

_____

_____

_____

_____

_____

_____

_____

_____

_____

_____

_____

_____

Brandon Adelman
Swampscott, Massachusetts, USA

June 1

D o you fight fairly, or do you let things inside you get totally out of control? Are you the "yeller" in the relationship? And that doesn't apply to just partners or spouses, but with family members as well. Do you find yourself saying the meanest things you can think of just to hurt the other person, or do you sit there silently and lead the other person into crazy and out-of-control behavior because you won't fight?

Do you point this out to them, "Wow, you are really out of control. Can you hear yourself? Do you think you *need* medication?"

These are the mean things that can come out of you when you are backed into a corner or feel as though you have been ripped off. Where does this meanness come from, and why do you swear to yourself that you will never go there again, only to end up breaking your word every time there is a fight?

Are you always feeling guilty after the fact, and out of remorse act too kindly toward the other person because of that guilt? Often we disregard what the other person has said or done because we feel so badly about the things we have spewed. Fighting can be so bad, and yet how do we get this relationship to grow?

Who gave us the idea that we have to fight? If there is a fight going on it means that one or both parties are unhappy with something. Often, we just cannot simply sit down and discuss our pain. We are incensed with raw, ugly feelings and they can feel so unmanageable. Do you really mean what you said during the fight, or are you just trying to get back at the other person and this is how you do it? Do you really believe that they feel the same way you do, filled with hateful thoughts?

Sometimes it is better to get these out yourself rather than keep them stuffed down inside. Often we find that it's the stresses in each of our lives that create the fight in the first place. In essence, we are letting out so much more than just the feelings around the fight. Most often the fight is about something stupid, but the intensity is not. Trying to cut down on damaging words is the goal.

Perhaps we need to create a board that allows us to leave notes for the other person, letting them know that we need to talk when they have time. This way we just don't hit them with our unhappiness. On this board we can just put up a topic like "household chores" or "food shopping" or "cell phone" to alert them of what it is we need to talk about. Make it like a meeting, not an execution, and try to find a good time to do it. If you have been boiling about an issue, you can certainly wait for the "meeting" to bring it up.

Do not start off with, "You did so and so . . .," but say how you feel. Many people will start off with, "I feel that you . . .," which again does not talk about your feelings but rather more about what the other person did. "I feel alone with the meal planning or childcare or decision-making" might sound silly and it may look that way, but it's much better than "I hate you!"

Letting your partner, spouse, children, or family members know about how stressed you are will really help.

Question: Do you react to negative situations or do you respond? Do not rush this answer. Think carefully about it.

_____

_____

_____

_____

_____

_____

_____

_____

_____

JUNE 2

Do you sometimes find yourself in a fight with your spouse or partner and you do not know how you got there? Can something as simple as a question from the other person cause a flare-up that begins to lead to disaster? Do you say things that are cold, harsh, mean, or downright horrible, and then feel full of shame afterward? This is really why saying "I am sorry" is so difficult.

No one likes to face their ugly side and admit they were wrong. You do not have to be wrong in your idea, but you can be wrong in how you handled feeling criticized. Perhaps you turned extremely defensive, so much so that you never even let the other person speak.

We are all so fragile and we are all so hypersensitive, why wouldn't this happen? It might not be possible for you to be quiet while someone is telling you off, but it also could be that this is just your perception and that the other person is attempting to tell you what is bothering them. This might just be about them and not you.

Breathe deeply and count to ten before you say anything! This way you will cool down the flame that has erupted inside you and you are less likely to ignite the other person. We won't do this perfectly the first time, but we can begin to become adults (and there are a few of us out there). We can become better role models and better partners if we work on being able to listen. Why is that so hard?

Question: Do you think that you have the type of personality that likes to fight? Are you argumentative or calm and understanding?

_____

_____

_____

_____

LARRY ROBINSON

JUNE 3

What are the components that I need in order to maintain a healthy relationship? Why do I feel anxious when I should feel peaceful? The needs that I have aren't wants, because if I do not have these then I have to question what we need to do in order to regain a strong relationship. These needs, by the way, exist in both men and women, although when men provide these needs they tend to feel stronger and more capable.

The first need is safety. This means that I have to trust my partner to be faithful and to provide for me emotionally. And we should always be working toward knowing what each other's needs are without constantly having to ask. And hey, if we listen carefully enough we will know what the other's needs are and we will no longer have to ask.

The second need is security. We need to feel that we are not sitting on the edge of financial ruin all the time and that we will back each other, without the hysteria and the anger, when one of us is having financial difficulties. We are in this together! And women need to help out, just as men do, when our family is in financial danger.

The third need is consistency. This means that we make rules for ourselves and our children so that we can all follow the same path. Do not make a rule for your child that they will see you break! Although they are not yet our equals, we want to teach them inner discipline, which is the ability to follow directions, make correct decisions, and finish things. We need to lead by example, not "do as I say, not as I do."

The last is stability, which is the feeling that we are together forever. Our families can withstand any crisis, and that includes infidelity, because we all make bad choices when we are unhappy. And we need forgiveness to preserve our families. Is ego more important than recovery and giving our children a stable home?

Too often we do not look at the entire picture as to what causes instability in our relationships.

Assignment: Follow these guidelines and watch your relationship thrive! Look at things as before and after!

LARRY ROBINSON

JUNE 4

Why do we grieve so much when a relationship ends and we are not the one who ended it? Why do we become desperate to fill that emptiness so quickly? Why, because we need to be needed! And maybe that's why we fell in love with that person in the first place.

Some of us have such poor self-esteem that we really don't bother to see who it is that wants us. Instead, we fall in love with the feeling of feeling wanted. How many of us fall in love so fast that the courtship, engagement, marriage, and subsequent divorce can all take place in a matter of months? We rush into relationships with our long-conjured-up "fantasies" about love and romance. We put aside our deeper feelings in order to rationalize why the other person does not show us the same excitement they did in the beginning.

We are still loved! That is our mantra. But when that blow finally comes and someone tells us, "I'm just not ready for a relationship," or "there's just something missing now," we forget that we've been feeling their detachment all along! Now we are so out of our minds with grief that we quickly forget those hints of disinterest and lack of sexual interest from the other person.

Well, stop! It does not matter who ends a fractured relationship. It needed more juice than you were able to pump into it, and it wasn't that you never asked, "What's wrong?" Sometimes we have to realize that it might not be who *we* are that ended a relationship, but who the other person is.

Are you too quick to jump to the conclusion that you will never be in another relationship? Well, get over it! There is no such thing as he/she is my *soul mate*. It is time to see reality. If the relationship didn't end, then neither would your suffering. Even though it maybe hadn't started yet, it was going to. Why would you ever want to be with someone who didn't want to be with you?

Question: Do you hold on to relationships even when you know it is done until you meet someone else? Do you see this as self-protective or selfish?

LARRY ROBINSON

JUNE 5

Are you depressed? Most professionals believe that there could be a chemical "imbalance" inside you that causes you to have mood shifts. If that was the case, we'd all be in trouble, because we all get depressed at times.

What if there were no time limits associated with depression and we were told that it was not just episodic, but rather a lifelong condition? Would we then go around feeling that we're permanently damaged and that there is no hope for us besides consuming all kinds of medications that produce horrible side effects? "Oh, I just gained all this weight because I'm on medication!"

Maybe you are still self-medicating even though you're on prescribed medications and nothing seems to motivate you. Would you rather isolate yourself than join the rest of the world? Has avoiding people become your main occupation?

What does the word "depressed" really mean? Visualize a picture of someone pushing something down inside of themselves, like 100 pounds of rock. How heavy do you think adding 100 pounds would be to your body? Pretty heavy, huh? It would cause you to drag yourself around and feel exhausted all the time. Sleep would be a great release from this weight.

We need to identify this pushed-down weight. The hardest feeling we have to deal with is anger. No one really wants to be viewed as an angry person, so we usually push it down inside ourselves. And that's when we start getting close to depression.

How much anger have you pushed down in your lifetime? For some, it is monumental and they use every form of numbing tool available to keep it down. No wonder they call it "chronic depression"! And if you've been holding it in your entire life, then that term applies to you.

Instead of being the victim of your feelings, take a good look at how angry you have been in your life and the different ways in which you pretend it's not there. Now you can see that you may have had depressed feelings, we all do, but that doesn't make you a depressed person. Never dealing with those feelings does!

Assignment: Challenge yourself to open the door of depressed feelings and face them. You know what they are; do not be afraid of them. They cannot hurt you. List them if it helps! Write about them!

_____

_____

_____

_____

_____

_____

_____

_____

_____

_____

_____

_____

_____

_____

LARRY ROBINSON

JUNE 6

Why do we "choose" the person we are with or have been with for our partner or spouse in life? Are they really our choice, or is there some destiny that is pulling us toward one another? How often have we seen a danger sign and not paid attention to it or purposely misread it so we could stay with this person? Were you ever warned not to stay and you ignored the warning? Well, it ends up that you were right not to listen, because this person has become part of your journey in life! We all want to run away or hide from our truth in life, but we have something to learn from this person and until we get it. We are either going to stay or leave until that lesson is learned.

We call it "chemistry" that binds us to that person, yet we do not understand exactly what causes us to need to be with that person. Chemistry is not just a physical or emotional or even a mental attraction, but it is more of a "gut" reaction, almost as if we feel a certain familiarity with that person.

Have you ever been with someone and said, "I feel as if I've known this person forever"? Well, this is the beginning of chemistry and it is both a wonderful feeling and a dangerous one. The dangerous part is that we might run into someone who is our opposite. They may be laid back while we are hyper, or we might crave adventure while they prefer staying at home. But there is a reason why we meet this person, and I am beginning to believe that it's a "meant-to-be" situation.

Look at your current partner or even the past ones you've had and see what the commonality is or was between the two of you. We have something to learn from this relationship, but we will definitely run into problems with it too. We are meant to be in this because there is a life lesson for us in it. And it is for us to determine what that life lesson is. When we do, it'll help us decide whether to stay because it's the right relationship or leave because it isn't. If you repeat the wrong relationship over and over again, then there is something you are missing and that is causing this repetition. And remember, repetition without resolution will cause us to remain stuck until we find the solution. What that solution is, well, that is your work!

Question: Are you someone who needs to be in love all of the time? Do you force relationships because you know you can make this person be the one?

_____

_____

_____

_____

_____

_____

_____

_____

_____

_____

_____

_____

_____

_____

JUNE 7

Why don't we tell our partners/spouses the truth? Why would we want to be considered liars as opposed to someone who is always honest with our partner? Are we deliberately setting ourselves up to look dishonest? First of all, who are you trying to convey something to? Are you afraid of the other person's reaction or does it go deeper than that? What is their reaction to perceived criticism? Sometimes it isn't what we have to say, but it can be a fear of the other person's reaction. Are they a volatile person who blows up at the least bit of confrontation?

Anytime we withhold the truth there is no way we are going to talk our way out of it when we are exposed. We either lied through the intentional act of omission or we outright just did not tell the truth. Therefore, we cannot defend this action by turning it around on the other person, especially when you know that they will turn it back on you! This is a setup for a big blowout, and watch out for what is said, for it will be shocking and nasty!

When people are "cornered" they will do almost anything in order to get out of that hotspot. The approach we take will determine how damaging the results will be. Pushing someone into a corner because you do not know how to reach them will cause your relationship to crumble in the moment. And if you string too many of these situations together, they will cease to end up as moments and instead turn into a way of life in the relationship. What a sad way of living, where we both cannot talk to each other without causing the other to fight back. Do not think, "Well, it is his/her fault because they are unapproachable!" It is a joint venture, where every action has a reaction!

Fixing this after years of repeating the same behavior is not easy, but whoever told us that relationships and communication was? We all probably fantasized about a perfect relationship, and now we are stuck in something painful and potentially abusive, but remember, we chose this relationship and now we are both responsible for fixing it.

There is no perfection, and it is never simply one person's fault. Do not set the other person up by saying, "There is something I need to talk about, but I am afraid that you will yell at me!" This is the coward's way, because if you know that the other person is a yeller, then you are setting them up when you say, "I knew you would yell, so what is the use?" Blame is not the name of the game in this situation, for you might as well point the finger at yourself too because your ability to communicate is just as negative! And do not think that you know how to reach this person, for you have chosen the wrong path over and over again. Tell them instead that your way of approaching them does not and is not working, and that you are no longer going to "hit" them with your issue the way you have been doing it. Ask them what would be better for them! Remember, the idea is to reach someone, not to be right!

Question: Think about who you are in a relationship. Are you truly honest or do you omit when you are afraid of a negative reaction? Do you try and be a pleaser or are you a fighter?

_____

_____

_____

_____

_____

_____

_____

_____

_____

_____

_____

JUNE 8

D o we really understand each other or do we fake it most of the time because we really have no idea what our spouse or partner is talking about? Can you picture yourself saying or thinking this, "You are the opposite of everything I am, but I still do not get why things are so difficult. Everyone always says it is about the communication. Well, show me then how I am supposed to communicate with someone who speaks a different language than I do? We evidently do not understand each other, so what do we do now?"

"You think that I do not try, but you are so wrong! I spent so much time going over in my head why things got so out of control. After all, all I did was ask you a question. My tone is my tone and I cannot change how I heat up so quickly when I feel attacked by you. And you tell me it is not an attack. I just asked you a question! Remember, it is all about the communication, so when I hear you it is an attack, yet when you deliver it, it is just a simple question. How do we get so far away from each other?"

If you remember, it has always been this way, but because you loved each other you ignored the how to in your communication. Now there is no communication.

Do you want to fix this? You both have to want the relationship to work, and not because of children but because you made a decision to be together. Right now you are not doing anything as a couple to fix it, so here is your assignment. For the next month you and your spouse are to take fifteen minutes a day and sit with each other and talk about your day or any other things that might bother you. While one person talks, the other listens. There is no interrupting or what we call "cross talk" (you are not allowed to challenge what the other person has said). One will work on listening skills and the other on delivery. Then you will change this around so each one of you gets a few minutes to talk.

If you both want to save this relationship then you will do this task. It is not easy, but one month is what is called for. There needs to be consistency in order to change behaviors that have been around for a long time. If you feel a need to question what someone has said, then ask them if they want feedback about what they have said. So many times we just want to be heard and are not looking to be fixed. There are no couples who cannot do this; there are just couples who do not want to do this!

Question: Do you really believe that you try to fix your relationship by trying to analyze everything or have you stopped caring? If you are single, have you given up too easily on past relationships?

_____

_____

_____

_____

_____

_____

_____

_____

_____

_____

_____

_____

JUNE 9

Why do we find it necessary to judge each other? What do we think we possess that makes us appear to be better than others? Do you think that you were put on this earth to find people that you believed were less than yourself in order to feel that you are better?

We are all guilty when it comes to judging others. It is almost a rite of passage that starts when we're very young and we begin to play with others. It stays with us until we realize that we are not better than anyone, just different! Thank god that we not only recognize differences in others, but accept them too and not believe that they should be like us!

The judgment of others is just a way of dealing with our own imperfections. If we can find fault with others, then we feel like we aren't so bad off ourselves. Isn't this a sad commentary on life? We are better than others! We are less than others! No, we are just different!

Sometimes, *different* is a hard word to swallow. We all, at times, need to feel powerful, and the way we go about getting power is by comparing ourselves to others. We have to come out on top or we direct ourselves to the bottom and feel less than others. Do you think this is a way that we keep ourselves stuck?

Only when you compete against yourself in order to better yourself is this a plus in your life. Spending time trying to beat out others is really a waste of time, for there will always be someone who comes along to challenge your position. The real test in life is to have a healthy competition with *you*! Challenge yourself to do better than you did before. This is what counts in life, not beating out someone else. Stop wasting time!

Question: Do you see yourself always competing against the world? How do you deal with losing?

LARRY ROBINSON

June 10

Why don't we let go of people who treat us poorly? What is the reason that we knowingly hold on to them without any regard for our own wellbeing? Are we just looking for the punishment and humiliation that comes with wanting someone who doesn't want us, or are there deeper reasons that do not allow us to let go?

As you are now learning, nothing is simple in life and there are no rewards for suffering, so why do we hang on to bad relationships long after things are done and over with? We never want to feel the closure that we so need. "Done is done," but not for some of us!

We hang on because somewhere inside of us is the message that we are not worth anything and that no one would want us. We feel we do not deserve to be loved, although we try to persuade the person to love us. We plead and beg for recognition by them to no end, only to continue to feel empty. We see ourselves as worthless if this person does not want us. Who does this person represent to us?

They represent our self-esteem! We allow someone who has treated us with a total lack of respect and disregard for our feelings to determine how we should feel about ourselves! We have placed everything onto their judgment of us, and that is where we are doomed.

Why would you want to let someone who doesn't want you determine your value? In bad relationships, sometimes it isn't about trying to repair something that has lost its life, but it is more about letting go! Why do we wait for the other person to end it? Why don't we take control of our lives and say goodbye? We could spend an eternity trying to figure out why we hang on, but that would only confuse us more. No, this is about knowing what is right and following through. Do it now before the pain of trying to stay becomes an addiction!

Question: Are you afraid to be alone? Have you ever really spent time alone when you were not in a relationship? How long could you last before you were out looking again?

LARRY ROBINSON

JUNE 11

Why is saying "I am so sorry" so difficult? Why is it that we have the hardest time with saying this to those we love? Are we that proud and are our egos so large that we cannot muster up the words to fit in our mouths?

Do we say "I'm sorry" so fast that it has lost all meaning, and yet we defend the fact that we have said it by snapping back and saying, "So now what do you want?" Are we truly *sorry*, or is that just our way of blocking having to deal with the fact that we have actually hurt someone?

Do we ever freely admit we were wrong without saying "you do it also"? What a sad story this is when neither one of us can say those difficult words. It is almost as if our mouths are filled with stones and we're trying to say "I'm sorry" with our mouths full. It cannot sound sincere or apologetic.

Do not defend yourself anymore. It is useless. If you truly believe you were right, then maybe you need to listen to how your delivery sounded to the other person. Was it intended to make them feel bad or less than? Remember, three-quarters of our arguments are about delivery and not the actual content of the fight. Listen to how you deliver your words and then see how the other person heard them. Are they clear and not blaming?

Always go back to yourself and not to what the other person has said. They need to be responsible for themselves, and it is not your job to point out their own behavior out to them! If you do not listen, then why on earth should they? The fight is no longer about what you initially fought about; it is now about how each of you handled it! Are you satisfied with your delivery?

Question: Do you say "I am sorry" with conviction and remorse or do you say it because you are supposed to? Does your heart hardened toward others when you are caught at something negative

LARRY ROBINSON

June 12

There are two kinds of suffering, one that we are exposed to from the outside world, such as natural disasters, and a second from violence upon our being or the death of a loved one. These outside types we have no control over but must work through nevertheless, while the other kind of suffering is that which comes from within. We are the only ones capable of changing that, and it is hard! This suffering comes out of our own "emptiness."

What does this emptiness mean and where does it come from? We can suffer when we look in the mirror and see ourselves as ugly. We can suffer when we become anxious about our future or worry too much about finances. There are so many things that will provide us with suffering if we let it.

We are not born suffering, because as babies we are only concerned with living in the moment as we adjust to our life on earth. However, we do begin to take on the suffering of our surroundings. We begin our "journey of emptiness" when we do not get out of our own way. We are constantly putting roadblocks up that *intensify* our suffering. We empty ourselves of positive energy and are left only with darkness and despair.

"Empty" is such a hard word. It has the image of blackness and coldness. And it is! In order to stop our suffering we must face ourselves and what we do not want to deal with. There is a choice, we either decide to work through the suffering and the emptiness that comes with it or wallow in it forever! And believe it, forever is a very long time! Understand that no one consciously chooses suffering, but when it comes to change we all back off at first. Do not be afraid to face yourself, for when you can forgive yourself for your negative actions in life you begin to release the suffering!

Assignment: List the issues that you are most afraid to face. Even though we have done this before, we need to do it enough times so we truly understand what we are facing. Think carefully of one solution to each one. Do not run away!

June 13

Why do we choose to want the person who makes our heart beat so fast that we feel as if we're having a heart attack? Why aren't we drawn to the stable, secure, consistent, and safe person, and instead want the edgy, *bad boy/girl*-type that seems to always cause us unhappiness? Are we out of our mind? Or is our mind simply tricking us into believing that this type of person will actually make us happy?

We might say that we are "blinded" by love, but that is the excuse that we give ourselves when we tread near the dangerous waters of love addiction. There are more times than I can write about when it comes to this "dis-ease" of the heart in which every decision we make is dependent on how that person is affecting our life. Love is not just blind, but to the contrary, it is insane when it comes to this type of toxic person.

We cannot resist the pull of this suicidal love. It drives us to the brink of despair for we know that these people are dangerous to start with, and yet the "want-to-be-wanted" person inside of us chooses the worst possible character for us. We choose the one who continually breaks our heart and shows no remorse for it. We set ourselves up for punishment because we cannot resist this type of person. How many of them have there been in your life?

You will say that you have no chemistry with people who do not "charge you up," yet these are the people who will love you and want to be with you. How many times do you need to be with someone who does not want to be with you! What are you really looking for? Is this what you believe love is actually about, or are you just such a hopeless romantic that you cannot resist this passion inside of you? Hopeless, yes, but "romantic"? You need to double check your definition of what you think love is about.

It is time to grow up and understand that nothing but lonely days are in your future as long as you continue to go after people you know are bad for you. It is not rocket science to learn how to bypass pain, it just takes enough times experiencing pain to get it! They are not for you!

Question: Do you truly believe that you want to be loved? It is very different from wanting to love someone. Considering you have been through so many relationships, why haven't you found "the one"? Take a good hard look at you!

_____

_____

_____

_____

_____

_____

_____

_____

_____

_____

_____

_____

_____

_____

JUNE 14

Are you a self-hating person? Do you always end up putting yourself down regardless of whether it is your fault or not? Has this always been the case for you? Remember, this cannot be a new issue for you but rather one that has followed you your whole life! We do not get new issues in life when we are adults, we simply just become more sophisticated in the ways we dish out the old ones. We "perfect" what we do to ourselves as we get older.

Do you unconsciously hunger for punishment? Is it almost impossible for a situation to come up in which you do not almost immediately take responsibility for it being your fault? Tiring, isn't it? Are you addicted to being the "bad guy"? Perhaps it is easier for you to take the heat for something than it is to stand up for yourself and point the finger somewhere else.

It is often the child in you that rushes to judge yourself before you think others will. It is easier to be the bad guy than to say, "No, it was not me!" Do you have the courage to drop the self-hating attitude?

Try to step back and look into the situation that you are trying to take responsibility for. Is it really your fault? You do know the answer to this, just as you know that you can be a coward when it comes to saying, "It is not me!" It is so much less of a hassle (hard time) to avoid confrontation and just own what isn't yours in order to avoid other people's junk! You do not see yourself as a coward, but your subconscious does and it is always whispering in your ear that you are a screwup. Do not be fooled into believing that you are the one at fault! It is just the inner you that is bound to destroy your value. Do not listen to your mind, listen to your heart. It does not lie!

Question: Are you someone who is self-hating but underneath that image you are hating everyone else?

LARRY ROBINSON

June 15

Are you always looking to take the easy way in life that requires the least input from you? Do you feel like you want life to be easier and so you choose the path that requires very little from you?

How much of yourself are you willing to put into "bettering" your life? Do you tell yourself that you are lazy and that you could do more but you will still, more often than not, accept mediocrity (something that is not that good but not terrible)? Are you really lazy, or is there something else going on that you have not wanted to look at? When you are doing something you like, are you accepting less or are you putting 100 percent of your energy into it?

Are you the type of person who feels that if you cannot do something perfectly then you will not do it at all? Would you rather be called lazy than incompetent? Let's face it, some of us can't help being perfectionists, and if we cannot be certain about accomplishing a task then we find some way out of it. There are so many times in life when we end up limiting ourselves because of our fear of failure. So there it is, out in the open, we are afraid that we will not be good enough to achieve success!

We can hide behind the perfectionist label, but the real issue is that we are afraid to fail! Our whole life has been built on the idea that we need to be perfect in life or else we will not be wanted. Well, think about this, because what you are in essence saying to yourself is that "Because I need perfection, I will not do or attempt anything that carries the slightest little risk that I might fail!" And what kind of way is that to go through life? How will you ever achieve any kind of success?

The fix to this issue is actually simpler than it seems. We have to take one step at a time and first acknowledge what our issue is and then attempt take one situation in which we fear failure and begin to overcome it. It is not as hard as you are telling yourself it is. In fact, you will feel so much better about yourself by attempting things and even occasionally failing than you will continuing to run away.

Assignment: Do it today. Pick a situation that you have been avoiding and begin the task of completion!

LARRY ROBINSON

Leaky Cauldron

I am just a leaky cauldron
I'm supposed to hold it tight
Keep it warm, stir it right
Wait for it to overflow
Because that's the way it is meant to be
But I was lazy all this while
Put a crack in it to flow a mile
Now fixed the crack and turned the tide,
Soon I will say I overflowed!

By Shrikanth Kapali Kurmathur, Mangalore, India

JUNE 16

D o we really pay attention to our partner, spouse, children, boss, or extended family when we are not interested in what they say? Do we sit there looking like we are surely paying attention while our mind is way out in left field (an expression meaning lost in our own world)? Are we really that *self-consumed* that we cannot let go of our universe even for a short time?

Yes, at one time or another we can all be guilty of this disrespectful behavior. It is very disrespectful to allow someone to think that we are really "into" what they are saying when in fact we could not care less. Remember, they might not know we are doing this but we do!

Where does this type of behavior come from? Is this another one of those childhood behaviors that we're plagued with? In fact, it may not be. We can get overly concerned about our own issues, and rather than tell people that we are having trouble paying attention we pretend to be concerned. Which would you rather have, someone pretending to listen or someone who has been truthful enough to tell you that they are not available to hear you at that particular time?

Why do we have to present such a "wonderful" image of ourselves when our reality is that we are complaining inside and wishing that this person would just go away? Rather than being honest with someone else, it is all about us! Why do we have to pretend that we're someone we're really not? It is okay to be unavailable to someone else, but it is not okay to fake it!

Learning to tell the truth goes way back into our family and school life. Being preoccupied is acceptable when you are a child, and that issue does come out of our environment, but today it is our issue to correct! Take the time to really listen to someone and you will begin to see that your problems are not as big as you think they are. Sometimes when you can actually give to someone you end up feeling really good inside!

Assignment: Learn to listen. The next time that you are in a conversation, try and really listen, not just hear the other person. Did you learn something? What happens in your mind when you try and listen?

LARRY ROBINSON

JUNE 17

Why do we fight in relationships? Is there truly a good reason for us to go to combat with each other over what many times seem to be something trivial? Do we say things that, while they may be true, we have held in for such a long time that by the time they come out they are filled with poison toward the other person? Is there such a notion that we can fight fairly?

When we take a step back and look at where we have been, do we see that there are no rules that we have been able to fight by and that each fight seems to be worse than the last one? We fight because we are either confronted with something we did or said, or something that the other person thought we meant when we didn't. The fight starts so quickly that before we know it we're engulfed in nasty stuff. Back and forth we go and the language escalates to a horrible place that we never dreamed we would see!

Have you ever thought that you are living out your parents' relationship, even though you have tried to avoid it? They were your role models, after all, and even though you swore you would never act like they did the same venom they spewed now comes out of you. Are we destined to repeat the past? And if we have children, are they likely to take over where we left off? And what is the aftereffect on our relationship when we have reduced each other to nothingness with our words? Sometimes words don't even feel enough and we push and shove one another. We give ourselves permission because our pain is so great and "they" caused it.

There really is no fair fighting! We are masters of our own destiny and that means that we have more control than we believe we do. Remember, we are trying to strike down the rejection, humiliation, anger, and meanness that come at us. Is fighting back the only way? And if it is, then we need to come up with some rules without destroying the relationship.

Some of us do not let go of past hurts, and that makes it much harder to let things go. A fight is not only about the present moment, but also about unresolved issues from the past. Sit down with your spouse/partner when you are *not* fighting and create a set of rules that both of you can follow. If either of you breaks the rules, then you need to force yourself

LARRY ROBINSON

to say so and then walk away. If you stay and engage you are doomed. Fighting is not necessarily bad; it just stinks. We have to get rid of what is inside of us. At times, writing a letter to the other person without trying to offend them is another possibility. In the letter, ask them to wait at least half a day before they respond to you and ask that it be in letter form also. This gives you both a chance to cool down. Remember, no one wants to fight; we just have no other route to follow when we are in pain!

Question: Do you consider yourself a fair fighter or do your feelings get the best of you? Describe how you think you fight.

_____

_____

_____

_____

_____

_____

_____

_____

_____

_____

_____

_____

_____

June 18

Do you rush from one relationship to another without very much downtime? Are you "shopping around" before you are even out of this relationship? Do you utterly hate being alone or are you always convincing yourself that you deserve more or think "Why wait?" and "Who cares?" Have you asked yourself whether you really wanted this relationship to begin with or did your "need to be wanted" outweigh your need to want the right person in your life? How many times have you picked the wrong person?

Have you chosen the wrong person, or is there something that you need to learn from this relationship? If you find yourself repeating the same type of issues with more than one partner, then you have not learned what you need to and you are destined to repeat it again!

You know that it isn't stupidity that keeps you involved in the same type of relationship, so what is it? Perhaps you are determined to make something work, not for yourself but because you were always given the message that you were a loser! So now you are out to prove that you can make something "nearly impossible" actually succeed. This, then, is not about love, but about showing others that you did choose wisely against all odds. Have you wasted an overabundance of time and energy trying to prove others wrong while inside you do know that they may, in fact, be on to something? Your anger at a parent can also certainly trigger this kind of "I will show you" attitude. The problem is that you continue to humiliate yourself while proving them right! It is most likely time to take off the gloves and concede that maybe they were right after all.

The type of relationship we all need is one that comes out of self-respect. If you do not respect yourself, then forget being involved with a respectful person. You will meet your opposition, and in this case, you do not want to! And if the person you are trying to change in order to meet your standards knows that this is exactly what you are doing, then you are in for one big fight! It will continue over and over again until you let go of your expectations. That is not who the other person is. If you are in a damaged place yourself, do you really think you will meet someone healthy? Think again, for without being healthy yourself you will continue your destructive cycle. You need to give up this insane struggle to fix and convert someone into an image that will appease somebody else. Remember, you got involved with them knowing who they were. It did not take rocket science to figure out pretty quickly that you screwed up! Can you at least own this?

Question: Find the similarities in the people you have chosen to be in relationships with. Put aside the positives and focus on the negatives. What have you learned?

_____

_____

_____

_____

_____

_____

_____

_____

_____

_____

_____

_____

_____

JUNE 19

Selfish! Is this who we are when it comes to wanting to leave a relationship? How often have we fantasized about leaving and meeting the "right" person? We can take fifteen years of a relationship and then decide that we don't want it anymore. We are done! No more taking it, no more wanting someone to want us who clearly does not meet what our expectations are. The cry becomes, "I will not have a relationship like my parents'," or better yet, "I want a relationship like my parents had! They are my role models, and this relationship is certainly not up to my standards." Time to leave! Have you really tried to save this relationship or do you keep telling yourself that the "grass will be greener" once I am out of this mess?

The problem we run into is do we really want to save this relationship that has not been worked on? Remember, the key factor here is that it has not been worked on! The amount of resentment has been so great that to even know where to begin letting go of it is almost inconceivable. When we look at this person we cannot see why we were ever with him/ her. We did love them! What happened?

We need to hold ourselves accountable for our part in the decline of what once was love. There is no couple who can say they really worked on it without both people trying. If only one person works on what they believe is right, then it only proves that the relationship is unworkable. Why would it be workable if we are only going by our own standards? The even bigger problem is that some of us brought children into this world. Do we even take them into account, or are we saying, "They will be all right, and taking them away from this fighting will be better for them"? No, children do not want to have their family destroyed, no matter how bad it is! We say this to ourselves in order to get rid of any guilt that we have in knowing that we are destroying their family. They do not understand husband and wife, they only know what father and mother are about. They would rather live in the craziness than have their family torn apart.

Can you truly look them in the eye and tell them, "I am so sorry, but Mommy and Daddy did everything they could to try to save their relationship so this family could continue"? You have to be able to tell

LARRY ROBINSON

them you tried! But did you? Have you gone to couple's counseling or talked to your priest, pastor, rabbi, or whoever you believe can give you advice? Have you sat down with the other person and both made the decision that we need to try and let go of the past and start listening to one another?

Assignment: Set a time, say six months, to work out some of the issues and write down the things that each of you need from the other. Exchange lists, and now it is up to each one of you to work on the list. When we do this we begin to rebuild the respect that has been lost. If you both continue to repeat the past, then you have defeated yourselves and really believe that it will be better with someone else. Truth is, it will not be, for unless we resolve the issues we have in this relationship we will only carry them into the next. This is your journey, so you had better understand that you are just as responsible as your significant other.

_____

_____

_____

_____

_____

_____

_____

_____

_____

_____

JUNE 20

Do you really listen to your spouse, partner, and children, or in fact anyone when you are involved in doing something for yourself? Do you choose what to listen to and pretend to be present when you are consumed by doing your own thing? How often do you fake it and get caught? If you haven't yet, you will, for people can begin to see if you are really listening. Do you know the difference between listening and hearing? When confronted with whether you are listening or not, how often can you repeat word for word what someone has said? But does it hit your heart?

Do we consider other people's problems important to us, or do we ignore the depth of their troubles or pain? So often we are trying to get a minute for ourselves and we do not mean to be dismissive or rude, but there is only so much time in a day. Here is a good example of hearing versus listening: a husband comes home from work really upset by his day. He was blamed for something that was not completed, though he did his part and someone else did not. He is enraged and needs to vent. His wife, who has been attending to kids all day, has a chance to go online and find a pair of yoga pants she wants but has not had the time to buy. As he is telling her his story, he realizes that she is not bothering to pick her head up from the computer. When he angrily confronts her about not paying attention, she repeats word for word what he has said. She now gets defensive and angry, and consequently a fight starts.

Listening is from the heart, and hearing is from the mind. We cannot listen and pay attention to something else. We may think that we can double task, but this is not the case.

There is so little time in our lives to really be present for someone else. We need to understand this before it is too late. The other person could shut down from us or even seek someone else to listen to him/her, for this has no gender attached to it. We all need to feel listened to. God knows that so many of us didn't get this when we were children. Maybe this is going on now with your own children. Well, if you show them disrespect by not taking the time to listen, why should they want

LARRY ROBINSON

to listen to you? What would it be like to live in a family where no one listens? I bet many of you already know the answer to that!

Assignment: Sit and try to be present while someone else is talking. Did you hear or listen to them? What is going on in your mind while you are trying to pay attention.

_____

_____

_____

_____

_____

_____

_____

_____

_____

_____

_____

_____

_____

_____

JUNE 21

Why do you think that we talk about other people behind their backs and that what we usually say isn't very nice? Why is that drive there, and do you think it is normal for all of us? Do you know anyone who does not indulge themselves in this act? Most people do this as if it is just what they do and without thinking too much about it. They might say something leaning toward the nasty side when someone leaves the room, and yet when the person reenters they are treated as "nice as pie." If the majority of us do this, then who is to say it is wrong? We do not truly mean any harm by it, and maybe it is just something to say because there is nothing else to talk about.

There are many reasons that this happens and it isn't just by chance! There are people in our lives who are jealous of us and we do not even know it. In fact, some of them don't even know it, but it cuts us down a notch and makes them feel better when they can find some juicy negative gossip to talk about. Unfortunately, the world around us is based on a "better than you or me" and "less than you or me" basis. Whenever someone feels less than you or someone else, their instinct is to put the other person down as a way of not feeling so inferior. Why is it that we have to measure each other in such a harsh way? Why aren't we able to accept the differences we might have and not judge others to make us feel better about ourselves?

Don't you think that we have become cold, hard people in a world that can show no mercy, where people are always being judged according to someone else's standards rather than looked at as unique in their own right? It is time for all of us to be accountable for this behavior. This is not a gender issue where we put it only on women who like to gossip. Men do it too! Isn't it time to go back to what our parents tried to teach us, "If you have nothing good to say about someone, then say nothing at all." Unfortunately, they most likely gossiped too!

Assignment: Where did we learn it from? It starts so young and it becomes woven into the fabric of our lives. *Mirror, Mirror* has a challenge for you: go for three days saying nothing negative behind someone's back, and that means *nothing*! Do you think this is an easy task? Think again, because we have trained ourselves to speak badly about others as the norm in our life. What a sad commentary on life!

_____

_____

_____

_____

_____

_____

_____

_____

_____

_____

_____

_____

_____

_____

June 22

This is not the time to ask you if you carry around a lot of guilt, but how much of it do you bear in life? We all have a certain amount of guilt that is left over from the past, but is it still in the past or has it been carried into the present? Why are we all so burdened with guilt? Are we just part of a greater picture of guilt from society or have we "developed" this guilt from our own personal experiences? And is this true guilt, or is it something that we're just calling guilt as a way of covering up another feeling that we don't want to deal with? What could that other feeling be?

Anger! It is as simple as that! Would you rather feel guilty or angry? The majority of us would rather feel guilty, for it is a more tolerable feeling for us to deal with. Guilt is not a "dark feeling," but one that can lead us into resolution of whatever it is that we feel guilty about if we accept that we have it. We may apologize for something that we didn't even do, but it does relieve this "false" sense of guilt. On the other hand, we cannot apologize for being angry because we do not have control over that feeling as freely as we do guilt.

Here is an example of anger versus guilt: one day Joan told her friend that she needed her to be there for her during a certain crisis she was having. The person assured her, in no uncertain terms, that she would be there for her since she had been there for her many times. When the time came and she was needed, she could not be there for Joan because she had set aside time to take her kids to a playground. At first Joan felt that anger rising in her, but it changed to guilt almost immediately, for how could she ask her friend to leave her kids to be there for her? Joan internalized the anger, which then turned to guilt in a matter of a minute! It does not matter whether she was right or wrong, what mattered was how she felt. Carrying that guilt around in her was very painful, for it distorted how Joan felt about other things. In fact, it covered some of her other issues, such as disappointment, rejection, and self-doubt.

Guilt is a killer! It probably is a greater destroyer of our health than anger is. Our minds become full of self-abuse and low self-esteem. The "How could I?" and "I am so selfish" thoughts dominate our minds, and it stinks! Deal with the anger or even the disappointment. You can tell

LARRY ROBINSON

someone that you are disappointed that they could not be there for you and it does not make you selfish. It simply makes you honest. You can still understand that the other person had to do what they had to do! It does not mean that you cannot have feelings about it. Do not play a victim who never has anyone there for you, because you are not! If the situation warrants it, stand up and let that person know not only what you feel, but also that you are not blaming them!

Guilt always leads to being a victim, for we very rarely experience true guilt. True guilt means we can express it only once for a specific situation and that we'll never repeat the actions we feel guilty about again. How could we feel guilty about something we do more than one time? If that is the case, and we continue to apologize for something that we chose to do, then is it really guilt or are we still using it to block our anger?

Question: Do you believe that you are a guilty person or an angry one? Describe how each might look to you if you were watching yourself in a relationship.

_____

_____

_____

_____

_____

_____

_____

_____

June 23

What happens when we feel that the love we had for our spouse or partner becomes a fading memory? How did we get this way when we started off with such passion and love? We promised each other that we would be forever, and yet now? We did not bother about those little things that could have irritated us in the beginning and that we knew we could handle. "I can change that" was our battle cry, for there was so much more that we fell in love with. Sure! It is interesting how that love begins to fade as soon as we realize that the honeymoon period of our union is over! Now we have to deal with reality and we are having quite a hard time.

What is the reality of these negative feelings we're having? Why aren't our feelings as strong as or even stronger than before we married or moved in together? Do marriages or unions end up destroying our positive feelings? "I didn't know this about you. Why didn't I see this earlier? If I knew that you lied constantly, would I have married you?" These are some of the declarations we make, usually to ourselves for fear of having to truly deal with these feelings. We put off the need to talk about them because maybe we need to wait and watch to see if we were mistaken. This is only a way of fooling ourselves, for what we feel is what we feel! We wonder, "Can I live this way for the rest of my life?" The answer is yes, you can, but in misery!

So often we use children as the excuse for staying in the relationship, but is it really the kids that keep us there or is it something deeper that we cannot recognize yet? It is deeper and it has to do with our own selfishness. There was a feeling right from the beginning for some of us that was not sure that this person was "the one"! Remember walking down the aisle or standing at the wedding ceremony thinking, "Should I really be doing this?" Oh yes, some had that feeling and now it is a reality that makes us sick. All you are going to do is detach and be distant and pick at the other person like a vulture with a new meal, that or pretend to be present when you are actually fantasizing escape!

Only you know the answer to the question of why. Did you forget that you are with this person not because you had that heart thumping "love feeling," but because so many of your previous relationships were with questionable people or those who lived on the edge? You loved that feeling of blood rushing to your heart and pumping out masses of charged feelings, only to be hurt in the end. You married this "boring" person because you wanted stability, security, safety, and consistency in a relationship, and you got it with this person. Now you must be genuine and look at yourself and stop blaming the other person for your failed expectations.

They were yours, not the other person's, and now you continue to hurt this person because of your own selfishness. They do not know where you are and why you pulled away, but be aware that they are hurt and angry. And you do know this but you cannot bring yourself back into that safe love. If you cannot get there on your own then you need to get some help to get there. You do know that left to your own devices you will swing back into one of those horribly addictive relationships where you feel nothing but insecurity. Life isn't necessarily about what we want, but about what we need!

Assignment: Ask yourself, "What is it that I need compared to what I want in a relationship?" Write down in two columns *needs* on one side, *wants* on the other. Do you see what is real and what is your fantasy?

_____

_____

_____

_____

_____

_____

_____

LARRY ROBINSON

JUNE 24

Do you know the difference between being called a "nice" person and a "genuine" person? Can a genuine person *be* a nice person, and can a nice person be genuine? Which one do you think you are and which one does the world see? For most of us, being nice is the acceptable one and the one that we get addicted to. We are nice!

Why do some of us prefer to be nice in the world at the expense of our own self-esteem? What does the word "nice" mean? Have you been able to define it? To so many of us the word has no real meaning, so when someone says that we are a nice person do you really know what they mean? Wouldn't you rather be called a tough person on certain issues or views? At least "tough" helps define you, but a "nice" person? Is this the passive-aggressive person we talked about before? Exactly what kind of person is this?

If being nice means that you give up a portion of your identity in order to please others, then who are you really? Do your own feelings count or are you too nice and think that "Maybe I will hurt someone by telling the truth"? This is the only life we have right now, and we decide to waste it by holding back our true selves? I am sure that there isn't a special seat in heaven (for those believers) set aside for those of us who are nice. Big rewards? Doubt it!

"Genuine" takes on a whole different role in our lives. Those of us who are genuine do not fear others' negative opinions of us, for we do not hold back telling the truth when it is appropriate. But it is not up to us to educate the world. Genuine always means being honest and true to our beliefs. A genuine person is real with how he/she sees life and deals with others. He/she stands up for their values and they are clear about who and what they are! They do not like confrontation, but do not fear it either, unlike the nice person, who would shy away from it. Being genuine (real) in a not-so-real world is difficult, to say the least, but we define ourselves by how we feel about life, not by pleasing others.

A nice person cannot really be genuine for they are always hiding their true self. However, it is possible for a genuine person to be kind, compassionate, direct, and even somewhat negative at times. But as long as the genuine person can take responsibility for their negativity and not blame anyone else, then they maintain real!

Question: How do you hide your true feelings from the world? Do you use addictive behaviors?

_____

_____

_____

_____

_____

_____

_____

_____

_____

_____

_____

_____

_____

LARRY ROBINSON

June 25

We all experience emotional pain. No one can escape its ugliness. We are tortured by the thoughts of deception, abandonment, and rejection. We want to believe that it will just go away, but it builds a home in our hearts and in our heads, and the head takes over. Yes, we do feel it in our hearts, but we knew that the situation or person who we wanted to believe in was not really being truthful, and now reality has taken over and we are suffering.

We suffer until we can bring ourselves out of despair. Until we can see the reality that we tried to avoid, we suffer! We suffer by hating ourselves, because deep inside we knew we were fooling ourselves into believing something that wasn't there. We suffer by the way it affects those around us and yet we cannot seem to stop it. Why are we so consumed by our suffering and pain?

We are so conditioned to suffer, and that is why we are hurting so much. It almost feels as if it is natural for us to suffer. Do you expect it? Are you someone who does not expect happiness in your life? This might be the hardest thing for us to admit. No one really wants to admit that they do not expect to be happy in life. Maybe that is why the emotional pain is so intense. We want to believe that we will find happiness, so when we do get disappointed we carry the pain way too far. We are suffering because of our failed fantasy of life and we suffer because we know our reality! Damned both ways!

Emotional pain is caused by wanting too much and not looking at the truth. If in the beginning we did look at the truth about who we get involved with, we would not be suffering because we would have gotten out. Our emotional pain is there because we allow it to take over. Some of you, even today, are holding on to emotional pain from many yesterdays ago. Who created that?

Question: How much do you hold on to emotional pain from the past? Does it rule your life, popping up when you least expect it?

LARRY ROBINSON

JUNE 26

How much of our life is based on the fantasies we create? Do we want to deal with reality or are we destined to keep on dreaming of what we want life to be like as opposed to accepting what it is? Are we always telling ourselves that everything is all right and not to worry, when in fact things are not right for us?

How often have we deceived ourselves into believing that someone is good for us when they are really bad? We want to believe that we are happy, and we want the world to see us that way, but in our hearts we know that we live from one fantasy to another. We would rather keep our false belief system going than deal with our reality, which others now see as ugly. In fact, sometimes we actually ban from our lives those people who are capable of seeing what we cannot.

We have always lived in a fantasy world. Let's face it; we hate to see reality when it breaks through the cover of our fantasy life. We cannot keep this fantasy life up because ultimately it will not be us who breaks off something that should not have started anyway. When the other person is finished with us, they are done! No matter how hard we try to hold on, their behavior lets us know that they do not care about our feelings.

Stop looking for the "impossible." Take a good look at what that fantasy of yours is and then look at the reality of your life. Can't you see that they are light years away from each other? You must tell yourself that you deserve better. No one deserves to be led falsely down a path that is filled with empty promises. It is our responsibility to take the time to learn the difference between what we want and what we need! Start to look now before your life is filled with one disappointment after another.

Question: Have you often fantasized about how your life could be different and never tried to make it your reality? Are you someone who dreams the dream but cannot live your reality?

LARRY ROBINSON

JUNE 27

D o you make promises that you cannot keep? Are you the type of person who is so eager to volunteer your time or energy to fill in for someone else, do things that others won't do, or take on projects when you are already overloaded?

You are looking to be liked! And it does not matter to you whether you can actually achieve the finished product, for at the time you volunteered you wanted the other person to be impressed with your *efforts* to help them. Often you do not even understand what you are getting yourself into. All you know is that you want the other person to see that you are a loyal, good friend or lover and that you will sacrifice your time and energy for them.

Our ego (the way our personality works) is shining bright right now and that is all that matters. We are valued and needed! Why are we so eager to take on something that, in reality, we don't want to do? We are needy, that's why!

We have this neediness inside of us that tells us that in order to be liked or wanted we must do for others! It is not about who we are but what we can do for others. This is our *diseased* thinking: "My value lies in what I do for others, not for who I am. I feel empty if I cannot be the best person, the most giving person, and the most selfless person."

That's a lot of work, especially when we often fall short of the goal we want to accomplish. There are even times when we have no idea of what we are getting ourselves into and then we have to come up with some excuse to get out of the situation. The very thing that we set out to achieve, value, is now negated through our excuse to get out of it.

What is the remedy for this? Do not place your value on the world. Yes, we all need to feel valued, but at what cost? Do what you believe you can do for others, but do not look for gratitude and "thank yous" as a way of feeling good about yourself. So often we do not even want to do the chore or project, but we say yes anyway. This is your issue and you are the only one who can change it. If you are so concerned that you will be looked at as less of a person if you do not do what you are asked to do or do not volunteer for something, think again about your motives, for in the end no one is counting how much you give!

Question: Are you the type of person who cannot say no to someone who needs something done?

_____

_____

_____

_____

_____

_____

_____

_____

_____

_____

_____

_____

_____

LARRY ROBINSON

JUNE 28

"I cannot understand why you do not hear the word 'no' when I say it. Do you have a hearing problem? If I wanted to do what you suggested, then I would have said yes! Enough is enough!"

The word "no" is one of the first words we hear as toddlers. Babies don't get to hear that word because they cannot move unless we move them, but as toddlers begin to walk they generally hear the word "no" as the first negative command given to them. They ignore it for quite a long time, starting their battle with us almost as soon as the word is said. They want to show us how strong-willed they are for they want their way, and nine out of ten times they get it. If a parent gives in because they can't stand to hear their child (that innocent little darling) scream and cry, then the child knows that if he/she can win once then they can win again! How well our parents enforced that word and continually gave us explanations that didn't include the phrase "Because I said so" determined how we deal with that word as adults.

As adults, many of us cannot tolerate that word. The word "no" can mean a lack of control in a situation or over a person. "No" means that we get denied something, and that can be horrific. It has much deeper meanings than just, "You can't have that." It can be interpreted as "I am not loved," and that is how life is then perceived. "If I do not get what I want, then I am not loved." How awful that so much is placed on the word "no."

We learn all about manipulation from that word. The battle never stops, and it just gets more sophisticated as we grow older. It actually begins to create stubbornness in us so that letting go becomes a trial. We aren't really able to understand why this happens to us unless we are willing to see that we cannot accept no as a valid answer in our life. Remember, in a relationship there cannot be any loser, for it will come up again and again until the issue gets resolved. Are you with someone who allows you to have your way constantly and then resents you for days and you don't know why? This passive-aggressive behavior kills relationships.

It is time to understand that when you are in a relationship it is not about getting. Children are "getters" because they want all the time! Parents are "givers" in that they want their children to *have*, but to not always be *asking*. Which one are you in a relationship? Do you and your spouse give equally, or is one of you always looking to receive something? Can you understand that sometimes when a person says no they are not trying to take something away from you, but instead understand that it is not a need but a want, and that some "wants" we can go without? Needs are what we provide for each other if it is possible, while wants are things more about us than the relationship! We should be able to take care of our own wants! Now, sure, it is great when we get a "want" from someone, but that is not always going to be the case!

Assignment: Decide what you and your spouse need and work toward that! Do not let wants get in the way because you cannot bear the word "no." Listen to one another. Take ten minutes a couple of times a week and sit down. Each person takes five minutes and talks about how they feel without interruption. This is the beginning of working on the relationship.

_____

_____

_____

_____

_____

_____

_____

_____

_____

_____

June 29

Y ou know that you have hurt someone and that they are suffering from your distance and righteous attitude, yet you cannot tell them that you were wrong. Why can't we say these two simple words, "I'm sorry"?

Maybe they aren't really that simple! No one is perfect, just as no one is always wrong. These are two given facts of life. We are not better or less than anyone, we can only claim to be different. "I am different from you, and you are different from me!" And *different* doesn't mean that I am thinking that I am the Dalai Lama and you are a street urchin. What it means is that I see things differently than you do.

Sometimes we can hurt each other in arguments and say ugly things to each other, yet we defend ourselves on why we said it instead of saying "I'm sorry." There is always going to be some excuse not to say it. Do you think that at the time we are saying something to hurt someone else we are actually telling the truth and that it does hurt? It is always better to walk away from such an argument and then think about what we have just said. We will find that it is a mixture of some truth and some anger at the time. And it is the anger that creates the need to get back at someone, for it hides the real feeling of being not good enough in someone's eyes. This rejection is the cause for retaliation, and boy can we do some damage when our egos are bruised.

Remember when we had to say we were sorry to our parents when we didn't do anything wrong? How many times did you hear them say that they were sorry for something they did to hurt you? You probably got some "bull" lecture as their way of not taking responsibility for themselves, or maybe they never even said it at all! Did we learn this from them?

Adults are not "required" to say "I'm sorry" to children, or in fact, even to their peers. How sad that we will continue this mode with our own children, or even worse, we will not say "I'm sorry" to them even if they screwed up out of fear of becoming our parents! Look, what's right is right! You do not have to be a perfect person who never does anything to hurt others. You just need to be "human" and know that saying "I'm sorry" for what you have done makes you a better person, partner, parent, or child! Who do you need to say you're sorry to before it is too late? Saying "I'm sorry" is all about giving to someone who has been hurt by you. Is there a better way for healing to begin?

Question: Do you repeat your behaviors that cause you to say you were sorry? Can you say *I am sorry* more than once?

_____

_____

_____

_____

_____

_____

_____

_____

_____

_____

_____

_____

LARRY ROBINSON

June 30

Did you listen to what adults thought of you when you were young and decided to give up on yourself? Do you believe that you could have done better in school if you had really given yourself the chance? Are you still beating yourself up about the past rather than seeing your potential now in the present?

Those of us who were too troubled with our lives, whether it was due to our home lives or being bullied or rejected by other kids, or even if we were athletes and nobody cared about how well we did in school as long as we performed on the field, where are we today? Here is a little story for you to really think about.

Once there was this skinny, geeky-looking kid who really felt bad about himself. He was truly screwed up. In fact, when he was fourteen his parents took him to see a shrink. But after the shrink met his parents (this was 1959), he was told that he could not be helped because his parents were too screwed up and that they wouldn't come back to therapy. Amazed at this, the kid said, "Why can't you help me live with them?" The answer from the shrink was, "I'm sorry, I wouldn't know where to begin." All that was left now for this kid was to get into trouble and get kicked out of school. And when he got caught cheating on his senior math final he was told that the school was going to graduate him, not because he'd completed his work, but because the teachers and administrators at the school had had enough of him! As he got his diploma, one of the teachers told him that he was the "biggest waste of time" and "too costly to keep in school." "You will never amount to anything; you couldn't even shine shoes," they said.

Being poor or abused or neglected is the motivation to succeed, not to give up. Think about how much you want to change. Start to do one small thing for yourself each day. It does not matter what it is, for what you need to remember is that changing even one little thing about yourself still changes you. And this is how change comes about. Change is not an event in our lives, it is a process! It is not an overnight miracle, but it is gradual throughout your journey and it does not end where you are right now. Age, gender, money issues, so what? Who cares? You have your mind, now use it!

Assignment: List your accomplishments. It does not matter how small they are. They count!

_____

_____

_____

_____

_____

_____

_____

_____

_____

_____

_____

_____

LARRY ROBINSON

Shayna Robinson
Chicago, Illinois, USA

"Do not worry at all. Can it add even an hour to your life? Just don't think about what you must do, but do the things you can do in the present time. Think less and act more with humility."

—Redz Urquiola Vara, Philippines

July 1

Do you know what "emotional happiness" is? Have you ever experienced a time in your life that was pain free and calm? Do you look for the chaos or the calm? This question is important for you to look at on your journey toward a peaceful and prosperous life. Too often we take for granted things that are too important for us to bypass. We all look for the easy way out. We must be honest with ourselves!

The hardest dynamic that we have to deal with is honesty with self. In order to achieve emotional happiness you must look at yourself! Emotional happiness is when we have forgiveness and compassion in our hearts and we hold no resentments or grudges. We begin to understand that no one is better or less than we are. We recognize the differences among people without judgment!

How much do you hold on to? Are you someone who "stews" about little situations and cannot, for the life of you, let go and forgive or even try to understand? Count how many of these situations are in your life. Each one is a step backward from peace of mind and a step forward toward chaos. This is your opportunity to begin the letting go process. You will ask, "How do I do that?" The first step is to accept the lack of peace in your life, while at the same time recognizing the role that you have played in helping create this chaos. It is not easy to not blame another person or situation for your emotional unhappiness. We all do this at one time or another, so you are not alone out there!

Question: What gets in the way of your emotional happiness? Is it you or the influence of the world around you?

_____

_____

_____

_____

LARRY ROBINSON

_____

_____

_____

_____

_____

_____

_____

_____

_____

_____

_____

_____

_____

_____

_____

_____

_____

_____

_____

_____

_____

_____

JULY 2

D o you fantasize about divorce or leaving your spouse/partner? Are you really unhappy in your relationship but stay because of the children and your fear of finances? Do you hate how your spouse speaks to you or ignores important matters that you want to talk about? Are you afraid of the confrontation that would ensue if you spoke up, or fear being beaten down orally or ignored?

These are not uncommon feelings in a damaged relationship. What have you done to try to change how you deal with this? You cannot change another person; you can only change your reaction to them. You are afraid of the fight and its repercussions, but the truth is you both need this fight! "Venting" is the only way you will begin to resolve the misunderstandings between the two of you. You cannot hold everything in until you explode with a tirade of meanness that will assuredly result in a defense designed to put you down.

We need to understand that both of us have been in pain. One person cannot be happy in a relationship while the other is miserable, and we both have different ways of showing unhappiness. This is the first step toward gauging where the relationship is.

The second step is realizing that you are not a victim and neither is your spouse, but that you are both guilty of repeating the same behavior without a resolution.

The third step is learning to let each other vent without defending or interrupting. There is no winner here, this is not a competition! And if you insist on turning it into one you both wind up losers!

Listening is always better than leaving a relationship! Work on this until you both get it!

Question: Are you a good listener or do you resist hearing how your significant other is feeling because you do not want to get in a conflict with him/her?

_____

_____

_____

_____

_____

_____

_____

_____

_____

_____

_____

_____

_____

_____

_____

_____

_____

_____

July 3

Why do we experience jealousy when we are in a relationship that is problematic? What is it that causes us to go off the deep end when our partner or spouse gives someone else the slightest little look? It doesn't necessarily have to be in a sexual way but it blows us apart! Have we always been this way, or is there a specific type of mate that causes this reaction in us? So often we are not even aware of the signs that will lead us into this "dis-ease" of the heart. This dis-ease makes us spiritually and emotionally sick. There's a deep emptiness inside that we so desperately want filled that we lose all sense of reason and become someone we would not want to know.

Jealousy is an emotion that we never thought would be a major part of our life. We did not set out to interrogate or spy or go through phone records and e-mails when we fell in love with this person. But was this love to begin with? Or was it just some fantasy that had this other person coming in to save us and make us feel better about who we were in life? They would be our savior!

If we placed this much value on who they were to be in our life, then we had to make sure they were honest about their feelings and were totally committed to us. Now, *totally* is such a strong word, yet it is one we can never really remove until we feel secure. If you are banking on the other person making you more valuable and a better person, then *security* will never come and we are doomed to repeat this cycle until we find the resolution that will free us.

No one can make us a complete person; they can only be an addition to our lives. We must be working on our life for ourselves, not just because we meet someone else. And often we stop the work because we have found "the" person that we feel will fill that emptiness. But remember that emptiness cannot be filled, for it comes out of our childhood and it is damage that is not repairable. It can, however, be dealt with better than we have done in the past. Just the recognition that our own sense of self has been damaged is the first step in letting go of that unbelievable person who has been placed in our lives to save us. Then we can start correcting the damage from the past. And what happens when this person screws up? Often our world can begin to fall apart, and the panic we experience is mind blowing!

Question: Do you deny at times that you are jealous? How do you get through that feeling? Does nothing bother you?

_____

_____

_____

_____

_____

_____

_____

_____

_____

_____

_____

_____

_____

_____

_____

_____

JULY 4

Do you feel as if your life is going nowhere? Have you been stuck in the same spot for what feels like an eternity? Is your life or relationship frozen in the past where there is no joy or sense of accomplishment? It sounds like you are depressed and that your motivation "took a vacation"!

Do you dream big dreams and are always telling yourself "It *will* happen! Just wait a little longer. I know it will," and yet life seems to be passing you by and you feel as if you have no control over time? Your life just keeps repeating itself. You sit there amazed at where the time has gone but cannot move yourself to find the right direction.

One way to look at depression is to imagine that you are standing on a hill and that there is a hammer over your head that keeps beating on your head until you are pushed down into the middle of it! Feelings that are beaten down are depressed feelings and they form a type of depression. This is also called *stuck*!

When you are in this place in life you are not destined to stay here. It is a clue that something else is going on, something that requires you to discover what it is and where it is coming from. Remember, there is no magic in life. You cannot wish away depression, nor can you go around it. You must face it head-on, and understand that while there are so many feelings inside of you that you want to ignore or make go away, until you deal with them they will remain attached to you!

If you look hard enough you will see that you have been carrying this depression since your childhood. It is time to face yourself and what it is that you avoid in life. Do not be afraid to see the *you* that is still clinging to childhood views of yourself and the world! It won't be pretty at times, but this is the way that you unfreeze. Facing your depressed feelings is the start of getting back on your life journey!

Question: Are you a depressed person or one who cannot feel anything for you are always finding ways to avoid the depression?

LARRY ROBINSON

JULY 5

D o you give up easily on yourself? Are you the type of person who has this great exterior attitude and who is gung-ho (up and ready) when you are about to start a project, but who gives up when it becomes difficult? Do you have this "pie in the sky" thinking that is so great that you will never achieve it? Well, maybe this is not because you cannot achieve your goals, but because you cannot maintain them.

Achieving success is not as hard as you think. If you have the right motivation and are a determined person, then you can achieve success. The question then becomes whether you can continue with it for as long as you need it.

So often inside of us is this negative mind that keeps whispering to us that we will not be able to keep it up. Some images and voices from our past have determined that we are failures and now we too have taken over that voice. It is no longer the fault of our past, which we constantly refer to, nor is it the fault of our dreams of what we will achieve when time is right in the future. It is our neglect of the present that is the problem. It is in the present where we can succeed and in the present where we can maintain our success. There are no excuses left if you think in these terms. Get your head out of the negative past and out of your "dreamy" future and pay attention to today! Today is all that counts! Live it and you will see success!

Question: Are you someone that starts things and does not finish? Do you think that is because you are lazy or you take on too much?

_____

_____

_____

_____

LARRY ROBINSON

July 6

How do we know if we really like someone? Are we still looking for that rush and that charge that we felt in high school, or are we hoping for it because we never got it? If you are younger than twenty-two, then you can really still get that charge, but it really is an unhealthy one because you don't really know that person and you only want him/her to want you!

Being wanted is fine, but by *whom*? Did you really take a good look at this person? Do you know their values? Did you take the time to get to know the real person, or only the image that you were dying for? Did you sleep with this person too fast and now the relationship will go through a courtship, engagement, marriage, and divorce in mere weeks? How many of us have experienced this?

The process is to build a comfort level and an ease of communication, and that takes a long time, usually until both people feel free enough to experience it. Why do we want to rush something that may be forever? Our need to be loved at this point in life (over thirty) needs to be second to our need to love someone. Children need to be loved; adults need to give love. It is so much better to truly care about someone else's feelings than it is to always want your own to come first. Today is a great day to let go of the needy love and experience the process of love! So go for it because it certainly hasn't worked the other way!

Question: Are you somebody who always rushes into relationships? What has been the outcome of you dealing with relationships that start so fast?

_____

_____

_____

_____

LARRY ROBINSON

JULY 7

A re you afraid to really love another person? Does it make you feel at
risk of being rejected? Some people create a false sense of love that
protects them from feeling vulnerable to someone else. Is that how you
are? What is it that makes us behave in a way that makes us look cold
and detached, even when we really don't want to act that way?

These are questions that you must ask yourself now rather than later,
for later might be too late. We may have chased the other person away
or they may have already spent years trying their best to get close to us
and have ended up leaving and no longer want the relationship because
they are burned out.

This is something that you have experienced most of your life. It
didn't happen just in this relationship, it happened through trauma
in your childhood. It is the baggage that we bring to the relationship.
Often we pick needy people who want to smother us and that only make
things worse for us. They do not realize that we run from too much false
love and yet long to give more. The needy person is not loving us, but
wanting our love instead and that makes us colder.

Perhaps we are always "testing the waters" to see if someone really
loves us, and they never pass the test. Have you ever thought that the
"test" is way beyond reality? It is almost as if we want them to fail so that
we are proven right in our refusal to be vulnerable. This makes us highly
oversensitive people who flinch at the first sign of disappointment. Put
yourself in your partner's shoes and decide whether rejecting someone
is better than feeling vulnerable. Love is about what we give, not about
what we receive!

Assignment: Look closely at how you approach love. Do you like to
be the giver more or the receiver? Ask your significant other if you can
switch roles for a week and see what the other side feels like.

LARRY ROBINSON

July 8

How do we deal with someone we love who lies to us and it isn't the first time but just one out of many? Whether it is about addictive behaviors or just small little things that have no real consequence in our lives, is the trust gone forever? How do we regain it when we just do not believe anything the person says to us?

All of us tell little white lies on a daily basis, but that seems to be excusable because we don't intend to hurt anyone. We just did not want to get into a useless confrontation. "How are you doing?" asks your spouse, and you answer, "Good, fine. Why do you ask?" Your spouse then says, "I just think that you look bothered by something," to which you respond, "I *am* fine." But the truth of the matter is that you are *not* fine and you are simply holding on to your anger because you do not want to start something!

Have you ever thought that this is the same reason why your spouse cannot approach you? We all are afraid of negative reactions to our darker behaviors, so we hide also. If two people are "hiding," then who is the judge in the situation? If you think that your lie is not as serious, well, have you considered that when you expose their lies that all your lies will come bursting out too, and that other person will now be hit with situations they don't even remember? Can he/she then believe that if they go to you with the truth they won't be crucified by your reaction, even though you have also lied?

Understand that no lie is healthy, and that one really is just as bad as the other. Start today and think of one thing that you have withheld from your partner and then tell the truth! Once you see their reaction, begin to discuss that the truth is really what sets you free, not the other person. They have to want their own freedom, and when this happens your relationship can grow!

Assignment: Think about lying as a way of protecting yourself. Make a list of all the small lies that you might have told to protect yourself from change.

LARRY ROBINSON

July 9

"Courage," what does it mean to us? Do you have courage to face tragedies and horror in your life? Can we hear that our loved ones are terminally ill or in some horrific accident and *not* make it about ourselves? Is your defense to brush it off and say, "Oh, you'll be all right," and then start to talk about something else? Or do you rush to fix something that you have no control over?

It is so easy to get an angry attitude, as if it is the other person's fault, and push away from them or tell them that because they did not take care of themselves this illness is of their own doing. "I told you this would happen if you continued to smoke!" But where is our courage during this time when it would be best to set aside our own fears associated with the possibility of losing someone we love and just be there for them? This takes an enormous amount of faith that you can feel for the other person and not personalize their problem as yours.

You need the courage to let them know that you will handle it no matter what the outcome and no matter what your loss might be.

Question: Do you make other people feel guilty for being in their predicaments or put them down by letting them know that they screwed up?

_____

_____

_____

_____

_____

_____

JULY 10

Do you know how fragile we all are? Do you feel as if you are the only one who feels more than others? Well, it is time to wake up and realize that we all are sensitive and that we all feel too much at times. Are you aware of how you speak to people? Do you think that you have a right to speak to them with disrespect, even if you feel they did something very wrong to you?

Speaking to people with respect gains respect! This even goes for how we speak to children. If we are always speaking to them as if we are better than they are, then we will get the disrespect back as an answer. We are not better than anyone! We can all be different and be in different places in life, but we cannot be "better." If we think that way then we think about life in terms of *better than* or *less than*, and that is not what life is!

Life is always a work in progress, and none of us have been given the "perfect" award. If you talk to each other with respect, then life looks less like who gets there first and more like a day at the beach! Are you *a day at the beach*? Ask those around you how they think about you. Speak to them! Use your courage to find out what they think. You are not the lone "feeler" in life!

Question: Do you think people see the real you or are you that good at hiding your true self?

_____

_____

_____

_____

_____

LARRY ROBINSON

July 11

Are you a person who makes decisions easily, and not just the difficult ones but the easy, everyday decisions? Do you need other people's advice before you decide what choice you will make? How many folks do you ask before you end up making the decision that you started out with, even though it goes against the advice you got from others? What a waste of time and energy!

Ask yourself, "Why don't I follow my own gut instinct?" Be honest, you need to hear what everyone else says but you are not really listening! You want people to agree with you, but if they don't, then you shut their opinion out!

There are very few people in this world who do not know how to make a decision, but there are quite a lot who are afraid of their own decisions. What if I am wrong? How will this screw things up? It really makes no difference because the majority of us follow our own path, and even though we ask, we already know the answer. Those of us who are still questioning but who follow someone else's advice, well, we have the perfect "out" if the decision is wrong. We did not make it, they did!

When is it time to take charge of our lives and be responsible for our own choices? Hell, the only thing that can happen to us is that we can learn from it! Follow this path and your ability to grow will amaze you!

Assignment: Describe the steps that you go through when you make decisions.

_____

_____

_____

_____

_____

July 12

D o you know the feeling of not being able to let go of a resentment? Everything inside of you says to let it go and start to love again, but no, you just want to keep that nasty feeling going! It is almost as if we like the feeling of being someone's victim. We are not concerned about what is going on with the other person; that is the last of our worries. We only care about ourselves and how *we* are the "victim."

Well, maybe there are two victims who are present. Did you ever think that the other person is a victim of themselves? Why would they want to hurt you? If they have been mean or distant or snappy, then they have their own reasons for it. Sometimes when people are really scared of something, even something that could take place in the future, they cannot deal with the intensity of their fear. Anger becomes a strong protection against their fear. Other times, when a person cannot deal with their anger they use fear and "shutting down" as a way of coping.

Do not rush to judgment when you feel hurt. Take a deep breath and try and see what situations are going on at the time. Is someone ill or is there a financial crisis? How does the other person deal with these issues? It is hard to ignore what you feel, but right now it is more about where the other person is, not where you are . . . Take what you feel and apply it to the situation and realize that at that moment life is not always about you!

Question: Are you always thinking about your issues and not about the other person's? Would you consider someone who does this selfish?

_____

_____

_____

_____

LARRY ROBINSON

JULY 13

Why don't I trust you? I love you more than anything in this world. You were my world, and I never doubted anything you ever said to me because you promised me that we would always be there for each other. Our word was golden and I felt safe with you. The first time I caught you in a lie, I shrugged it off and said, "We all make mistakes." I did not want to pay attention to that tiny uncomfortable feeling deep in my gut that was telling me something was wrong. After the second time, I knew in my heart that we were on a bad path. I blamed myself and questioned what I did that you had to lie to me. I made it all about my self-esteem and not about you. You were my partner and you were supposed to be able to tell me the truth.

But when I caught you lying in situations in which there was no reason to lie, I knew that I wasn't the one who was screwed up and that it was you instead! I sank to my lowest level of despair because my love for you had not changed. How could I not love the person I swore to love through good and bad? Well, this was bad, and you only gave me excuses and became defensive when you got caught.

Now I am resorting to actions that I never would have believed I would take. Sometimes I cannot even stop myself, I have to know! And now I am lying to you! If we could only talk to each other, then maybe, just maybe we could change and begin to understand what went wrong. Please tell me the truth! I know I can handle anything if you trust me to. I will work on not getting so hysterical if you will work on the truth. You see, it is the trust that we did not build upon that caused you to want to lie to me and for me to spy on you. I know that we are better than this!

Question: Could this be your story or one like it? If so, write a little about it.

July 14

D id you wake up this morning with that *queasy* feeling in your stomach? Are you already fearful of the day and you do not want to get up? Are you lying there with your eyes wide open and wishing that you could fall back to sleep and forget that today ever existed? Well, this is the beginning of your anxiety.

The "edge" is already on you, so your family had better watch out and see that they do not set you off! Everything that you planned for yesterday remains half-finished and you already have a planned list for today, and that's without yesterday's accomplishments. Do you feel overwhelmed and disgusted with yourself? I bet you do, and God knows this is your routine every morning!

Why do you continue to set yourself up to feel like a failure and disappoint those you made promises to? You know that no one believes that you can complete anything without either leaving a mess or forgetting what you started and moving on to a new project. How many of us say, "But I have ADHD," and use that excuse over and over again?

Do you think that you set your expectations of yourself too high and that you are really just resisting yourself? Whatever happened to "one step at a time"? It is more important to finish one project than it is to start twelve and accomplish none! Make today your day to feel like you belong to this world, and do that by setting one goal that you can and will accomplish! Enough of your excuses and the self-hatred that comes as a result of them. Today, I am OK!

Question: If you were to set one goal for today, what would it be?

_____

_____

_____

_____

LARRY ROBINSON

I am guilty, I am guilty, I am guilty, or are you? How many times have you said "I am sorry" for repeating negative behavior? How often has your bad or irresponsible behavior hurt you or someone else? When we say we are sorry, does it give us permission to repeat the negative behavior?

So many of us do that. It is almost as if we do not have any remorse for the behavior itself but only for being caught. In all sincerity, you can really only feel guilty once and commit yourself to eradicating the act rather than repeat it. After we have gone through our *mea culpa* (admission of fault), why do we then continue the behavior?

The answer to that is that we must really want to, because if we really took responsibility for our actions and their resulting consequences, then it would be something that we would never repeat again! We would commit ourselves to removing it! It is not productive to use the words "I am sorry" if you know that you cannot commit to them. Those words are said usually to just appease someone else. And even if we initially believe that we won't do it again, we should not try to explain why we did what we did. This only begins to rationalize and explain the psychology of our bad behavior. And the truth is that there is no explanation if we're going to continue to repeat it. Saying "I am sorry" is a commitment, not an excuse!

Question: Do you believe that when you say you are sorry you really mean it, or is it a way for you to run away, only to repeat the negative action again?

_____

_____

_____

_____

Let Time Do the Healing

by Ti Na Agassi
Macao, China

There is this feeling inside of me
That is hard to explain.
My heart seems to be dancing
Every time that you are near.
But I sense this is not right,
For someone else owns your heart.
You walk hand and hand,
She owns you day and night.
Please, God, give me the strength
Because I know I should be moving on.
Say goodbye to this crazy little feeling,
Let time do the healing.
I wish I did not know you,
You just broke my heart in two.
Poor fragile heart of mine,
You will be healed in time.
I don't want to hurt anymore,
And I don't want to hurt anyone.
So I will choose to leave,
I'll find my love on the way
So please, God, give me the strength
Because I know I should be moving on.
Say goodbye to this crazy little feeling,
Let time do the healing.

July 16

Have you ever been in an argument in which as soon as you confronted another person with something that was troubling you they immediately said, "Well, you do it too"? For example, you say to your partner while you are watching the news or on an important call, "Please let me finish what I am doing," and they just continue to keep talking. It doesn't matter whether you are talking to your boss or watching a program that you had been anticipating for weeks. When you confront the other person, their first defensive remark to you is, "Well, you do it also!"

We call this "turning it around," and what that means is that by reacting defensively like that the other person has now made the issue about your behavior instead of theirs. This is definitely a no-win situation, which more times than not leads to a good fight. It is always important to state first that "I dropped the dime," meaning "I get to speak because it is my issue with you right now. If this is an issue that bothered you, why did you wait for me to bring it up?"

It is essential that we give each other the respect of bringing up an issue without the "turn around." How many of you have experienced this in all your relationships? This is a given for all of us. If we give respect, we will receive it!

Question: Do you believe that you give respect to others by listening to them, or do you only pretend to and wish that you could be the one speaking?

July 17

Why do I lie? I created an image of myself when I was a child and I wanted the world to like me. There was something in me that had a double life. It was almost as if I formed this little wormhole into an alternate universe and there I was "king of the kingdom." When I came back into my reality, I felt lost and empty, and so I started to lie! I told people exaggerations about my life and the adventures I had. I told people these untruths so that they would want to get to know me. I wanted to hang out with popular kids. I guess you could say I was a social climber, and that kissing butt got me to where I wanted to be, but never to a place where I felt authentic.

I lied to my parents all the time. I thought I didn't care, but in the end I turned on them rather than expose my truth, the truth that I was a liar! I wanted the people closest to me to believe in me, and so when I screwed up, I lied. Unfortunately, this process destroyed their faith in me. The very thing I wanted, which was to be liked, was replaced by just the opposite, and I wound up feeling friendless and unloved!

What is the lesson here? The lesson is that people will love you for the truth! Sure, they may be angry at you at first (that is one of the biggest consequences of lying), but they will eventually come around and get over it. They will still love you, perhaps even more! How can you love a liar if you do not know what is real? There are no more excuses. Tell the truth and see what the reward is!

Question: Can you identify with this story? Which parts are about you?

_____

_____

_____

_____

LARRY ROBINSON

July 18

C an I say "I'm sorry" and *not* forgive you? How often do you say "I'm sorry" and think that you mean it, but feel a little empty after saying it? "I'm sorry" is an automatic response to a confrontational situation. And if your heart is still *frozen*, then why did you really say it?

We are mostly "conflict avoiders" and do not want to get into it with each other, and you all know what I mean when I say "get into it"! The selfishness and meanness starts to flow and we say things that we do not mean just to hurt one another. We feel violated.

When we argue or fight, we may not be ready to let go of the residual anger when we're finished but still we apologize to each other, knowing full well that the resentment is still there. In order to sort through our feelings, we need to call a "truce," during which neither of us can say those words "I'm sorry," which we really don't mean yet. Go off by yourself and look at the disagreement or fight and examine who you were in the situation. Did you like who you were? Do you understand the other person's feelings? Are you being stubborn?

When you can answer these questions honestly, and this goes for both of you, then you can begin the forgiveness process. And it *is* a process, not an event. We do not have pain and suddenly say, "I forgive you. I am sorry." No, let the truce be there. It will help your recovery.

Question: Are you one of those persons who are always apologizing for something that they didn't do? Why do you do it?

_____

_____

_____

_____

_____

LARRY ROBINSON

July 19

Why can't we make our own decisions? Why are we always feeling insecure about what we decide to do? We seem to always want others to approve of who we are and what we decide! This has caused us a great deal of pain, for we now doubt everything we do.

We are constantly looking to be right in front of others, but we seem to need their approval even if what they tell us does not go along with what we have decided. We can easily become frozen with our own decisions for fear that we will not receive the approval we are looking for.

Ask yourself, "Am I afraid to disappoint everyone and therefore become afraid to make my own decision?" Most likely, you are! And it must have been this way most of your life. As children we are always looking for approval from our parents and what they tell us has a great impact on our ability to make decisions. That was as children. Are you still looking for their approval as an adult?

Most of us who have trouble making decisions will say yes to this question. We are stuck in our childhood and still afraid to disappoint others. This is why we ask so many people whether they think we should do this or do that. In the end, no one suffers from our decision except us. It is time to grow up!

What this means is that we must begin to make our own decisions and start dealing with our own mistakes, even if we have to go against those we love who tell us we are wrong. There is that expression, "No pain, no gain," and that is how we must view decision making. We do not learn if others make our decisions. We end up angry at them, for we do know at some level what our intuition tells us. You only need to approve of yourself, because others do not live your life. You do know what is best for you!

Assignment: What does your decision process look like? Describe the steps you use in order to complete a decision.

LARRY ROBINSON

July 20

How easily are you hurt by someone that you care about, whether they are friends or family or a life partner? What is it that sets you off and that wounds your heart and causes you to retreat from that person? What makes you so sensitive that you hide your feelings as if they needed to be constantly guarded and protected? You will not show the other person that they hurt you!

What causes us to run away from telling someone how bad we feel? We nurse (take care of) these negative feelings inside ourselves as if we are carrying a great secret that needs constant care. We feed it and nurture it, and it makes us feel better.

We have conversations with ourselves in which we tell the other person how we really feel, and there is some pleasure that we receive from these mind conversations. "How dare you!" becomes the main topic, and we go after them with so much poison!

We are presenting an image to the world that we are tough and that what the other person has done to us does not affect us, but our reality is screaming something completely different. We are boiling inside and it feels as if there is no relief from this torture. We go over and over it in our heads. We are "stewers"!

To "stew" over something is like putting our feelings in a slow cooker and having them slowly cook all day, in some cases for many days. Our minds are preoccupied with this stewing inside. This is our torture! We are distracted and cannot be present for others when we are in this situation.

Learning how to tell someone how we feel is the goal for us! Taking the risk that we may or may not be rejected for expressing our feelings is scary, but it is so necessary if we are to find our own wellbeing. If someone cannot handle how you feel, do you question their friendship or love? Maybe it is time to take back control over your feelings and decide that you have a right to how you feel. True people in your life can hear you without offering judgment or criticism. It is time to grow again!

Question: Can you name issues that you have stewed over or are still stewing over in your life?

_____

_____

_____

_____

_____

_____

_____

_____

_____

_____

_____

_____

_____

_____

_____

LARRY ROBINSON

July 21

Are you consumed with fears and no one really knows? Is the image that you present in life one of looking secure and able to handle the most difficult situations life throws at you? Do people look to you for advice because you seem so cool and easy about resolving things? If this is the case, then you are in trouble because your big meltdown (falling apart) is drawing closer. And it is not as if you have not had meltdowns before. The issue is that no one sees them but you!

How often have you felt false because of the way you believe the world sees you? First of all, you are not alone. There are many of us who can identify with this issue. The thing is that we are alone with it and we cannot talk about it because we are afraid to feel or be seen as weak.

The longer we hide from our own fears and cover them with false pride, the more afraid we become. Who told us that we could not be afraid? We all have fears, but some of us feel that our sense of self relies on the fact that we are always strong and fearless in our approach to life. We suffer inside with so much more than just our fears. We now suffer with the lie that we continue to put out there. It is a double dose of self-hatred that we receive. And if you haven't been in touch with your self-hatred, you are now!

It is long overdue that we see this issue in our life and decide to say, "No more!" We are determined to rid ourselves of an image that is fearless. We will not show the world that we are incapable, that is not the goal; but instead we will show the world that we can face our fears by being honest about them. This is the one and true goal. We are not meant to be better than others, but we can be different!

Question: How much do you struggle with this issue? Do you tend to run away from it?

LARRY ROBINSON

July 22

D o you believe that there will never be anyone who loves you in your life? Are there times that you feel that no one will ever know your goodness or your value as a person? Have you secretly given up and feel that no one can be there for you? This is not the case!

Life has many obstacles for us to face, and we all go through certain trials in life in order to become better people. Learning to be with ourselves is one of those trials. Remember that nothing in life is static, which means that nothing stays the same. Things are always changing, and we must be strong enough to handle our lives and the changes that will come.

So many of us are impatient when it comes to "having it all," and do not think that it takes a lot of work to really care about and be happy with another person. It is work! Do not let your fantasies rule your life. To truly care about another person we have to be caring about ourselves first. If we believe that when someone comes into our life we are all done working on ourselves, well, do not deceive yourself, because the real work has only just begun!

There is no "magic pill" that removes all our woes. There is just the learning process of loving someone else, even when we do not like their behavior. There will be many times in your life when you will doubt your feelings for the other person, but this is where your strength comes in. We need to remember why we loved this person to start with in order to accept who they are.

It is so easy to give up and let defeat take over. There are times that we will have many opportunities to meet and get to know others. Do not rush this process and make them into the fantasy person that you have been waiting for. Take your time, for if this is the right person you will have a lifetime together. Whereas if you are impatient, then you might end up with someone you do not truly know!

Assignment: Think about all the relationships that you have gone through. What do they all have in common that has tricked you into believing that they are the right person for you?

LARRY ROBINSON

JULY 23

As we go deeper into ourselves, the issues that we find are not going to be about how others treat us, but rather about who we are in this world. It will take a lot of courage to take responsibility for our behavior, as opposed to us continuing to blame it on the past or others. Be prepared to look inward without judging yourself, but instead try only to observe yourself.

Are you someone who exaggerates (makes more out of something than it actually is)? Do you find that you can take something that may have started out as a minor issue and expand it into a major "storm"? Are you that person who talks so much about what is going on in your life that others start to shy away from you?

There is some need inside of you that longs for attention, and the only way that you have been able to receive it is by placing yourself in the throes of some great crisis! How much energy do you waste trying to get that attention? Do you realize that people who previously may have wanted to be there for you can see what you are doing? Too often we claim to have no idea as to why our friends or family have pulled away from us, but we never really look at ourselves in these situations because we're the ones who have created the crisis, and now we're upset because things have come full circle and it is now real! How many of these must we go through before we see the light of what we have created?

We refuse to believe that people could actually care about us for who we are rather than what we claim to have done or what we say has been done to us! We are so desperate for recognition and love that we automatically exaggerate situations that cause us some pain. It is almost as if we need these situations to be part of us. Sometimes we have told our story so many times that we actually believe them ourselves!

It is time to take responsibility and admit that you need this false attention, and that from now on you will not seek sympathy from others! No longer will I exaggerate situations in my life! It does not really matter where this comes from because the past *is* the past. What does matter is that you have been doing this most of your life and it has only caused the opposite effect: isolation and despair!

Assignment: List the ways in which you look for attention. Remember, they could be little things that you never thought would affect your life but they surely do.

_____

_____

_____

_____

_____

_____

_____

_____

_____

_____

_____

_____

_____

_____

LARRY ROBINSON

July 24

W hy do we think or say things to hurt other people? When we are in the heat of an argument, what causes us to flare up (ignite, like starting a fire) so fast that it even shocks us at its fury? Are we truly mean spirited people or is there something deeper that causes this furious reaction?

You can hurt someone just by thinking terrible things about them. It is not that there is some magic that we can produce, but a thought can be almost as destructive as a deed. We distance ourselves with the thought of being mean to someone else, even though we are pretending to really care. How false is this!

We are defensive people in that we have been hurt, or in many cases, believe that we have been hurt so many times that we are always on guard to protect ourselves. It is so intense at times that before we even hear the whole sentence we are lashing out at the other person who we believe is ready to hurt us. Often, when it is later and we have calmed down, we discover that the other person was going to say something completely different from what we thought. How humiliating for us to have to stand there and listen to how our words wounded someone else when all they were doing was offering us advice!

Our "sensitivity" is at the root of our meanness. We are always sitting on the edge of chaos inside our heads. Someone begins to speak and one word, just one word, can set off an explosion inside our heads that comes bursting out like an erupting volcano. We are destroyed in that moment and our only recourse (solution) is to strike back with all our hurtful words. We have not really heard what the other person has said; we only assumed that it was a put-down. We are now humiliated, for we have shown our true weakness by our horrible response.

When someone is talking to you and you know that you're capable of erupting very easily, quickly take a deep breath and count to ten! Breathe in and out very slowly and listen to the words of the other person. Do not jump to defend yourself, for your tongue is starting to get that nasty taste of meanness. For years you have been subjected to this horrible illness of hypersensitivity (overly sensitive). You experienced this as a child when your parents spoke to you or when teachers called you out. It is almost as old as you are. This is something that you can fix. Be aware of yourself in conversations and what you are beginning to feel!

Question: Look closely at yourself. Are you a defensive person all the time, some of the time, or no, not at all?

_____

_____

_____

_____

_____

_____

_____

_____

_____

_____

_____

_____

_____

LARRY ROBINSON

July 25

What causes us to feel indifferent toward certain people in our life? Why do we end up saying, "I could not care less about what he/she does or says because I am fine without them"? "Indifference," how can we define this feeling?

The highest form of anger you can reach is indifference. When this feeling takes over your mind, your heart is shut down. No longer will you allow yourself to feel pain from someone else. They are dead to your feelings. You can walk right by them and feel nothing. In the past, all you felt was the pain of your anger and hurt, but now you just do not care!

How did we get to this place of indifference? It takes so many painful encounters for us to end up feeling emotionally abused. It does not matter how many times we tell the other person to stop the behavior that is hurting us. They continue and continue and continue until we are so angry and the pain is so strong that we have to shut down any good feelings we have.

It is important to remember that when we feel indifferent we feel neither good nor bad feelings toward the other person. We feel nothing! We no longer care about confronting this person or situation. We are feeling nothing!

Breaking indifference is one of the hardest feelings we are faced with to resolve, and that's if we're even interested in resolution anymore. Often it becomes so dead inside of us that our ability to resolve dies also.

You must be able to see your indifference for what it is. It is your protection against pain, but it can also begin to take over your life if you are not careful! Remember, you have shut your feelings down, and when you do that it sometimes takes hold of other situations as well. We must learn that this feeling is never going to go away, and not just from the other person, but from ourselves too. Think about how many people you can end up feeling indifferent toward. Indifference is the highest form of anger we can get to. It takes us beyond being able to forgive! How sad for us!

Assignment: How much of your life has been focused around feeling indifferent? List all the situations that you can in which indifference was an issue.

_____

_____

_____

_____

_____

_____

_____

_____

_____

_____

_____

_____

_____

_____

LARRY ROBINSON

July 26

D o you set expectations for yourself that are too high? Do you always set the bar (level) of achievement way beyond what you are really capable of and then beat yourself up for not accomplishing it? Why do you think that you always seem to set yourself up to fail? Whenever we set the goal higher than what we can actually accomplish, we are creating low self-esteem in ourselves. And that is when we often start saying the worst possible things about ourselves, sometimes to the point where we actually begin to believe them. Doesn't it seem foolish to continue to do this?

There is something in us that never feels good enough. No matter how much positive feedback we receive, we never feel that we are living up to our potential. The problem is that we do not really know what our potential is. If we are always feeling defeated by our false sense of value, then what measure do we take to see the truth? Is there anything in our life that we can call "valid" when we have set our goals so far beyond what is reasonable for us?

Children are always looking for approval. It is how we begin to form a positive sense of self. We look to our family, teachers, and friends to tell us that we are valuable, smart, and lovable. What happens when we do not get what we need? Remember that as children we cannot see reality in the same way adults can. If we grow up and never realize that perhaps the reason why our parents could not value us was because they never really valued themselves, then we are locked into our childhood of not feeling good enough. We are still looking for the world to give us value.

It is time to set the record straight. We are as good as our effort. When we overwork ourselves and have expectations that are too high, how could we possibly feel good about any of our achievements? We are doomed to feel like a failure. We are the only ones who know our strengths and weaknesses.

Start to think what is reasonable, and understand that you can set the bar too high. Bring it down to where you can feel the rewards of being successful. Each time this happens you will begin, little by little, to erase all the negative feedback you have heaped on yourself. The goal here is to be proud of who you are rather than always looking to others to tell you that you are okay.

Question: Are you someone who can give yourself positive feedback or do you spend a lot of your time being a negative force?

_____

_____

_____

_____

_____

_____

_____

_____

_____

_____

_____

_____

_____

LARRY ROBINSON

July 27

D o you think we love the wrong person? Are our choices based upon a fantasy of who the other person is, or rather by some chemistry we have with this "love of our life"? Do you believe that you were destined to meet this person in your lifetime? Are there truly mistakes that we make in choosing our life partners?

In order to understand choices we also need to understand the word "chemistry." *Chemistry* is not just a physical or emotional attraction to another; it is a deep bond that goes far beyond our conscious self. Sometimes it is almost as if we've acted like a part of the animal world and "sniffed" each other out. Our first feelings of attraction were far beyond what we expected and gave us a rush that we do not easily forget. In fact, it is that rush that keeps us attached to that person. No matter how difficult things appear to be, that rush stays. In some cases we can become addicted to that rush, but it is not necessarily the other person that we continue to want, instead it is the rush that stands out in our mind.

Within that attraction lies the promise of "happily ever after," and because of this we cannot seem to let *go*. This prevents us from making the decision that the relationship has too much pain attached to it for us to survive in it. In the wake of all the destructiveness that is attached to this, we have asked ourselves, "Are we doomed to suffer?"

If we approach each relationship with the idea that we did not make the wrong choice, but that we instead have something to learn about ourselves through the experience of it, then we have a better chance of growing emotionally. It is rare that anyone's first relationship is going to be their last. Perhaps we are meant to grow through a series of relationships until we do get it! Often, we jump too quickly because our need to feel loved overpowers us.

Approach each relationship with the idea that things change, and that if your relationship survives the changes and each of you grows, then it is the relationship. If not, you will meet someone else. Yes, if you met this person there will be another. There is no such thing as my soul mate in life; there are just a lot of souls out there looking for their mate.

Question: Do you feel that you always love the wrong person? What attracts you to them?

_____

_____

_____

_____

_____

_____

_____

_____

_____

_____

_____

_____

_____

_____

_____

LARRY ROBINSON

July 28

When do we know that it is time to end a relationship and move on with our lives? We can become so afraid of thinking that we will be alone that we resist leaving. It is our own insecurities that keep us in poisonous relationships. Let's face the fact that we feel weak and insecure.

Do you believe that we do know when to "call it quits" but give ourselves tons of excuses as to why we must stay? The children, finances, shame from our family, we could go on and on, but the real issue is that we would rather be in a terrible relationship than face life alone. Is being alone, and even lonely, worse than being in a relationship where we get no respect and are treated like an inferior?

Here is a list of some of the reasons to leave a relationship: when we are consistently lied to; when there has been infidelity; when there are numerous addictions that the other person refuses to deal with; when there is physical or strong emotional abuse; when we live with someone who wants to live a "single life," yet who comes home to children and wife/husband and expects to be treated royally; when we are never listened to and our opinions are tossed in the trash; and when the other person gives us no value. Now, see if you can add to this list!

If you confront the other person with both your feelings and references to issues included on the above list and you are still ignored, then it is time to leave! Maybe you will only separate, but your will must be strong enough to let the other person know that you will not stand for this behavior any longer. There is no one who can justify any of the actions that are mentioned above. Know that you are being manipulated and sometimes blamed for their inexcusable behavior.

It is time to take a stand and stop seeing yourself as a victim. The only victims in life are those people who have been raped, robbed, or murdered, or swindled through fraud. The rest of us use our fear as our excuse!

Question: Do you tend to stay too long in relationships that are bad for you out of fear of the future? Are you afraid to be alone?

LARRY ROBINSON

July 29

Are you always feeling cheated by life? Do you watch other people find success while you are always struggling to get ahead? Do you find that you measure yourself up against others when there is no need to be competitive? Do you judge their relationships and secretly feel envious and jealous of what they have? Are you a true *victim* of life?

Here is a chance to be very honest about yourself. If you are really going to grow emotionally, then it is important to be able to look at yourself without judging your own feelings. It is not easy to be responsible for feelings that at one point in life you blamed others for. As we go deeper into those darker feelings that we hide from ourselves, the more we will find that honesty is our only weapon against them. We must fight all our demons and wipe them out of our hearts, for they have infected the way we look at life.

We secretly tell ourselves that those who have more than we do are not good people and we start the process of putting them down in our heads. We are relentless in the things that our minds create about them. We convince ourselves that we know that they do not deserve what they have! Our meanness has taken over and our goodness disappears deep down inside of us. We are frozen in our feeling cheated and we at times can let everyone around us know exactly how we feel. Of course we are careful not to show our envy or jealousy, but it can creep out of us.

The longer we wait to challenge ourselves and ask why we are like this, the longer we stay in the darkness. And we can really let that darkness invade our lives, as well as the lives of those around us. It is time to stop being a prisoner of our own thoughts.

Start to look at what you do have and not just what you believe you are lacking. No matter how small you think it is, it is yours and it is positive. Catch yourself in the habit of comparing and stop yourself before it completely takes over. Realize that you are so much better than these jealous, dark feelings. Do not punish yourself for having them, but accept what they have done to you and allow yourself to forgive you. The fact is that we all know that these feelings are bad, yet we continued to let them take over our beings. No one is better than you, just different!

Question: Are you someone that looks at the glass of life half full or half empty? Now be honest, for it is so easy to run from the truth!

_____

_____

_____

_____

_____

_____

_____

_____

_____

_____

_____

_____

_____

_____

LARRY ROBINSON

July 30

What happens when we fall in love? We become transformed into the person that we always wanted to be. Light with our thoughts and deeply invested in our hearts, we sometimes get so excited that we fail to see reality. How often do we tell ourselves, "This is it!" The truth is, we fall in love with *being in love*!

We can feel the rush inside of ourselves when we believe that we have met the "right" person. This can happen after the first date. We are crazy about this other person and we know that this person is a "keeper." The problem is that we are following our dream rather than our reality! We do not even know this person, yet we already are planning our future with them. How can this be?

Chalk this one up to desperation, and it can lead us down a very dangerous path. We end up investing way too much energy into someone we hardly know. At this point we are blinded by love and fail to see the position that we have put ourselves in. Even after a few dates that have given us a glimpse into the other person's reality and shown us things that would normally turn us off, we refuse to accept the truth! The truth is that at this point we are not coherent enough to be making good decisions for ourselves. All we know is that this person was put into our lives to fill in the emptiness and loneliness that we have always felt. How misguided are we?

When we are younger we can withstand this notion of what love means to us, but as we grow older our hearts cannot tolerate the despair that we feel when love goes sour. We set ourselves up to experience intense pain over someone we hardly knew. Our misery is self-induced and it is not, at this point, about the other person. For all we know our fantasy of them might have chased them away. Maybe we gave ourselves too quickly, expecting that this love would be consummated through sex. None of this really matters because we still end up in the same place, *alone*!

If love is real, then it is not about how fast we move but about how much we want to deal with reality. Take your time, for if this is the one then you have a lifetime with this other person. Do not try to force your feelings on yourself or the other person. Get to know this person, especially when there is a conflict. If we ignore learning about how the other person deals with conflict, then we are setting ourselves up for disaster. Knowledge is powerful! Can you see that?

Question: Do you get seduced by your fantasies of what a relationship should be rather than what it really is: work, hard work?

_____

_____

_____

_____

_____

_____

_____

_____

_____

_____

_____

_____

LARRY ROBINSON

July 31

What do you think true friendship means? Would you consider yourself a true friend? We all can be confused by what this really means.

Let's talk about what is not a true friend first. A true friend is not someone who talks behind their friends' backs. We do not wait for someone we care about to walk away from us before we start to talk negative about them. A true friend does not hold their feelings in when they feel disappointed or hurt or even angry at their friends. A true friend is not a "fair-weathered friend" (one who only wants to be friends at their convenience, calling when there is no one else to be around). A true friend does not judge others' decisions and does not shy away from the truth.

If these are characteristics of what isn't a true friend, then what is one? A true friend is able to stand by their friend no matter what the situation is and not judge them as people. Yes, at times we must judge behavior for we can certainly differ as to what we think is morally correct, but we do not judge their soul. A true friend is not afraid to tell the truth to their friends, even if it can hurt the other person. It is not the kind of hurt that tears at their insides but to their ego which a true friend might say: "I do not think you are looking at the whole picture," while the other person becomes angry or hurt by the honesty. They will get over it if they are telling themselves the truth.

A true friend is there when needed the most and that is not always when they think we need them. The love that is present in the friendship should be enough to be able to listen to each other. There is no right or wrong but always a challenge from our true friends. Who else knows each other enough to present that challenge?

We should want that challenge in our life and look at it as love and caring (most likely after the initial anger on feeling unsupported dies down).

If that anger in them does not go away and they remain angry at us for our wanting to challenge them out of love, then maybe WE NEED TO QUESTION THAT FRIENDSHIP!

Living up to what a true friend is, is a difficult commitment for this is what it truly is, a commitment. Through life, those that deal with honesty keep their friends forever. Are you a true friend? Do you have true friends?

Question: Can you answer the above two questions?

_____

_____

_____

_____

_____

_____

_____

_____

_____

_____

_____

_____

LARRY ROBINSON

Isabella Walsh, Limerick, Ireland

AUGUST 1

Are you someone who gets into fights with others? Is your relationship one that is consumed by bickering or fighting? Do you end up feeling as if it is your fault that the fight happened because you cannot control your temper? Is the other person just standing there, making you look like a fool? This is so damaging to your self-esteem, for you will feel guilty and responsible because you were the one who lost it!

This is not the truth! The other person is acting what we call passive-aggressive, and knows that by standing there silently it will drive you to screaming. How unfair, but you are being set up. Ask yourself, "Why can't I control my temper?" You are being pushed to your limit when the other person knows you will end up hating yourself.

Fighting is sometimes necessary in a relationship. We cannot be afraid of the fight, but there has to be some rules, and we need to follow them the best we can. First of all, who is right? Is it the person yelling or the person not responding? The answer is they're both wrong! This is so important to recognize.

It will become a standstill until we are exhausted of energy. There is nothing wrong with raising your voice. It is a natural occurrence when we feel unheard. We are trying to make a point and we are getting a wall. It is not okay to remain silent! We might need a moment to take in what the other person is trying to say, but we don't need silence throughout the argument because it will surely turn into a fight. Silence can translate to, "I don't care how you feel."

There are three types of couples:

1. The temper-temper couple: they are always fighting
2. The temper-passive couple: always ending in "still in guilt" or still angry
3. The passive-passive couple: this couple hates conflict and avoids fighting, but never resolves anything

Question: Which one are you? Which do you think is the healthiest one?

AUGUST 2

It seems like we never want to stop the party in our life. Remember in high school how we couldn't wait for the weekends to come so that the party could begin? "Who's getting the party favors for tonight?" we'd ask our friends every Friday.

Have things really changed for us in the present? We are not teenagers anymore but we still want the party to go on. How many of us still make plans to party with a couple of friends on the weekend? Do we ever do anything that does not include drinking and smoking or some kind of drug aimed at making our weekends "better"? What are the differences between now and our teenage years other than that now it is legal, while back then we took risks?

Do you tell yourself that you do not take risks with your life today? Do you believe that you have control over how much you drink and drug and that you know when to stop? Right! How many of you don't remember what happened the night before and what you said or did? Oh, maybe it wasn't as bad as that, but did you make a fool out of yourself? What has changed from then to now? A fool is a fool, whether you are a legitimate sixteen-year-old or a forty-year-old who is still acting sixteen!

How often do you lecture your children about not drinking or drugging and then *you* go and do it on the weekends? Believe it: they see you high or drunk. You are their role model and they will mimic your behavior. And how are your hangovers the next day? Do your children have to tiptoe around you because your head is splitting? All of these issues seem so unimportant to you right now, but where does your partying end and your responsibilities to your family start?

We all have our ways of "medicating." When we were teenagers we wanted to block out the sound of our parents' voices. They were constantly yelling at us about what we didn't care about, so we medicated. Weekends were for drinking until we didn't hear those voices anymore. For some of us, it took blacking out or getting stupid to the point where we could only crawl home! Have things really changed *that* much? Has your "medicating" become an addiction and you do not even realize it?

LARRY ROBINSON

Question: What is your way of partying to ignore your feelings? We can call this *medicating ourselves.*

_____

_____

_____

_____

_____

_____

_____

_____

_____

_____

_____

_____

_____

_____

_____

_____

_____

AUGUST 3

Does your life always seem to be caught up in chaos? Are you someone who has the best intentions and takes on multiple tasks, only to always end up in some sort of mess? Do you start out with the great attitude of "I can do anything" and end up in tears or beating yourself up? Face it: you have no sense of organization.

Some of us start off as children with certain "requirements" from our parents when it comes to taking care of our belongings, as well as certain chores that we are expected to complete. And we do know the consequences that will come if we fail to produce. As strict as we remember our parents being, what do you think the outcome of that requirement was for us?

We could take it in two different directions. One direction is that we become super compulsive about cleanliness and order. Everything has to be perfect, and we go over things to make sure that we got it right! We can drive others crazy with our compulsions and we end up doing everything because nothing seems to meet our requirements except when we do it ourselves. This is our "burnout" situation, and while we often complain, we refuse to change this behavior.

The other direction is chaos. Believe it or not, we do not want to be responsible for anything, although we do not know it at the time. We start off with so many wonderful plans and end up completing nothing and feeling like a "waste of time" person. Inside of us there is a block about what is expected and it hides itself in our subconscious. We are not aware that we are angry from our past and the expectations others put on us. We do not understand that we almost always set ourselves up to fail! This is why we take on so many things and repeat this pattern over and over again.

Growth starts with awareness. We must be aware of what our issues are and why they are there, and the first step is to force you to just do one thing at a time. The awareness of moving from one task to another without completion has to be in the forefront of our minds. Set a single goal and concentrate on the fact that this one goal is all that is required! Now, watch how you struggle to stay focused on that goal. It's difficult, isn't it? But we must push through with this in order to realize that underneath it we have the ability to achieve success. We must face our own rebellious self!

Question: What is the most chaotic (one that causes you a lot of pain) issue in your life that you want to change? Try and look at this as a major issue that perhaps a number of little issues come out of it.

_____

_____

_____

_____

_____

_____

_____

_____

_____

_____

_____

_____

_____

_____

August 4

D o you plan your future? Do you have a "five-year plan" that you are working toward and have made a commitment to, and try as hard as you can to stick to it? Are you someone who is driven to accomplish goals in your life?

Try to picture in your mind what that five-year plan looks like. Have you planned it out in your mind or are you waiting for the "right" moment to begin? If that is the case, you are a "want to want to" person.

When you are in this situation you still have not made a commitment to your life. Yes, you are contemplating the next step, but something is holding you back. Your determination is lacking and your ability to take control over your life is missing. What are you waiting for? No one is going to come into your life and give you the opportunity of a lifetime!

We make our lives work, no one does it for us, and that is the truth! When was the last time that someone came into your life and gave you unlimited possibilities for your future? So often we are told to live in the present, and that is a true statement, but we need to have a vision of what we are going to be doing in our future. Without anything to work for, we stay frozen in our life journey.

Plan, discuss, and *put into action* what you want for your future so that you are working to gain not just money, but something that gives you a sense of self-worth and a feeling of accomplishment! Both men and women need this in their lives.

Do not wait until it is too late and your life has passed you by. Take charge today and form a plan and do not care whether it is immediately doable; just begin the journey down this path.

Question: Are you someone who plans out their life or is just too beaten down by it to really care what happens next? Are there no plans that you make for your life?

LARRY ROBINSON

August 5

How do we make up after a fight that went out of control? Did you say things that were mean and hurtful, but which only came in the heat of the moment? Did you raise your voice or scream at the other person? Who do you remember that did this in your life?

When we are engaged in a fight, think carefully about how you said things. Did you really mean what you said, or was it just to hurt the other person? How would the other person know when only you know? What if what you said was only meant to be used in a destructive manner so that the other person got angrier and more defensive? Most likely you did mean what you said because you were carrying it for such a long time that it came out in this fit of anger and meanness and now you are stuck with telling someone how you feel in a destructive rather than constructive manner.

Well, either way your feelings came out, and so did the other person's. Maybe you both said things that you meant but would never say out loud. These are things that we felt inside ourselves that were our private thoughts, which we experienced when we were alone, possibly after our spouse said something "off the cuff" that ticked us off but which we had seemingly gotten over. The reason is that it went into the back of our mind really quickly. The issue is that during a fight that door to these fleeting angry feelings opens up and out they come. It is almost as if we had no control over it and neither does our spouse.

In order to make up you first have to allow yourself to open that door as a manner of cleansing that junk that's in there. The both of you are now so much freer because you cleaned it out. The "I'm sorry" is not about what you both said, but how you said it to each other! Take some time and let yourself and your spouse cool down and you will feel a sense of relief inside you. If the other person is still hurt, then give them time to think about themselves. Do not feel guilty because that will erase what you needed to say. In a fight we need to blast each other at times or else we will be too weak to get it all out. Do not fear the fight! If your love is unconditional then you will love each other again. If you

LARRY ROBINSON

hold a grudge it is because you could not accept what your spouse had to say. For better or worse, you are together forever!

Question: What kind of fighter are you? Do you blast out your feelings and emotions, or are you shut down emotionally from the other person?

_____

_____

_____

_____

_____

_____

_____

_____

_____

_____

_____

_____

_____

_____

AUGUST 6

S tubborn, stubborn, stubborn! Do you know one person who isn't stubborn? Do you see people not challenging what other people say and just going with the flow of someone else's opinion? Even if that person seems to agree with everything others say, don't be fooled into thinking that they are not stubborn.

"Inside stubbornness" is actually worse than someone holding their ground and refusing to move. At least you know their opinion! The "inside" person, who lets you think that they are agreeing with you, is acting passive-aggressively. They actually find ways that prevent movement on an issue without directly confronting you. They are the supreme manipulators and never quit looking like they are not the ones who are holding on to things.

Where does all this stubbornness come from? If you look inside yourself you will see the child in you throwing a silent tantrum with your parents, siblings, or friends because you do not want to lose! "Winning," as a child, was everything! We had to win or we would not be liked enough, loved enough, or respected enough. These are delusions we formed as children. A child's perception of reality isn't always true. It is how the child sees it, and they hold on to that belief with an iron determination.

When two people experience stubbornness at the same time, a fight will most assuredly break out. Someone will give in, while the other will never really know if they got their point across or if they just were fooled into believing that they were right! The only way that we can get through this is to assess ourselves and see what the truth about us really is. Always trying to win is such a waste of life, time, and energy, because in the long run who really cares? There is no reward in the afterlife for being right, only for being truthful! So the next time you experience stubbornness, figure out why you are so persistent on winning, and then let go!

Question: Are you someone who can let go not winning all of the time? Are you really stubborn enough to ruin a friendship over being too stubborn?

AUGUST 7

How do we "make up" after a fight? Sometimes the fight continues just to prove to the other person that you are right and they are wrong, but this keeps the fight ongoing and the anger still flying. Most often, the fight's roots are much deeper and stem from unresolved issues from the past and the fight only allows the deeper issues to surface. This is not unhealthy, it is just painful, because then the accusations get tossed back and forth. "Why didn't you speak up? Why are you hitting me with these now, three months after the incident happened?"

How afraid are we to be yelled at or rejected because we feel hurt or anger from the treatment we have received? This is not a gender-based feeling either, it is instead an "everybody" feeling. There cannot be a winner in a relationship, for if there is then someone loses, and that makes the relationship off-balanced. The best we can achieve with each other is to understand how the other person felt. Remember, there are two sides to every story and your partner reacted out of their feelings, not necessarily because of you.

We have to stop the attacks and really try hard to let the other person have their say without interrupting them. We so anxiously want to defend ourselves that we speak over each other to the point where no one gets heard. This requires patience in knowing that the other person will finish and then you can speak. Listen carefully to his/her feelings, and understand that this is how they felt.

Feelings do not have a right or wrong attached to them. It is just what they perceived the situation to be and why they felt hurt. You will get your turn to speak as long as you allow the other their right to explain to you how and why they felt hurt. When you hear this you will either know that it was not what you had meant, or that you now understand why your behavior hurt them. They will also understand why you reacted the way you did. This is resolution that will lead to a better understanding of each other. Now there are two winners!

Question: Are you someone who believes in right and wrong when you argue? How do you resolve a fight with this opinion?

LARRY ROBINSON

August 8

D o you ask for help when you need it? Are you the kind of person that is determined to do everything on your own? Well, you are not alone. There are so many of us out there for whom it is almost impossible to ask for help. What makes us this way? How often have we screwed up a project at home or at work because we were too stubborn to ask?

But is it stubbornness, or is it a feeling of needing to be invaluable to everyone that drives this? We live by the mantra, "I can do it," and if we run into problems we will constantly obsess about finding the answer, while saying that we have it under control if we're asked about it in the meantime. Big lie!

Sometimes we rush to put something together without even referring to the directions. We are labeled ADHD, but that is not the really the case. We just want people to know how capable we are. Sometimes we make ourselves look foolish around the mess that we make out of something, and when we do we either blame the other person for "nagging" us or proclaim that something was wrong with the project. It was not our fault. And we not only humiliate ourselves, but we also attach a secret weakness to our sense of self-esteem that says, "If I cannot do this, I am a failure!"

Where does this need to be capable come from? Look back early in your childhood to a parent who had no tolerance for you to learn. Does the phrase "Put it down, you can't do it; I will have to" sound familiar? Well, how many of us had parents we could not ask for help? Are we repeating their pattern? Asking for help when we cannot solve a problem is our strength, not our weakness. The weak person uses pride and stubbornness to stay weak. The strong person knows that getting the project done right is more important than pride. Which one are you!

Question: Was there one parent who was especially critical of you? Did you always try and please them? Did you turn to the other for comfort?

AUGUST 9

Jealousy, the root of a great deal of pain. Do you see yourself as a jealous person? Do you understand what it means? There is a difference between jealousy and envy, in that if you envy someone for the new car they bought, then it is something that you could set a goal to achieve, for it is attainable. Jealousy, on the other hand, is about a loss of control over a situation or a person, during which we fear that we will lose it or them!

It becomes so important for a jealous person to have power over the situation, and at the slightest sign of weakness their insecurity gets going and they begin to manipulate the person to want them! They might start flirting, or even eyeball others while they are with their partners.

Jealousy can look very different to each of us. There is the person who, on the outside, is so happy for the other person's success but on the inside can be plotting to gain back the control that they believe is teetering on the edge. This person is never overtly critical, but in an underhanded way criticizes the other person. It can take on a very caring tone, but the real intent is to topple the other person's happiness. And then there is the person who picks a fight with the other in order to feel superior to him/her. They feel that if they overtly put the other down, then they will not feel inferior. How many of us know people like this?

There also is the person who tries to outdo us. No matter how happy we can be over our success, the other is boasting a bigger success. How annoying is this! Further still, there are those people who constantly need to talk about themselves. You know, the person who calls you up and asks, "How are you?" and before you can answer starts to talk about themselves and goes on and on, and at the end of their speech says, "So what's up?" Whenever we encounter these people it is very important to realize that they are "toxic" and that we need to set an invisible barrier between us and them in order to keep their poison away.

Jealousy can ruin relationships and create enemies. Where there once was friendship, now there is either a direct, open verbal badmouthing or a silent, deadly wishing for the other to fail. We need to be happy for each other, for we grow and learn at different rates. Wasting time being

LARRY ROBINSON

jealous keeps us stuck. Time to face the jealousy and find out what we have rather than always comparing ourselves to others and what we don't have.

Question: What is most recent thing that caused you to be jealous? How did you deal with it? Is it still causing you pain?

_____

_____

_____

_____

_____

_____

_____

_____

_____

_____

_____

_____

_____

_____

August 10

I 'll do it tomorrow! I know I will! I have promised myself that I will take care of my body. I will call the doctor. I will call the eye doctor and the dentist. I know I will, tomorrow!

Are we kidding ourselves when we say that we feel great after very little sleep or fitful sleep? What about when we have to get up numerous times in the night to pee? We feel great? We will call the dentist tomorrow; the pain in our tooth isn't that bad. We feel great!

There is this lingering feeling of uneasiness inside us, and when we are not defending ourselves, our body is telling us, "I do not feel great." We are too afraid to admit this to ourselves and dread what might really be the case. Is that why we "fantasize" that we have heart disease each time we have heartburn, or cancer when our kidneys hurt? Are we stressing ourselves out by not going to the doctor? And then we say to ourselves, "But I am not one of those people who rush to the doctor when they have the slightest pain. I never rush to the doctor!"

Stress will go to the weakest part of our body and sit there until we have either rid ourselves of it or created more pain. Do I cause my own pain at times? Do I really believe that my body is invincible and that I will never get sick? I haven't had a cold in years. I haven't felt well in years either. Will I learn in this lifetime that my body needs my help and that it doesn't always take care of itself? Tomorrow, I will definitely call the doctor!

Assignment: How well do you take care of your health? Rate it from one to ten, ten being superb and one being not at all. List your diseases or ailments. Do you think you could be healthier?

_____

_____

_____

LARRY ROBINSON

August 11

Living together, what a surprise it is to all of us! Where did the word "bliss" go? We are all so naive to think that we are going to meet the same person whom we planned to move in with. When we are dating we show the best to each other, even when we spend the night together. Some women even get up before their boyfriends and redo there makeup to look fresh and pretty in the morning. Some guys run to the bathroom so they will not let morning gas appear. Oh, how wonderful it all seems!

We live in an alternate universe when we assume that other people do not have their secret little habits. Why would we ever expose them before we live together or get married? (And oh, just to let you in on this, perhaps it is a mistake not to live together during the engagement period, just to work out these issues before the wedding.) Our habits are our habits, and it takes a lifetime to really remove them.

We all have to learn to accept each other for who we are, not for what our fantasy of the other person is. Living together is the first step toward "forever." I guess since relationships are built on that word, how many "chickens" are there among us who give up too quickly and decide, "This is not for me"? If you remember that we can change anything if we really want to, then you start off on the right foot! Know that everything about us comes out when we live together, and that includes the good, the bad, and the ugly. By the way, I didn't know that you were perfect!

Assignment: Make a list of your habits that you think another person would have a difficult time living with. Are you tolerant of other people's living habits?

LARRY ROBINSON

August 12

Can we really forgive each other? How many years of anger does it take before a relationship dies? We store each hurting stab inside ourselves and rationalize that it didn't hurt, but yet our resentments many times only go "undercover" with our denials.

We look around and wonder why *that couple* seems so happy, and yet we really do not even know their reality! We become jealous of people we know nothing about, for we fantasize that anything might be better than what we have!

The truth is that we never really look at who we are in our own relationship. And don't even try to tell yourself that you do, because you will always have a "but" ready to add, inferring that it is the other person's fault that you act the way you do. "You made me do it," is one of your favorite responses to your spouse or partner.

Well, pardon me, but no one *makes* us mean or selfish! That is our problem, not anyone else's. It is not our partner's now, nor can it be anyone else's later! Never!

Assignment: Describe what your best and worst traits are in a relationship. Do you ever wish to rid yourself of the really bad ones and do not know how, or are you the type of person who says, "you get what you see"?

_____

_____

_____

_____

_____

_____

AUGUST 13

Are you one of those people who "wants to *want to*" change? It just becomes a mind trip when you tell yourself that you need to put down your addiction, but maybe not just yet! Do you tell yourself it really isn't harming anyone else and that you don't necessarily do it every day? Why have you given yourself permission to stay stuck?

You demand that your children change their behavior, while you are lighting up a cigarette, pouring a drink, rolling a joint, or worse. They surely know the consequences of their behavior. Do you know the consequences of yours? They do not respect you and soon it will be too late. It is said that addicts are many times selfish people. Well, get off the couch and begin to see who you are! "You can do anything you put your mind to," is what we tell children. I guess it is a fake statement, for why should they listen to hypocrites?

Prove society wrong. Do something for someone else and you will see the amazing reward you get for giving! You say that you want self-esteem, well, giving to someone else is the beginning!

It is time to grow up! Yes, that is what addiction can be, it keeps us stuck in our childhood while we try to raise children. Some joke! Stop pretending and be genuine with yourself before you pass on your weakness!

Assignments: List the addictive behaviors that you have held on to most of your life. Can you trace any back to childhood? How have they interfered with your life?

_____

_____

_____

_____

AUGUST 14

D o you feel really lonely inside? Do you have a smile on your face while you are feeling *reject-able* in life? Do your insides feel different from what you show on the outside? Have you given up on yourself in thinking that there will ever be someone meaningful in your life?

You are not alone! There are so many of us who feel as if there will never be anyone who will love us. It is one of the most painful situations we can have, and there is little anyone can say to you that makes things better. "Don't worry, someone will come for you. Just be patient!" Isn't that a horrible statement? We whisper to ourselves, "How do they know?" We begin to compare ourselves to everyone else (at least those in relationships) and we come up empty and sad.

Did you ever think that maybe it is your attitude that keeps people away? If someone does show interest we pounce (jump) on them as if they were our last meal. We devour (eat up) their attention and begin to smother them with our neediness. We think that we are loving them, when in actuality all we are thinking about is, "I am finally loved!" Do you then wonder why it is that they run away?

The problem is that we do not love ourselves and we are overanxiously waiting for *the* person to magically appear and take us out of our misery! This is so unlikely to happen. When you hate *you*, why on earth would you ever think that someone else will love you? And that's when the defeated feelings begin.

This is the time when a light bulb needs to go off in your head. How many times do you have to go through this before you "get it"? No one loves someone who smothers them. You hate it when someone else does it to you because it is a turn off, not a turn on! It is time to focus on yourself and deal honestly with who you are, because until you build a better sense of self, you will not meet *the* person!

Question: What is it about yourself that you think another person could not tolerate? Are you satisfied with who you are?

"Knowing and affirming your self-worth will help you to let go of relationships that no longer serve you. Pray, go within, and ask God for strength to let go and move forward. The only way to allow someone into your life who is right and healthy for you is to let go of the old, realize your self-worth, and create space for a beautiful new soul to connect with on a deep, spiritual level. Wishing you all love, happiness, and the ability to see how beautiful your light truly is."

Rick Staula, Brooklyn, New York, USA

By Dan Williams
Bournemouth, England, UK

There's nothing worse than
Losing who you thought
Was your best friend.
They just wake up one
Morning and decide they
Don't like you anymore and
Just leave you. Ignore you.
Hurt you. Break promises
And forget all those
Memories. It is truly sad,
Especially when you did
Nothing wrong. Don't worry
About my feelings though,
Nobody else does.

AUGUST 15

Are you someone who is always comparing yourself to others? Do you look to see what they have compared to what you have? How often has your wellbeing been determined by measuring yourself up against others? This is a very difficult and painful trait to possess. This can rule your life and you might be totally unaware that it even exists.

Once we begin these types of comparisons there is no stopping us. We do it with everything we have, whether it is looks, money, love, friendships, you name it—we will compare ourselves to others. We are truly discontent with ourselves when we are doing this.

This has been going on since we were children. It is not something that just pops up as adults. We did not feel very valuable as children, and often we were compared to others and heard, "Well, Damian got all A's on his report card. Why didn't you?" And we felt the sting of it! It went right to our hearts and it made us cry internally. We were not good enough!

Let's face it, we have spent so much time comparing ourselves to others that we really do not know our own capabilities. Isn't that sad? How misguided we were to think that we would feel better about ourselves by beating out everyone else. The real problem with this is that there will always be someone who comes along who will be better than we are. This is our demon in life, for we can never just rest comfortably and appreciate what we do have! Our whole life can become consumed with this craziness and we do not know how to stop it! We are not even sure we can!

There is a solution, though, and that is we need to begin to look at what we have accomplished on our own. We may think that there is nothing we have done on our own that is worthwhile, but that is because this "comparing ourselves to everyone else" trait of ours has gotten in our way, and it is blocking us!

The first step is to accept that this is a damaging issue for us. We need to look deeply at this and find its origins. How far back can you remember doing this? Most likely you will not see yourself without it, for it runs so deep and goes very far back. Next, find your accomplishments, no matter how small and insignificant they may seem. Remember that even though you are looking at yourself you may still revert to comparisons, so catch it before it takes over. When you do this, a new world will begin to open up for you and you will see the real you, and then all this comparing will become a thing of the past.

When you run a race, it hurts your time to turn around and see who is behind you. Go straight forward and remember to compete only against yourself!

Question: Are you the type of person who compares themselves to everyone else? How damaged has this made you? Do you ever stop yourself or do you think it now is an automatic response?

_____

_____

_____

_____

_____

_____

_____

_____

_____

_____

_____

_____

_____

LARRY ROBINSON

August 16

D o we really know what love is? Are we always in search of it and does it seem to turn against us every time we think we have found it? Are we constantly disappointed in what we really wanted from another person and feel as if all we do is put out love rather than receive it?

To truly love someone else, we need to be able to give unconditionally without thinking about, "What about me?" When we say *unconditional love*, it does not mean that we give constantly and receive nothing. It means that we always need to return to the unconditional love when we work issues through with the other person. Love *does* have a condition when we are upset with our lover, and that condition is not whether one of the two of us right or wrong, but that we remain committed to listening to each other and actually hearing what the other person has to say. To truly listen to another person is in itself an act of love. To not cut the other person off as they are speaking is an act of love. To breathe deeply before saying something that we will regret is an act of love.

There are very few of us who do not want love. Do we all need it? Well, that is for each one of us to decide for ourselves. The idea of love is so different from the reality of it. Yes, it has pain attached to it, but where does the pain really come from? It grows out of our disappointment with not living out our fantasy of what love is supposed to be. Let's face it, love is hard, but it is also beautiful!

When we are able to put another person's feelings before our own and not think about what we are getting in return, then we experience true love. When we accept the other person for who they are rather than who we want them to be, that is love.

Love is always a work in progress. There is no end to loving someone. We are different from each other, so accepting this reality is loving. We will always be challenged by love to understand each other. When this happens, a most beautiful healing takes place between us!

Question: Do you believe in unconditional love? Have you ever felt it and sustained that feeling with someone else?

LARRY ROBINSON

August 17

Do you know what the difference is between holding resentments and keeping a grudge (deeply internal negative feeling)? How often do you feel resentful toward someone or some situation and have it eat away at you daily? Are you someone who cannot let go of the resentful feelings that you harbor inside? Are you the type of person who does not confront your resentments?

It is important to know the difference between "resentment" and a "grudge." A resentment starts off being a minor issue, and one that, despite the fact that we try to ignore it, often begins to eat away at our mind and eventually begins to fester (negatively go over and over the situation). It can cause us to stew (cook our negative feelings for long periods of time). Until we confront the resentment we are not free! In fact, we can add more resentment to this one if we are not careful. Anything the person we are resentful toward does becomes subject to us feeling more resentments until we confront the initial one. How dangerous can this be?

A grudge, on the other hand, goes much deeper. It appears after we believe that we have confronted the resentments we feel. When we find no satisfaction or resolution surrounding the original issue that we had with the other person, and they continue to exhibit the same behavior that we are resentful toward, then a grudge develops. Grudges are not forgettable, and in most cases, not forgivable. No matter how many times we tell ourselves, "It's no big deal," we are lying to ourselves, and that dark, angry feeling of bitterness comes back! A grudge is bitter, and we do not have the ability to let it go!

Now, the reason we cannot let it go stems from our continued failed expectations regarding the other person. A good example of having a grudge can be the feelings we have toward someone who has lied to us and hurt us deeply with those lies. At first we hold the resentment, but when the lying happens over and over again we form a grudge. We do not really label it as such, but we definitely feel it! Our attitude can even become one of indifference toward the other person. Yes, we can be fake and act pleasant, but we know that the grudge is there and that we will no longer be vulnerable to the other person.

Question: Have many of your resentments turned into grudges? Can you go back in your life and list them? Are they still active today? Do you believe that we can love someone and still hold a grudge? Grudges can be our way of protecting ourselves from being hurt. Our best option is deal with resentments as they come up. That is the only way we become grudge-free!

_____

_____

_____

_____

_____

_____

_____

_____

_____

_____

_____

LARRY ROBINSON

August 18

Why is it that we can feel so sad and lonely when we are surrounded by people who say they care about us? What is it that causes us to feel so isolated from everyone, and yet we put a smile on our face while our heart is breaking? The sadness is overwhelming!

This is our *demon* and it has been chasing us for as long as we can remember. It surfaces and makes us feel that our feelings are unacceptable and we become afraid to let anyone into our secret, darker side that always tells us that we are not good enough and that no one will ever love us.

As children we were not allowed to have certain feelings. Our parents would not or could not listen to our fears and concerns. We were always put down for any negative feelings we had, or we had to pretend that everything was okay when we were filled with fears and anger. We believed that there would never be anyone there for us. Even when we met *the one*, we became afraid to show our true feelings for fear of rejection. This is the pain we carry in life.

Enough! We have had enough of this sadness that covers our pain and loneliness. We are the masters of our own life, and we are the ones who have deemed our feelings to be too difficult for anyone to understand. It is that dark side that has always interfered with our happiness. But wait, perhaps we never give anyone a chance to be there for us. We determine who we open up to, and we have chosen *no one*! Our sadness now becomes imbedded (deeply rooted) inside us.

Let go of the past! It has determined our destiny and now we need to get angry at that side of ourselves. We are better than this! We have formed a habit around our sadness so that when we see others we believe that they are a lot better off than we are. Any habit can be broken, if you really want to break it!

Assignment: List the issues from your past that still have not been dealt with. Are you someone who lives in the past and cannot see the future?

LARRY ROBINSON

August 19

How much of our life do we live in a fantasy world? Why are we so determined to make some "dream" come true when we do not even know what the reality of it is? We live in our own fantasy world, whether we are male or female, and when reality hits us we are devastated (destroyed).

Why is it that we cannot live a true life? How many times has our fantasy world disappointed us, yet we continue to return to it as if it will never fail us again? Are we so afraid of reality that we constantly have to create a world in which we get everything we desire and "live happily ever after"? How foolish are we?

The reason why we create such a world and hardly let anyone into it, usually out of fear that they will tell us how foolish we are, is because we are so afraid of rejection and emptiness. We are constantly filling ourselves up with false expectations in order to satisfy this incredible hunger for love that is inside of us. The fear that we will not be loved is overwhelming.

It is time to stop this fantasizing before we get older, for as time passes so does our chance at true love. Get it out of your head that you can change another person to be the one that you want. If you cannot accept another for who they are without trying to impose your fantasy person on them, then move on!

Your life does not go on forever. You are missing out on knowing how to love and receive love by living in this fantasy world. Do you really believe that you can change another person? How unfair are you in your present relationship in trying to impose your standard, which has been born out of your fantasy world, on the other person? We can fulfill our dream of love, but that only comes out of the hard work we do together, the end result of which is a stronger, lasting love.

Question: How many people in your life have you tried to change into your fantasy person only to have them eventually leave you?

LARRY ROBINSON

AUGUST 20

Where does our motivation go? Why is it that we can start off doing something that needs to get done and then just become full of excuses for why we cannot do it? We go from one excuse to another, giving ourselves the freedom to quit. How often do you quit on yourself?

Sadly, the answer to that is *more often than we think*! There are so many good intentions that cross our minds, but we are often so full of ourselves and consumed by responsibilities and commitments that we often fail to even recognize that we either start or stop something. We have every intention of completing these tasks, but something always pops up to block us before we have completed them. Why does this happen to us? It only makes us more and more angry and defeated by ourselves, and that is when we start the journey downward toward low self-esteem.

This issue affects both males and females, for creating low self-esteem has no gender attached to it. We want so much to be liked and needed that so many times we do not even listen to what is being asked of us. We simply raise our hand to volunteer or to assist a loved one and end up feeling inadequate when we don't follow through. Do you think that we fix this, or do we continue to repeat this in our lives? We lose our credibility (belief in our intentions) and are now seen as fake. Despite our good intentions, we not only end up disappointing the person who needed us, but start to view ourselves as losers too!

So then it is time to learn our lesson. We are not liked for what we can do for others. Understand this! We are the ones who are looking for value from the world. Why else would we volunteer to do something that we really do not know how to do? Why would we take on the needs of others when we don't even have enough time for our own lives? We kill our own motivation by overcommitting ourselves to the point where we have to back out. We are our own worst enemy. If people only see us for what we can do for them as opposed to who we really are, then they are not friends in the first place. They are simply "users."

Do not be fooled any longer! Do not take on what you cannot achieve. This does not make you a loser, but instead something a whole lot better: an honest person!

Question: Do you value yourself or are you always needing validation from others? Explain.

_____

_____

_____

_____

_____

_____

_____

_____

_____

_____

_____

_____

_____

LARRY ROBINSON

AUGUST 21

W hy do we become filled with doubts and indecisions (inability to make choices in life)? Does every decision cause us to feel anxious and we go over it in our minds until we are mentally exhausted? Is the decision still bothering us even though we thought that we finalized it? We just drive ourselves crazy!

We need to face the fact that we doubt everything that comes into our life and that it has always been this way. We cannot decide on anything! Things that are easy for others are painful for us to decide. We make a big deal out of everything and drive those around us nuts with our constant need to have feedback on every decision we are trying to make. We cannot stop ourselves at times.

The anxiety we experience is overwhelming, and it never seems to stop. Sometimes the tiniest little decision can quickly turn into the biggest crisis. We find that people tend to stay away from us when we are in this intolerable place. And though they even give us the feedback we want, we are still not satisfied!

Doubt and indecision have been our companions forever. As children we were always afraid that we were doing it wrong and were often criticized for the choices we made. If nothing we ever did was right, then why would we think that we could make good decisions?

It is time to let go of this tortured piece of ourselves. In order to do this we need to not go to anyone for advice, for that is not our idea but theirs! Herein lies the problem. We cannot trust anyone with our decisions or doubts. They might give us the right answer, but we will not usually follow it because it is not ours. There are so many times that we actually have the right answer but refuse to believe that it came from us.

This is the child in us who is full of fears and self-doubts. We need to recognize that this is childish behavior; that is the first step. Next, we need to breathe in and then breathe out slowly, and in that breath blow out the anxiety. Once you do that you will feel much freer to see whether your decision fits the situation or not.

Change will happen when you see that you have been operating out of fear. There is no one to judge you except you, and you can often be too harsh on the child inside!

Question: Are you someone who fights change and wants to stay in the same safety zone in your life always?

_____

_____

_____

_____

_____

_____

_____

_____

_____

_____

_____

_____

_____

AUGUST 22

Why do we continue to suffer in bad relationships? What causes us to continually try to save something that is dead? How can we be so out of touch as not to see what everyone else sees, that the relationship is poison? Why are we constantly making excuses for the other person, while deep down inside we know the truth?

Are we that broken that we need to stay in something that gives us an enormous amount of pain just so we can believe that we "have someone"? No matter what the cost to our own self-esteem, we continue to try to change the other person into someone we desire. Have we ever thought that we might really detest this person for the pain that they caused us, but just do not want to see it?

We cause our own pain! This is the truth that we do not want to face. We have given this person many chances to be a better person and they have failed us every time, but we still believe that through loving them we can change them into who we want and need them to be! How foolish of us to think that we can change another person! Why did we choose this person?

Not only did we pick this person, but we will also continue to choose unwisely until we value ourselves more. Do not believe that we didn't know who we were getting involved with. Oh yes, we did! We were just too stubborn and we were determined to have it our way. The signs were there from the beginning but we ignored them. We put them in the back of our minds as we continued to be emotionally abused by someone we "loved."

This was not and is not love. This is us not wanting to see the truth because we are too busy fantasizing about what wonderful things are going to come our way. It does not matter at this point what the psychology is around our choices to hold on to someone who hurts us (and this affects both males and females alike), what matters is that we continue to stay! Don't you think you have had enough of shaming yourself?

Question: How have you caused yourself pain in relationships? Do you continually repeat the same mistakes with all relationships?

_____

_____

_____

_____

_____

_____

_____

_____

_____

_____

_____

_____

_____

_____

LARRY ROBINSON

August 23

D o you feel hopeless about life? Does everything you do seem to fall apart, or at least you believe that it does? Are you one of the millions of people who see things half empty rather than half full? Does your mind control how you see yourself?

The mind can be so powerful. One minute it is singing our praises and the next it is whispering terrible things about us in our ears. Of course we believe it, and why should we see things any differently since it has always said the same things to us, "You are a loser"?

Where did all this negativity come from? Has it ever been any different? In our childhood we were the child who was never praised and who always felt like we were being compared to others. It doesn't really matter whether this was true or not because that was how we saw it. The whispering never stopped, and now, as adults, we have no true value of ourselves. We even protect ourselves by predicting that we will fail at whatever we do, just so that if we do fail we can say, "I told you so!"

Perhaps we were the type of child who just needed more encouragement or more praise. This did not make us losers per se, but it did make us less secure. Not every child has that strong sense of self. Sometimes parents do not recognize exactly what their child needs and there is no one to tell them. How long do we live this way? Hearing only the half-empty side of life as opposed to the half full is so destructive to our growth,

It is time for us to grow up. As long as we hear the same negative things we did as children we are stuck. And anything negative that we still believe about ourselves as adults is "childish" thinking. It has no place in our lives anymore. Catch yourself thinking this way and change it! Replace it with something positive. Know that you do this! No longer let the darker side of yourself predict your future. This "stinking thinking" has rented space in our heads for too long. If you continue to think this way, then you are not allowing yourself to grow emotionally. Your life is in your hands now! You are not your history, but you do need to learn from it.

Question: Are you afraid to grow up? What benefits have you received by staying emotionally young?

_____

_____

_____

_____

_____

_____

_____

_____

_____

_____

_____

_____

_____

_____

_____

_____

LARRY ROBINSON

August 24

Are you the type of person who cries a lot? Do you tear up whenever something bothers you or you are angry about something? Do people see you as someone whom they cannot talk to because you are always on the verge of tears? This has no gender attached to it for it hits both sexes.

When you hear something that gets your blood boiling, does your body heat up? Do you remember as a child that you were always crying when something bothered you? This happens to so many children who cannot verbalize their anger. The only thing left to do is cry. The crying releases some of the intensity from the feelings that have built up inside. Unfortunately, as children we do not understand what is going on and it begins to make us feel weak. Children truly have no outlet for their feelings and do not realize that crying can be a form of anger.

This overwhelming feeling does not leave us after childhood. We become conditioned to using our tears as a way of expressing ourselves. Even though we know that it is a destructive way of facing our pain, we continue to do it out of habit, a habit we have a difficult time ridding ourselves of. How many times have we been embarrassed by this mechanism? Who will take us seriously when all we seem to do is cry?

How many of us either do this or know people who are caught up in this childish behavior? We are looked at as fools who seldom have anything worthwhile to say because our tears take over and make us look unstable. No matter how much we try to explain away this behavior no one is really interested in what we say. All they see is what we have presented.

It is time to learn about communication. The crying is our habit, but it is not written in stone that we are stuck with it forever. We must breathe deeply when we feel the crying begin to approach. We must label it for what it is: anger! Breaking bad habits are what growing up is about. This part of us just never had the opportunity to grow. How many relationships have we ruined because we could not express ourselves? How often were our feelings negated with "Here you go again"? We must take ourselves seriously in order to stop this bad habit.

Do not let anyone call you out on this again! You still have your voice, so use it!

Question: Are you someone that takes yourself seriously or do you still engage in childish behaviors?

_____

_____

_____

_____

_____

_____

_____

_____

_____

_____

_____

_____

_____

LARRY ROBINSON

August 25

Why are we always going from one relationship to another? Most of the time when our relationship doesn't feel like it is working or our expectations are so out of whack, we are already looking for the next relationship. Why should we bother to work on something that we believe is the other person's fault?

Perhaps this is what is called being a "relationship addict." We cannot tolerate being by ourselves, and when there is the slightest sense of something not working we are "moving on"! We never really tell the other person that we are actually finished until we have secured the choice of our next relationship. We are not easy to be involved with!

Our expectations of what the other person is supposed to fix in us are way beyond reality. Because we live in such a fantasy world, we do not give anyone a real chance to know us. All they get to see is the best part of us at the start of a relationship. Yes, we put on the act, but the sad thing is that we do not even know that it is an act. We are so convinced that the person we're with is "the one"; that is, until they show us something that we do not like. Do not misunderstand, we do not leave right away, but we begin to shut down against the other person and our hearts begin to get cold.

We have become addicted to relationships because we are so afraid to let anyone get close to us. Why is it that we cannot tolerate true intimacy? Somewhere inside of us we believe that we are not worth very much. Did you ever think that this could be the reason why things do not work out for you?

If you see yourself as this person, do not despair, for there is hope. We must be able to accept this part of ourselves so that we can begin to allow ourselves to be vulnerable to another person. Breathe deeply and allow the other person to see you! Relationships are not about what you do or how you look, but about who you are. It is time to let another person close. As much as you cannot tolerate the closeness, go slow and it will start to feel more comfortable. Try to stay out of your fantasy about the other person and see instead who they really are! It will work!

Assignment: Start with something small that you withheld from another person and introduce it as a topic. Do not make it dramatic, but refer to something that you may have omitted as just part of the conversation. It is no big deal, just say it.

_____

_____

_____

_____

_____

_____

_____

_____

_____

_____

_____

_____

_____

_____

LARRY ROBINSON

AUGUST 26

Do your moods go back and forth from being happy to feeling so sad and down that it is tough to get out of bed? Are you the type of person who is one minute completely excited about something and then the next totally pessimistic? Do you confuse yourself with this kind of behavior?

Mood swings are present in all of us. There is no one who is completely balanced and who can handle everything, both positive and negative, that goes on. There are times when we all feel confused and unsure about ourselves, and this does not necessarily have to be a bad place for us to be. If we think about it, it can be an investigative (exploring) time for us, for sometimes we need these doubts to really check out and research our decisions. The swing of your mood will often depend on how well thought-out your decision is.

Many times, our first reaction is to get very excited because we feel as though we may have found the right answer to either a situation or something that is bothering us. But when we take the time to think about it and we take a step back and actually look at the solution we have come up with, we realize that there is still something missing. This can really pull us down, and we have now created a mood swing.

Mood swings can happen to us often, and they can make not only those around us but even ourselves think that there is something wrong with us. What is wrong is that we do not think things through well enough! We can understand the main idea of what to do, but we have not thought it out entirely. Unfortunately, until we accept this behavior in ourselves we are destined to repeat this until we find the resolution.

Take your time! You do not need to prove anything to anybody except yourself. You can think something out and see all sides of it rather than rush to judge your solution. Stop trying to impress everyone else with the speed of your decisions and figure out whether or not something will really work before you decide! Remember, this is about feeling good about yourself through your choices and how you figure things out, not about impressing others!

Question: How much thought goes into your decision making? Do you rush them or do you linger and take too much time with them?

_____

_____

_____

_____

_____

_____

_____

_____

_____

_____

_____

_____

_____

_____

LARRY ROBINSON

August 27

Are we truly honest with ourselves about our feelings? Do we tend to not want to see the reality of our situations and mask our feelings with beautiful thoughts rather than truth? Are we just incapable of dealing with our negative feelings when we are involved in a relationship?

Are we so "love struck" that nothing will take away the dream we have formed around another person? We do not like real! We hide the truth, not only from the world but also from ourselves. We are so determined to play out our fantasy that we cannot, and oftentimes *will not*, even attempt to look at reality. We are the "excuse makers," and we will defend our relationship no matter what the truth is!

Why are we so dishonest with ourselves and why do we keep our pain locked inside even though we do know the truth? Twisted somewhere within us is the faint glimmer (weak light) of reality. We run so fast because we do not want the truth invading our make-believe world. How long can we really go before we collapse from the weight of our pain?

We have never felt good enough to truly have the relationship we always dreamed of. We take crumbs because we do not believe that we are worth very much. Anyone who can show us what we want to believe is love captures our broken hearts. Remember, our hearts were already broken before this person came into our life.

People who do like who they are do not take less than their expectations. The rest of us feel so low at times and become so desperate to be loved that it does not matter who it is that we allow to love us. This is us creating our own pain!

We are not as blind as we lead the world to believe! We do know when someone is abusing our feelings or is not an honest person. Stop looking to be loved! That time in life when we hoped that we will be loved has passed, and it is now time to learn how to love. And we cannot learn it with someone who is constantly hurting us. When we learn how to truly love someone, then love returns to us. Children need to be loved first in order to understand love. Adults give love, and we need to place that as our priority.

Learning to love another person for who they are is the way we receive love. Can you honestly say that you love the person who is hurting you? If you can, something is very wrong!

Question: Do you think you love too hard? Do you understand that by loving too hard you might not be loving someone at all?

_____

_____

_____

_____

_____

_____

_____

_____

_____

_____

_____

_____

LARRY ROBINSON

AUGUST 28

Are you the type of person who beats themselves up? Are you always criticizing yourself and finding fault with everything you do? Do you often compare yourself to others and in the process feel that ugly tingle of envy and even jealousy? Are you never satisfied with your performance in the tasks you take on?

How did you become so picky about yourself? Why do you always see the glass as half empty rather than half full? Do you ever see any redeeming qualities about yourself, or is everything always negative and critical? This is so painful to walk around with. You can never say anything positive about yourself, and you forget what it's like to be able to take compliments in life.

When we have this issue we make everything we do a competition. We cannot see anything in front of us but winning. Even when we take on challenges that are way beyond our reach we are relentless in our abuse of ourselves. We will not quit, even when there is no chance of us succeeding. And this is not because we are incapable, but because we have strayed very far away from our own reality that would typically warn us when something is too hard!

Life is way too short to never come up on its positive side. What is your rush for perfection? Do you even know that there is no such thing as perfection? We can only try for it! Who do you know that has actually reached it? And this is not to say that we should not do our best, but be realistic with yourself. If you want to compete, then compete against yourself. This is the way to improve yourself. And remember, there will always be someone who will come along with a more improved skill set than you have. What reward do you think you will achieve if you can never relax and are always beating on yourself?

It is time to find the place inside of you that is self-accepting, and it's time to relax a little bit and enjoy life! It goes by so fast! Where will you be if you do not understand this? Slow down and stop the war on yourself!

Question: How have you viewed perfection as a negative in your life? Think about what perfection means and how often you beat yourself up for not attaining it.

_____

_____

_____

_____

_____

_____

_____

_____

_____

_____

_____

_____

_____

_____

LARRY ROBINSON

August 29

Do you look at what other people have and think "I could never achieve that!" Does it make you want to quit on yourself and, thus, you end up with this defeated attitude? This topic about success and failure, envy and jealousy, will be with *mindful thinking* for a while. Until we begin to understand that there is nothing that we cannot do if we put our energy into it, this topic will keep popping up.

Jealousy can be such a horrible feeling inside. It takes so much out of us to "put another person down," and that is what we do when we are jealous. You see we have to destroy their accomplishments in order to hide our own lack. How "small" does that make us?

Envy is a much healthier feeling, for when we envy someone, we still can strive to achieve what they have if we desire it enough.(I love your new car so I will work harder to get one!) But jealousy is a whole different story. Jealousy pushes us to despise those we believe are better than us. It makes us mean and ugly at times (remember looking in the mirror, if you are jealous do not expect to like the way you look) and only wants to find fault with the other person so we can feel better than them.

As long as you are always comparing yourself to others you will experience jealousy. Let's get this correct: We are only different from one another. As long as you insist on dealing with the "better than" and "less than" in life, you will go NOWHERE!

You are your own person. Your life does not depend on how others see you but how you see yourself. STOP COMPARING and start looking at WHAT YOU HAVE and build on those. If you tell yourself you have nothing, then you have nothing! We all are equal, but at the same time, each of us is unique. Find this uniqueness and you will begin to grow. There is no "I CAN'T!"

Question: How do you deal with being envious of someone else? Does it ever turn to jealousy?

LARRY ROBINSON

AUGUST 30

How to we let go of someone whom we believe we love yet cannot get along with? It seems that all we do is bicker and argue over the same things and neither one of us is willing to change their ideas. What if we have been together for years and we cannot make a commitment to each other because of these differences? How painful it is to let go, or is it really?

After going through the same struggles almost weekly, would we believe that we would continue to love the other? Perhaps this is our excuse because neither one of us can really make a commitment to the other, nor are we willing to support what the other really wants. Do you really believe that this is love, or is it more of a conditioning that we both share that allows us to accept failure rather than what we both say we want in life? If neither person is willing to compromise, then why would we see this as love? Unconditional love is on parts, not just one or the other. If you both cannot give to each other for what the other needs, then why do you call this love? It sounds more like an addiction, for it never ceases to stop repeating the same pattern. True adult love is what we give to the other, not what we receive, and so when two selfish people try to form a relationship they are bound to fail.

There are many of you out there who have sacrificed a lot in order to support your loved one, and you are lucky because you have gotten what you've needed over the long run. Well, good for you, but there are those of you who just cannot give true love. This is your damage and not the other's. Maybe it is time to wake up and really see what you have lost because you wanted to be given to more than you wanted to give. What a shame!

Assignment: Take one issue that is between the two of you and try and walk in the other's shoes. Try and understand what they are feeling and do not make it about you, but about them. This is difficult but not impossible.

LARRY ROBINSON

August 31

How anxious a person are you? Do you worry about everything and need to feel in control of every situation in life, even at the cost of intruding in other people's decision making? Do you read a book and at the end you have no idea what you read because your mind is always focused on something else? Is it impossible for you to take a break and sit quietly without getting up repeatedly to stick your nose into someone else's business? Are you the type of person that worries about tomorrow, next week, and even next year and who creates a crisis before one happens because your mind is always in the future?

Here's a story about a mother and father who were recovering alcoholics. They were so afraid that their son would drink that they kept him in the house throughout his entire high school career. They allowed no weekends out, any friends over except those in the neighborhood, and they did not allow him to drive. They thought they were keeping him safe. He got high honors in school because he had nothing else to do but study. As soon as he graduated from school he moved out of his house. Three weeks later he died of alcohol poisoning. His parents were devastated. But what really killed him?

If you suffer from this anxiety you probably have an anxiety disorder. Where do we get such fears, and how are we supposed to live? This anxiety in us is old, and most of the time we will find that if we trace its history it will take us back to childhood. As children, some of us took on the image of being tough, reckless, and a daredevil. We were constantly trying to hide our fears by doing just the opposite, putting ourselves in danger. On the other hand, some of us were the good little child who always did the right thing and never said a word. All of our fears stayed hidden, and we swallowed everything and the result was anxiety.

Anxiety always comes to us when we hide feelings, and it comes big and does not stop until we try to discover what is underneath it. It is a clue that we are troubled, and if you do not view it as an aid or a signal or a clue, then it becomes a way of life. Once you see it this way you free yourself from wreaking havoc on everyone else.

This is your issue and you must see it this way. Do not be afraid to look at yourself, for anxiety can lead to unbelievable emotional and physical illnesses.

Assignment: Have you been plagued with anxiety? Try and see if you are angry when you are not anxious. Can you see a relationship between the two?

_____

_____

_____

_____

_____

_____

_____

_____

_____

_____

_____

_____

LARRY ROBINSON

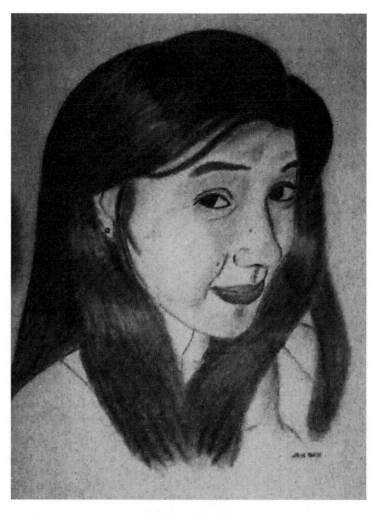

Jem Rose Maitlong
Philippines

September 1

"I don't understand why you cannot help me. I have always been there for you, and then all of a sudden you're too busy to help me move? I don't understand you, and after I've sacrificed so much of my time and energy for you. Why are you being so distant and mean to me?"

Can you hear the voice of a "victim" in the above quote? A "victim of life" is someone who needs to remind others of what they have done for them and who continues to complain about their own life. Their biggest weapon is guilt and they have no problem inflicting it on the next person in line who has "failed" them. In fact, nearly everyone has failed them and they will not hesitate to remind you of that failure. They like to combine two feelings to get the other person to feel really bad. The guilt is one, but the other is less obvious, and that is anger.

They get us to feel angry but also guilty at the same time. This combination really freezes us so that we ultimately become their servant. We hate listening to them, and they are right, we really don't want to help them because we've had to hear over and over again how much they've been through in life and how lonely they are. We have repeatedly heard about how no one cares about their life anymore!

We have all had someone in our life who has exhibited these traits. Most often it is an elderly parent, especially mothers, who cannot let go of their children. Why do they hold on? They are afraid of being alone and having to face themselves. Each one of us must face ourselves at some point in our lives, and it is usually toward the end of life. We start to panic and look into things that we do not want to know about. If we have a child, then we can continue to remind ourselves, and them, that we gave a lot and that it is now someone else's *turn*. "Take care of me!" is the message that is given out to those around them. And they mean it! They forget their fear at times and create havoc all around them because that fear becomes bigger and bigger the more they're ignored. If you thought you could shut them out, forget it! You will be (or already have been) hounded by them and you now know that until they die you will get no relief. You must be willing to change your reaction to them in order to remain sane.

How do you change this? First, you recognize that they are human and afraid, but you probably already know that this is an uncomfortable situation for them to be in because they've been this way your whole life. But it is time to stop being their child and see, instead, the child in them! Remember that when you get around parents you definitely become their child and they treat you as they always did. But you are not their "baby" or "little person" anymore! They are now actually looking for safety from you and you can provide it by not feeding their fears.

There are very few of us who can "kill off" a parent before they have died. And by that I mean that because of some major unresolved issue they were already dead to you in your mind. But that will not happen, because that guilt will appear again and make you fall to your knees! Can you imagine what it would feel like if they died and you didn't have closure? Would you really be able to go to their funeral when you had already killed them off? I doubt it!

There is only one way out of this and that is to do the right thing for ourselves. When we come to that place we will see things a little differently, and they become more vulnerable to us. Go beyond their complaints and into the heart of the matter. They are afraid of death and do not know how to either deal with it or tell us. Do not let yourself be taken advantage of, but remember to find a balance of not too much and not too little attention. You will then see a different side of you from the one that runs from them!

Assignment: Describe the ups and downs of the relationship with your mother and father. Look to see how they deal with their feelings. Which one are you like? Which traits have you inherited?

_____

_____

_____

_____

LARRY ROBINSON

September 2

Are you really committed to changing your life, or are you an "I want to want to" change my life person? And what this means is that the thought about you changing constantly stays in your head, but you never take action! It is like being in an alternative universe where you can actually see the change. You see yourself living the change and living as a happier person, but again, it is not real because you have not fully committed to changing your life. Well, the first thing you need to do is to come back into focus and join the rest of us, because most of us are daydreamers and big talkers.

Our lives keep spinning out of control, and every time we believe that we are actually achieving change something pops up that brings us right back to the beginning. We rush too quickly to fix something that has gone wrong and miss the point. You do not "fix" things, because that means they are *only mended.* You actually have to commit yourself to a better life, and sometimes it is more important to take one step at a time than it is to take on a major overhaul, which can often result in you becoming overwhelmed.

How many of us say we are going to take on all of our addictions at one time, and then wind up not even being able to resolve a single one because there are just too many to deal with? "I am going to lose weight, stop smoking, and not party as much." Which one of those has worked? I thought so, not one!

These pages are written for you to begin to challenge yourself with your life issues. They are not an answer, but rather a beginning to finding one that is your own answer! A coach is a guide for your journey, not the answer to it. You have to figure out what it is you are striving for, and your coach will give you the plays you need to score healthy, valuable points along your journey. And it never stops unless you give up on it.

There is no one who cannot change their life, only those who elect not to work on it. Do not tell yourself that you are so depressed that you cannot, because you're only kidding yourself. And if that really is the case, then get yourself some antidepressants to lift some of the "down" in your life. But at the same time beware, because if you are on medication and you're waiting for the big change to happen, forget it. There is no "magic pill"! Work with it and you will grow. And if you self-medicate you will never change, because you are only stuffing your issues down into your mind, where they mate and grow new ones.

This is the fall, a time when everything changes again. This is the time to let go. Write a list of all the things you want to let go of and then prioritize them. Let us begin together, one at a time, to walk the path of change! Make this commitment to yourself! There is no "perfection," only recovery in life, and you are going to recover your life!

Assignment: If you were to make a commitment to changing one thing in your life today what would it be?

_____

_____

_____

_____

_____

_____

_____

_____

_____

_____

_____

_____

LARRY ROBINSON

SEPTEMBER 3

D o you respect money? Do you know what it means to value what you have and to live within your means? Has money become your god, meaning that it will be the "cure all and end all" of your problems? Are you someone who believes that you respect money when in actuality you have become a slave to it? We often confuse money with happiness! You can be happy without an excess of money, but can you be happy with more than you need? In fact, for so many of us this is what keeps us in bad and destructive relationships. We either are afraid of losing our lifestyle or we believe that we cannot earn what we need. Money is by no means a friend!

Money is the root of a lot of pain in our lives. Yes, we need it to survive and even thrive, but how much does that entail? Do you feel like you have spending habits that are out of control? Has this been a way for you to cope with your unhappiness or try to "keep up with the Joneses" (an American expression that says we need to do better than our neighbors)? Do you work hard and still never seem to have enough? This could be because spending money is the "charge" in your life, and without the charge you feel empty. Have you substituted money for love? If you have, it actually means that you would stay in a loveless relationship because of your lifestyle or your inability to recreate it. Maintaining your lifestyle, you see, is more important to you than loving another person. And notice that I said *loving* rather than "being loved." You have been loved before, but at some point you determined it was not enough. Getting carried away with material possessions became more important to you than being a loving person. This is our shame in life.

The most wonderful thing about life is that we can change things. We do not have to be a slave to money, for with it comes a loss of freedom, and that is the freedom to make the choice for ourselves that we do not need money! You might say, "How could that be? I need money to live, and I am dependent on my spouse or partner to support me." Well, that is still a choice that you make. And if it means making your life, your children's lives, and your spouse's life miserable because of money, then there is definitely something wrong with this picture! No one but you have said that you cannot take care of yourself or make decisions or even earn a living for yourself. You have been brainwashed if this is the case.

Do you really want to achieve your own success? Even if you believe that you cannot, read this entry over and over again until you realize that it is not the lack of money that holds you back, but the lack of a true belief in yourself. Believe that you do not need more than enough money to be happy! Yes, money helps, but it cannot replace what is missing for you. Take control today and begin to realize that you can do anything you set your mind to, even making money without it controlling you!

Question: How have you viewed money in your life? Is it a positive or negative? Do you never feel that you have enough? Is money a major issue in your relationship?

_____

_____

_____

_____

_____

_____

_____

_____

_____

_____

SEPTEMBER 4

"I want to love you more than anyone could ever love you. You are my world and I your universe."

Don't you wish that you could say this about your own relationship? Why is it that this statement is only seen as a fantasy of what we wanted when we married rather than what our reality is now? Couples come into counseling beaten down by the life that they have created. Some feel hopeless that they can change, yet do not want a divorce. What happened to that wonderful feeling of love that was there in the beginning? Why did it disappear and we got left with anger and resentment? We no longer discuss things, but instead react to each other with indifference or meanness. Just the looks that we can give can tell us how disgusted we are with each other.

Actually, we are afraid of each other; afraid of what we have to face by telling the other how we are really feeling. We lie and say, "I'm fine," when asked if anything is wrong, but in reality the person who is asking doesn't really want to know, while the person answering does not want the confrontation that is likely to come about if they actually tell the truth about how they really feel!

Do all couples get to this point where we cannot listen to each other any longer? If there is no respect shared between the couple, then yes, they do. What then brings us to that place of disrespect?

We really do not know our spouse until we live with them. We do not know what one person brings with him/her into the relationship from their past, nor do we know what the other has experienced. Our attachments to the lessons we learned as children, which are not conscious, dictate our automatic responses to conflict with our partners. In observing our parents in their relationship, it is almost as if we inhaled the negativity that we saw between them and acted it out in our own relationships. Since the learning processes that both have experienced are so different, there are bound to be struggles over who is right and who is wrong. Soon we have stockpiled enough negative feelings that the slightest disagreement can turn into a vicious fight. Any thought of respecting the other person goes out the window and we are left with resentments and hurts.

This does not have to be the way things are, but it is more the norm than not. How do we change these behaviors that we have been so rooted in? How often do you feel hopeless that you will not be heard or will be put down for your opinion?

Assignment: Sit down with your spouse/partner and allow each other five minutes to talk about their day. Do not challenge anything. Allow the other to speak and wait for your turn to speak. Learn to listen. How does this feel when you have this space set aside for each other?

_____

_____

_____

_____

_____

_____

_____

_____

_____

_____

_____

SEPTEMBER 5

Are you consumed at times by self-pity? Do you even know what it means? So many of us cannot even look at this issue because we're afraid it might make us look like we are consumed by ourselves. Well, that's just it, we are and it is so difficult for us to admit it.

What is self-pity and how did we get this issue in our lives? We never started out in life feeling sorry for ourselves, but we certainly can end up there. Self-pity is an issue that hits all of us at one time or another, and it is there to serve as a clue to our unhappiness. We are definitely missing something in our lives in order to get to this place where we make our life all about what has gone wrong for us.

Self-pity can go deeper than what the surface tells us. It is actually our cry for help, and we do not even know that is what we are looking for. Others think that we are always making life about ourselves, and on the surface we are, but there is more to this than just being in the spotlight (the center) of life. So much of the time we feel empty and neglected. We feel as if no one will ever understand us or recognize us, and once we make the focus about ourselves we cannot stop! It becomes like an addiction and it shows no mercy for us or anyone else around us. We are looked at as selfish and needy.

When we are in self-pity mode we need to be guided to stop and look at where we are. And rather than continuously humiliate ourselves by looking for validation (to be recognized), we need to look at ourselves! No one can fill that emptiness. It is leftover from our childhood, when the only way we might have received attention was if we were sick or rejected by others.

We so desperately need to be valued that we put ourselves in the opposite place. We are now seen as, "Oh no, not her/him again! Don't they ever get tired of complaining?" It is time to stop this and grow by keeping our issues out of other people's lives. We alone can fix ourselves. No one can do it for us!

Question: Do you secretly feel that you are always against the rest of the world? Do you feel that no one understands you?

LARRY ROBINSON

September 6

A re you someone who feels afraid a lot? Do you wake up afraid in the morning and lie there in bed scared to start your day? No one knows that you experience such fear, for you know how to cover it up.

This is not new to you, and as you get older the fear does not get weaker but instead takes on a whole new space inside your head. The fear itself can be terrifying, and you are alone with it because no one wants to hear another person talk about their fear! You have become an expert at hiding it.

When you were young, it was the bogeyman (night monster) who came to you and whispered scary things in your ear. Now, you whisper to yourself all the negative thinking that you can feel and now you are worse about scaring yourself than the bogeyman ever was! You have become your own worst enemy!

The fear you experience comes from the feeling of being unprotected as a child. Your feelings were not listened to and you might even have been laughed at many times for having fears. Parents can be very hard on children who are fearful. The most important thing is that you are no longer a child!

Instead of giving into your fears and remaining frozen, stand up to them and face them! You will be amazed once you determine that you can do this. The fears actually get weaker as you get stronger, and what once was a huge fear now seems silly. There is no monster hiding under your bed, there is just you who have become conditioned to your own fear!

Assignment: Make a list of everything you are afraid of. Now list the issues that you have held on to from childhood and the ones that came into being when you reached adulthood. Are they different?

_____

_____

_____

LARRY ROBINSON

September 7

D o you always feel let down by other people? Are you always feeling as if your expectations must be off because people do not live up to their promises? Are you constantly putting yourself down because others fail you and you make it your fault? What then did you do wrong?

How often do you ask people to do something for you and end up feeling abandoned and unimportant? Have you ever thought that perhaps your expectations of the other person are way off the mark? It is important to think about who the person is that you are asking for assistance before you actually ask them for help. Did you forget that they always have some excuse for you that make it impossible for them to be there for you? Is this their fault, or do you need to take responsibility for asking the wrong person?

Who wouldn't feel rejected by someone who fails to follow through on a promise? But are you someone who sets yourself up to be disappointed by others when in fact you need to be looking at yourself and who it is you choose to be there for you?

Perhaps this is about how stubborn you are in refusing to look at your reality. You keep choosing the wrong people to be there in your life. What are that other person's limitations? Do you even know? They might be all about themselves, and although they may have the right intentions, they do not have the right "heart" to follow through. They are limited, and yet you take it to heart and make it about yourself.

Enough is enough! The world does not revolve around us as much as we really want it to. Growing up means that we have the ability to see who others are before we set them up to fail and we fall into our "rejected self." No matter how much it hurts to realize this, isn't it better than constantly feeling like there is something wrong with you? Look and think before you ask for the impossible!

Question: Do you dream about what it would be like to have someone there for you but are always disappointed when they do not meet your expectations?

LARRY ROBINSON

SEPTEMBER 8

What is it that makes us feel so abandoned and rejected? The most minor act from another person can cause this enormous flare-up of rejection inside of us. What has happened to our strength and determination that we can take care of ourselves?

We can hang on to every word or action that another person says or does, and yet we interrupt their action by interpreting it as a personal assault against us! Are we crazy or is this real and it is just that our feelings have become programed to pick up the message as unwanted and unworthy? This has been going on for as long as we can remember, and it does not look like it is going away. Are we destined to suffer the pangs of rejection forever?

So often we rely on the world to make us feel better about ourselves, and the end result is that we are at the world's mercy. We want so much to be valued and approved of. Any sign that this will not happen sends us into a panic, and to make matters worse, we are relentless in our need to change the feeling that we are not wanted. It no longer becomes about how the other person feels (even if we read them wrong), but all about us instead!

It is time to grow and see that the world is not that interested in rejecting us! We reject ourselves and interpret this as rejection from others. We are so sensitive to others that before they even finish a sentence we already feel rejected.

Where else did this idea that we are "reject-able" come from but our childhood? There are a multitude of reasons for this, but at this point it really does not matter. What does matter is that we have this *plague* and it is up to us to see reality instead of creating a false one!

Assignment: Do you always think that people think less of you? Are you someone who never can give yourself positive feedback?

LARRY ROBINSON

September 9

Why do we hold on to issues or situations or even people for such a long time? How is it that we cannot let go of pain and instead play with it as if it is a game that we have to win? We must win or else all the things that we felt about ourselves that were negative will be true!

Those of us who cannot let go are stubborn people. We have to get that other person to want us no matter what price we pay. We cannot see who they are, for we have placed our value on their acceptance of us. We do not care how much pain they have caused us, we continue to hold on!

"Stubborn," say the word to yourself. First, start off slowly and softly and then increase the sound you make until it is really loud! Did you do it, or did you think it was stupid and rushed past it? If that is the case, you just proved to yourself that you are stubborn and that you only really do what you want to do! Now, if you were told to jump off a bridge, then you would not be stubborn. You would be wise not to follow. You have to be the one to determine what is really right for you or not.

How much pain can our stubborn self tolerate? An enormous amount if we are truly stubborn people. We wonder to ourselves, "Why does life treat us this way?" But the answer is not about life, but about how we treat ourselves. We cannot see our reality when we are caught up in it. The first step in changing this is to accept that this is who we are! Once you do that it becomes so much easier to let go of bad people or situations!

Question: What is one thing that your stubbornness just cannot let go of? It plagues you like a terminal virus but you still obsess over this situation.

_____

_____

_____

LARRY ROBINSON

September 10

We are back again to forgiveness. This, without a doubt, can be one of the hardest issues we can experience. We have been hurt and the feeling goes into our soul. We cannot stop the pain of what was done to us. We think that we want to forgive, but our heart is heavy with feelings of betrayal and rejection. Our sense of being abandoned goes very deep.

Forgiveness is not an exercise that we are supposed to complete. There is no rule that says we must forgive those who have hurt and tricked us. We must allow ourselves to be angry if we are going to get through this pain in our heart. We need to recognize that the pain is real and not listen to those who tell us, "Don't worry, you'll get over it!" Sometimes we do not want to get over it!

Why would we hold on to such pain when we certainly can work on letting it go? We need to be the one who says, "I am done with it and I need to move on!" Remember, forgiveness is a gift that we give those who have harmed us, and we are the only ones who can determine when that happens.

We must learn how to gain control over our pain. Each time we go back into our pain we end up experiencing the hurt once again. Only when we are depleted of the poison that we were left with can we begin the healing of our heart. The important thing is that we are always in control of it. We just do not know it!

When we truly for the wrong done to forgive someone us we do not need to let them back into our lives. That is our choice. We know that we will not forget the pain. The forgiveness is not for the other person but for us, because it frees us from the situation that occurred. We do not have to forget! Free yourself of repeating the pain!

Assignment: Make a list of those people that you still need to forgive. What reasons do you tell yourself why you cannot and should not forgive them?

LARRY ROBINSON

September 11

Why do we judge ourselves as better than or less than? How did we get to that place where we proclaim ourselves as being better than others, while viewing ourselves as less than those we deem to have more than we do? What a cruel thing it is for children to have to go through this before they are even old enough to realize they are victims of this screwed-up world. Why should any child have to view themselves as less than another or better than a neighbor?

We are guilty of instilling this in them. We make them compete to be better, or we drag them down to make them feel inadequate. Do we mean to do this? Maybe it is a reflection of ourselves, and maybe it was passed down from a previous generation just as we pass it down to our own children. We make this world what it is! We teach our children what we have learned, and it isn't always pretty! Maybe we try to instill good values in our children, but we also teach them dishonesty, racism, and how to buck the system. So what are they to believe? Are we the role models we think we are? Do we chastise our children for the very things they see in us?

Today is a very sad day as we remember what happened on 9/11/2001, but have we changed since then, or have we become more bitter and "holier than thou" in our attitudes toward others? We created 9/11, all of us in the world, collectively. We judge how other people live and pray, and we think that our way is better than their way, no matter who we are! Do you get that!

Today, just take a moment and close your eyes and envision a world of serenity. Yes, I know that is a fantasy, but give yourself that luxury and then give someone you love a hug. After that, give someone you don't even know a hug! Make that vision real, if just for a moment!

Question: What are you thankful for? Do you stop enough times in your life to think about what you have rather than what you do not have?

LARRY ROBINSON

SEPTEMBER 12

D o we really understand what disappointment is? It is not like any other feeling we experience because it has no true *roots* to it. When we get angry about something we have the situation in front of us and it directs our feelings toward someone or something else.

Disappointment stands alone and has no ending to it unless we stop it ourselves. Often we do not know how to deal with disappointment because the feeling attached to it is no more than. "I am so sorry that it did not happen," or "I feel sad that we cannot go on vacation." That is it! It has no other meaning than "I hoped, I wished, I wanted." These are the statements that disappointment produces, no more and no less.

When we do not know how to deal with disappointments we push them to the next level. Now we feel down, depressed, and empty because of the disappointment of not succeeding at something or receiving something. Anything that has disappointments attached to it can lead to feeling like a failure. And boy, is it ever easy to turn a disappointment into a failure!

Because we do not recognize disappointment as a true feeling, we give it more power than it needs. It is almost as if we need it to be greater than it really is. We can even make mountains out of molehills (an exaggeration of making something out of nothing).

Next time the feeling of disappointment comes up, do not try to find a "greater" feeling than it really is. Instead of saying to yourself, "I wish I had gotten that job" or "I wish I had made friends with that person" or "I wish that date was better because I was really hoping something would come of it," just say, "Whatever!"

"Oh well!" needs to be our response, because life goes on. And if we take every disappointment to the next level (depression, anger, sadness), we are creating pain where there does not need to be any! Disappointment is not pain; it is just what it is! Now, say the word and that is the extent of the importance that we will attach to it!

Question: Are you still harboring obsessive feelings about something that you were disappointed about from your past? Do you get heated when it comes up again in your life?

_____

_____

_____

_____

_____

_____

_____

_____

_____

_____

_____

_____

September 13

Are you a competitive person? Do you need to be first or right in everything you do? Do you need to win? Is it more of a need for you than a want? These are questions that if you answer honestly and really look inside yourself you will find the true answers to as to why this goes on.

Does your anxiety rise when you inject competition into your life? It is certainly fine to be competitive, but when it becomes an obsession and gets out of hand, then we have problems. We become relentless in our pursuit to win! Winning becomes everything, but the problem is that it is not enough! We have to win at everything and we burn ourselves out with the neediness we feel when we are in danger of not winning. What failures we must be if we do not win!

Our whole sense of self is then based on our reliance on winning. We are nothing and no one if we do not win! How dangerous is this to you? Are you no one and nothing unless you shine all the time? Do you alienate others because of this out of control drive that rears its ugly head when you smell competition? Do you lose all sense of what is fair and right when this comes up for you?

We must face the fact that there will always be someone who comes along who will be better than us. We need to learn that in competition we compete against no one but ourselves in order to better who and where we are! If you run a race and turn around to see who is behind you, you take away from yourself at that moment! Set your goal to beat yourself! This is the true competition. What truly matters in life is that we do the best we can and that our goal is to achieve improvement!

Pressure to perform and get recognition is why we can get so out of control when we enter into competition. Make this a beginning for you to compete only against your own record or grade or whatever it is that you believe you must win. You will be amazed at how much better you really do when you take the pressure off of yourself to beat everyone else!

Question: Have you been accused of being competitive and denied it? Give an example of your competitiveness and how it plays out.

LARRY ROBINSON

September 14

Rejection! How it hurts! Why is it that we take it so hard when we are first going out with someone? Why do we take it like it is the end of the world? There are so many different ways in which we can be rejected and so many different ways in which we handle it.

We all get rejected in some way or other every day. Think about it: someone is too busy to talk to us and we can feel rejected. We don't get that promotion at work and we become real angry and feel passed over. Our spouse is in an "edgy mood" and we take their silence as a rejection, even though we never bothered to ask them what was wrong. Our children yell at us and we feel rejected. We could go on and on about different ways we get rejected. Let's face it: we are too sensitive. How do we go through the day personalizing everything that comes our way? God, we are down and feeling so alone. This makes it really important to check out how you dealt with rejection as a child.

Children have no understanding of other people's emotions. Some are apt to take everything a parent says that doesn't meet their needs as rejection! "You don't love me!" is usually how they deal with the word "no." If they begin to feel that way in school when they raise their hand and are not called on or aren't picked for a team, then they begin down the path of rejection. Without the right help in working these issues out, why would they be any different when they are adults?

Remember to ask yourself, "Why would I want to be with someone who doesn't want to be with me?" Self-esteem really plays a huge role in how we deal with rejection and we need to keep a firm understanding that we are strong enough to deal with not being wanted! If both parties in a situation are unsure of wanting the other, then why do we then take it as rejection when they go first and tell us that they are not interested? Check out your ego. How big is it?

Question: Are you able to see yourself as emotionally immature at times? Are you still feeling like a child when it comes to acceptance and rejection?

LARRY ROBINSON

September 15

*I*ntimacy, we all crave it and know that it was what we promised each other when we started this relationship. "I want you. I want to be so close to you and know that we can be best friends." This is how we felt. Making love in the beginning was wonderful. We responded to each other as if we had always been together and knew the depth of our feelings in our actions toward each other. We didn't have to tell each other what felt good, *it all did* because our love was present.

What happened that in no time at all foreplay was gone and things just started to feel mechanical? Neither one of us really took the time to talk to each other. There was nothing wrong with sex until it too was 1, 2, 3, and over, and neither one of us wanted to hold the other, have warm talks, or cuddle. It was "I need to wash up" or "I'm hungry." The worst was just rolling over and falling asleep with our backs to each other! How empty it all has become.

What brought us to this place where we no longer feel that charge we had with each other in the beginning? Well, that charge cannot last forever, but it needs to be replaced with true caring for the person we are spending our life with. This caring comes out of respect and gratitude for how we have handled the ups and downs of our life together. Yes, there is unconditional love, but only if you work out your resentments and begin to understand who each other is. We are not the same person! We do not handle things the same way, but that does not mean one of us is right and the other wrong. Whenever there is that dynamic, someone loses, and in a relationship no one can lose. Understanding equals winning! Look at your relationship and look at who you are! Would you make love to you if you were the other person?

Assignment: Make a list of all the issues that you have had with respecting your partner/spouse's feelings. Do you not want to listen at times? Do you ignore the emotional impact that the feelings have on your spouse/partner?

LARRY ROBINSON

Photo by Stephanie Cavallo
Falmouth, Massachusetts, USA

"When you are in a relationship and you are giving love and respect to the other person, and if you are getting it back, then it is a perfectly balanced relationship. Do not look to see how much you give and how much you are getting back. . . . Numbers look good in math, not relationships."

—Jaya Manjo Bhaskaren, Gwalior, India

SEPTEMBER 16

Where does shame come from? Why do we experience it so intensely when we have done something wrong? Is shame a learned behavior or is it something we are born with? Have you ever fought with someone and said things that you thought you would never say and the aftereffect is a deep sense of shame and humiliation?

These feelings are often ones that eat away at the core of our heart, so why do we go back and do it again? It is almost as if once we start this "shame cycle" we cannot get out of it until we have reached our bottom, which is different for each of us. Our bottom is a very disgusting place for us, and reaching it takes truly knowing that you have wounded someone with your words or actions. This is when we can experience that shame. It is only when we have destroyed someone else's self-esteem.

What happened to us to cause such wrongdoing inside of us? All of this behavior came out of our childhood, where we were berated by our parents for doing something they believed was shameful. They would shame us with familiar phrases like "How could you" or "Why would you be so bad?" They were so frequent, in fact, that they caused us to have low self-esteem. We heard them over and over again and it was pounded into us that we were shameful children, and eventually we carried this feeling into adulthood, where we repeat this cycle of shame and remain numb to its real effect. It is only when we break the other person that we feel the shame of our actions, which in turn triggers the stored shame from our childhood!

It is time to recognize that we were not horrible children but were too much for our parents to handle, so we got the blame. Do not repeat this cycle with your children, spouses, or partners. Remember that you understand all too well what that feeling of shame is all about! When you stop shaming others, you will begin to love.

Question: Are you someone that has shamed others? Do you not think before you speak and end up feeling ashamed about hurting someone else with your words?

LARRY ROBINSON

September 17

D o you remember having a best friend in high school, the person who really knew you and you, them? Do you remember all the times that you would talk to each other about things that no one else knew and how you could trust them to the end of times! This was the person whom you dreamed with and the one whom you sneaked cigarettes and drank with when no one else in your group knew about it. You knew your secrets were safe with them and you never doubted their loyalty; that is, until someone came along who had more to offer them than you did. Maybe it included joining a more popular group with more prestige, or maybe it involved an upward social-climbing position in school. Do you remember how horrible and betrayed you felt?

This happened to almost all of us with one person or another. The worst was when your group turned against you! Well, how much has changed today in terms of friendships? You are the trusting soul, the one who is loyal to the end. Then why do you pick people who use you until they move on to bigger and better things?

We pick these people because we want them to want our friendship! We don't bother to see who they were friends with before and why they are no longer friends today. Why don't you wonder why? Well, it could be that you are drawn to people whom you want to want your friendship rather than see who they really are. When you do not take the time to learn to trust someone and then they disappoint you over and over again, your motive for the friendship has to be questioned. Maybe you actually gave up friends to be friends with this person, and maybe things come back to us when we have ulterior motives about friends.

Your best friend should be your spouse. Why would your friend know more about your feelings than your spouse? Ask yourself why does social climbing even happen!

Question: Who is your best friend and why? If it is not your spouse/ partner, do you see something wrong with this?

LARRY ROBINSON

September 18

Are you an appreciative person? Do you value what you have achieved in this life? Are you someone who is thankful for family, friends, and what you have earned? Or do you still think about what you do not have?

There are so many of us who see that glass as half empty rather than half full. We see it in everything we do. We see it in our spouse's behavior and we see it in our children. We are always complaining that nothing is satisfying and we want more! It doesn't come out in direct form at times, but you'd best believe that your family can simply just look at your face and know!

Do you compare what you have to what others have? Do you feel that you are less than if you don't measure up? Or if the roles are reversed and you actually have more than others, do you let people know what you have?

This is not about "things," it is about how you feel about yourself! You have never felt good enough in this life. You measure your value by what you have obtained, not by what you can give. The person who has kindness and compassion on the inside is a wealthy person. You can say that it doesn't "put bread on the table," but maybe the half-full person strives for enough for themselves and does not feel jealous about what someone else has.

The person who is half-full is not obsessed with material things, but they are *givers*. When was the last time you didn't think about yourself, but instead looked at the world and said, "What can I do for this broken world?" When have you followed "well done is better than well said"? Make this what you are and learn that giving is how we are thankful for what we have!

Question: Which type of person are you, "well done" or "well said"? Are you always saying you are going to do something but never actually doing it?

SEPTEMBER 19

What if you do not know that you are an addict? How often have you been out and do not remember what you did that night? It all becomes a fuzzy mess inside your head. Oh, you know how to rationalize that you partied too much, but there is a lingering feeling inside that you lost time in your life. You wake up and do not know how you got home, or even worse, whose bed you are in and what really happened! Now, this might be the extreme for those who are truly addicted to alcohol or drugs, but there are so many kinds of addicts who do not even realize that they are addicts!

There is the person who comes home every night and simply must have their glass of wine. Even if it's only one glass (which usually ends up a half or full bottle) there is a driven compulsion to have it. Take it away for a week and see for yourself. There is also the addict who only drinks on weekends and who from Monday through Friday doesn't touch a drop or take a pill. These people often say, "We are the responsible people. We know how to control our pleasures!" These are the "weekend addicts" who start Friday night and go straight through until Sunday. Does this sound familiar when it comes to yourself or someone you know?

Then there is the abuser, who doesn't touch alcohol or drugs for long periods but who routinely goes out on a bender three or four times a year. They save it up and they are "binge users." There are so many more to talk about, but you know who you are, unless you're in denial, in which case you'll convince yourself that this doesn't even apply to you.

Which one of these are you and what effect is this having on you and your family? Are your children growing up to be adult children of alcoholics or drug users? Great, they can be afraid of life for the rest of their lives. Stress and your life brought you here, and as long as you continue your life will spin out of control. This applies to both men and women, and do not point fingers unless it is at yourself. Now it is still not too late, but tomorrow might be! And do not blame genetics! It is only a possible path. Take the responsible step and look at yourself!

LARRY ROBINSON

Assignment: Do you really know what your addictive behaviors are? Remember it takes looking at ourselves very closely to understand our addict ways.

_____

_____

_____

_____

_____

_____

_____

_____

_____

_____

_____

_____

_____

_____

_____

_____

September 20

A re you somebody who is extremely hard on yourself and cannot stop it even when you try? Does this condition cause you to be demanding and place greater expectations on those around you? During the times when you are caught up in this nightmare of not doing enough or not feeling good enough, do you lose it with others who you are close to because you think you are failing?

There is something in all of us that takes us back into childhood and which determines how strong this issue is. Some of us have above-average expectations of ourselves and we are determined to do better. This feeling is based on our own knowledge that we could do better but that we can tend to get lazy. Now, most of our laziness comes out of our adolescence, during which our hormones controlled so much of our behavior (which, by the way, parents forget), but some of us are driven by shame! We feel shame that we "bagged out" on ourselves and that we made bad decisions as teenagers and would not listen to anyone about why they were bad. Some of us, too, got no supervision and no direction, and so as young people we stopped caring about ourselves, and now, as adults, we try to make up for all the willfulness that we exposed to others. We knew it all!

Now we are trying to fix our past by beating ourselves up in the present for not being good enough. If we do not feel success in the present, then it validates all of our past. We need to take a good look at that shame and realize that teenagers are not supposed to make good decisions, and that they need only to learn from their mistakes. Did you or are you still stuck in your childhood trying to prove your value?

Take it slower and realize what you have rather what you don't have. Judging yourself only means that you end up judging others harder. You are okay as long as you stay out of your past and live in the present of your life. The past is only there as our lesson, not our burden to bear.

Question: Have you learned from your past mistakes and have emotionally grown or are you still obsessing over them?

LARRY ROBINSON

September 21

Are you an anxious person? Do you hide it by taking on more tasks than you should? Is it impossible for you to sit still until you are utterly exhausted, and then, when that opportunity (chance) arises, does your mind start racing, thinking about what's next? This must drive you and everyone around you crazy!

How does one get so anxious? Is it inherited? Were either of your parents this way? If they were, then you probably have a combination of nature/nurture that you must contend with. The current situations in your life present a great opportunity for this anxiety to "blossom." Why are we so anxious? We all are trying to right a wrong inside of us, just as we are trying for that perfection that we so much want to achieve. We exhaust ourselves to gain the recognition that we feel we never truly got. And as much as we get, it is never enough!

It will never be enough because we fail to understand the true feelings that are going on inside. Let's face it, we are angry, and that anger moves around inside of us in the form of anxiety. We are angry because no matter what we do it is not good enough for anyone. That is our perception of reality. We want the world to see our great deeds, but there is never enough acknowledgement for us. We watch as others sit around while we do everything, and yet we ask for no help. I bet this gets to you! Does it make you angry?

If you avoid your true feelings, then anxiety will take over. No one can offer to help because you refuse it and then walk away angry. Face it, this is your issue! Unless you are looking for an early death or a mental breakdown, ask for help. If that doesn't work because no one believes you really want it, then take control and stop everything and do nothing until you are heard! Take responsibility for setting this up and delegate to others. And if you think you have something to lose, and then think again!

Question: Do you see yourself as an angry person or as an anxious one? Can you see a connection between the two feelings of anger and anxiety?

LARRY ROBINSON

SEPTEMBER 22

Would your family and friends consider you a patient person? Can they ask you a question more than one time and not have you show them your frustration? Do you wear an expression on your face that lets folks know that you are answering a stupid question and it is not the first time? This makes people not want to ask you anything, for they already know how you are going to react.

Do you ask people questions they cannot answer because the answer lies days ahead? Do you need to know something before it happens, such as asking your partner, "Honey, why is the woman in the movie being chased?" when the movie just started? Your need to know can ruin the movie because your partner is getting frustrated, not only because you are "ahead" of the movie, but also because they must now pause for a minute to answer you! You can hear them mutter something under their breath and you know it is not a compliment! Why do you need to know?

Your anxiety gets in the way, and in order to soothe it you cannot control your impatience. When we are like this we forget that the other person is watching the same movie we are and that we aren't sitting there by ourselves. Sometimes this can be a symptom of needing to control *everything. When you know in advance* what is going to happen you can relax, but at what expense?

Think about whether or not you are a person who needs control in everything. This is a way of quieting your anxiety and not trying to run the show all the time. It is usually misunderstood, but behind your back people might be calling you a "control freak."

Patience comes in different forms. Sometimes we need to be patient with people and not get angry at what we believe to be stupid questions, and sometimes we need patience for the impatient people. Hey, in the long run there is nothing to lose!

Assignment: List all the situations in which you needed to be in control. Understand that this control may have always been in your life.

SEPTEMBER 23

W hy aren't you sick and tired of helping other people all the time? So much of the time your efforts are not accepted and all you do is feel drained and undervalued. When people want to talk to you, do you rush in with a "fix it" attitude and give them solutions to their problems? Were you asked for solutions, or did that person just need to vent out what was bothering them?

Those of us who are "fixers" feel totally inadequate when our suggestions go unheeded. We feel empty and then a surge of anger rushes at us. Why does this happen to us and why aren't we heard? At times, our helping others even gets in the way of us taking care of our own families. This is such a shame for us because we end up "failing" on two fronts. Our family is angry, while the others don't listen!

Does your identity rest on who you fix? Is that how *you* get your fix? We are called "codependent." We need to be needed so much that we put our own needs second and make the rest of the world more important than ourselves. There are never enough problems for us and never enough rewards. There will never be enough fixing for us to feel better.

Fixing ourselves is what works, because you cannot fix another person. Empathy, compassion, and caring are what we can give! Start with yourself and you will be able to be codependent no more! Make your life real, and then you can be there for someone else.

Question: How have you been there for others in the past? How would you like them to be there for you?

_____

_____

_____

_____

LARRY ROBINSON

September 24

Why do we exaggerate when we are feeling like a victim? How often have you or someone that you know made a situation worse by not exactly telling the truth? When we feel victimized we want everyone to know how awful the situation was that we found ourselves in. Have you ever embellished your past by telling something or writing something about yourself that made you look a little "larger than life"?

Why are we so afraid that we are not going to be good enough to pass the test of society? We make up a false self that excels in whatever it is that we want to achieve. We do not really look at this as dishonest, but just a little "off color." Despite the fact that deep inside of us we know the truth, we tend to tuck it away in a little box inside our mind because we know that nobody is likely to check the facts. And at some point we will have told this untruth so many times that we will actually begin to believe it ourselves! Some would call this "pathological lying," but there is no intent to hurt anyone else except ourselves.

When you build your life on a lie, no matter how small, it will prevent you from ever feeling that you are enough. Does this one lie give birth to others? You have to ask yourself this question and determine whether your life is valid or not. If you can see your own truth, then you can start right now with a commitment to being genuine. Remember, you are the one who hurts yourself!

Question: Do you believe in yourself? How do you knock yourself down so much of the time?

_____

_____

_____

_____

LARRY ROBINSON

September 25

When will I be enough? When will I be enough for my parents, husband/wife, teachers, or boss? When will I be enough? I never seem to please you because there is always a "but" after every compliment. As parents, you rarely say that you are sorry. And if by chance you do, then that is always followed by something critical that erases the compliment.

"Sorry" is almost always a foreign word to partners. "You made me act this way!" No, I did not, you brought who you are to our relationship. And while I might have fed your issues, I certainly did not create them!

How weary I can become due to my fear of your disappointment in me. I feel transported back to times when I was either very little or a teenager, when all I heard was, "You are not enough!" I do not think that I am damaged to the point of not knowing how I feel when it comes to disappointing you. It is not rocket science to see your face and know that it does not match your words. Life does not ever seem to be about me, but always about you! I am so weary of the fact that you cannot be pleased. Why do you think that I do not get motivated or have an "I do not care" attitude in school or work? Why would I want to make a great living for you? I am not enough!

"Well, you walk in my shoes and see how it feels, and then maybe you will understand how it feels to never be enough. Do you like it? If not, then do not impose your ideals on me! Let me be who I am and give me some positive feedback and I will come through! Regardless of you, today I am enough!"

Assignment: Read the above declaration and make it about yourself. Read it many times until you can believe in it! Jot down things you would like to add to your life regarding how you want people to see you.

LARRY ROBINSON

"Kindness," when was the last time that you were actually kind to someone you really love? What was the last kind word that you said and really meant it? And I am not talking about the obligatory "I love you" with a peck on the cheek as we run out the door. I am talking about from your heart, because this is your family, whether it is about husband and wife, children, mother and father, or partner.

All too often we take for granted that love is there, so why then are we so stingy when it comes to giving it out? And you must feel it from your heart and not from your head. Love is not an obligation, it is a blessing. And all too often we don't appreciate that blessing!

Why not try and tell someone you love exactly what they mean to you! Enough of this rat race of life in which we do not have any time to tell our children each morning that we love them and that we are proud of them. Why are we all so afraid at times to feel love? I bet you can look at your loved ones from a distance and know love, but the risk of expressing it can be too high for you! And what if the people you love disappoint you, do you avoid feeling vulnerable too? Kindness is not about the other person, it is about who you are! Are you a person who is kind?

Question: Can you answer the above question truthfully? What does that person (you) act like when they are being kind?

_____

_____

_____

_____

SEPTEMBER 27

Why do we hate ourselves? What do we carry around that makes us feel so insecure and self-loathing? Do we hate what we see in the mirror today compared to how we felt yesterday? If this is the case, today we see our hair as awful and our weight as having increased, and frankly, nothing about us looks good. We wear our ugly feelings and see them in the mirror as distortions of our bodies.

Our bodies do not change overnight, but our feelings do. Do you try to walk around with a smile on your face all day, but when you get home you immediately pick up that drink as soon as you walk through the door or start to graze on food, roll that joint, anything to escape the fact that you feel like a fraud? If this is the case, then you are filled with feelings that you would rather not see. Isn't it much easier to take it out on ourselves than deal with the "dirty" feelings inside?

No one knows that you are fake, only that subconscious of yours that is waiting to explode with all these negative feelings. And good luck to your spouse or children who are likely to become the recipients of an angry tirade unleashed through your subconscious should they say or do something wrong once they get home!

Today is the day in which you no longer have to feel fake. You can start by listening to your inner self (your heart) and understanding that your feelings are just yours. They do not have a right or wrong attached to them. Remember, this is a process, so do not be discouraged that when you begin to speak up people may react in shock when you start to challenge them with your ideas.

Question: Have you ever been called a fake person? What caused you to act that way? Why do you think someone saw you that way?

_____

_____

_____

LARRY ROBINSON

September 28

Who am I? How many layers will it take for me to expose my true self to you? I know that I could not be myself as a child, for there were way too many people with expectations that I could not or would not meet! But why is it so difficult to show the real me? Can I show me my real self?

By taking one small step at a time, maybe I will relearn that I am okay, and that it does not matter if the world does not approve. I am not here to please the world! I need to learn this lesson over and over again. I am here to be who God meant me to be! It is my journey that I am on, not yours and not theirs. Once I realize that I do have all the components of goodness in me, I can successfully fight off my darkness.

So today I now understand that I am going to be me! I cannot be you.

Question: How many different "selves" are there in you? Describe each one.

_____

_____

_____

_____

_____

_____

_____

_____

LARRY ROBINSON

September 29

D id you love your child this morning? Did he/she go off to school feeling safe and secure with you, or was this one of those mornings from hell? Do you struggle every morning with getting your children dressed and out the door? Well, if you think you had a bad morning, think about what they went through! And now they have to sit quietly in school for eight hours and pay attention to their work. Can you do the same? You rarely get caught thinking about the morning, but they always do! Now, it may not come out in the form of disorderly conduct, but it surely will affect their grades.

You all say the same thing, "I hate mornings and I don't know how to change it." Well, you can if you really put your mind to it! If there is a problem with children picking out clothes, either teach them what colors go together or help them choose, but do not choose for them! This is where the struggle begins. So what if they do not look exactly the way you want them to? Is that so important? For whom?

They need to learn someday, and at least they're telling you, "I want to be in charge of something in my life!" Eventually, and with your guidance, they will learn!

And if they won't get out of bed when you tell them to, get them up an hour earlier. So what if you lose an hour of sleep? You'll survive! They will hate it, but all you're really doing is giving them the choice of getting up now or when they're supposed to. If they are slow getting into the car, give them till the count of three and then drive off. Can you imagine how that will feel? Then go back and get them and tell them that you're going to do this every day until they understand that you mean business!

Did you hug your child this morning? Will you miss them while they're gone? Repetition without resolution stinks, and neither of you deserves the chaos!

Assignment: If you have children, how much tolerance do you have for them?

Can you handle the stress of your life? There are always the everyday stresses of life, like family, work, ongoing relationships, and children. But what happens when we have an added stress that is overwhelming? When a tragedy strikes or an illness occurs or there is a loss of an important relationship or job, add this to your everyday stress and you can become emotionally frozen or even crippled!

Our life energy is the most important part of our physiology and psychology. And when we can no longer make decisions or motivate ourselves, we are in deep despair. We feel as if our life energy has been drained out of us and we do not understand how to move. Family and friends get tired of hearing our woes, even though they know that we struggle. They only can take hearing so much, so in essence we add another stress to our lives, that of being the problematic person. We begin to feel more isolated and depressed. We avoid our spouses, partners, children, or careers, and getting up in the morning is horrendous. "Just let me stay in bed for five more minutes," is our cry.

Have you become a victim of yourself? Are you convincing yourself that you cannot motivate yourself and that you are a failure? Well, that is what your mind tells your brain. When has your mind ever told you something good about yourself? Listen carefully to what it is telling you and do not let your mind control your life. You can do it! Get up and force yourself to listen to what it tells you. Fight it until your heart can take over, and then you can face anything! There are no victims inside you, only a strong mind that wants your energy!

Assignment: List ways in which you have been a victim of your life? Do you always have the *poor me's* going on?

_____

_____

_____

"Love" is letting go of *fear*. That is true. When one understands the importance of loving ourselves and others and embraces *love*, then *fear* is *squeezed out* . . . fear cannot abide in the experience of "Love." Life is not simple, but it is *amazing* and *gratifying* when we realize how precious it is and live accordingly . . . breathe in love and out gratitude . . . seek like-minded authentic friends and encourage yourself and others . . . Be at peace, avoid chaos . . . Be patient with yourself . . . *consider writing your own journal.*

An excerpt from the journal of Mary Singleton, Kentucky, USA

Photo by
Stephanie Cavallo
Falmouth, Massachusetts, USA

October 1

When we do bad deeds as children, such as lie, cheat, or steal something small, do we feel shame or do we think we got away with something? Do you realize that we are born with something called *tabula rasa*, which means "blank slate"? We do not possess guilt or shame!

As soon as we come into this world our "slate" starts to get murky. It is up to our parents to teach us guilt or shame by the way they speak to us when we are caught doing something wrong. Screaming, "What did you do?" at a child will tend to make the child's eyes turn downward, and this is the beginning of shame. What if we ignored this behavior and instead asked, "Why did you do this?" in a matter-of-fact voice and posed it as a question rather than a direct statement? Would we bypass the shame and think that everything we do is fine? Everything is *how* it is said rather than *what* is said.

Some people are lacking shame. Do you know those people? Do you know children who puzzle you for they do not seem to have any reaction to their wrongdoings? Children can still learn guilt and shame until they reach about six or seven, but can adults learn it later in life? What do you think?

Do you believe that there is evil in the world? If a person does not feel anything toward others, do you consider them evil or just blocked? If, as a child, we experience too much shame or guilt, do we automatically experience shame when something is done wrong, even if we had nothing to do with it? Perhaps we are so wiped out from our childhood that we can no longer feel anything because we were mentally abused by an adult who needed a scapegoat for their own anger. Does this make us evil or "bad seeds" because we no longer feel anything?

In this world, as it is today, we see many people whom we judge before we even understand why they act a certain way. Our spouses, bosses, family members, children, and friends are all at our mercy at times when it comes to us judging them. Yes, there are evil people in this world who do horrific things, and who do not need our judgment because their acts speak for themselves. But those who do the much lesser deeds that skirt society's rules, are they evil or are they just misguided? Allow yourself to sit with this. Haven't we all done things we're ashamed of? Do you think that makes us evil or just dumb!

Question: Do you believe that there are evil people in this world? Have you met an evil person? What scared you about them?

_____

_____

_____

_____

_____

_____

_____

_____

_____

_____

_____

_____

LARRY ROBINSON

OCTOBER 2

The relationship is gone, over, *kaput!* We are alone once again. It seems as if this rollercoaster ride never ends. So what comes next for us? We don't want to go through the pain of a relationship again. We swear, "Never again," but we cannot stand the loneliness. How do we begin to cope with it?

Many of us cannot tolerate the loneliness after the end of a relationship and we decide that we are just going to "party." Nothing serious, maybe even find a "friend with benefits" because we don't want any strings attached. We go on the hunt for sex almost immediately after the breakup. We figure if we can put enough sex between us and the other person, then it will make our pain easier to deal with. Not so! The sex becomes great at first, but it is still not enough. We seek more and more of it to medicate our isolation or loneliness, but it does not work! And now instead of just loneliness we add feeling to our list of pain, emptiness.

"Driven sex" can become out of control. And if alcohol is added to the mix, then we can go down a dark path and end up with people we normally wouldn't even consider being around. But we talk ourselves into it by thinking that something is better than nothing! We lose ourselves in the need for sex, and now it really isn't about a relationship but about feeling a sexual charge, which even when we get it only leaves us wanting more. Now we cannot feel anything in our hearts and we have accomplished our goal, which is to feel nothing! This is sex addiction!

There are other forms of sex addiction aside from just the sexual "acting out" with another person. Some of us immediately go back on dating websites and use this as another way to meet the next "victim" in our "journey of pain." We might flirt with multiple people at one time, date three or four people, and yes, even sleep with them all. Are we crazy? Well yes, we are, and we are caught up in such an incredible need for attention that our morality sinks to depths we have never seen. We can actually burn ourselves out to the point where we are depleted of our sexual energy and we are now seeking that special one again.

For many men and some women, pornography becomes our next escape. We do not see it as addictive, just normal, because we are not hurting anyone and simply need a release. Addiction to pornography can be as poisonous as any other addiction for it is a progressive one that leads us down some of the darkest paths we can find. It starts out with normal sex, but can end up in places we never expected. It causes all sorts of problems around ED (erectile dysfunction) and helps to destroy future relationships. We are not porno stars, we're real people!

The answer to all of this is twofold: first, become sober and refrain from sex for a while until you get through this "love addiction," and second, join a twelve-step program, such as SLAA (Sex and Love Addicts Anonymous). It might freak you out, but a fellowship program is the best support you can receive for this addiction. And remember, you are not alone!

Question: Have you gone on sexual "binges" when you have been hurt after a breakup? Do you become sexually anorexic (no sex at all for long periods time) after a breakup?

_____

_____

_____

_____

_____

_____

_____

_____

_____

_____

LARRY ROBINSON

October 3

"I don't think I can do it! How do I begin my life again after such a painful time? I feel so empty now. And when people tell me I need to get on with my life somehow, I just want them to leave me alone. No one can tell me anything I don't already know, so please just leave me alone!"

Starting over after a destructive relationship can be torture for so many of us. Our self-belief has diminished to practically nothing, and our fear of being alone has all but consumed us. Part of us wants to rush out and get into a new relationship as quickly as possible because we need to feel that we are still wanted by someone else. It does not matter who broke up with whom in this case, for the need to be wanted after being in such a terrible place for so long has eaten at our self-esteem.

Often we will be "gun shy" and not want to meet anyone anytime soon, for we feel that we could not trust another person again. This is what happens to our self-esteem: it is shot! We have feelings of despair, and not just because someone else hurt us but because we are not very proud of who we have been in the relationship. We have badmouthed our partner so much that no one really knows how horrible we were in the relationship. We said and did things to purposely hurt another person and it doesn't really matter what that person did to us. It didn't warrant us stooping as low as we did, and yet while we were doing it we got such great pleasure in being the other person's "victim." But think, were there really any victims?

Starting over does not mean entering into another relationship. It means self-evaluating who you were in this last one and what you can do to make yourself a better person. Have you ever heard the expression "we meet people in life for where we are at"? Well, that is what happens if we do not change our own behavior! If we are still angry and feeling like the victim of our partner, then you'll find the same type of partner the next time! Over and over we will go until we look inside ourselves!

Are you beginning to swear off relationships because there aren't any "decent" people out there? Are you? Can you actually say that you liked who you were in all your relationships and that it was always the other person's fault? Learn from your experiences and listen in your mind back to what the other person screamed at you about yourself. Most of it was true, despite the fact that it was said in anger! Pay attention to it because it was another person's feelings about your behavior. Nothing is easy after heartache, but if you look at your life as a journey, then each person on it was meant to teach you something about yourself!

Question: How would you evaluate who you are in a relationship? Do you like yourself? And if so, why? If not, why?

_____

_____

_____

_____

_____

_____

_____

_____

_____

_____

_____

_____

LARRY ROBINSON

OCTOBER 4

"I just don't know where the time has gone; it seems to have flown by. I wanted so much to go back to school and now it is just too late! I am so disappointed in myself. I seem to do this with everything. I remember when I was in high school there wasn't anything I couldn't do. I was National Honor Society, a three-sport athlete, and president of my class. I loved being there. Nothing could stop me! I flunked out of college and suddenly I started to go downhill in sports. This seems to be the story of my life. Oh, how I wish I was that kid back in high school again. I remember when . . ."

Do you live your life only in the past? Is that where you had all your successes and could be proud of yourself? Are you one of those people who were stars in high school and never really went beyond those "glory days"? Are you someone who unknowingly drives people crazy by always bringing up your past victories and yet can't see beyond that stardom into your present?

We have had those victories and now we cannot seem to stay in the present. The present is where our life is, and we now have to compete with the world to find our place in it! This is so difficult, for we have to fight to stay in the present in order to build a healthy and secure future. Are we spoiled, or has the past confused us when it comes to knowing the difference between what was and what is? Back then we did not have to learn to struggle to gain acceptance, for it came with the sports and academics. Maybe we are afraid of growing old and we keep ourselves attached to the past in order to hold on to our youth!

We accomplish nothing when this happens. Are we truly afraid of the world and the consequences it brings when we are not living up to our potential? Maybe that potential was based on how the world viewed us and really had nothing at all to do with how we saw ourselves. Was this the "myth" we carried, that we were only as good as our hometown made us? Never having to work for anything did not prepare us for the future.

Do you wonder why you would rather stay in the past? How sad we have become because we have watched others move on and become successful and yet we sit frozen in our past. It is time to let it go! How, you wonder? Well, you were the one who made National Honor Society! Maybe the sports part of you is gone, but your brain isn't! Now is the time to use it before it also stays stuck in your past. Now is the time for you to begin to live in the present and start dealing with the issues that have been created. It is not too late! Living in the present is the only place that allows you to create a future! So don't just stand around, move forward and you will find your path in life!

Question: Do you live on your past experiences and are afraid of new ones? How does that affect your life? Do you always talk about the past as if it was still alive?

_____

_____

_____

_____

_____

_____

_____

_____

_____

_____

_____

_____

LARRY ROBINSON

OCTOBER 5

What happens between two people to make the charge go out of a relationship? Do you remember how excited you were when you first met? The waiting for phone calls and the anxiety that went along with hoping you'd get that call, and when you did the other person was eager to hear from you? It was so sweet, the gradual unfolding of our lives to each other!

We hoped that maybe we'd finally met the "right" person, someone whom we could confide in, our best friend! The sight of each other made our hearts race and the joy that we felt by being next to this person was like a drug. It was a "high" that nothing really could equal. And as we courted and so carefully said the words "I love you" to each other, we did not pay any attention to that little tingle of fear that was rising inside of us.

So we got engaged and began to plan for this special day. Silently we said to ourselves, "Why doesn't he get more involved?" or "Why is she so stressed out?" It was as if we did not know how to relate to each other. Again we had to rationalize or ignore those feelings inside of us and we could always come up with a good reason, which was that it was the anxiety associated with the build-up to this day, which was at times overwhelming. And finally, when the day arrived and we still had the anxiety, we were forced to ask ourselves whether it really was the wedding that was causing it or was it the word *forever?*

Did we really understand what *forever* meant? Do couples who make this commitment begin it at marriage, or is the marriage just simply a celebration of their work leading up to the actual wedding itself? Oftentimes the commitment starts after the marriage, and this becomes a difficult journey for a couple to undertake. So many issues are not worked out or even discovered until after the marriage. Why does sex change after marriage? Do men just want more sex and women less? That was, in most cases, not how we started out. What happened to that beautiful girl who wanted me all the time? What happened to that guy who understood me so well?

We changed! After the "ball" is over we now deal with finances, in-laws, the birth of children, and parenting styles. And we now have to start all over again trying to go about getting to know one another, only this time without that charge of *newness*. "I don't understand why you behave this way. Why is your anxiety so out of control? Why don't you care about how I am feeling?" We begin to hold on to our ugly feelings. Sex becomes a chore, while listening becomes unbearable at times. What happened to the thrill of you and me? How do we get it back?

There is an answer to this. To begin with, we both must want it back. Look at your life together and look at what you have been through. Nothing ever stays the same. Know that you started a journey together and that it is meant to be tough. Life is tough, and when we look for the easy way out we fail in our journey. And most of the time when this happens it is too late to really start a new one, for we will only repeat what we did not learn. And for those of you who fantasize about *new*, well, it is just what it is, new, and that is only until it too grows old. Then we are forced to confront that maybe we ran away too fast and didn't bother to see what we had, only what we didn't have!

Assignment: List ways in which your relationship has changed since you two were first together. Talk about both good and bad changes!

_____

_____

_____

_____

_____

_____

_____

OCTOBER 6

Remember when you were a child and stayed up all night scared out of your mind that there was something lurking around in your closet or hiding under your bed? When we were children and we had angry, hateful feelings, they could take on the form of a "monster." This is the bogeyman. In a child's subconscious is the fear that someone heard "I hate you, Mom. I wish you were dead." Well, guess what? The bogeyman heard it and now he is after you!

How many times did we want to hide or run to our parents for a feeling of safety? Today, as adults, we still have a bogeyman, only it is not a monster but our subconscious instead. Residing in our subconscious are all our negative feelings from the past and even the present that we do not want to deal with. We do not know how much is there until someone says something critical or mean to us and then suddenly out pops a tirade that we had no idea was coming! We cannot control the force of what is coming out, and often we shock the "recipient" of our outburst. Unresolved issues now take the form of our own meanness, and we do not understand why. For some reason it can even feel good to let loose on the other person, but the aftereffects always leave us feeling empty.

What can we do to rid ourselves of our inner bogeyman? First, find and identify what is going on in your life in the present and what situations you have that you have not dealt with. Second, ask yourself why you are not confronting these situations and/or person(s) that you have identified. See what relationship they have to your past and then you will see that ever-lurking bogeyman who is there to remind you that you are no longer a child who does not know how to deal with life, but rather an adult who doesn't have to be afraid to look inside.

Question: How has your inner bogeyman interfered with your growth? Look back into your childhood for the answer.

LARRY ROBINSON

OCTOBER 7

A re you stubborn? Do you hold on to situations even though you falsely state that you have let go of them? Do you hold old resentments against people and yet still put a smile on your face when you see them? This is an old issue that you have not resolved. Think about how many of these you have in your life and how it always interferes with feeling good. We walk around searching for "normal," but feel so heavy inside. Are we really genuine people or do we always live in a fake world of pleasing and smiling while we fume inside?

We are both! We can sincerely care for another person and even love them but still hold on to our resentments. We feel wronged in life, but that can go back into our childhood when our sensitivity to criticism was developing. Internally we saw everyone as our enemy, while externally they were our friends. Our need to belong and to be "a part of" was so great that it became too dangerous for us to let our feelings out! And besides, our stubbornness would not allow it! At times we actually got pleasure from not telling people how we felt. It was our secret!

Our stubbornness created a sense of isolation inside and it made us feel friendless and empty. Sure, we could be other people's friend, but we could not let anyone get close to us for fear of them finding out our secret. It is time to free ourselves from this oppressed place. What if we die with all these resentments inside of us? Begin today to let go of anything that is older than one month. No one would remember the situation because it never was discussed. Let others know that your sensitivity and stubbornness is yours and that they did not make you feel that way. Those feelings are yours to work out. Do not blame others for who you are!

Question: Have you ever been so stubborn that you lost a relationship over it? Explain.

LARRY ROBINSON

OCTOBER 8

Family, sometimes you cannot live with them and you really cannot live without them. Growing up, we all have tons of complaints about our parents and siblings. God knows that we have a right to complain. Did we ever really feel understood or praised enough? Validation meant a lot to us, and we had our own thoughts about who we were. Did we ever really get listened to without a parent interrupting us to tell us their truth instead of ours? We grew up believing that the process would lead us to becoming their equals, but we discovered that we were still viewed as their children, who still needed their "guidance." We still could not make decisions on our own that were good ones, and we still had to listen to their endless criticism about how they would solve our problem!

We didn't learn that we very rarely thought their advice was worth following, and yet we would still go to them with our problems, maybe hoping that they would finally understand who we were. They were never going to change and we were not the ones to do it. We had to change our reaction to them.

When we do not have them anymore, we miss them, even now after they have been gone for all these years. Why, you might ask! Because they were our family and now we still want to ask their advice. We now are sorry that we weren't smart enough to accept them for who they were. They did accept us in the end because we were their family. Accepting them for who they are is our work in life. Not theirs!

Assignment: List ways in which your parents still drive you crazy. Remember, we cannot change them, only our reaction to them. How would you react to them if you truly believed that you only could change you, not them?

_____

_____

_____

LARRY ROBINSON

OCTOBER 9

When do we decide that life is not just about fun? How old are you and what kind of charge do you still need in order to like life? Being a husband or wife isn't enough, is it? Parenting can get so intense and draining; why can't we still have fun?

Fun is your way of running away from being an adult. It is not that we cannot enjoy moments in life, but when fun takes over, we sometimes find ourselves disliking our partner or spouse because they promised to have fun with us and that is not always possible. And this is not gender determined because both males and females want an escape from the rat race of life, and fun is the answer.

So let's explain what fun is. Drug and alcohol-fueled weekends, just like in high school, and blackouts, which have no filter, so that you say or do anything you want without caring about the repercussions. Are these fun? Whatever happened to your dream of having a family and being successful? You might now be in your thirties, but you still want to be eighteen!

We rarely know what it is to have fun when we are not "high" on something. Perhaps you will try today and begin to understand that there are different ways of having fun and you do not have to be drugged to achieve it.

Assignment: Look at the ways in which you have fun. List things that you can do that are fun without drugs or alcohol.

_____

_____

_____

_____

LARRY ROBINSON

I mage! Image! Image! Are you someone who cares more about how you present yourself to the world than how you really feel? Do you want people whom you don't even like to care about you? Is your life such a secret that you have no one who really even knows how you feel, not even your spouse or best friend? Well, maybe it is time to come clean with yourself and face the fact that inside you feel fake!

"Fake" is such a harsh word, but it is the world that you created because you never felt good enough about yourself to really stand up against those whom you believed looked down on you. We spend way too much time trying to impress the world with false images of ourselves, and we impose this on our children also. Those kids who see through you rebel against you because they can see the falseness.

This is what you teach children: "Go with the flow and do not take your own position on life because the world will turn against you!" Do you remember sucking up to the popular kids in school, or even telling yourself that you didn't care about how they felt about you, when deep inside you were stabbed with pain?

Maybe it is time to reevaluate who you are and decide that this might be the last chance you have to be authentic! We get to a point in life where we think that we cannot change, but all it takes is your commitment to you and for you to stand up and speak your truth! It is time to tell the people who talk about everyone else that you will not judge anyone else any longer! Are you afraid that you will lose friends? Are they really friends, or do they talk about you when your back is turned?

Make today the day of change for yourself. No longer will you respond to others out of your fear of rejection but from your determination to be an authentic person. Start small with little issues and voice an opinion that is yours. Do not be afraid of the challenge.

Question: Can you be yourself with others or do you need to put a "face" on to be yourself?

October 11

When is a relationship over? A relationship is over when we repeat the same pain over and over again without a resolution. Here is a list of issues that need to be present in order for a relationship to be in the throes of death. If you feel that the majority of these apply to you and your relationship, then you either need to rush to seek help or call it quits!

1. A relationship is over when you would rather eat than have sex.
2. A relationship is over when you would rather be in a separate room than sit with your partner (the usual excuse being that we don't like the same programs).
3. A relationship is over when you hate the thought of going to a restaurant because you know that there will be no conversation and that one or both of you will be looking around the room, possibly even focusing on another person while the other is talking.
4. A relationship is over when you cannot stand kissing the other person. You used to love how they tasted, but now you cannot tolerate it.
5. A relationship is over when you would rather sleep alone or stay downstairs until your partner is asleep.
6. A relationship is over when either one of you continues to bring up past anger and hurts every time you argue.

These are just some of the issues that cause our soul to suffer.

Question: Can you name other situation in which you would end a relationship?

October 12

I s nothing ever good enough for you? Are you always looking to see what others have and thinking that you either have more or less? This is a difficult topic to discuss and it will take a great deal of honesty to answer the questions. We are all guilty of this at one time or another, but when it comes to admitting it, well, that's a different story.

It is important to start with: do I think I am good enough? Do I spend more time comparing myself to others than I do paying attention to the areas in which I am weakest? Ask yourself if you are the type of person who is secretly not happy for others' successes, and yet put on a face that says you are. "Fake" is what is going on at that moment. And we do not start out as fake, but we can really get into it when it comes to covering up our envy or jealousy.

If you were to study this negative trait in yourself, how far back can you trace this in your life? Were you the type of child who was always unhappy with yourself and thought other children were better off than you? Did you talk to yourself about how you hated them for succeeding, while putting yourself down for not doing so? Do you realize that by always looking outward you were defeating yourself?

It is time to stop the nonsense that comes with this issue and begin seeing what you have rather than what you do not possess. Yes, this is a childish issue, but if it has followed you into adulthood it is now time to put it away for good! Spending your life wishing you were someone else is a big waste of time and energy. Learning how to accept who you are is the most important part of you growing up. Do not despair, you are certainly not alone. Hopefully others will help you identify this in yourself through their honesty. We help each other when we help ourselves to honestly look inward. Do not wait another moment, for life is flying by and you do not want this issue to become your life!

Question: What traits about yourself do you wish you could return? *Mirror, Mirror* talks a lot about this for the reminder always needs to be there!

October 13

D o you wake up in the morning with an empty feeling inside you before you even get out of bed? Does your mind start racing before your eyes are even fully open and then all of a sudden it hits you, that heaviness that takes over and leaves you with a feeling of deep, deep sadness? And this is different from the typical depressed feeling you get. This is sadness, and it overwhelms you and makes your heart begin to ache immediately.

This is not depression, for our hearts are not affected by depression, only our minds are. This heavy feeling of sadness is like no other you have experienced. Depression is a welcome relief from this lost, empty, "I do not know what to do" existence that we now take on. There is no help, no one to rescue us. No matter what anyone tells us we cannot lift this sadness. There is no "magic pill" and no salve that we can rub on us to heal this sadness.

The only savior we have here is time! Remember the expression that "time heals all wounds"? This is the real truth with this kind of sadness. You see, sadness is one of the stages of grief that we all have to go through at one time or another. Whether this is due to the end of an intimate relationship or friendship, the death of a loved one or even a pet, we do not avoid this feeling.

Now, yes, we can "medicate" this sadness. We can try to block it out with drugs or alcohol, or try to find someone else to fill in the empty feeling, but until you face the sadness and understand that it is not an unhealthy feeling but one that comes with being human, it will not go away. This sadness tells us something that we do not want to know but must face regardless. We are hurting!

It is time for us to move on with our life. There are times that we can hold on to the sadness just because we are afraid of letting go of the person or situation that caused the sadness to start with. This is our fear of starting again. But the truth is that we actually need this sadness in order to understand that we're capable of feeling. So many of us want to deny our feelings and put up in their place this big front that it is "no big deal," but the truth of the matter is that it is a big deal!

LARRY ROBINSON

We can survive anything if we take each loss as a lesson that we can learn from. This is your life. Nothing stays the same! Change is always going to happen. Learn this lesson and your sadness will eventually go away!

Question: How do you deal with your sadness? Are you someone who uses addictive behaviors to medicate yourself or do you face it head-on?

_____

_____

_____

_____

_____

_____

_____

_____

_____

_____

_____

_____

_____

_____

October 14

Are you an addict? Do you have multiple addictions that you deal with on a daily basis, and as soon as you put one down and think you are free another pops up and you are back to square one again? Are you constantly telling yourself that you will stop drinking, eating, smoking, drugging, and numerous others that are always trailing you? What is it that keeps you in your addictive cycle?

The addictive cycle starts out with desire. It is just a little thought that enters into our mind, but it starts to grow. When our mind really gets hold of it and tells us, "Oh, it will only be this once and I so need to feel better," we are hooked! The next part of the cycle is the preparation. We buy our booze and we hunt for our drugs. We start to look at food differently, not as something meant to nourish our body but as a feast that we'd like to binge on for days. We never see the consequences until after the party is over, and we feel empty and devoid of everything good.

Well, unfortunately this is the result of addiction. We want to shut out the pain, but we also shut out all the good that is inside us. And when we shut down our feelings we lose the ability to be selective. We can no longer tell ourselves that we want to feel this but not that! Addiction has now started up, and do not think that you are "home free" just because you might not pick up the next day. It is in your system now and it will creep back in and take you by surprise. Addictive behaviors, once started, are much harder to stop again. We want to be able to say we "slipped" back into our addiction but that we are now back in control of it, but that is not so easy once your addictive self is back in the picture.

This self, your addictive self, is your worst enemy. It has no conscious and does not care about you at all. It is selfish and hungry for the dark side. It sees you as its tool and it manipulates you into acting out in ways that really turn you off, and yet you show no control over it. Not until you admit that you are an addict will you begin to get it under control. We have no idea who we really are until we are humbled by our detestable actions.

LARRY ROBINSON

Question: Has your addictive self ruined work and relationships for you? How?

_____

_____

_____

_____

_____

_____

_____

_____

_____

_____

_____

_____

_____

_____

_____

_____

_____

OCTOBER 15

Do you feel lost in life and without one, clear direction that leads to your rightful path in life? Are you someone who has many great ideas about what you would like to do with your life but who accomplishes nothing? Do you end up feeling like a big failure in life?

What causes us to lead our life this way? How often have we been somewhere and thought, "Wow! This is it! I know exactly what I want to do!" only to end up starting all over again, and only this time with one foot already in defeat?

We are dreamers, and that is the real cause of our failures in life. We want things to be the way we want them to be! We do not really understand what it takes to fulfill a commitment in life. We start with the best intentions, but we have no patience with ourselves to learn or to even make mistakes. We do not know how to continue to strive for success when we believe that we will fail. We have no confidence in ourselves.

The reason why we feel this way is not because we cannot accomplish anything in life; the reason is our out-of-whack (unrealistic) expectations! We never stop and think about what it will take to make a success out of ourselves with the tasks we set up. Instead, we rush in and then run out just as quickly when we see a touch of failure rising!

Be realistic! Do not fantasize about being something, especially when you have no realistic idea of how you will be affected by the work that it will take to get there! Research first, and then see if you have it in you to achieve this success. Never rush your choices in life to the point where they start controlling you, as opposed to you controlling them. Once they control you insecurity rushes in and it becomes easy to quit. This is your life. Find your passion by eliminating those things that you would not want to do. And listen to your heart, not your mind, because your heart will lead you in the right direction. Trust in your heart!

Question: Do you listen to your heart or your mind when you are setting expectations for yourself? Remember, your mind can control your actions while your heart will ultimately give you the truth.

LARRY ROBINSON

Photo by Isabella Walsh
Limerik, Ireland

". . . As much as I know I cannot change anyone but myself, I still try, and every time I get further disappointed when I fail. Even though I have the knowledge, the emotional pain that comes from emotional neglect from a loved one is so damaging and hurtful. I try just a subtle comment to invoke change, and it backfires instantly. It can be so challenging to stop looking outside of myself for love and happiness. It really takes practice!"

—Carrie Culbertson, Nantucket, Massachusetts, USA

October 16

Just when we thought it was gone, it appears once again in all its ugliness. It takes control of every fiber of our body and mind and we become its slave. Our anxiety is back and winning once again.

What causes this painful process that starts to throw added decisions and things that we have to do in our way? We cannot sit still, our mind begins to race, and we are overwhelmed by life. We take on way too much at this time. The anxiety has now begun to control our lives and it shows us no mercy!

Anxiety is another form of depression. It just takes on a totally different characteristic from the frozen depression that makes us and the world believe that we are lazy and uncaring. This depression bypasses laziness and creates the racing mind. We cannot sit still. We cannot focus. We cannot make decisions that we can follow through on and we continually beat ourselves up for what we have not accomplished.

Sometimes we don't even remember when we haven't been like this. It seems as if our whole life has been a rollercoaster ride (up and down and moves so fast) and we cannot seem to get off of it. After a while it is almost normal for us. Believe it or not, we can also get charged (like a stimulant or drug) by it. We run on the anxiety and it rules our decision-making ability. How good are your decisions when you are in this place? Feeling anxious is our demon and we are its slaves!

Assignment: Try this exercise and this will help you determine whether your anxiety is ruling your life. Sit in a quiet place and close your eyes. Try to clear your mind. If you begin to think about sitting and whether you are doing it right, then your anxiety has taken over. Go back to clearing your mind (settle down into the sitting) and see how much "craziness" comes into your mind. This is what it is doing all of the time.

It is time to learn to sit still. Try to sit for five minutes every day. If you can do the five, try to increase the time by a few more minutes the next day or so. Learn to listen to your mind. This is the way that you slow it down. If you do not pay attention to it, it will ruin your day, filling it with needless worry. We can do this. Take back your life!

_____

_____

_____

_____

_____

_____

_____

_____

_____

_____

_____

_____

LARRY ROBINSON

OCTOBER 17

How sensitive are we in relationships? What are the rules that we have unconsciously set up to determine when we are hurt by the words or actions of someone else? Does the other person even know what those rules are? Do you think it is how we speak to one another that set off the struggles in our relationships? Do we become frustrated too easily when someone else is too sensitive?

We can be either in one camp or the other: too sensitive in reaction to the other person or too frustrated with the other person's heightened sensitivity. "Didn't I just tell you that? God, why do I continually have to repeat myself?" This statement will definitely meet up with someone who falls apart at our frustration! Is this the never-ending struggle that we cannot overcome? This is neither a male or female issue, but one that is interchangeable between the sexes. You can be a man who is too sensitive and a woman who gets easily frustrated. This causes bickering (arguing) that can go on and on without resolution.

The end result of this kind of fighting is two stubborn people who fail to see how the other is feeling. Remember, if one wins, the other loses, and there should not be a winner in a relationship. Relationships are about balance, not winning. This can cause deep resentments, which add a new negative dimension to the relationship. What then is the answer to this dilemma (hard problem)? We could go on and on with the most perfect communication but that will not heal us. No, the true answer is *acceptance*! We need to accept who each other is. We start this way: the too-frustrated person begins to work on patience. Breathe when you are listening to something that could drive you crazy. Do not let the other person feel that they are a bother to you. The too-sensitive person works on not reacting so strongly to the other person's words. They do not cause your sensitivity; that is yours to own. You see, in the end you cannot change another person, you can only change your reaction to them!

Question: Are you someone who fights a lot with your significant other? Do you yell loudly or are you the shutdown type of fighter where the other person gets crazy trying to get a response out of you?

_____

_____

_____

_____

_____

_____

_____

_____

_____

_____

_____

_____

_____

_____

LARRY ROBINSON

OCTOBER 18

D o you sleep well, or are you the type of person who as soon as you put your head down on the pillow your mind begins to race? So many thoughts flood your head that anytime you attempt to close your eyes another thought races in and pops your eyes open. Do you lie there and become totally frustrated with your inability to sleep?

Another painful way in which you are deprived of sleep is when you fall asleep and maybe one hour later you are wide awake, and although you know that you are tired you cannot get back to sleep. How horrible is it for you to lie there and know that you have work or school the next day and the night never ends? And if that isn't bad enough, you lie there awake while your mind is in complete control, constantly telling you about all the things that you have put off that need to be done, and like yesterday! It is relentless in telling you how inadequate you are and that you never will fall asleep. It constantly reminds you that you will be exhausted and feel useless in the morning.

There are some things that we do to not sleep. If you eat before you go to bed your ability to metabolize (burn up) that food stops. You have overworked your metabolism and the food just sits there turning to fat and keeping us up. Not good! If you watch television or listen to the radio, you are activating your mind so it does not rest and you are bombarding (flooding) it with material to keep it thinking and you awake. If you go to bed angry, that is a definite *keeper-upper*. The anger plays over and over in your mind until it wears you down.

You need to tell yourself when you get into bed, "I am tired!" You are giving your mind the message that you want to sleep. It will try to stop you by putting negative thoughts into your head, but you must tell it to stop! When you close your eyes, take slow, deep breaths in and out. And count each breath as a way of clearing your mind. This allows you to gain control of it. Fight your mind and you will win. Let it control your head, and well, you know the answer to that!

Question: What kind of sleeper are you? Some people think that when they close their eyes they are "dead" to the world, but that also could be restless sleeping.

_____

_____

_____

_____

_____

_____

_____

_____

_____

_____

_____

_____

_____

_____

LARRY ROBINSON

OCTOBER 19

Are you filled with worry? Do you worry about everything that happens or is going to happen in your life? Are you a secret worrier, where no one knows what you really do to yourself with worry? Is it impossible for you to stop?

When you are a secret worrier, you present a self that appears well put-together (appearing that you are easygoing and not a worrier). Everyone thinks that you can handle everything that comes your way with a smoothness and easiness. You are someone who people can admire. The problem is that your image and your reality are miles apart! What people see is not the true you who worries about everything. They only see what you present. Inside you can feel like a fake.

There is no one whom you can turn to when this is going on. How could you expose your fears and worries when you present the opposite? Face it: you have no one to turn to who can be a support to you.

How do you change this situation in order to get the support that you need? Most of us do not! We cannot let down our defenses enough to let someone into our dilemma (problem). Here are the facts: we let someone in and appear as someone who "faked" having his/her stuff together, or we are totally alone with our worries and without support.

Carrying this issue around is very dangerous to your physical and mental health. Why would you need to have this image? There is something inside of you that needs to be needed and cannot show any true needs yourself. Whatever the reason for this, it does not matter. It is wrong to do this to yourself. Let someone who does not need you know that you have fears also. Just by opening yourself to someone else you begin to remove this issue.

Do not be afraid to tell the truth. It actually makes people more comfortable with you if they think that you are not better than they are. You worry about things just as they do. You can still be a support, just not someone who knows everything!

Question: Are you someone who pretends that they do not need help from others? Are you too set in your ways to think you need help?

LARRY ROBINSON

October 20

D o you carry around regret in your life? Are you always thinking about the past and what you could have done differently in a situation or a relationship? Do you condemn yourself for what you should have done over and over again?

Let's face it, you cannot stop feeling regrets in life. When this occurs we cannot truly grow emotionally, for we are stuck in the past. And because we are stuck in the past, we do not see any positive future for ourselves. Therefore, we are constantly bouncing back and forth between the past and the future. So while all this is going on, what happens to the present?

We do not live in the present! This is where our life is, and yet we are so consumed by what went wrong and what will happen that we miss the moment in our life that is the present! Our life then becomes one big repetition of condemning ourselves for the past and being fearful of the future. All our energy is sucked up in this pattern, and we find ourselves feeling hopeless.

Often, we use the past as an excuse not to move forward. We tell ourselves that, "I am through with relationships," for we cannot tolerate the pain that they bring. Well, why wouldn't we feel this way if we do not learn from our past?

Learning from your past means applying to the present that knowledge that you have accumulated through life situations that you have experienced. This means not jumping into your future with negative thinking, but remaining in your present and wanting to have better success the next time around.

It is way too easy to tell yourself that you are through with relationships. And yes, you will remain someone who lives with regrets if you fail to learn about yourself. Forget focusing on the other person, they are just who they are. Focus on yourself and want to be a better partner, person, husband, wife, parent, friend, etc. Remember, this journey is all about your life, not someone else's!

Question: What have you learned about yourself on this day in October?

LARRY ROBINSON

OCTOBER 21

What happens when friendships go bad? Where did it go wrong? Suddenly your BFF is no longer there and you have no idea why. They refuse to answer your e-mails, text messages, and phone calls, and one day you realize that they have blocked you on Facebook: the epitome of insults. At first you say nothing and you rationalize about some ridiculous circumstances that must have come up, but then you hear from mutual friends that this person is bad-mouthing you. What do you do?

Typically, our first reaction is to feel rejected and hurt by this betrayal, but as we sit with it we start to feel our anger slowly rising. We did nothing to cause such venom! But maybe if we really think about it, is it possible that we crossed some line that we felt we had their permission to cross? Think about it, did you violate their privacy by saying something to another friend that you assumed would be all right? Did you believe that it would okay because they were friends also? Did you clear it with your friend? Did you mention something perhaps about your friend's parenting or housekeeping skills that embarrassed them?

You might have a "big mouth" and not even realize that you have spread some hurtful gossip about that person. Do you think that you need to talk about others to make yourself interesting and popular? Were you like this in high school and never changed this behavior? Well, now probably is the time to really look at yourself and realize that immature behavior might have cost you a high price. This is not popularity, it is mean!

Assignment: List ways in which you are a good and not-so-good friend. Do not take this lightly, for it is easy to do so.

LARRY ROBINSON

OCTOBER 22

Do you respect your marriage? Are you someone who takes your wedding vows very seriously? How many times have you thought that you married the wrong person because they do not live up to your expectations of who your spouse should be?

Well, there are no should-haves in life. We each make our own decisions based on how we feel at the time. If you remember, your vows were said with tears in your eyes. Well, where are those tears now? Do you sit in judgment of your spouse believing that you married beneath yourself, or do you feel empty because in your eyes there is nothing but boredom in your marriage?

You have given up the belief in your vows, and so has your spouse. It is time to step back and look into your marriage and see what kind of partner you are. Nothing is simple in this life. Parenting has destroyed "husband and wife," and neither of you any longer puts energy into working on intimacy or the connection between the two of you. Bedtime is not one of joy and closeness, but now one of exhaustion and distance. Whose fault is this?

When you decide that your love is so fleeting with your partner, then it is time to put down all your defenses and start to work on loving again. What is the use of repeating your parents' crazy marriage? Look inside and not outside!

Question: What has been your part in the downfall of your relationship? If you are not in one now, what happened in the last one you participated in that did not work?

_____

_____

_____

_____

LARRY ROBINSON

OCTOBER 23

How often do we take time for ourselves? Has someone made you feel guilty about being a stay-at-home mother while your spouse is out working to provide for your family? Has someone ever told you that you cannot take time off from work because you will look lazy? How often do we get caught up in this guilt or anger? Sometimes it is a toss-up whether you feel guilty that you are angry or angry that you are guilty! How often do we take the time to honestly appreciate what each of us does for the family or the couple?

Not often enough, that is for sure, because there is always someone complaining that we don't do enough. You see, guys always feel that women who stay at home have all the free time in the world once their children are in school or the baby is asleep most of the day. All husbands should spend a month, not a week, taking care of the wash, cleaning, painting, gardening, and cooking, let alone the children. And all women should experience what it feels like to be the sole provider for the family and the pressure it puts on your husband. You take his job for a month and feel sick, but still go to work for fear of losing your position.

The truth is that neither job is easy! The reason why we have so much addiction in life has a lot to do with that anger and guilt that paralyzes us and we need some sort of self-medication to ease the problem. We wonder why obesity and alcoholism are so rampant in our society. Perhaps if we took the time to appreciate each other and really gave the credit where it was due, then we would feel like we were sharing the struggle together. Isn't it time?

Question: Are you a supportive person to your partner or do you get angry and jealous over what you believe their life is like?

_____

_____

_____

LARRY ROBINSON

October 24

Do you know how to manage your finances? Are you someone who occasionally goes on spending binges and then has to lie about it out of shame? Has this happened to you repeated times? And after each time it happened, have you promised yourself that, "This is it," only to find yourself a week later doing online shopping or out at the mall or buying scratch cards or lottery tickets? Do you find that you cannot stop even though you promise and promise? How many times have you paid off your credit card debt and then created it again? Some people spend most of their life in debt. How much money do you think you would have if you didn't do all that spending?

You are a "spending addict" and you do not want to believe that your mind is controlling how much you spend! None of us want that shame and humiliation that are the consequences of our addiction. We need help, but first we have to help ourselves.

Listen to your mind! Do you really need what you are buying, or do you simply just want it? Now is the time to look at needs vs. wants. Be honest and side with your heart and not your mind, for when it comes to indulging yourself your mind is always looking to take control. If you cannot stop it and take control yourself, then find a group that will help you before you find yourself alone, with no love and no money. You see, we have a hole in us, and we tend to try to fill it with things. It is time to fill it by giving love, and that will allow us to put our selfish spending in the trash!

Question: What would you say your money issues are? Are you a saver or a spender?

_____

_____

_____

_____

LARRY ROBINSON

OCTOBER 25

How do we know that we have met the right person? How many dates does it take to decide whether you want to see this person again or not? Are you the type of person who rushes into a relationship very quickly because it feels so good to be wanted that you fail to get to know who it is that wants you until you're already hooked? Maybe it is time to stop making these same choices over and over again and begin to stop, look, and listen!

There is a three-date limit. On the first date, decide whether the person talks too much about him/herself. This is a bad sign, and do not rationalize this and say, "What a great communicator this person is." If they do not ask you about yourself, then this will be what goes on in a relationship. It will always be about the other person. But on the other hand, if the time is shared and you feel a good chemistry with this person, then date number two is fine.

If the second date doesn't go as well as the first date, put yourself on notice. If it is really awful, then end it there. But if you think the other person might be a little quiet or may just be having an "off" night, then date three is okay.

If on the third date you find yourself a little bored, then at the end of the night you can simply just thank the other person and say, "Goodnight." And offer them your cheek only! No kissing! If they call you again, you can say that you really enjoyed their company but that for you there just wasn't enough chemistry.

Now, let's say that you make it to the third date and your interest builds, well, then what? Now it is okay for *the kiss*! And the kiss is so important because if you do not like the way someone kisses, you can bet that you will not like the sex either! You cannot teach someone how to kiss the way you like it, even if you feel that this person is very nice and that the chemistry, physical attraction, and the sexual energy is just too important to pass by.

Tomorrow will be what happens after the kiss!

Question: Have you ever stayed with someone even though you hated the way they kissed? How difficult was that for you?

_____

_____

_____

_____

_____

_____

_____

_____

_____

_____

_____

_____

_____

_____

OCTOBER 26

W hen we left off yesterday we were at the end of the third date and we were confronted with *the kiss*! Now, assuming that went well enough, today, in part 2, we want to talk about what happens *after* the third date and you find that the chemistry, both physical and energywise, is still very potent.

The most important commitment we can make here is to not rush things! Some people will say the most wonderful things about someone they have really just met, and some will actually try to convince both you and themselves that this person just might be *the one*! But what "one" are we actually talking about here? We just met this person and already a lot of us are planning our future? If you have been burned before in relationships (and who out there hasn't?), then how or why would you even think this?

Repetition without resolution means that you are very likely to repeat the same thing time and again. We must hold back from that feeling of being wanted and allow ourselves to decide whether we want this person for who they are or because they want us! This is the biggest mistake we can make! You have to genuinely feel your own value first before you can place value on someone else's feelings for you.

Now, go ahead and date the person but do not promise anything! But if you cannot help yourself, just remember that if you decide to have sex too quickly, do not think for a minute that sex automatically "seals the deal." The sex, you see, is likely to be your fantasy and not necessarily the other person's.

This is the time when you need to find out a lot more about that person, and you can still even date others if you want. There is more commitment coming in a few weeks, for if you decide that this person feels right and they are in the "same place" as you are, then we can move to part 3, which is about seeing someone exclusively! See you tomorrow!

Question: Have you moved too fast in starting relationships? Has it been you or the other person who rushes things? Explain how.

LARRY ROBINSON

OCTOBER 27

We now can look at this person and realize that after spending quality time together we may now be thinking about not seeing anyone else. We have spent enjoyable time laughing and being affectionate and had great discussions about life and love, and we now feel we are ready to date this person exclusively. But there is so much more to this!

This is about becoming serious with this person and wanting to see if we can form a loving relationship. And it is one of the most anxious times, for if we are truly serious then it is a major step in our life. We are not testing the waters any longer, and our hearts are invested in the relationship. Remember, both people need to be in the same place. Any sign of "game playing" at this point is not a good one. We are in the process of building another layer of trust. And there can be no lies and no excuses. Feelings are now becoming vulnerable, and both men and women do feel the same way during this time.

It is not until this period that we introduce our new "loved one" to our families or children. We have all made the mistake of doing this too quickly and regretting it afterward. Settling into the relationship now begins to feel as safe and secure as it needs to as you go along. But if you don't feel safe and secure, then it is most likely your own issue of intimacy that is popping up and you just need to slow yourself down. Remember, there are no wedding bells yet, and a simple, smooth feeling of comfort is all you are looking for. If you haven't rushed into this, you are more likely to get the support of friends and family, and that always helps. Remember, this is the beginning of a possible journey together, one that could possibly lead to the word "forever"!

Question: Do you believe in the word *forever* even if you find yourself unhappy in relationships? Would you stay in a relationship because you made a vow that uses the word *forever*?

LARRY ROBINSON

OCTOBER 28

How many goals that you set for yourself have you accomplished? How often have you told yourself that you are going to achieve something and it dies in your mind, only to be followed by another goal that is buried next to this one? Have you really reached your potential in life, or are you just a dreamer or someone who just feels defeated? How old is this, and please don't try to tell me that it started in adulthood, because it didn't. This starts in childhood.

So many times we hear that we have so much potential that we want to stay in bed forever. We just do not think we can live up to that statement. Have you asked yourself why? Are you just lazy, or is there something else that stops you from becoming the best that you can be? We have all heard success stories about kids who overcame great economic odds or physical disabilities and become huge successes in life, so that means that we do not have those as excuses, because no one is better or worse off than we are. They are just different. So what is the problem?

No one is truly lazy, that is something our parents tell us, and after a while we prove them right. They do not know how scared we really are and that we feel defeated so early in life. Well, stop pitying yourself! It is never too late! Do you hate your job and feel stuck in it? Well, that is what you have accepted from yourself. You don't think you can better yourself! It is never too late, no matter what you think.

There are no more excuses that you can give yourself. How many have you already had? Ten packs of cigarettes can start you on one course at a community college. It may sound weird to say that, but it is true. It does not matter what you take or if you just audit a class. You think you cannot do the work, but you never thought you could and gave yourself the excuse that you didn't care! Now is the time to prove to yourself that the world is wrong about you. Now is the time to prove that you are wrong about you! All it takes is a little motivation and real desire from you to do this! What's the matter? Are you afraid of a little challenge?

Question: How do you challenge yourself to do better in life? Or are you someone who gives up on *you* easily?

_____

_____

_____

_____

_____

_____

_____

_____

_____

_____

_____

_____

_____

_____

OCTOBER 29

If we believe that tomorrow will be better, we can bear a hardship today. Do you understand what *hope* is? Do you have it, or are you that negative person who lives in the moment of your pain and thinks that this is the best you can do in life? Are we all living in a hopeless society, in hopeless families, and in hopeless situations that we do not believe will change?

Why do you think you became hopeless? Did you experience this as a young child? Was there no one in your family who was a hopeful person? Maybe we are the products of parents who saw no hope in life because they came from that unhappy place where life was always a struggle. Is this a generational issue, or did some traumatic event happen in your life to create this despair in your life?

Do you really believe that you cannot change this attitude, or are you just waiting for it to miraculously change for you? Well, it will not change on its own. It will take a close examination by you of how your grandparents and parents viewed life, as well as a closer look at what your own attitude toward life is. Children are very rarely born negative. Remember, I once told you that we are born with a *tabula rasa* or a blank slate. Well, this is what I meant, in that we have no negativity at birth. So this will tell you that negativity is not a naturally born issue, but instead one that comes out of your background. Do you want to change this? Are you addicted to negativity? It is time to learn what the above quote really means!

Question: How often do you think that you get disappointed and give up your faith that things will get better?

_____

_____

_____

LARRY ROBINSON

October 30

D o you know what an *aware person* is? Are you an aware person? Are you someone who is always thinking of the future and never stays in the present in your life? If this is true, then you are not yet aware. To be aware is to be in the moment. It is an observation of your life right now, not in the future as so many of us run to. We are always thinking about what will happen tomorrow and avoid the present in our life. We question everything we do. The answers are always coming out of us, but are they really the answers to our unresolved questions or are they simply excuses that we make for not listening in the moment?

The one thing that people who are aware do very well is that they know how to listen! They not only hear what someone else is saying, but they also listen to the emotional meaning. When someone is in distress, they do not always show it. Sometimes we see them hide their pain by always being angry. I bet you know someone like this. Our tendency is to stay away from this person, but what we really need to do is listen closely for the unspoken message. Then we will be able to feel their pain.

Awareness is not about the future, for the future is not a sure thing, no matter how much we focus on it, plan it, or dream about it. The only thing that we can be sure of is the present. Do you ever catch yourself drifting into the past? Stay away from it! Nothing good happens if you are only focused on what was rather than what is. When we are in the past we cannot see what our present emotions are. The only possible way we can grow is to be in the present. Do you ever feel as if you sabotage the moment?

Do you think it is true that we all avoid the moment when there is pain involved? This is where our growth begins. Do you remember the expression, "no pain, no gain"? It is so true. Learn to tolerate your emotional pain and you will begin to see the roadblocks that are preventing your growth. It is not a pleasant place to be, but it is better than eating, drinking, smoking, and all the other vices we use to medicate the present. Remember, if you are not aware you cannot really be there for another person. Unless you learn first how to be in the moment of your own life, how can you tell someone else what to do!

Question: Are you an aware person? Do you think that others see you this way or as someone with their head buried in the sand?

_____

_____

_____

_____

_____

_____

_____

_____

_____

_____

_____

_____

_____

_____

OCTOBER 31

Are you a free person? Do you know what "inner freedom" means? And if so, how has it played a role in your life? Do you stand up for your beliefs? Do you even have any idea about what your beliefs truly are? Do you practice what you preach? Can people turn to you because you are a person who lives according to what they believe in and serve as a role model to others, or are you the person who says, "Don't do what I do, but do what I say"? This is the most difficult way that we can live our life, because no matter how diligent we are there will be times when we can definitely come across as a hypocrite. No one believes someone who doesn't follow their own belief system. How does this happen to us?

We start out with the right intention, but when it comes to delivering our beliefs we very often become frozen due to our fear that it will not be the right belief. This tells us how insecure we really are. Are we just "preachers" in life who spout off our beliefs with nothing to back them up, or do we have that sense of freedom inside to not let it matter who believes us or not? We must believe what we feel inside, for there is no right or wrong about our feelings. Anyone who tells us that our feelings are wrong is trying to take our freedom of self-expression away. Do we just give it away, or do we fight for the right to our beliefs? And who cares if we are seen as weird or looney or radical because we believe something that those around us think is absurd? So what? No one has the right to put you down for your beliefs. You are the one who needs to express yourself! What does it matter to someone else if you do not share their beliefs? Isn't that what being free is all about?

This is a hard world to live in, and I'm sure that there are few who would disagree, but ask yourself this: would it be easier to go with the flow of everyone else or to stand up for your beliefs? You are truly mistaken if you believe that it is easier to just follow everyone else. The bottom line is that your feelings identify you as an individual in life. And if you cannot be heard and valued for who you are, then have you wasted your life by dodging the conflicts that come with freedom!

Question: Are you someone who will fight for what they believe in? Can you find something in your life that you could say you fought for?

_____

_____

_____

_____

_____

_____

_____

_____

_____

_____

_____

_____

_____

LARRY ROBINSON

Christina Alvarado
Ulote, Heredia, Costa Rica

November 1

Who really doesn't have an eating disorder? How can we live in such a tempting, unhealthy world and not get addicted to something? It does not matter if it is McDonald's or chocolate or cheese or having to eat organically healthy all the time, any of these can certainly turn into an eating disorder. Apologies to those who feel offended by this, but anytime we become obsessed or compulsive around food, we create an eating disorder and there is damage to others we are close to.

We cannot judge anyone with this problem. No one starts out life saying, "I really want to be obese" or "It is great to be anorexic or bulimic!" We develop into this for a variety of reasons, but it no longer can be blamed on anyone else. It is our responsibility to either work on this—and yes, it takes your lifetime—or just let it be and accept who we have become! Stop comparing yourself to strangers walking down the street with the mindset, "Well, at least I'm not as bad as that." Yes, you are! You are for you, not the world!

We know we cheat on diets all the time and that we obsess about our clothes size. We are also constantly trying to hide what is there already, and when it is time for intimacy we always need the lights off.

Men and women, young adults, and even children suffer from this problem of being overly conscious abut weight. Therefore, we need to help ourselves by committing to becoming examples of how to do it right. Commitment is not as hard as we think it is. How can you watch your child blow up and say, "Well, it's just in our family"? Yes, a family of obese people is not easy to take, but we tend to rationalize everything and it is time to stop!

Take one day at a time. Diet addicts, put down the diets. You know how to eat! The question is, do you want to?

Question: Can you honestly say that you are not addicted to any food? When do you consider your eating is out of control? Has this been a hidden issue for you?

LARRY ROBINSON

November 2

What is more important to you, the need to be wanted or to want someone else? Do you know the difference between the two? How often in your life have you wanted someone to want you so badly that you did not even realize who you got involved with? By the time you settled into a relationship with that person were you questioning why you wanted this person in the first place. What caused you to rush into this relationship without having a courtship? Did you go from one or two dates immediately into a relationship? When we have dated someone for a couple of months, we can then determine if this person really is who they say they are as opposed to what our fantasy of them is.

And what about the times when we've wanted someone so desperately that we failed to see the warning signs of a noncommittal person? The entire time we were with that person we became someone we didn't even recognize! We would always comply with what the other person wanted, and had to keep our own feelings bottled up as if they were poison. Did we keep telling ourselves that things would get better and that soon we'd see signs that the person felt the same way, or were we kidding ourselves and later found out that this was just another one of those unavailable people we always seem to get involved with? Pain and rejection almost feel normal in these types of relationships, and to be honest, why would we feel any different if we continue to reach for the unreachable? How sad we become when it finally starts to dawn on us that maybe this unhappiness is our destiny.

What is wrong with us? Aren't we entitled to happiness in life, or are we always settling for less than we deserve? But that's the problem. If we are the settling type, then we are getting exactly what we deserve! We obviously do not think well enough of ourselves to actually believe that we are capable of more! And why are you in such a rush? To whom are you trying to prove that you are lovable?

Again, you need to look at your choices and see if there is a pattern to this madness you seem to keep repeating where you end up feeling that you are better or less than the other person. All in all, this stinks, and it ends up making us wonder why we want to be in relationships at all!

LARRY ROBINSON

Question: Are you always willing to settle in a relationship that does not feel right to you? Do you secretly long for something that you consider better?

_____

_____

_____

_____

_____

_____

_____

_____

_____

_____

_____

_____

_____

_____

_____

_____

NOVEMBER 3

What causes us to lose control of ourselves when we meet *the* person whom we have decided is the only one for us? Is this normal, or is there something a little "off" inside of us that allows us to create this "storm of passion" that erupts in our hearts? Is it our heart that is affected by this new love, or is it our mind that is once again playing with us and causing us to think like this person is going to be with us forever?

How could we possibly know after just meeting this person whether they are truly the right person for us? We're already picturing our lives with this person, thinking how beautiful our children will be, the kind of home we will build for them, etc., etc., etc. And nobody gets spared from this, no age, race, gender, or sexual preference! It does not discriminate! We all can be affected by this. But this also can create a very strong "dis-ease" within us, this thing called "love addiction."

Love addiction is one of the hardest addictions to break or even recognize, for that matter. And you say, "What do you mean that I'm 'love addicted?' What the hell does that mean?" What it means is that somewhere in our minds we believe that there is someone out there who will make us a better person and save us from all the misery we have experienced in life. This person will be the "be all and end all" of our experience, and without them we're nothing! This "dis-ease" can happen many times throughout our lifetime and make us believe that we are so unlovable that *no one* can stay with us. This toxic feeling in us causes us to lose our identity and create a needy, begging, manipulative person who will go to no end to achieve the goal of being loved by this person, and sadly, in some instances it can even involve violence. But the point is that this is not the real us!

Where does this condition come from? When we were babies we were in the bonding stage with our mothers for the first six or seven months, and this is the time during which we can be spoiled to no end, for we are forming the seeds of learning how to love. If we come from a disrupted background where alcohol or drugs or even poverty are involved and where mom is working all the time and there's a disruption in our bonding, we,

LARRY ROBINSON

at that age, do not know what is missing but we feel empty nevertheless. And later, sometimes as early as when we are in our teen years, we might turn to alcohol or drugs to fill that empty feeling. Underneath that will be that love addiction that we need in order to feel love.

For some of us, that initial "charge" that we feel and that quick rush into a relationship is forming the love addiction. Remember, this is a warning sign! Move too fast and you'll be suffering for a long time! In order to have a healthy relationship, you must have a healthy self.

Question: What are some of the signs you have seen that create toxic (poisonous) relationships for you? Do you hide from them or do you actually confront them?

_____

_____

_____

_____

_____

_____

_____

_____

_____

_____

_____

_____

November 4

Have we ever considered that loving another person could be an addiction? Do you believe that love can make us sick when we cannot seem to change another person in order to meet what we believe are our needs? If we are addicted to another person, would we know what those needs really are? We have to remember that we do meet our opposite in life, and that whatever our issues are the other person fits right into them. If we are driven, they are laid back; if we are happy-go-lucky, the other person is too serious; if we are caretakers, the other person might not be what we can handle, so anyone who thinks that their partner or spouse is lazy, unmotivated, or unavailable, well, they might just not be capable of handling having all their needs met. Now, I know that some will say, "That's crazy," but if it wasn't true you would not be with that person and you would have left a long time ago.

Whether you believe it or not, we actually do know who we're with! We know it before we commit to them, but that charge has already gone off in us and we rationalize that we can handle them or change them or fix them. It is now just a little voice in our head, but later it becomes a blasting headache!

Challenge yourself for a moment. Is this the first time you haven't been involved with someone whom you ended up taking care of? Were you a caretaker in your family, and did you feel taken advantage of? If you can answer these questions honestly, then you are a codependent addict. We would need to understand that this is an addiction, just like alcohol or drugs or any of other things we use to numb ourselves. When we are constantly thinking of others before ourselves, and we cannot manage to stop, we are in trouble! We do not want to look at ourselves and we use the other person or people to distract us from our own issues. And if we look hard enough, we will see that it has always been that way. It is important to remember that we do not get new issues at thirty years old! We have, instead, just brought a "mature" version of the ones we developed in childhood. And without this recognition we have no real chance for recovery when it comes to having our own needs fulfilled. We wouldn't even know what they are!

LARRY ROBINSON

Sometimes we need a support system to help us make this life-altering change, for we have to remember that every addiction is selfish, even taking care of others! The best support for this is other people who are in the same situation. CODA, which stands for Codependents Anonymous, is a fellowship of people who understand what it is like to be in your situation. Remember, this is just a different act of the same play in life. Counseling helps you to get underneath it, but before you look at yourself you have to go through recovery from this addiction. You don't need to leave the other person as much as you need to find yourself! If you are addicted to putting others first and you don't believe it, then your pain is still tolerable.

Question: Are you isolated from other people because you are too afraid to let them know that you suffer? Is your image of yourself important for you to break? Can you open up to another person about how you really feel?

_____

_____

_____

_____

_____

_____

_____

_____

_____

_____

NOVEMBER 5

What does it take to "renew" love with your spouse or partner? How long have you felt that disconnection? Most couples can experience that disconnect because one person cannot tell the other that everything is "fine" if in your heart you know you are being lied to. How many times have you validated the definition of insanity, which is doing the same thing over and over again and expecting a different result? We are all guilty of this. Do not let anyone ever tell you, "Oh, that's not my issue!"

This disconnect can go on for years without either person truly pushing the other to want to fix this problem. The thing is, the longer you do not deal with it the more distant you grow apart. In no time you will experience the "roommate relationship." This one really is hard to cope with because we have no idea what's going on with the other person's life and they don't know where we are. It results in short answers and an edgy feeling when you are together. There are so many things that could be mentioned, and I am sure that you will bring your own situations to light.

This can also have a profound effect on children. They can feel the detachment, but have no idea what it means! They could blame themselves because they react to their parents' anxiety or bitterness. They really do let us know what is going on, if we just would pay closer attention to why they are acting out.

The *reconnection* begins when we are at our bottom. Nothing feels as empty as this. Having an affair looks like the only way out, but that in itself causes a whole new bag of issues. It is not a matter of who brings this up, but we definitely can revert to acting like children, waiting for the other to "go first"! Once we do bring it up, we can decide to either work on this or understand that the disconnection is so great that we just have to leave. But it is not easier to start with someone new. A new person is not a better person to work out your issues with, they are just a different one. It is very painful to allow yourself to love this person again. Yes, the amount of pain was horrific to you, but you are both responsible for the disconnection. It does take the both of you.

Assignment: Take slow steps. Make it light and easy. Dress up for each other and make a date night. Find something common you share before you go out so you have a hidden agenda to keep the conversation fun. Connect!

_____

_____

_____

_____

_____

_____

_____

_____

_____

_____

_____

_____

_____

_____

_____

_____

Have you ever experienced a broken heart? Do you know *that* feeling that starts in your toes and creeps up into your body and then lands on your heart as if it was a ton of bricks and makes it impossible for you to breathe? And the only relief you get is when you cry!

And cry we do as if someone turned on a faucet inside of us and forgot to turn it off! Songs, restaurants, beaches, books, movies, all the things you did with someone you loved are always flashing before you as if you have a nonstop movie playing in your head. The bad thing is that you cannot turn it off. You wake up to it as soon your eyes open and it is your last thought before you go to sleep (if you even can). Face it, life feels so ugly and you do not feel like a day at the beach!

It feels as if we will never get over this loss, but wait, who says that? Are you saying that one person, who didn't even like you that much, has that much control over you? No! No! No! You need to get out of that pity party you are having and recognize that it took two people to make the relationship and two people to destroy it! Do you remember all the pain you experienced being with someone who was not emotionally available? Would you rather go back to that, or do you value yourself enough to want to move on? Look, if you met this person, you will meet another. There isn't just one person out there whom we are meant to be with.

Take back your heart; it is stronger than you think. Take back your life and shine again! Get off your butt and see that life has so much more to offer you when you let go of bad company! No one can break your heart except you by continuing to dwell on the impossible and fantasizing that the other person wasn't really so bad! You deserve more! Do not dare to think of what today is by mourning the past. Love yourself!

Question: Are you someone that lives in the past? Are you always crying about lost relationships and ignoring your life in the present? Do you never see the future?

NOVEMBER 7

Do you fool yourself into believing that you are all right with the way your life is going? Are you someone who always needs to be the one with the best relationship and the greatest kids and the job you always wanted? Do you bypass negative situations and generally refuse to deal with them for they tend to disrupt your fantasy world by injecting a harsh dose of reality? Do you know people like this? It is endless the way they need to talk about their lives. It is almost as if they cannot stop themselves because to really look at their reality might be devastating. Can you look at your reality without going into a deep sadness or depression?

We all have this issue but to different degrees. Some of us are in such terrible denial that it is the only way we can cope with life, while others can have just a touch of this. What this means is that we do not always deal with our issues in a relationship. What makes it so that we cannot face our reality?

There are no mistakes in life, only choices. And if you made a choice about this relationship, then it is possible that you are meant to be in it? Again, this is your journey! Do you ask how and why mistakes even exist if this is your journey? No, you have something to learn about yourself from this life that you have created. Hiding behind a false happiness is also part of your journey. Dig a little deeper into yourself and you will see that this false self is not a new issue, but rather one that you brought into this part of your life! Have you ever walked by a mirror and glanced at the person you saw in it and wondered to yourself, "Who was that?" Often we do not see ourselves for who we are, but for what and who we want to be!

The steps you need to take in order to change this part of you, the false self, are as follows: you need to be honest with yourself. No more trying to fool yourself into believing that everything is great in life. You have your issues, just like the rest of us. There is no shame in having doubts, fears, disappointments, or heartache in life. Next, you need to have a plan for yourself that translates into a plan for recovery. It is essential that you see yourself in a recovery process. There is a point in your life where even you

LARRY ROBINSON

cannot tolerate this happy self! What a great notion, that we can be in a recovery stage. This enables us to not be so hard on ourselves because we can see a light at the end of this tunnel of falseness.

Assignment: Do you believe that you can have a false self? Do you ever leave a group of people and feel as if you have been fake? We also need to journal about our life and our feelings as we recover. Go back into your past and start to see when this false self emerged. Write about who you believe is under this guise of happiness. Do not judge yourself! This cannot be emphasized more! There is no judgment that you can make about you that is new. If you see this, then you are in the beginning of recovering you! It will feel so great to shed the false self and just let you emerge. Do it!

_____

_____

_____

_____

_____

_____

_____

_____

_____

_____

NOVEMBER 8

Why do I want you to be someone else? So many times I thought if only you were kinder, prettier, or better-looking; if only you were richer or wiser or more successful. If only you didn't work so much; if only you weren't so anxious all the time. If only, if only, if only . . . Then who would I be? Do I rely on you to bolster my self-esteem? Do I think that if you had any of the above qualities that I would be a better person? If only that were true then I would have found the right person!

Oh, how misguided I am, for it is not up to you to make me a better person. I know my image would improve if you were those things. I could walk around pumped up and feeling better than most, but I would be lying to myself. You do not determine who I am. I do! It is my work in life to become all the things that I want you to be. It is my responsibility to accept myself and you, and appreciate what we are, who you are, and who I am. I know this is my work. Never let me put you down for what I want you to be. I am with you because I fell in love with you; not to make me better, but to make me see all of your good qualities. Today I will tell you one hundred times how much I love you and how much your love means to me!

Assignment: Write your own declaration of love to a loved one. If you are single, to one that you wish for. This exercise is to help you see the positive in your life!

LARRY ROBINSON

November 9

"Why is it that anytime I have something I want to say you tell me 'later'? Right! As if later ever comes! But when you have something that you want to say you want me to drop everything and let you speak? There is something wrong with this picture. Can't you see that?"

Relationships are almost never balanced, for there often can be an inequality in how and when we listen to each other. Men and women have different views of what is important and what can wait. We are often confronted with right and wrong choices in situations with our partners regarding whose way we are we going to do something, and it can sometimes turn into a game of "one-upmanship." We get extremely confused over something we believe starts out as a simple question and almost always turn into a major battle. Usually one partner will freeze up, while the other is hot as coals over a fire. This combination is a hard one to overcome, but a necessary one to conquer!

We have to be able to listen to one another without becoming defensive to the point where we often end up saying things we don't mean. Oftentimes we are reacting, not to what is said but to how it is said to us. The tone that someone uses is a dead giveaway as to how they are really feeling! Where did we learn such horrendous behaviors?

A more important question is do you want to stop it? We might say that we "want to want to," but to really stop it we have to feel the poison that comes out of us and want to be rid of this form of communicating. Learned behaviors are really difficult to break, especially if we have had role models in life that showed us this *is* the way to communicate. Remember that for a man his father is his role model whether he likes it or not, and for a woman it is her mother. We have them inside of us! Call it "emotional genetics," but it does exist! Haven't you ever said to yourself, "I will never be like him/her," but inevitably out they come in our arguments? We can even pass this on to our children if we do not catch it before they absorb it. Which way of communicating negatively do you do?

LARRY ROBINSON

1. "Whose way do we do it?"
2. "I'm right and you're wrong!"
3. "I am better than you, you are less than me."

In order to stop this behavior you first have to look at yourself from an emotional distance. It is necessary to accept that this issue is yours before you can resolve it. Remember that you do not act this way out of spite, but out of habit and conditioning. Once you realize you do this, and then it is your responsibility to catch yourself doing it! And it is not resolved overnight, for there has been so much repeat behavior.

Give yourself a break and let your spouse or partner know that you are working on this. Acceptance and mindfulness are key ingredients in fixing this issue. Both you and your significant other need to work on this together, for if anyone is guilty of communicating in one or more of the above examples, then the other person will react defensively. Decide today that you want to treat your spouse/partner as you would wish to be treated, with respect and honesty!

Question: Which of the above three characteristics do you possess? How have you expressed these negative traits to others? Can you honestly identify them in yourself?

_____

_____

_____

_____

_____

LARRY ROBINSON

November 10

"Why can't you respect me? Why is it that you never tell me where you are going or when you will be home? I just do not understand why you treat me like I am nobody in your life. I have always been there for you no matter what was going on and all I feel from you is disrespect."

Does that statement sound familiar to you? "Respect" is probably the most important word we can use on each other in a relationship. It does not come easily, and you can love someone and still not respect them. Why do we get ourselves into relationships where we are taken for granted? We want the relationship more than we want the person! We put up with such intense pain just to be wanted by someone who will treat us as second-class citizens. We have no self-esteem and they know it! If we let them know all the time how much we love them and need them without asking, or even demanding respect in return, why shouldn't we be treated like we are indentured servants?

This has no gender to it. Men do this to women and women do this to men. As long as we allow this type of behavior to exist, our children will learn it from us. Why do you think your son or daughter treats you the way they do? You showed them the path to disrespect! Now it is time to understand this behavior and change it! It is incredibly difficult to get inside the mind of a young child. Their perception of reality is often wrong, and their sensitivity to us is so strong that sometimes we can even look at them with love and they can interpret it as dislike. It is almost impossible to teach a four-year-old about their feelings.

If we do not act respectfully toward our spouse or partner, we begin to teach our children how to disrespect us and other adults. It really is "monkey see, monkey do" for children. We can give them everything they ask for and feel like good parents, but we cannot tell them to respect us without showing them what it looks like! "Well done is better than well said" is the old saying, and sometimes we are just "well said" people.

Did you respect your parents? What valuable lessons around respect did they teach you? Do you respect yourself or are you just someone who puts on a show? Who do you want teaching respect to your children? You are what they have in the beginning to understand it. If you do not bother to show respect to their mother or your partner, then they are lost also. It just repeats itself from generation to generation.

Disrespect is a gateway to failed lives. We never grow or move away from where the last piece of respect was injected into our life, if any. Stuck in the quicksand of despair, we sink slowly and without the ability to breathe life back into ourselves or those around us. We create an atmosphere of losing, and it does not get better unless we begin by respecting ourselves.

So how do we go about respecting ourselves if there was none to start with? The first step is the recognition that we want the ability to respect, and honesty is really at the beginning of the path of respect. No matter how bad you think you might be, bad was yesterday and now today you have the opportunity to begin the truth. Telling the truth and respecting oneself are interchangeable! One cannot exist without the other. After reading this, make today a chance to get back on your journey in life and find that self-respect! And then you can teach it to others!

Question: In what ways have you sabotaged your life? Are you always looking at your life as half empty rather than half full? List three positives about your life.

_____

_____

_____

_____

_____

// I am always there for you no matter what! Where are you when I need you? I never tell you how to run your life. Where are you when I need you? Why is it that I no longer want to go to you with any problem I have, for you will make me feel like I created it?"

What happens in a relationship when you no longer believe that your partner or spouse is really there for you? Why can't you tell them something without getting a fifty-cent lecture on "You knew that this would happen; you set yourself up for it, so get over it"? There is something very wrong here, and what eventually happens is that we start to disconnect.

The disconnection is unconscious at first, but there is a little bit of distance that you feel when you are around the other person. You feel a little less open with them and you are not sure why. And the next time you want some support you hear something like, "I feel sorry for you, for you seem to need a lot of approval from others."

Well, maybe we never got any from anyone and we figure you are the best we have. Why is it that we can listen to you and try to soothe you, but you can never do that for us? We do not understand what you believe support really is. It is almost like you do not want to take the time to listen before issuing some snide remark. We don't even know where it comes from and yet you hold your ground like a soldier who refuses to give up. Can we count on you to be our friend or does it only work one way?

Now the disconnection is no longer underground but at the "fighting" surface, and we have become numb to our feelings. We are silent on the outside but full of rage on the inside, and all you will do if we open our mouth is call us too needy. We needed you, where were you? And now that this disconnect is so strong, what will happen to our life? We will not come to you again and you will have to feel what we feel!

Is it really possible to mend this disconnect that has been going on for such a long time that any thoughts about intimacy are now gone forever? Healing takes a recovery period and both partners need to understand this. We do not flip our feelings around because someone simply says they are sorry, nor do we want to make them feel better by accepting it. It is okay not to accept an apology until we are ready to, but you must tell your partner that you will work on the acceptance. To leave someone hanging out there is just as bad as saying, "Too bad!"

Everyone experiences hurt, and there isn't a time period that says when we are over it. There is still a hidden anxiety that it will happen again and a trust that has to be rebuilt. This time the connection is slow to renew itself. We all can remember when it was, "Oh, don't worry" and "I'll be fine!" That was a long time ago, and it will take a lot more before we can say that again. Everything that happened will make us think whether or not we really even want to mend the disconnect. But no relationship is perfect and no relationship can heal itself. It needs communication, forgiveness, and time to heal.

Is your relationship in a disconnect? Why have you let it go this far without communicating about what to do to repair it? How has it affected the rest of your family? Do you fantasize about being with someone else? And if you do, then why would that be any better? After all, if this one didn't work out and at least 50 percent of the problem was you, all you are going to do is bring it to the next one. No, there is no perfect relationship, only a chance for recovery!

Question: Are you someone who dooms themselves in a relationship? Are you always feeling a disconnect with your spouse/partner but never address it? How long do you go before an explosion happens?

LARRY ROBINSON

NOVEMBER 12

"I am sure I gave that to you. I put it on my desk and marked it *urgent*, so I do not understand why you didn't get it. I remember you telling me when you needed it. What? No, I am sure I did it! Oh god, did I do it or did I just think I did it?"

Are you a procrastinator? Do you always have a pile of things to finish, a new project that you have not started yet, or so many "made promises" that you did not get to that people cannot rely on you anymore? There are so many of us out there who are like this that we could fill another universe and there would still be a waiting list to get in. We are not people who cannot leave things undone. We are not reliable people. We are not lazy; we only appear to be. We just cannot be trusted to accomplish what we promise.

The problem really is that we do not trust ourselves enough to complete tasks or requests. We are the lost and forlorn, for no one really respects who we are and would rely on us if in trouble. We mean well, but there is something wrong about how we approach life. We do not see life like the "step-to-it" person who has something finished the day they receive the request. They get it, we do not!

How many times have you beaten yourself up for disappointing yourself or your spouse or children or even friends? How many jobs have you lost because you could not finish your work on time? Oh yes, this is not a new issue!

Look back into your life and see how many times this happened when you were young. Back then you really didn't think it was an issue, although everyone else did, but today it is such a different story. Today we have people who rely on us and we have proven to be a disappointment. Why is this? We do not want to be, but one way or another nothing changes for us. Has your marriage or partnership ever been at risk of dissolving because your spouse cannot take it anymore? Do home chores like cleaning the gutters get continuously put off? Does your thinking along the lines of "I'll do it tomorrow" eventually become very costly for you when things finally break and you are forced to take things seriously? How much has it cost you to be the procrastinator? I'll bet you a pretty penny! How did we become like this?

There was no one who taught us inner discipline. We were children without boundaries. We made our own decisions when we were young, and after a while we did not listen to anyone. We were basically left to our own devices when it came to homework or chores. Our parents were either both struggling to make a living or so self-centered that we were left to ourselves. We had no curfew and were not disciplined for bad behavior. We might have been the "rebellious" children who no one could control. They gave up on us so easily that we didn't care then, and now we do not have the confidence in ourselves to take steps to correct what happened in our past.

We need to get over this. How long do we sit around bemoaning our out-of-control lives before we do something about it? Do you think you have ADHD? I do not think so. You were an emotionally neglected child, or perceived that you were, and you were beaten down by yourself or others for most of your childhood. Well, you are no longer that child! You grew up, and unless you want to remain a child/adult, you will start to seriously look at yourself. You need to begin to understand that because you believed you were not good enough to have any kind of self-esteem, you have been living this way for most of your life. You allow your mind to tell you negative thinking about yourself and you still want to believe it! Well, why would you have any success if you listen to the "bull" your mind repeats over and over in your head? Your mind is not your friend! Look into your heart and you will find you! Look into your mind and you will find nothing good!

Assignment: Do you pay attention to what your mind says to you? How often have you not listened to your heart but followed the negativity of your mind?

_____

_____

_____

_____

LARRY ROBINSON

NOVEMBER 13

"Why did you make me feel that I was worth nothing and that you could not care about me at all? Why did you lie so many times when I begged you to tell me the truth about where you were? Why did you do this to me?"

Why do we really cheat on those we say we love? Why is it that we experience no guilt when we are carrying on an affair? We act as if we deserve it or are entitled to have it. We are in bliss and then return home either as wonderful as can be or looking for any little reason to fight with our partner, almost as if we can then feel justified in our cheating. We know that we are not happy in our relationship, and we are pretty sure our spouse or partner is not happy either, yet we say nothing because the thrill of the affair has captured our feelings. Nothing matters until we can sneak a call to our "new best friend" with our spouse or partner in the house! How much hate do you think we really have for our loved one when this happens?

Do not kid yourself into believing that you love your spouse but just needed to be able to speak your real truth with someone who could understand you better! Isn't it difficult to talk nonsense and "bull" about your husband or wife when only your side is what is being heard? At one time or another, when we are unhappy we might fantasize about what it might be like to be with someone else, but to actually act on it must take a great deal of misery or hate.

We say we are always misunderstood or not listened to by our spouse, but in actuality that is how we want it, because the *idea* of an affair is so great that we cannot stop ourselves from committing this act! After a while we become so used to the infidelity that we make it part of our life and it is our "new normal." And it does not matter whether it is an affair, running to massage parlors, watching pornography, or creating an online affair, we have crossed a very dangerous and desperate line. We risk so much over absolutely nothing! It is a choice between a "charge" that lasts for only a few seconds and a real connection that lasts forever!

Hurting someone you promised to be there for forever is so selfish. Step back and recognize that the face in the mirror is you! Do you like

LARRY ROBINSON

what you see? Can you see the honest, genuine person, or do you see the devil?

Question: Look into the mirror and describe how you see yourself. Are you the person that you say you are? Do not look at your features, try and look beyond to what you see inside yourself. Yes, we all can see inside if we try!

_____

_____

_____

_____

_____

_____

_____

_____

_____

_____

_____

_____

_____

_____

_____

November 14

The "game of life" is so difficult at times that it makes you want to say, "What the hell is going on?" We are constantly confronted with situations that we don't want to face, and sometimes we are blind as to how we got there. We do not really pay that much attention to this game until we get either too involved with someone else's or trapped inside our own. What is the "game"?

Of course we all want someone else to be at fault for where we are or who we are or what happened. How often do we really hear people say, "This was my fault," or "I am responsible for what happened to me"? The biggest blame is on our parents, whether they are alive or dead. If they are alive, we harbor anger toward them for not giving us enough love or what we needed as children, yet we continue to play the role of "child" to "parent." "Yes, Dad and Mom" is our mantra, and even though we are grown adults we still respond to them as if we are children. We remain afraid to speak our mind to these "holy saints" who were always right!

The only time we can blame them for making our lives miserable is when they are dead and cannot answer us. How brave we are to let the dead not rest with our lament about how horrible they were to us. There was no resolution to those relationships, that's for sure! So here we are, left with a bad taste in our mouth, and they cannot speak back! We make our own life! We make our own decisions! We are masters of our own destiny!

Not our parents, our spouses, our children, or our friends are responsible for where we are in life. If we stay with a partner who cheated on us, they are not to blame for our decision. If our life is so unsettling with them, then we should leave them or never have allowed them back in our life! If we still remain insecure in the relationship, then that is not their fault. Our insecurity is ours, and fear is no excuse to stay. And don't place the blame on your children because you decided to stay! You stayed for you! They do not ask for this turmoil. We give it to them!

Take responsibility for your choices. Remember, we are not those little children who were looking for validation. No one can validate our choices in life, and no one but ourselves can take responsibility for them.

LARRY ROBINSON

"Passing the buck" leaves us empty and alone, for if we do not honor the truth, then no one will honor us. Blaming the world for your life condition is so easy, just lie back and point fingers at whoever you deem the culprit! How sad we must be to have to cheat in this game of life!

Assignment: List all the ways that you blame others for your troubles. Think carefully, for the answers are important.

_____

_____

_____

_____

_____

_____

_____

_____

_____

_____

_____

_____

_____

Can you sit with yourself and quiet your mind? Do you get so distracted with your surroundings or a noise in the room that you lose your focus? What *is* your focus? Is it on you, or are you running from yourself?

Think about what it would feel like to sit quietly with yourself and think of virtually nothing. Clearing out all the garbage that enters into your mind every waking moment would be so refreshing! No, you cannot sit for more than a moment before a flood of thoughts rushes into your mind. There is no escape from your self. The self is chasing after you to challenge you to sit with you and you will have nothing to do with it! "Why," you ask your self, "are you so persistent in having all these intrusive thoughts enter into my thinking?"

"I don't want to think about where I am in my life," is your battle cry. You are a winner because you outsmart the self by keeping your mind on thousands of little nonsensical issues in order to keep out the bigger ones. You know, those bigger ones that relate to your life and unhappiness. How many times have you outwitted your self? It won't get you when you are going to sleep because you don't allow sleep in. You keep your mind going until you are so exhausted that you pass out! "Ha, got you again, self! So stop chasing me!"

Sometimes you feel it creeping in when you're trying to read, and when you finish a page you have no idea what you just read! Some say this is ADHD, but the self knows better that it is just you having another battle with it. There is no peace of mind, there is no silence, and there is no understanding as long as you keep running from your self.

Stop now and understand that what you are afraid of is the truth. Your self always knows the truth, and that is why it chases you. It wants you to listen to your inner thinking and find your feelings. It wants you to stop thinking that the world hates you and that it is you who is hateful. Your self has witnessed so many judgments of you and others that it understands your loneliness better than you do! You think it is because you can't do enough for others or that you have a cold heart or you try too hard to please, but these are not the reasons for your isolation or loneliness. Your loneliness comes from never telling anybody the truth about how you feel. You are the fake! Your self sees this and tries chasing after the authentic you, but you have not been ready to stop running. Aren't you tired yet?

It has been a lifetime and you still cannot sit quietly because you are too afraid to look. Nothing is more frightening than having your self always chasing you. But instead of running away, try to slow down and let yourself be caught. If you do, you will find that the self will only serve as your guide to a better understanding of you!

We are all running at times, and we all are being chased. When you stop, your journey in life continues and your mind begins to quiet itself down. You begin to see a different person from the one you thought you were. You grow and you begin to understand more people because you finally understand you! Look in the mirror and see your self!

Assignment: Make a list of all the ways in which you try to avoid issues in your life. The most important thing is to be honest with yourself.

_____

_____

_____

_____

_____

_____

_____

_____

_____

_____

Eric Krouss
Marblehead, Massachusetts, USA

November 16

It is done, finished, over! How do I cope with my life now that I am alone again? I cannot believe how much love and energy I put into us. And you just said, "I don't feel the same anymore."

The first thing I ask myself is, "What did I do wrong?" Why do I rush to judge myself first before I really look at what was happening between us? You have ended something so easily and I am suffering and you are free!

This is often the case when a relationship ends. This is the "aftermath." We are left with so many questions and no answers that fit. The first reaction is, "I cannot make it without the other person. How do I get on with my life?" Well, do not let anyone tell you that "Time will heal all wounds," or that you are "better off without the relationship." This is not support! This is more pain! It is pain because you did not end the relationship. You were still holding on to some sort of hope that you would work things out.

Everyone who has experienced rejection, no matter how bad the relationship was, does not want to have it end this way. You might ask yourself, "Why didn't I end it when I knew it was dying?" It might be that you didn't really want to face life alone again. Starting over is half the fear in the aftermath of a relationship. But the big question is *can* you start over again, and *will* you pick the same type of person? The truth is that until you begin to see who you chose and why, you will repeat yourself.

How many of us have chosen the same type of person over and over again? They might have a different story but they will certainly remain in our path until we figure out that repetition without resolution will result in us making the same poor choices. You need time now to heal and to understand you!

The aftermath sometimes rushes us into wanting to find someone to fill our emptiness immediately. Usually that person is someone who wants us so quickly and who gets intense so fast that we realize that this person is the opposite of the other. And the opposite doesn't mean better, it just means that we have exchanged one who didn't want us at all for one who can't get enough of us. This person will tell us "I love you" two weeks into dating! Soon we realize that we don't want this either. We also might go the opposite way and become a "dating anorexic." We announce, "I will never get serious with anyone ever again!" and we spend so much time avoiding dating that we give up on it entirely. Again, this method of coping will get us nowhere.

In the aftermath we need friends to be with us who will not talk our heads off about dating or the old relationship. When we need to talk about it we will, with no pressure! We need to make it okay to spend time alone. It is essential that we understand that we had a life before this relationship and that we'll have one again! Wouldn't you rather be with someone who wants to be with you than be with someone who doesn't?

Don't just sit around doing self-destructive behaviors either. Do something good for yourself! Learn that being with yourself is better than being with someone who might want you but who still leaves you feeling empty because you do not feel the same way. You will know when the right person comes along because you will feel at ease with both yourself and the other person. There will be no, "Do they like me?" It will be, "Gee, I really feel comfortable with him/her. I like the way I feel when I am with them."

Question: How did you survive the aftermath of a broken relationship? Is it still dragging around inside of you?

_____

_____

_____

_____

_____

_____

NOVEMBER 17

Does it just hit you sometimes that you are so alone in the world, even if you are surrounded by people who love you? Do you feel isolated from all the people you love? Have you always felt this way but have hidden your despair from those you think know you?

You have been hiding behind an image that you have created and now you cannot tolerate it. Is this really you? How did you create a persona that you do not even like? We cannot live in our reality because it is not a pleasant place and it is where our secrets are. As children we began to create a person who could easily become fake to the world as a way of survival. "I am happy." "I am funny." "I am serious." "I am generous, and I care more about how you are than I do about myself!" On and on we could go with our false images, when behind this is the lonely child/person.

We have looked to all sorts of addictions, like alcohol, drugs, sex, work, love, food, and you name it, and we can try to find some solace in them, but they do not stop the loneliness. They only intensify it!

Have you ever thought to yourself, "Why have I been so afraid to see the true self in me? Do I hate who it is? Maybe I have always felt I had to be validated by everyone, and by looking for it I pleased or tried to please everyone but me. How could I feel valuable if I was not being me? How could I be valuable if I *was* me? I was too afraid to take that chance. When it comes down to it my loneliness is the product of never being myself; of never voicing my real opinions and instead swallowing my self and becoming passive to the world around me. When do I take my stand and become authentic? *Now!* It is now before I slip away into nothingness. My fear is coming from my manufactured self, and I can no longer muster up the phoniness. If I am alone, then what difference does it make to have my voice heard! I might not feel so lonely anymore and I will have my best friend beside me, and that's me!"

Assignment: Write about the self that you wish you were. What is different about that self from who you are now?

LARRY ROBINSON

November 18

If there is a habit or quality in your mate that rouses unattractive traits in your disposition, you should realize that the purpose of this circumstance is to bring to the surface those poisons that are hidden within you so that you might eliminate them and thus "purify" your nature.

"Perfection," this is what I saw when I met you. You had such a way about you that I thought we were just meant to be together forever! Did I know what forever meant? Not at all! To me, forever was something I only dreamt about. In my dreams I saw that partner alongside of me, rocking in that chair built for two and watching the sunset in the twilight of our lives. There was *never a thought of you in those pajamas,* which I sometimes I believe are your entire wardrobe, or your hair that's piled on top of your head as if it was sprouting wings! Nor did I believe that you would picture me chewing potato chips with my mouth wide open, driving you insane as we sat and stared silently at the TV for the eighth millionth time.

And how many times did we talk over each other, never quite hearing what the other was saying and probably not that interested to begin with? We were always engaged in who is right or who is wrong, and each time one of us "won" we actually lost because we made the other feel bad.

And then I ask myself, "If I had known all of these things beforehand, would I have still married you and promised myself to you forever?" There is no doubt in my mind that I would marry you over and over and over again, because you know me and I know you, and no one will ever know us the way that we know each other! You are perfection. Maybe not what I thought perfection was supposed to be, but what it really is! Our struggle and our love, which have no "normal" attached to it, are perfection because they are ours! Yes, we are a perfect fit for that rocking chair!

LARRY ROBINSON

Question: Do you understand that forever is something that couples have to work on? Do you work on your relationship to create the forever feeling, or is it still just a fantasy that never truly happens?

_____

_____

_____

_____

_____

_____

_____

_____

_____

_____

_____

_____

_____

_____

_____

A re you desperate to be married and to experience "the American Dream"? Why is it that the man/woman that you have your heart set on does not keep his/her interest high after the "honeymoon period" of a relationship is over?

Who said that you were on a honeymoon to begin with? We all call the falling-in-*like* period the *honeymoon period*, where we think that everything about our new partner is cute or acceptable. But we are not really seeing the whole person during that time, only what we want to see. Is the other person hiding their true self? What you see about the other person is true, but it takes a long time to really get to know someone.

Falling in love is a *process,* not an event. Most men work from the outside in, looking at the sexual side of a woman, and when they feel that the woman is willing they will approach sex. If the sex is good, then the relationship will continue. But this is not love! This is about sex and feeling good. How long do you wait before you will have sex with a man you like? Are you afraid that if you do not go along with his program that he might not want you?

Many couples have had sex on the fourth date and the sex was great. The problem with this is that the relationship starts out with sex and is therefore based on the "quality" of the sex. This can make the honeymoon period really great, mostly because there are no evident problems yet in the relationship. As soon as a problem between the two arises and there is a split in the difference of opinion, then the sex becomes only mediocre.

This is not necessarily the end of the relationship, but rather the beginning of a "settling in" period. Yes, the man says, "She turns me on," but he does not necessarily want to deal with what he perceives as her issues, and so the "hot" guy turns somewhat "cool." He falls into a more complacent position, and the charge of "new and wonderful" begins to slip away. What is the answer to this problem?

We rush into relationships because we all want to be wanted. Do we ever get to know how the other deals with arguments or with negative feelings? Sex has become a driving force in the relationship—often, way too early—and we do not know enough about each other to be truly secure.

Do you remember the expression "Why buy the cow when the milk is free" (giving too much away for free)? Think about how relevant that statement is and ask yourself who is this guy you gave yourself to before he understood your heart and you his? Remember, women work from the inside out, and if you don't really feel your heart, then you are living his life and your insecurity will always follow. If you build an emotional connection without the sex your chances of finding happiness with each other is so much greater. There is a lifetime to explore lovemaking with each other. You might be giving the milk away before the cow is truly up for sale!

Question: Are you someone who rushes into relationships? Do you think by having sex quickly you are sealing a relationship? Or do you end up feeling bad about yourself and even rejected later?

_____

_____

_____

_____

_____

_____

_____

_____

_____

_____

November 20

Why is it that we are always setting each other off as if our partner believes we intended to? How often were your words met with extreme defensiveness rather than the understanding you were looking for? Both males and females suffer from this disease. Becoming defensive is second nature to a lot of us. What does it really hit inside? Defensiveness is our protection from feeling guilty or from low self-esteem.

Let's look at this example: a wife approaches her husband and says that she needs to talk to him but that she is afraid that he will get angry and start to yell. Already the defensive self is feeling on edge because she has told him something that he knows to be true. She continues to tell him that she ends up never being understood. At this point, his anger is starting to erupt. First, he wants to know what she wants to say, and secondly, he cannot tolerate what he believes to be her constant criticism. When she starts to tell him, he immediately yells at her and defends himself and reaffirms her belief that she cannot talk to him. And she says, "See, I knew you'd yell!"

Question: Who cannot identify with either of them? What do you believe the answer is to their problem? Which one do you identify with and what example can you give in support of this reasoning? Who do you believe to be more defensive, men or women?

There are probably too many situations, which would likely take years to work through, but let's try and identify some others. Do you believe this will turn into a "who's right and who's wrong" issue?

_____

_____

_____

LARRY ROBINSON

November 21

When an infant is in need of attention, it emits a certain sound in its cry. We know by the sound to go to the baby. If we do not respond right away, the crying gets louder and we can detect anger coming from the baby. But what if no one responds? The baby is left alone and no longer do we hear anger but now we hear fear in its cry—fear that can then lead to *terror*. Abandonment has taken over. How does this relate to us as adults?

It informs us that the first feeling we experience when we don't get what we need or want is anger. Anger is the hardest feeling for most of us to deal with because it almost always entails a confrontation with the person whom we are upset with. It also can lead us to that feeling of terror from the possibility that what we say will end up chasing the other person away and we will be left alone. This raises the stakes enormously for us because it triggers our subconscious, which has stored all our feelings of unworthiness, low self-esteem, and abandonment.

Have you ever seen a child you are reprimanding start to cry before you are even finished talking to him or her? Anger can be a very hot feeling, much like a fire, and tears (water) cool down that burning feeling. Crying enables us to hide from our true feelings. Shutting down, which is another form of anger, is a defensive reaction to a situation, which causes the other person to feel rejected. How often do people freeze out the other person because they do not want to show their true feelings or take responsibility for their actions? They ignore the other person until the situation is dismissed out of pain and fear.

Question: How do you deal with your anger? List some ways that have worked and some that have backfired and made things worse.

_____

_____

_____

LARRY ROBINSON

November 22

"Why is it that we fight so much? Every other day it seems as if you want to end our relationship. And if I do something that you do not like you say you need a break! How many breaks will it take before I walk away from you and I am done, finished, out of here? I am tired of trying to be the bigger one in this relationship and the one who always ends up apologizing. When do you start taking some responsibility for your part in our mess?"

Commitment is something that many of us struggle with. What is it that causes us to want to run every time there is an issue between two people and we have to be responsible for our behavior? *Commitment* is a "forever" word and action, and we have a difficult time honoring it when we are always running away. Forever seems like an eternity, and we can be easily frightened away with that word just by itself.

What kind of commitments can you keep? Are you the type of person who one minute is madly in love and the next doubting why you are in a relationship? Do your words mean more than your actions? This is a problem for any of us who want a long-term relationship. We "want to want" one, but when it comes down to it we panic and are afraid of the word and the action. Sometimes we may even be considered "commitment phobic."

How does one become phobic around committing to a relationship? This is something we observe in childhood. We usually do not come from stable homes, and what we see as children can scare us as adults. Fighting, hurtful words—we watched all of it and our ears took it all in. We need to face the fact that we are afraid to fight. We have the "flight" and not "fight" way of dealing with our lives. Running away has always been easier.

It is time to stop acting like the child who wanted to run from his/her family. It is time we learned that we can be angry with someone and not have to pack our bags each time we experience conflict. Life is about conflict and resolution, and we can never have resolution when we're running away! Yes, it is painful to stay, but it is so much more painful to flee. Stay put, you do not need to run! Adults can resolve conflicts

LARRY ROBINSON

while children have no choice but to be beaten down by them. Today we become adults and stay the course!

Question: Are you someone who can follow through on commitments? Have you ever run away from one? Are you still running?

_____

_____

_____

_____

_____

_____

_____

_____

_____

_____

_____

_____

_____

_____

NOVEMBER 23

A re you someone who is filled with guilt? Are you that person who feels responsible for everything that happens, especially when it has a negative outcome? Are you someone who carries shame along with all that guilt?

Guilt eats away at us like a vulture (birds that eat the dead), picking us to the bare bones, and it shows no mercy. It has no gender and no age, but it has sharp teeth that tear us apart, and we let it! We have no defense against it. We are consumed by guilt.

How did this happen? What have we done to deserve this life sentence of feeling too responsible for every little thing that goes wrong? Do others really feel the way we do, or are we just unique?

We are not unique, and we share this "dis-ease" with millions of others, except we do not like to talk about it. We are the "volunteers" destined to take on this enemy while keeping it away from others. You see, there is a part of us that has gotten used to feeling this way and we do not see a way out of it! In fact, sometimes we may even feel beyond even wanting it to stop!

Many of us were shamed as children. We had parents who were relentless in their criticism of us and who were constantly pointing out our flaws. We were blamed even when we were not even present! Someone had to "take the fall" and we were selected. We did not put up a fight. We were always seen as "less than" and we lived our life that way.

Childhood is over! We are adults now and we need to stand up for ourselves and remove the label of "guilty as charged"! Anything that we feel is leftover from our childhood is the perception of a child, not that of an adult. If we look hard enough at reality, we will see that we were victimized into feeling responsible for other people's negative actions. Enough is enough! It is time to wake ourselves from this nightmare of feeling guilty and start to get angry over what we were put through!

Assignment: List all the ways that you have felt guilty about your behavior in the past. Are you still holding on to the guilt?

LARRY ROBINSON

NOVEMBER 24

Do you sleep well? Are you the type of person who longs for sleep so much of the day that when you finally arrive at bedtime you cannot fall asleep? Does your mind go wild and does the "war" begin as soon as the lights go out?

What is this war that so many of us struggle to conquer? Why do so many of us feel defeated and give up to a monster that shows no mercy? We belong to the "sleepless!" We are those people who cannot sleep and who struggle to close our eyes for more than ten minutes at a time. We lie there and pray that we will fall asleep, but no one is listening to us. The loneliness at two o'clock in the morning is devastating. It almost feels like all our demons are holding an all-night party and we are the guest of honor!

After a while we give in to this conscious nightmare and every night we prepare ourselves to be persecuted (chased) by our demons. Is there no rest for us?

There is no rest if you let your mind control you! As soon as you put your head down on your pillow it begins, or better still, you let it begin and the senseless thoughts take over. And we certainly can become "addicted" to not sleeping. Can you beat up this intruder and kick it out of your life and feel victory?

You must first decide that you will not let your mind control you. Detach yourself for a moment and look at what your mind says to you. There is your enemy, right in front of you, and you give up so quickly! You are negative before the light goes out and all your internal mental fussing about not sleeping even takes over!

Assignment: You must tell yourself that you are tired and are going to sleep. Get it into your mind that it listens to you and stop it from racing by saying to it: STOP IT. Do not give up, for it takes time to change a pattern. You might have to say it over and over again, but remember your mind tires also.

LARRY ROBINSON

November 25

Are you the type of person who looks like you are all put-together (have all the answers to life) but feel so different on the inside? Do people view you as someone they can go to with their issues or problems, but they tend to not want to know who you are? No doubt this must make you feel lonely and frustrated, but it is you who has set it up this way.

People who tend to want to listen to others and who always have the "right' advice for others can be some of the loneliest folks around. You will easily feel ignored and unwanted when you are not included in other people's plans. You can feel used and tend to start viewing people as ungrateful because you feel unrecognized due to the amount of energy that you have put out for others.

This is your issue, not theirs! You are the one who has set it up to not need anyone by making your life look so put-together. When we are in this space we cannot let others know how we feel because we would end up looking like we were seeking a reward for being there for them. How often do we not want to take on this role?

How sad for us that we cannot ask others for help when we are feeling as if our own issues are being ignored while we're taking on everyone else's. We do like it this way. The only problem is that reality is really hard on us. We can feel stuck in a very emotionally disturbing place, for we have to cope with our own issues and tend to suffer by ourselves. "Keep that smile on!" That is our motto (way of dealing with life)!

Assignment: Well, it is time to stop this nonsense! You can either choose to keep living this way or you can start to slowly come out of this condition. Let someone know that you know how they feel because you can feel the same way! This is at least a beginning! Making the "identification" lets them know that you experience the same feelings. Open up a discussion about ways that you both could resolve the issue. Do not try and be the only one with an answer. Let the other person lead. You will be amazed at how people will begin to respond to you!

LARRY ROBINSON

NOVEMBER 26

Thanks-*giving*

Thanksgiving

A time for all of us! Whether this is your holiday or not, let's take advantage of this time and give thanks for something in our lives that has made us a better person! I will start, and please let's show the world what it means to say "thank you!"

Mirror, Mirror is thankful that you took the chance and believed enough in this book that you went out and bought it.

Assignment: Please write a comment on what you are thankful for!

_____

_____

_____

_____

_____

_____

_____

_____

_____

November 27

D o you feel as if no one is listening to you? Are there times when you say something that you think is important and you get no response? You might as well be talking to the wind!

Do you get really excited about something, yet when you try to tell others they seem disinterested? And when you finish your sentence they change the subject? Do you feel as if you are just a shadow that people can step on without any consequences? If you can relate to this, then yes, you are a shadow! If it is that easy for people to change the subject, and it happens to you a lot and not just with one person but with many, then there is something wrong with how you are delivering your statements or ideas.

It is possible that in your excitement you can overwhelm others. You may be so into what you are saying that you might not be letting anyone else speak. It is not that you do not want to hear what others feel about what you have said, but your eagerness wipes out their desire to comment. Remember that this is not a one-shot deal, but something that happens to you quite often!

Whenever you get the one-word responses to what you are talking about or the simple "uh-huh," then the other person just cannot listen. They have now "drifted away" from your speech and are now impatiently waiting to hear the period at the end of your sentence so that they can talk about something else.

You need to stop complaining in your head that no one listens to you and start listening to yourself. What are you hearing? Is it one person going on and on about something that perhaps the other person is not even remotely (slightly) interested in? Pay attention to your "audience" and make sure that they are available to listen. Do not assume that everyone is as eager as you are to share news or views. You know that you have been in the same place that you put others in. We all are capable of talking too much at times, but give yourself a break and see that for you it might be all of the time!

Assignment: Listen to yourself when you are speaking to others. What do you hear? Are you always complaining or negative? Do you realize that this can turn people off?

_____

_____

_____

_____

_____

_____

_____

_____

_____

_____

_____

_____

_____

NOVEMBER 28

"Lonely," the word hits us in the heart so quickly that we do not even know what happened. Here we are facing the emptiness of our life. Empty! We desperately need someone, anyone to fill us up.

How bad does this feeling get? The answer to that is *very bad*, so bad in fact that at times we think that we are sinking deep into the *quicksand* of life. We feel that we have no one *there* and that there is no one who understands us. We're convinced that there is no one who will listen to us or make us laugh. We are so isolated that we do not know how to cope with loneliness.

We pray and we ask a higher power to fill us up and to let someone be there for us, but the answer does not come, and we wait and wait until we feel angry and then turn away from our belief in something greater than ourselves. No, this is all about us, and we are angry and so disappointed. How could this be? What did we do to deserve this emptiness in our life? We cry, we yell, and eventually we turn our backs on the world because we believe that this life has let us down.

Wait a minute! Are we that needy? Do we have to have someone "there" all the time? Without someone, is our life over? Have we no goals or ambitions to better ourselves? Or does life depend on having someone there? Perhaps each one of us must go through feeling empty before we can really have someone in our life. We must be able to make our life work whether there is someone there or not. We must see our own strength rather than rely on someone else to fill us up. We can be alone and not be lonely!

There is also a difference between being alone and feeling lonely. Being alone just means that at this point in our life there is no one there, whereas being lonely is a feeling that we cannot be with ourselves. We need someone there to take the spotlight off of ourselves. Perhaps we each are meant to experience the feeling of aloneness, and it is when we become comfortable being with ourselves that we can truly accept another person in our life!

Question: Can you tell the difference in yourself between being alone or lonely. What are the signs for both for you? How long can you spend time with yourself?

November 29

Are you the type of person who is laid back in life? You seem to be easygoing, free from too much worry, and less anxious than a lot of other folks. Nothing seems to get under your skin, and in fact some people marvel at how you handle life. But they really do not know you, and perhaps you never bother to truly look at yourself. The truth is that you have created an image of yourself that is controlling your life. You are the "guru." The problem is you have no one to turn to and you can never ask for help.

How alone does this really make you feel? Do you sometimes feel isolated and lonely because you have to hide how you really feel? Even the people you are closest to do not get that you are hiding your true self! Now, please do not misunderstand what the true self really is. The true self is not a big giant mess with many hidden issues, but it is, instead, just a normal person with normal issues. The problem here is that the issues do not feel normal to you. Issues are not normal when they are stuck deep inside you and you do not have the courage to break down this "nothing gets to me" attitude.

It is time to understand yourself better. You will ask, "How do I let go without looking like a weak person who has presented a false image to the world?" There certainly are issues that you can handle well, but there are other issues that you are stumped (confused) about also. You need to be able to say to people, "I wish I had the answer to that problem, but I do not." This is not telling people that you are inadequate, but that you are in the same place they are. This allows you to ask someone else, "What do you think?" And it does not matter whether what they have to say is right or wrong, but the point is that this allows you to be an "equal" with others, and not someone who has all the answers.

You will breathe easier when you take this pressure off yourself. Imagine how burdened you have felt (at times, not even knowing it) carrying everyone else's problems around inside of you! You can still be there for people without having to be so laid back!

Question: Do you ever fake being laid back but are a mess inside? You can write the truth here.

_____

_____

_____

_____

_____

_____

_____

_____

_____

_____

_____

_____

_____

_____

LARRY ROBINSON

November 30

"Tension," another invader of our peace of mind! It creeps up on us like an animal stalking its prey, waiting silently in the background of our lives and then pouncing on us, devouring our minds with anxiety, worry, edginess (ready to snap), and an obsessive song in our heads that never lets go of its grip on our hearts. No one escapes its hold!

Tension is a byproduct of stress and it always attacks our body, mind, and spirit. It can cause us to say and do things that we normally would not think of doing. When tension is present, sleep disappears. We lie there in bed with our minds racing on to so many issues and problems that the only way we end up sleeping is when we are so exhausted that our body takes over our mind and we "pass out" or we have to medicate ourselves to sleep.

Tension attacks the body and tightens it up so that we cannot heal anything physical that is bothering. Remember, sleep allows the body to heal, and without it we are at tension's mercy, our body tied up in knots. Try healing a backache or a cold or anything physical when you are tensed up. It just will not happen.

Tension attacks the mind to the point where we do not see things clearly. It does not allow our minds to rest, and that is what we need in order for our minds to stay rational and clear. And it truly magnifies the stress factor in our lives. To walk around with tension inside of us is extremely painful. It takes our spirit and drains the energy from it.

To deal with tension we must learn to breathe deeply. Put it into your mind that you are going to blow the tension right out of you. Breathe in and go deep into your body, and if you need to, scream it out of you. See how much you have absorbed from others and chase it away. "Get out!" is the mantra we need in order to free ourselves from it. Remember, it takes time to condition yourself to have a new way of dealing with life. Do not despair! You will achieve it if you keep consistent and do not give in to your tension.

Question: Do you see that tension can come out of not dealing with your anger? Look at some of the things that you are worried and tense about and see if you have been exceptionally angry about something else that you did not deal with.

_____

_____

_____

_____

_____

_____

_____

_____

_____

_____

_____

_____

_____

LARRY ROBINSON

Isabella Walsh, Limerick, Ireland

"It is not that people are not sorry truly and deeply. Change is a difficult thing to do. It takes time and lots and lots of thought processes focused on that particular issue, that particular action. One can be deeply sorry, yet with the day-to-day life experiences that can put you in the same thought process or mindset it is hard to correct your actions. Sometimes even if you are making progress, it takes both parties to address why the issue is happening and what they can do to minimize or correct the behavior."

—Dino Brienza, Maspeth, New York, USA

December 1

What makes us so afraid of rejection? Why do we fear the thought of being alone when we can already feel so alone in our relationships?

We both seem to live separate lives, which cause us to pass each other all the time. How sad our hopes have become. This is not what we signed up for! Do you remember when you felt so happy to have this loving person by your side, and you never thought you'd end up with a roommate with rings attached to both your fingers?

Well, while you sit there wondering why you put up with this, a fear creeps into your mind. "What if he/she leaves me? I could not tolerate the rejection. I would feel so abandoned." Aren't you feeling it now? Does it take the absence of someone else to let you feel alone?

If you have children, there is also the excuse that leaving would "ruin the family." Well, if you really think about it, isn't it ruined already if the children do not see their parents happy? Do you think they are unaware of the distance and tension they feel coming from the two of you? Okay, let them suffer the consequences of your behaviors, but you will use them as ways not to stir things up between the two of you. Remember the children, we say! But we need to work the rejected feelings between one another just for the fact that we did bring children into this world. If you can look your children straight in the eyes and tell them you did everything you possibly could to save your relationship but you could not, then and only then can we consider ending our relationship.

No one wants to start something that maybe they cannot finish. But we need to try and understand each other. If we do not work out what the issues are between us, everyone loses. We have nothing to lose by trying to talk to each other and heal!

Question: How do you deal with rejection? Do you sit silently crying inside or do you walk around angry all the time, jumping out at others, for your pain is too great?

LARRY ROBINSON

DECEMBER 2

D o you live your life out of the "hurts" from your past? Do you go over and over again what happened to end a relationship or job and try to figure out what you did wrong and why you cannot let go? Does your anger well up inside of you and not allow you to move on? When something painful happens in your present, do you immediately rush back into your past, and in the process embrace a mindset that is "flooded" with regrets, remorse or anger, and a violent reaction to a deed done against you? This is a problem!

Do you "stew" about your past and find yourself wandering through your mind, waiting for it to pounce on something that is so old that when it finds the perfect situation the pain seems like it happened yesterday? This is what happens when we are stuck in our past.

How did we get there in the first place? We never intended to hold on to this pain for eternity, but that is the way it feels. Old, new, they get so mixed in together that it is no longer easy to distinguish which is which. All we do know is that the suffering begins! Remember, we do not ask for this added pain, we just never learned how to resolve our pain in the first place. Now, think about how much pain you have held on to and why your life seems overwhelming to you at times.

Sometimes we have to take a different approach to this longtime enemy called "living life from our past hurts." Do you know how some of us can literally become hoarders with clothes and possessions and then call ourselves "collectors"? Well, we can also collect pain! Think about going to your closet and throwing out everything you no longer wear or have use for. It isn't easy to let go of because we think "Just maybe I might wear that next summer." We can do this with emotional issues, too. Whichever ones are no longer resolvable or outdated, just throw them away! Get a huge bag and start with your childhood and then go through it and toss out all your issues that have no resolution. You have no idea how light you will feel.

LARRY ROBINSON

Question: Are you someone who stews and does not let things go? Is there a list of times, places, and people in your head who have hurt you that you can access anytime and make yourself and others feel bad? Do you keep everything to yourself and act like nothing is wrong when in fact you are really hurting inside?

_____

_____

_____

_____

_____

_____

_____

_____

_____

_____

_____

_____

_____

_____

_____

December 3

"I have not finished yet, I still need you here! Why would you pick this time to leave when there are still so many things left unsaid? How can I make decisions on my own? And now, what do I do when I feel bad? Please, just a little longer!"

What happens when we lose our parents? After all, it is the norm in life, for each one of us gets old, gets sick, and then dies. But what if you have been so dependent on one or both of them that now you are alone? And what if the parent you are closest to dies and you are now left with the parent you either never got along with or whom you really never knew? How do you deal with this death?

They always were there for you, sometimes even too much, but even though you knew that you still wanted their advice. We all have to remember something, and that is that after a certain age, such as twenty-five or so, we no longer need parenting, despite the fact that we still might want it. Of course there will be great grieving for this loss, but when were you supposed to start making decisions on your own? When were you going to start being capable of choosing a partner without the need for anybody's "okay" but your own?

We all lose our parents, and at some point we will lose both of them! We will be orphans, in a matter of speaking, but that is the course of life and we cannot stop it! We all have to recognize this and we need be thankful for the amount of time that we did have with our parents rather than mourn what we have lost to the point that we are incapable of carrying on in our own lives.

Maybe you will actually find a partner in life now because your parents are no longer around to keep you "safe" and in the role of a child. Now maybe there is a need for you to have your own family that didn't exist while your parents were still here. As hard as this is to hear, it is the truth!

Sometimes we leave things undone with our folks, and that is very hard. When a parent dies and you have had a poor relationship with them but you still served them well, it is possible to resolve that anger after they have died. If you were angry at them and you ignored them,

LARRY ROBINSON

or if when you spoke to them you found that you just couldn't stand the constant whining and complaining to the point where you distanced yourself from them, then you are left with guilt. When this happens there really is no resolution for feeling guilty. You need to accept what the relationship was and accept that neither of you realized what needed to be worked out. This is the sad part.

If your parents are still here, then maybe you can do better with them. Remember, they cannot change at this point, only you can! When parents die we are "free" only to the extent that we allow ourselves to be. It is really the time that we can be adults instead of someone's child!

Assignment: We all will lose our parents one day. Write a letter to each of them and tell them what they have or have not meant to you. If they have passed, write a letter about missing them or not.

_____

_____

_____

_____

_____

_____

_____

_____

_____

_____

_____

_____

DECEMBER 4

"Did you see how she talked to her children? I can't imagine how those kids feel. She didn't even give them a chance to speak. What a terrible mother she is!"

"Look at the way he promotes his child in Little League. He's the league president, so why should his kid get special preference? I don't care if his kid is that good, he should show by example that his child gets no extra promotions!"

How often have we heard these kinds of "judgments" made by others or even by ourselves? They are passed daily by the majority of us and without any thought about what we are really saying! We are passing judgments on others and we feel no remorse or "afterthought" about what we are doing. It becomes part of our everyday conversation with others, and they "participate" as much as we do.

Why are we a society that needs to feel better than others? Do we feel that much less? So much of our life is spent either trying to feel better than others or feeling like we are not as good as the rest of the world. Where did this idea come from? Were we raised with this notion that we needed to be better than others? How did your parents feel about themselves? Were they jealous people who made themselves feel better by putting down others and never acknowledging the success of others without a negative criticism attached? Did they throw it in your face about the success of other kids and your lack of it? Do you do this to your children?

Comparing children is so unfair, for each child is different from the rest. Do you see your child as unique and a success in his or her own right, or do you look at them and wish they were more like other children you may know? Do you judge people by how much income they have or by the car they drive? Do you judge people? And how do you feel about others judging you? After all, what's fair is fair, so why should you go without judgment when you spend so much time giving your opinions about others? What kind of world do you want to live in?

It is easy to say, "Well, everyone does it," and you are probably right, but that doesn't make it acceptable. Think about how you want others to see you! Better yet, think about how *you* want to see you! Thinking in terms

LARRY ROBINSON

of love and compassion toward others can feel so much better than finding fault in order to raise yourself up. There is no one who is better or worse than you. We each are different and in different places in life. Encouraging each other is so much more productive than putting people down!

Take this time in your life to stop the comparisons and negativity. Give your child the praise they need so very much for whatever they do that is good. Make your family a place where each person feels their value! Never let anyone, adult or child, go to bed with a "stinging" in their ears about how they were judged. Who are we to judge?

Question: How has your negativity affected your interactions with others? Do you feel lonely so much of the time for it seems as if people keep away from you? Do your judgments keep coming back even when you promise yourself not to judge?

_____

_____

_____

_____

_____

_____

_____

_____

_____

_____

_____

"What brought us together? Was it the incredible physical connection that we had together? Was it the fact that we could talk to each other so easily as if we had been friends all our lives?" What brought us together, for today it feels so different?

The way people first meet is not the way their relationship will be. All relationships go through different stages of development, which are the same as for a child growing up. We have the "infancy stage," where all we did was "coo" and smile and touch each other. It was like a dream in which we were never so happy, nor did we want for anything. There were no worries, and we responded to each other as if we lived in our own world.

The next level was the "toddler stage," where we took tiny steps toward talking about the word *love*. We did not want to rush things, and it was very wobbly but we managed to stand up together and hold each other. It was the beginning of knowing what really felt right about being together. We could agree on practically anything, and if we didn't, no problem. And it was easy to *give* to the other person.

Next we ventured into the "latency stage" of our relationship, where we really loved being together but needed our friends just as much. We were very confused about how to balance both at the same time. One of us always allowed the other to "Do what you need to, it is fine," and it was meant with sincerity as long as attention was still paid to the us. Going out with the guys or girls was still our "playtime" and we needed it. In fact, both of us needed it. And even though we still might rather be with one another, we had great friendships and we didn't want to lose them.

As we entered the "teenage years" in our relationship, we started to see that the "perfect dream" was not so perfect after all. We started to see each other as different from when we first met, and "different" took on a whole new attitude. What we perceived to be communication in our infancy stage was now gone, and we were left with an empty feeling that told us we were not being understood by our partner. The sense of togetherness was fading, and we were spending more time apart than together. Rationalizing as best as we could, we slipped through this stage confused and with a growing uneasy feeling of "What is going on?"

As we entered the "adult stage" and "marriage," we realized, after the "party" was over how unhappy we really were and how lonely the relationship had become. We wanted more than what we had and we were so disappointed in who each other had "become." But wait, this relationship was taken for granted. Each one of us took the other for granted! There were no talks about how each of us was feeling, and if there were they were ignored!

There was something else, however, that we did not recognize when we "fell in love," and that was a piece of that chemistry that we were reminded of constantly inside of ourselves. It was a feeling that was very old and very scary, for we were dealing with our parents' traits inside us, and our spouse was dealing with this too. We were drawn unconsciously to the other person by our history. We were meant to be together. It was almost as if your spouse's father married your mother, or vice versa. And how many times had you said that you would never be like your father or mother?

We are together in life to learn to "shed" those parts of ourselves that we hated in our father or mother and that we have, like it or not, become. The only person who can tell us that is the person we married, because they do know us. Truth is, they know us better than anyone! They see and feel the ugly pieces of us that come out, which, though once hidden, have now been exposed. Good! We need this to happen so that we become better people and rid ourselves of the negativity we inhaled from our parents as children.

Do not despair, for you must go through this! If you don't, you will leave this marriage blaming the other person. While if you choose to stay and work on being honest and genuine with each other, you will find the true love you thought you had. Your children will also see how a relationship can and does work! You will both leave this life knowing what it meant to truly love and be loved! How much better can it get?

Assignment: What are some of the factors that brought you together with your past or current relationship? Was it love at first sight or a slow getting to know one another? Are you the type of person that falls in love with love?

LARRY ROBINSON

DECEMBER 6

A ren't we all looking to be better parents than our own were? Didn't we swear that we would never do what our parents did to us? We are going to be the new generation of parents who give love and more consistent attention than we got. God help us if we let our child cry the way our parents let us cry. Why wouldn't it be okay for our child to sleep in our bed? Hell, we could never assume to charge into our parents' bedroom and demand to sleep with them. Their room was sacred!

Why would parents want privacy and a place to talk alone or be intimate? It is outrageous for us to even imagine that our children need their own room and their own bedtime. They need to be able to make decisions at age two, like when they "decide" to go to bed. We need to be able to stand behind their decisions in order that they respect us more than we respected our parents for demanding that we have a specific bedtime. Under no circumstances are we allowed to sleep in their bed. We are stronger than our parents because we do not need to sleep through the night! We enjoy the fact that our children can kick us and slap our faces as they push us to the edge of the bed. And as for them crying, no child should cry if they want us! We pick up our children at the first sign of crying and soothe their little hearts. We cannot imagine how upset they can get from throwing a tantrum and gasping for breath until we rush in and save them. We feel that this is traumatic for a child and can scar it for life.

We see how awful our parents were at parenting and how much better our children are. We were a little afraid of our parents and we would never talk back to them without severe consequences. Now we want our children to be our "equals" and to yell at us when they feel we are wrong. They will have the final say, and we will listen to their complaints and treat them as equals! Our children will voice their negative opinions to our friends and family because they should not be considered "less than," no matter how rude they are!

This is the "new manifesto." It says, "Attach your child to your hip and never put it down." And after all of this we now know that we are "better" parents than our parents were. Just ask our children. But wait,

I forgot. They have a "Do not disturb!" sign on their door and they will be very upset if we bother them. Please wait for them to finish, and then we can ask them if they think we are cool!

Question: What kind of parent are you? Do you give in too much as a way of avoiding conflict, or are you too strict? If you are not a parent yet, what traits do you think you need to have?

_____

_____

_____

_____

_____

_____

_____

_____

_____

_____

_____

_____

LARRY ROBINSON

December 7

Why do I feel so alone in parenting? What happened to that dream we shared about raising beautiful, wonderful children and having a great family and a better one than we grew up with? Why did you think that I knew more about parenting than you did? Wherever did you get that idea? I have been given all of the responsibility for raising our children, and do not think for one moment that I do not feel your judgmental looks when you get home and I am frazzled! I hear the tone in your voice at how frustrated you are with me!

You can walk through the door and be the hero while I am the villain all day. Even when I need your back because they just won't listen, I see you glance at them, conveying the message "wow," as if I am crazy. Well, you win! I am crazy, crazy to think that we are in this together!

When you come home all you do you complain about your day. What about mine? You take for granted every day that my role is easy compared to yours. Well, I am just as tired and just as beaten down as you are. I am the "shrew." I am the bad parent and you are the "loving" parent. Well, they outsmarted us. They play us off one another. I see it, why don't you? Oh, and I forgot, you want to be the good parent. You ask me why I am cold. You want to be close to me. Right! When you see my life and understand that I am the backbone of our family, then maybe I will stop resenting you. Do you get it?

Assignment: Do you need a question on this one or can you identify with this day? Explain!

_____

_____

_____

_____

LARRY ROBINSON

December 8

A major feeling that can hit us as we open our eyes in the morning is anger. We awaken to the scorching hot feeling that takes over our entire body and mind. This is our "demon," and we easily surrender to it. We are the victims of our own "stewing." We are cooking up our day before it even begins! What a delicious mess we are making.

And this is not just about the anger we experienced yesterday either. In fact, it is far from it. This is about all the anger that we have never dealt with! Some of us have such a difficult time dealing with it that we rush to sadness and despair, but the truth be told, we have been angry for such a long time that we cannot even remember when it first started!

Some of us can't even identify that it *is* anger, for we are burdened so quickly with the heaviness of our feelings that we cannot raise ourselves up to see the truth about what we feel. No one wants to be an angry person, and in some cases we feel we cannot even allow the feeling to happen inside of us. We walk around fighting our minds in an effort to stop the chatter inside our heads, but nothing works.

The truth is that nothing will work until we stop and recognize that we took the right to have these hot feelings away from ourselves. We pretend that everything is okay, but people are always asking us, "Are you all right?" And we always respond with a "Yes, I'm fine!" Until we are strong enough to face our anger, we'll continue to "cook" our feelings until we get to the point where cannot even determine what they are! All we will know is that we are not "fine"!

Be brave and start to think about the situations in your life that have caused you pain. You know they are there, and by at least recognizing them you free yourself enough to start to deal with them. Either you need to learn forgiveness or how to confront these painful situations. You can do it.

Assignment: Take one step at a time. Write down everything that bothers you and then go through them step by step. Determine which are valuable, as well as those that are not worth anything. Throw out the worthless ones and then let go and begin your emotional growth!

LARRY ROBINSON

DECEMBER 9

We have talked about sadness and anger when we awake in the morning, but there is one feeling that is the hardest of them all to face and that is fear! Do you wake up in the morning and open your eyes, and when they adjust to the light does a cold, empty chill meet you at that moment? Do you stare at the ceiling, unable to move? That is when you know "it" is here, "it" being that fear that you feel every morning when you wake up,

So many of us, whether male or female, have this sinking, hollow feeling upon rising each day. All the feelings of aloneness can overtake us in that moment. We now remember how truly lonely we are. Perhaps there once was some brightness, and maybe it was during a period when we thought that we were loved and loved back. But that time has since passed and all we have now is this emptiness in our hearts that we're supposed to use to fill ourselves up. But wait, we cannot fill what feels empty with nothing, for we have nothing inside! This is the ultimate fear, that we will be alone forever.

Sometimes we can feel as if nothing changes in our lives and that we are "destined" to be alone. This is what our mind says to us and it beats us up with the sound of the word "alone." Our hearts are so blocked that all we have left is our treacherous (dangerous) mind to listen to and it keeps saying, "No one wants you! No one will ever fill in this empty feeling that has been following you all your life. Face it, you are a loser."

Yes, you will be the "lonely person" if you allow yourself to listen to your mind! Fight the damning words it whispers in your ear and wake up and get out of bed and tell yourself, "I can be alone today! Today I will be all right."

All you need to do is to start! Do not wait a day longer or else you will prolong your own suffering and fear will be your companion. Say, "Get out, you damn fear . . . get out!" Let this be your new morning prayer or mantra, or whatever you want to make it. You are in control of how you feel! Do not let your fear control you!

Assignment: List in priority your fears from greatest to least bothersome. Which ones do you feel incapable of handling and keep coming up when you least expect them?

_____

_____

_____

_____

_____

_____

_____

_____

_____

_____

_____

_____

_____

_____

LARRY ROBINSON

December 10

Have we forgotten to remember our fellowman? Have we become so rude and detached that we fail to recognize human suffering? *Suffering* is not a matter of degree; it is instead a matter of "difference." We cannot determine who suffers worse than someone else. We cannot make that judgment. We don't even recognize when our own family or friends are suffering because we do not take the time to listen! We are too busy being greedy or selfish or angry to even bother. How did we become so shallow and uncaring?

It is a difficult life we all live, and for some there is only struggle and pain. We do not know what it feels like to not be able to feed our children or to have a roof over our heads. We are too worried about whether our golf game will take place or if we'll get accepted to a beach club. Do you ever wonder what someone who lives without heat or food might say to you?

Suffering is not about being popular or whether your golf game is off or whether you wake up with a hangover from a night of partying. Suffering knows that you will not know what tomorrow will be like! Suffering does not know whether you can feed your family or whether you will find a job. There are so many ways that people suffer. Why not take a moment and look in the mirror and ask yourself, "Can I consider myself a giving person? Do I take the time to remember that I am fortunate and others are not?" Maybe today you will learn something!

Assignment: Help someone today. This does not mean go and find someone. That person is right in front of you.

_____

_____

_____

_____

LARRY ROBINSON

DECEMBER 11

We don't get it! We do not understand what *violence* means, and we judge the world by it. We steer clear from judgment of ourselves by denying that we can have violent actions or even violent thoughts inside us. What makes us think that we're so special that the "buck stops there and not here"? Do you think that it is because we think we are too important?

How often have you screamed at your spouse and said things that you regret and that you would never want the world to hear? One might think from your words that you were violent. How many times have we snarled at our children and screamed things at them that would crush us if someone said them to us? There are children out there who hear things like, "I wish you were never born." Now, I am sure that most people who would say that type of thing probably assume that the child knows they don't really mean it, but can we really be sure about that? What if the child doesn't understand that and then goes to school and acts it out there? And then we say we have no idea why they behave the way they do! Right!

We have to get real and we have to think about who the next few generations of children will be. If you do not take a deeper look at yourself and realize that you are part of the world's problems through your private actions, then we are lost and we create more children who do not feel! It already is a cold world; do not create the Ice Age!

Question: Do you have a violent streak inside you? Does it scare you? Have people told you that your temper scares them?

_____

_____

_____

_____

LARRY ROBINSON

DECEMBER 12

No one is prepared for tragedy. We never can be. When we lose a loved one, no one can tell us that they "understand" how we feel, because *we* don't understand it! That unconscious insult goes right to our bones and we want to shout out, "Shut up!"

Each one of us is alone with our grief. And even though others share the grief, it is ours alone. Even our brothers and sisters cannot understand how we feel. Maybe we're harboring our own secret guilt that stems from something we were angry about and never resolved, but what we have to remember is that we have no control over life, and so the love we felt for this person will have to be enough.

We need to grieve; our strength is in our ability to let go and feel whatever we can over this loss. We will grieve for a long time, and when the time is right, we will also let go. But now is not that time.

Do not fear your feelings! Too many of us do. Weep, scream, and even condemn God if you need to! This is about you and no one else. What the rest of us can do is feel your pain and know that we are there when you need us. We will not belittle your feelings; instead, we will understand that these are yours and we will not take them away from you. We do understand!

Assignment: Have you lost someone and cannot get through the grieving process? Begin to talk to that person as if they were here and let them know how you feel about losing them. It is a beginning of the "letting go of grief" process.

_____

_____

_____

_____

LARRY ROBINSON

DECEMBER 13

Fidelity, what does it mean to each of us? Men and women can have different views of what it truly is. Who is right and who is wrong? A relationship can have only one answer, and that is when another person's feelings are hurt!

How can we say that just flirting around with others is okay when our partner or spouse is in pain over it? It can cause them to do sneaky things, such as checking cell phones, e-mails, and texts hoping that they will not find strange messages from people who think that it is okay to correspond with married or partnered people. What do you really think the goal is here for the person doing the snooping? Do you think they really want to find evidence of flirting, or are they hoping they do not?

What about emotional affairs? Is it okay to talk to a person of the opposite or same sex about your spouse or partner? If you are unhappy, why aren't you talking to each other? Sure, it is easy to talk to someone who can lend an ear, especially if they are single and want you, and you *do* know it! We all know when someone is interested in us, even if we are not in them. It feels so good to feel wanted!

Well, get over it, because you are putting your whole life at risk and your family cannot handle this trauma. The actual affair crosses every boundary there is, and only an extremely loving spouse or partner will be able to muster up the strength to tolerate it. But make no mistake, even if your spouse or partner is tolerant, they will never forget it and will not trust you for years to come. Is your life so meaningless that you're willing to risk everything for someone you don't really know? Think before you act. But if you do decide to proceed, be a genuine person and tell your spouse rather than have them go through the embarrassment of having to catch you!

Question: Have you ever contemplated having an affair? What brought you to that point? Are you still there? Do you believe that your fantasy of an affair will fix your pain?

LARRY ROBINSON

Jessa Mulman
Marblehead, Massachusetts, USA

"It is so frustrating trying to figure out what the other person *expects* from you. They expect that you should already know if you love them. It becomes vicious when you have little self-esteem and you think that you have no other way to love and be loved is to fulfill their expectations."

—Joanne Chisholm-Lake, Palm Bay, Florida, USA

December 14

D o you ever have to deal with someone in an argument or a fight who just won't answer you? Does it blow your mind that while you are full of heated emotions the other person seems to be somewhere in outer space? You could hit them over the head and they would still not respond! I bet it makes you angrier!

How are you supposed to deal with this when you are bursting with heated emotions? Sometimes we call this *passive-aggressive*. The "passive" part is when there is no response, and the "aggressive" part is that they know what your reaction will be! You fall into their trap so easily and you wind up looking like the insane person, while the other person sits whistling a happy tune. Now, maybe you might not look crazy, but to be sure on the inside you feel it.

"Rude" is not the word for this behavior, because each time you are upset you will not be heard. We say repetition without resolution means that each time we repeat something it gets harder to resolve. You have to be one step ahead and know how that other person will respond. Say what you need to say, and then walk away! Why stand there and look like the fool?

Now, you can bet that they will hear you, but they will also be expecting you to stay and try to fight. But surprise, surprise, you're not going to do that! You're going to walk away, and when you do it will send them a clear message that you are not willing to buy into their meanness any longer. And that's exactly what it is, *meanness*! Walk away, walk away, and walk away! Let them feel what it is like to stand there and feel stupid!

Question: How often have you let people take advantage of you? Why does this happen? Do you feel completely defeated and even indifferent to others?

LARRY ROBINSON

DECEMBER 15

So many of us do not realize that there is a connection between mind, body, and spirit. We think that only the privileged class talks like that, and that we cannot relate to it. And what does it really mean anyway? Is it some of that New Age bull that requires a translator in order for you to understand it? And why have so many people put so much stock in this, when just like the rest of us they are out partying all weekend but come Monday they act "holier than thou"? What does this concept mean, and how does something so strange even apply to us?

Let's start with *mind*. Your mind is separate from your brain. It is the one that talks to you in your head. Have your ever heard it say anything that is not damaging, judgmental, or negative? Do not believe that your mind is your friend! It is always whispering in your ear things that your gut tells you not to do. And since we hardly ever listen to our gut, we end up all too often realizing that we knew the right answer all along and chose to ignore it. When our mind is balanced, which means that we control it and are able to push away all the negative junk, then the mind is calm. Negative is out!

Next, let's look at *body*. What do you put into your body that is dangerous to both it and to your mind? Do you drink a lot, do drugs, or even overeat? Well, this definitely makes your body poisonous. We call it "toxic" because it not only throws your health into danger, but it also creeps into your mind and causes unneeded negativity. How can we feel positive when we are physically feeling either hung over from the booze, drugs, or food? And yes, overeating *does* give us a hangover. When we are care about our body, then we care about ourselves. And that is when our mind and body become balanced and calm.

Lastly let's look at *spirit*. What does this mean? Is there something greater and more powerfully good than us out there? Is this God, or is it something that we have no faith in but are just supposed to believe in right now? The truth is, *spirit* is what you believe it is. No one can make you believe in anything that you do not trust. Maybe spirit is a higher self in you, that part of you that knows the truth but is always ignoring it. Maybe spirit is a greater energy in you that allows you to fight for

LARRY ROBINSON

your good life. Whatever you want to call it, if it is missing from you then it leaves an empty space inside you. And make no mistake, your body and mind both feel that emptiness.

When you put your faith in a higher power, you bring calm to the "whole" you. This is your life journey. Do not think that you can successfully ride out the storms of misfortune into the true experience of goodness when you have no balance in your life! It just doesn't work that way!

Question: Do you understand what balance means? In what ways and situations is it missing in your life?

_____

_____

_____

_____

_____

_____

_____

_____

_____

_____

_____

Loneliness

by Marjorie Laderas Tiozon

Glancing at beautiful scenery
Watching those birds hanging on a tree
Seeing two people who are madly in love
Together with the feeling I can't bear to have
And I just have to look away
'Coz the tribute still hurts my way
Bursting tears that are always hiding;
Hiding in a place that no one can see
And it really means to me
Wind blows, suddenly it became dark
I'm still grieving and losing a spark
Clouds carrying a huge rain were about to pour
Still, my heart won't endure
As rain comes, small tears flowed through my eyes
Seems like a melting ice
I just can't help but to cry and groan
And it is so hard not having a companion
Just to understand my situation
Yelling at someone else to seek help
But no one was there to be kept
Everything sets to loneliness
And I think, it is helpless
The feeling of wanting someone to lean on
Keeping a promise, I'm still holding on
But I think, it's time to let go;
Then I wandered to the place where I am
I see a clearer view of someone approaching me
But in the end I was wrong; it vanished all of a sudden
Knowing the truth, it was only a mirage;
A mirage that never came true
How can I ease the crucial pain I have,
When the only thing I need is to love and be loved?
Fighting the urge of not wanting someone, but I lose

LARRY ROBINSON

The painful scenario is I just accept my real situation;
A situation that needs a hesitation
When does this heavy rain stop?
How many times do I have to go with its thousand drops?
I'm tired of waiting for someone;
Someone who will offer the umbrella just to protect me,
From the rain which is continuously landing through my eyes
So I walk away and leave this place
And I ended up in a mussed room
Glaring at the window; It's gloom
Outside, the rain hurled itself against the glass
Just then I realized as I looked down, both my hands were clinging
That was the time I, myself, was comforting my own loneliness . . .

DECEMBER 16

What does being in harmony with a spouse, partner, or family member mean? Do we even understand what the word really means? Actually, *harmony* can be defined as a natural goodness, and it is the opposite of a person who does not get along with himself/herself and he/she is always at war inwardly. How can we really get along with someone else? Until we reach that harmony within ourselves, we have a great difficulty being truly comfortable with another person. If we are constantly finding fault with others, then we are usually always finding fault with ourselves too. We can get bored and tired very easily, often even tired of life itself. If we do not find harmony within our own hearts, we cannot and will not find it in someone else.

Let's use an example of what is and is not harmony within a relationship. As we now know, we often find that we choose our opposite to be in a relationship with. The outgoing person meets an inward person, sometimes even an antisocial. The "neat-nick" meets the "mess-aholic," and the person who still has the first cent they ever made meets a person who has a spending addiction. Now, these are not harmonious, but we would go crazy in a relationship with someone just like ourselves. But we are always trying to change the other person to be more like we are. Remember, we cannot change someone else; we can only change our reaction to them. How often have you failed at trying to change someone and found yourself in a heated battle? There is no winner.

There was a couple, and she brought to the relationship her anxiety over her fear that there would never be enough money. She grew up in a house where money was always under lock and key. Her mother was a tightwad and she always went with very little. He grew up in a house in which money always caused bad arguments between his parents, for there was never enough. He disregarded the value of money and didn't care about spending. Was this relationship a setup for disaster?

Yes, it was. For many years all their real fights were about his spending and her anxiety over it. They fed one another and could not resolve the issue. It went round and round in a vicious cycle that almost ended their relationship. So how did they achieve harmony? They sat down one day after a huge fight and came to the realization that they fed one another. He fed her anxiety and she fed his spending, or vice versa. Achieving harmony, you see, would mean that she would work on her anxiety and he would work on his spending. They were finally in harmony with one another! He hated how he was always having to work to make up for the money he spent, and she was always regretful about what her anxiety did to the both of them. Now they had something that they could both work on.

Assignment: Sit down with your partner or spouse and figure out how you are opposites and the ways that you "trigger" each other. This is the first step toward bringing harmony to your relationship!

_____

_____

_____

_____

_____

_____

_____

_____

_____

_____

_____

December 17

Are you sad all the time or at least a majority of time? Do you hide this from family and friends? Are you disappointed with your life and feel like there is no outlet for your sadness? Do you think this is depression, or have you been sad all your life? Look back into your childhood and see if you were happy. Chances are you were not! Sadness is something that starts at a very early age, and it is different from depression. You see, when we are depressed we usually are holding down anger, but sadness is not about holding things in. Instead, it is about always being disappointed in life. Try to remember your first disappointment. It could have been a promise from your parents about going someplace and when the time came to go they didn't even remember telling you. What can a child do with that? At that age we really cannot get angry with our parents, at least not outwardly, and we turn the disappointment into sadness.

Maybe now you will understand that all the disappointments in your life have made you a very sad person. It is now almost as if we expect the negative result and say to ourselves, "I told you so," when things don't turn out the way we want them to. With all the negativity that we have stored, now we give off the vibe that, "I don't care if it isn't going to happen anyway. No one ever takes what I say I need or what I say I want seriously anyway, even though I always bring it up in advance to their making any other plans. But if you really don't want to do this, then it's okay with me."

Well, think about this. How would you deal with this person if the situation was reversed? Face it, your sadness (from your disappointment) has made you no fun to be with! It is time to hop on the change wagon and catch the negativity before it comes out and replace it with a positive vibe!

Question: Are you afraid of change? Have you unconsciously committed yourself to staying the same? Do you believe that you cannot change?

LARRY ROBINSON

DECEMBER 18

D o you tell yourself that you like being alone? Are you that person who is constantly telling yourself that you do not want or need a relationship, and that your dog or cat is enough for you? Do you hang with a group of singles who are also alone and who support you until one of them gets into a relationship and then they disappear from your life? Have you always thought that you were a loner and that you were much better off without the headaches that come with a relationship? How many relationships have fizzled during your life and each time you told yourself that you really didn't care for that person anyway? What about on the flipside, are you that person who was so wounded over a failed relationship that you are too afraid now to have another? You tell yourself that you never want to experience that pain again, but in reality you just never got over the breakup.

If this or any of these people are you, then you are never going to have a successful relationship. Oh sure, you might use someone for some companionship or sex, but without that *connection* you will definitely get bored. There will be no love in your life, and you are making sure of it! Now yes, there are people who are alone, but do you think that being alone is really the purpose of life? You just live by yourself, grow old by yourself, and then die. Doesn't that sound horrible?

Never give up on yourself! Why can't you handle the pain of a breakup when you were not happy with the relationship to begin with? So the other person went first and pulled the plug, and you couldn't handle the rejection of someone you supposedly loved? The truth is, chances are you probably wish that you had had the courage to end it first!

Growing up is difficult no matter what age we are. But if we keep repeating the same patterns it isn't the other person's fault: it's ours! We chose that person and we didn't do anything different from what we normally do, and that's the problem. We, once again, did not communicate our feelings and then we felt ripped off because we didn't. And better yet, we chose someone who was so screwed up that it made us look good. It is time to get on the ball and look at who you are in a

LARRY ROBINSON

relationship. Honestly, knowing yourself, would you be in a relationship with you? Try to remember this, that when you finally come around to liking who you are, you're going to have no problem meeting someone who is in the same place!

Question: How often have you wanted to leave a relationship and backed out on yourself? Are you afraid to be alone, or do you still have hopes to saving your relationship?

_____

_____

_____

_____

_____

_____

_____

_____

_____

_____

_____

_____

_____

DECEMBER 19

Is there a difference between laziness and depression? Do you think that you are a lazy person, or do you think that there is some underlying depression that causes your laziness? What do you think causes your laziness? Were you spoiled as a child and needed others to do things for you? Were you someone who always felt that you had to do things for everyone else and now you want it done for you? We do not have any idea that we are truly lazy, but we do feel entitled to have someone do something for us. Parents can put a lot of responsibility on children to do for them. You would not consider yourself lazy after a childhood of doing for others.

Do you lie in bed in the morning listening to the chaotic scene that is going on between your spouse and your children and not get out of bed? Your spouse can think of that as lazy, but do you? You are thinking of all the hassles that await you when you get to work, and you become frozen in that bed. You do not have to have a family to feel that stuck position. You can also be a single person, student, or married without children and not want to get up in the morning. The world sees you as lazy, but you do not. You know that you are repeating a bad place for yourself, but you do not want others to know how you feel. You are depressed over your life. There is no motivation in you to start your day. Your life seems not to be in your control, and all you can hear in your head is your name being called or the assignment that you didn't finish being called in, or your boss upset that you did not finish something. This is not laziness; this is called "defeat."

These are not new feelings to you, but rather ones that have plagued you for most of your life. In fact, many people have thought you were lazy, but now we know that they were wrong. Your sense of self has been off since as long as you can remember. You start things, but do not finish them. And with so many projects that go unfinished, why wouldn't folks see you as lazy? But wait, the real answer here is that you are defeated very easily. You never seem to be able to stay in the present, and instead are always rushing ahead into the future! And what you see there are all the things that you will not finish, so you figure, "Why should I bother to go any further?" Isn't it easier for you to let people

LARRY ROBINSON

think that you are disorganized or lazy rather than depressed? Well, stop it now and begin to face this issue yourself!

Laziness can be an offshoot of depression. We can "mask" our inadequacies by appearing to be lazy. You always needed to be pushed, and that was not laziness but needing encouragement, which you did not get! Fear now plays a big role in your life because you could not face things alone. Well, you are not a child anymore and there will no longer be someone there to hold your hand through finishing projects or work or responsibilities. Recognizing this issue is the beginning of following through with completion. This is one issue where no one can help you, so do not look for that support. In this case you need to give it to yourself. You need to take things one step at a time and guide yourself through each stage of completion until you have succeeded. You can do it!

Question: After reading this post, are you a lazy person or is there some underlying depression in you?

_____

_____

_____

_____

_____

_____

_____

_____

_____

DECEMBER 20

Are you a "right or wrong" person? Do you have an opinion and you will not change it no matter what? Do you end up in frequent arguments with your spouse, family or friends? What causes us to take that position and not be able to let it go? Have you ever found yourself cutting someone off who is trying to tell you what they think about something and you say, "No, I don't want to do that," before they even finish? So much of the time the other person will just give up, but will also harbor a barrelful of resentment toward us. What makes it so impossible for us to hear what someone else has to say?

Do you find yourself ever feeling bad because your behavior has caused the conversation to be over, and even though you apologize the other person tells you that they're not interested in your apology and that they are done with you? They stop wanting to participate in discussions. Is this because we are selfish, or is there something deeper going on? We certainly look selfish, but having everything our way is really not our goal. If that was the case, why would we bother talking to anyone?

This is about wanting to establish our identity. Unfortunately, and usually without even knowing it, we are using other people to validate ourselves. We sometimes need that control because we do not have it with others. We are wrong in our approach, because rather than create an identity that says "kind and flexible," we create one that says, "bully, and always right."

On this issue, you do not need to know *where* it comes from. It is just there. The question is, do you want to fix it or are you comfortable with it? The *fix* is to be able to listen to yourself and hear who you have become. This you can change, but remember, this is not a "want to want to" type of change, but rather an "I want to and I need to" change!

Question: Would you consider yourself someone who needs a lot of control? If so why?

LARRY ROBINSON

DECEMBER 21

What does trust mean? Do you truly trust another person's word, and can they trust yours? Does being trusted become hard for you when you have addictions that you are confronted with and you *lie* about what you are doing? Do you believe that your business is your business, even though it might affect your spouse's or partner's life?

Can you trust your spouse or partner to hold true to their promises, or do they continue to lie to you when you ask them not to get into your business? Do they have a right to do this because it causes them anxiety, even though it has nothing to do with them? Are we responsible for someone else's anxiety, and are they responsible for our shame? Do they hold themselves higher than you when they confront you with something that they told you they would not do? Do they use, "Because I needed to know" as their excuse? How can we be in a relationship in which promises are broken by both parties all the time?

There is something about these types of relationships that has a very strong effect on each person's *karma*. Karma is good or bad deeds that happen when we are or are not working on ourselves. There is a specific karma for relationships. Yes, it takes into account that each person brings into a relationship their own baggage, but unchecked it becomes part of the relationship. And we're not the only ones who need to work on our ability to tell the truth so that we can be trusted. Our spouse or partner needs to work on this too. If one person in the relationship holds themselves higher than the other, then the bad karma will continue. When each person is taking responsibility for their own actions, then the karma can be positive for they have changed the pattern of the relationship.

Remember, we meet people in life *for where we are at.* We do not meet someone who is better or worse than we are. This is life, so why would we want to be with someone who thinks they are better than we are? For that matter, why would *we* think that way? No, life gives us what we need to learn, not always what we want!

LARRY ROBINSON

Question: Do you believe that you were meant to meet your partner? Is there something that you believe was *spiritual* in your meeting? Explain!

_____

_____

_____

_____

_____

_____

_____

_____

_____

_____

_____

_____

_____

_____

_____

_____

December 22

Are we too concerned about how others see us in life? Do we sacrifice the feelings of our spouses and children to the image that we have created of how we want to be seen in life? Do we care too much about being the best rather than allow for human error or faults? Will you ever surrender your attachment to what other people might think of you, or are you committed to this way of life forever? When we place others' feelings about us before what is real, we live a false life. And because we place more importance on what the rest of the world sees, we are constantly hiding the truth. As a result of this, the truth that appears normal to the rest of the world no longer looks normal to us! We have to be better than everyone else in our circle of life.

Do you allow yourself to keep an open mind about what others see about your life? The answer to this question is usually no. Even in the face of tragedy we cannot let the world see us as weak. We keep that upper lip stiff no matter how devastated we really are, and we never air our dirty laundry. In fact, we never truly want the world to see that we have any dirty laundry or weaknesses. Usually it is when someone really close to us gets in trouble that the stage we live on collapses and we are exposed for who we really are. It is at this point that we're forced to make a conscious decision to either come clean or continue to hide our negative emotions from the world and instead wallow in a morass of self-despair behind closed doors. These are our attachments in life, and they drain us of feeling positive and free.

Can you free yourself from judging others' thoughts and ways of life, or are you so attached to them as a source of comfort that you cannot let them go? Perhaps we have needed these judgments to make us believe that we are better than we really are! What would we do without them? Are we *collectors* of people or things to give ourselves a better image in life? Do we believe that the more we have, the better we look? Can you let go of these attachments to find a less complicated way of life? All these attachments have done is created a truly difficult life for us. And so ask yourself this question: when our life is done, what do we really take with us? And the answer to that is that we take nothing!

LARRY ROBINSON

Question: Are you a judgmental person? If so, do you feel that you are always being judged?

_____

_____

_____

_____

_____

_____

_____

_____

_____

_____

_____

_____

_____

_____

_____

DECEMBER 23

C an you be alone? Can you be really alone and feel the peace that is presented to you, or do you get antsy and cannot sit still? Being alone means that there is no one there and it is not the same feeling as being lonely. When you are lonely you long for someone to be there, and being lonely is frightening to some people for they cannot sit with themselves. When this happens they take the opportunity to immediately let their loneliness and panic take over. And the panic can come in so many different ways that often we aren't even aware that we are panicked. We start cleaning or washing clothes, or we turn on the TV and start bingeing on our favorite substances. Oftentimes we take to the telephone and bug people for hours on end. Why does this happen to us? Why can't we sit in silence for a few moments and listen to our mind?

Oftentimes when we are left alone our inner anxiety about ourselves and our lives takes over and begins to stir up feelings that we do not want to deal with. These are not usually good feelings that arise, but past memories that we have repressed or run from. At times the anxiety blocks us from confronting those feelings and issues from the past, and this leaves us with unresolved feelings that we do not know how to deal with, and they frighten us! They might tell us what an awful person or bad child we are, or how bad a parent we are for something we did or thought. What we need to remember here is that we cannot resolve the past, but we can understand that we are not that person today! We all have to learn from our past in order to live more quietly in the present.

Assignment: Take some time and sit with yourself today. Listen to what your mind is trying to convince you of and fight back! Do not let your mind rule. Your heart is still kind and compassionate, and that is what matters. Learn that acquiring the ability to forgive yourself and others is what will ultimately give you the ability to be alone and at peace with yourself!

LARRY ROBINSON

_____

_____

_____

_____

_____

_____

_____

_____

_____

_____

_____

_____

_____

_____

_____

_____

_____

_____

DECEMBER 24

How are you with taking care of your money? Are you the type of person that saves constantly and does not allow yourself anything for fear that you will not have any money left for tomorrow? Maybe you are the type of person who is constantly insecure about money and you track your partner's finances to make sure that there is always enough money. Does this behavior cause arguments between the two of you? Do you like to go on shopping binges and tell yourself that you deserve it, or are you the type of person who has money "burn a hole through your pocket" and it slips right through your hands as soon as you receive it? Doesn't it feel "great" to have no money for the weekend? Are you always borrowing until your next paycheck and it has become a cycle that you cannot break? If nothing else, repeating this behavior over and over will not only leave you with the sense of shame that comes with never having any money, but it will also eventually lead you to feeling as if you have no security and no sense of a future.

Whether you want to believe it or not, you have a spending addiction! This is just as serious as any other addiction because it has the potential to ruin your life and bring your family down. We just don't recognize the amount of money we are spending. Some of us just go out there and buy things that we will really never use, too. How many of us have clothes in the closet with the price tags still on them? Do you think we will ever wear them?

Inside of us there is a giant hole that seems to never be filled. We buy in order to try to fill that hole up, but there never *is*, nor will there *ever be*, enough money or possessions to fill it up. Is it love that we're looking for? At one time that would have seemed like the right answer, but what if we get enough love from family and friends and still have this need to spend? Do you know the high you get when you buy something that you think you really want? It feels like a wonderful drug that takes us away from our problems and we can "spend till we drop." The problem is that the aftereffects are usually just as bad as waking up with a hangover, except a hangover eventually goes away but the bills don't.

LARRY ROBINSON

We need help, and that is the only way to fix this problem. We need a support system that is always going to be there to remind us of what the consequences will be while assuring us that the right path is for us not to spend. We need to change our lives now!

Question: Have you ever looked at your finances before and seen how much you really spend? Do you get shocked when you actually look at your spending and realize that you live beyond your means?

_____

_____

_____

_____

_____

_____

_____

_____

_____

_____

_____

_____

_____

December 25

What kind of day is today for you? Is it a quiet, contemplative day, or is it a day that feels like an anticlimax to all the running around you have done buying presents and baking goods? Did you buy for people you really wanted to, or did you put yourself in an obligatory position where you felt that you "had" to buy for some whom you do not even like? Are you overextended with both your money and your energy over just this one day of the year, or are you content with yourself because you love to give? Do you love giving presents? Why is that?

If you are not Christian but of another faith or even have no declared faith, what kind of day is this for you? Are you feeling left out of something truly important to so much of the world, or are you thankful for your own belief and wish others to be thankful for theirs? This time of the year can be very alienating for some, and it does bring up losses from our past, like relationships and people we loved who have passed on, or maybe we cannot afford the type of holiday that we really wanted.

Do not measure your self-worth by the amount of money you spent or the "greatness" of your presents. Value your ability to give, and not just for today but every day, because people are in need not only today but on an ongoing basis. Have you determined what "giving" really is, or are you stuck somewhere between guilt and anger about the feeling that you "have" to give? When you truly give from your heart, a most beautiful feeling will come over you. You will know this feeling, for it is "divine."

Assignment: Do you think that you can go through this holiday without spending so much money? Offer to do things for someone else as a present. List ways that you can give to people without spending needlessly.

DECEMBER 26

When is the partying in our life finished? How many of us keep saying that we'll deal with our alcohol or drug or whatever addiction we struggle with "tomorrow" and "tomorrow" just never seems to come? We might be the type of folks who don't even recognize our addiction and yet we are constantly hounded by our love ones to "put it down!" We believe that since we don't use very often we are not addicted. How many times a day do you think you want a drink or smoke or whatever your choice is? We can lie to ourselves, but we cannot lie to our heart, for it knows that we listen to our mind and that it gets overruled in that struggle. We are blinded by our belief that we can handle a little without ever being tempted to go further. That is, until we are lost again in the progression of our addiction.

What kind of excuses do we throw out to our family and friends about how we are just using occasionally? How angry do we get with them? We tell them it's their issue and not ours. And technically we are right; it is their issue for they cannot control what we do. They need help in understanding how and why they are so codependent on our disease that they block out what their own issues are, and we know it! They need their own program, like CODA, which is "Codependents Anonymous." This is where they get the support to either leave us alone and take care of themselves, or leave us for good because we choose drugs over our families.

What is the answer then? Do we throw out the "baby with the bath water" because we do not want to listen, or do we really take a look at what we are doing to not only our life but also to the lives of those dear to us? Do we affect our children? Will they grow up either looking to medicate themselves as we seem to do, or will they be adult children of an alcoholic and have many of their own unwanted issues to deal with later in life? This is our future, and the damage that we later deal with is so horrific that it can push us deeper into our own darkness.

Assignment: Please, look at *you*, not what others tell you. You are the only one who really knows. How many times in the past have you lied to yourself, never mind to others? No one can tell you who you are! Only you can do that! It is so important to accept who we are so we can change ourselves!

_____

_____

_____

_____

_____

_____

_____

_____

_____

_____

_____

_____

_____

DECEMBER 27

The dark side of us! How cruel it is to our heart, for it wipes away our goodness and leaves us in despair. The dark side is our innermost thoughts that no one really knows except when we explode and all the negativity that we have stored up inside comes rushing out, flooding us with mean and abusive thinking and even actions! This side of us is the horror movie inside our heads that we are the producers and directors of.

Everything that is negative and scary about how we think is stored in the dark side. We can call this our "subconscious," and it is not a pretty place; it is our *demon*! If we allow it to control us, we are doomed to have pain in our life. When we were children and we could not label our angry and rage-driven feelings, it became our bogeyman that caused us to have horrific nightmares. The bogeyman was real to us then and it is real now.

The thing that is different now from when we were children is that we are strong enough to not let it control us. We have the strength of our hearts to fight off its isolating effects. We cannot avoid the dark side for it is there inside of us, but we can recover from it quickly when we can identify it. Remember it is where our jealousy, rage, hate, speaking badly about others (the list can go on and on), is hidden. We are the only ones that can change this. Recovery is our only salvation!

To start the recovery process we need to begin to practice kindness and compassion. For the next three days we will not allow ourselves to say anything unkind about another person. This is difficult because we have no awareness even that we are doing it. It is almost as if we have incorporated negativity as a way of life.

We also will not tell a lie. This might seem absurd, but do you realize that we tell little lies all the time? We do not need to tell people our problems, but how often has someone asked you, "How are you?" and the answer was "fine" when that was not the case. Just say, "I could be better but I am working on it!"

Remember that the dark side is part of our journey. We are certainly not perfect, but who said that we could not do better? Begin your healing!

LARRY ROBINSON

Question: Do you find yourself having difficulty staying out of the dark side? Do you look at life with a negative approach, or do you give yourself a chance to see it with an open heart and mind?

_____

_____

_____

_____

_____

_____

_____

_____

_____

_____

_____

_____

_____

_____

_____

December 28

Are you someone who has positive willpower? Do you set a goal and drive yourself until you finish it? Maybe you are that person who has a really gung-ho attitude and who even builds up tremendous anxiety and excitement to start this new challenge, but as soon as you run into trouble you bag the whole idea. Can you easily convince yourself that now is not your best time to start a diet, give up cigarettes, get to the gym, or stop any of the bad habits and addictions you currently have? Do you tell yourself that you will get to it later when your energy is better? There is just one problem: once you fail at it the first time you do not really want to fail again. You have lost that willpower that was so essential in your ability to start things in the first place. Did you really want to *have* the willpower, or were you kidding yourself and unconsciously working against success? Remember that success in itself is not impossible to achieve, it is maintaining it that is really the core problem. You need that willpower for a very long time in order to maintain your success.

In order to achieve your goals, you cannot kid yourself. Willpower is an energy that we create that is our determination and drive combined, and it allows us to continue along the path of success no matter what obstacles we are presented with. In fact, there is no challenge we'll encounter that is not going to require willpower. The greater the will we have, the greater the energy we create to find our right path. There really is nothing that we cannot accomplish. There is no addiction or bad habit that we cannot let go of!

We all tend to take on too much to start with. Who told us that we had to be perfect and stop all bad our habits at once? "Today I am going to go on a diet, give up cigarettes, stop smoking pot, and start working out for the New Year!" Sure you are! And while you are doing all of these tasks, I suppose you want to change your job or move too? Do you see how we can sabotage our own will? Do not think that you do not have enough energy for success. Your willpower has become frozen because you overloaded it. Slow down; take one thing at a time. If you want to go on a diet, find one to start with that will not be so difficult.

LARRY ROBINSON

Find one that doesn't force you to give up too many of the foods you love. So what if you only lose six pounds in six weeks? Later you can take something else away from your favorites list and apply that to this diet. For each addiction or bad habit, go slow but steady, and you will discover a willpower that you never knew you had!

Question: Do you believe enough in yourself to accept you and let go of negative behaviors? Which behavior will take the most willpower for you to let go?

_____

_____

_____

_____

_____

_____

_____

_____

_____

_____

_____

_____

_____

Why do we allow people in our lives that hurt us? Why is it that we cannot stay away from them? We know that they are poison to us, but we cannot seem to let go. Every time we catch them in a lie, they persuade us to take them back and they swear they never will do it again. How many times have you heard that statement and given them another chance, only to be hurt again? And we're the ones who end up feeling crazy because somehow they continuously convince us that we are at fault for their lies or cheating ways!

These people manipulate us by telling us that we're not good enough partners, or they concoct these lame excuses, like "I just never had enough experience because you were my first, and I needed to find out if I truly wanted you. Now I know I do." And we buy into these crazy excuses hook, line, and sinker every single time! Now, invariably we come to our sense soon afterward and we call ourselves stupid and out of our minds for falling for it again, but we still continue to do it!

We *do* have something wrong with us. And it is *us*, not them. They are just being who they are! If you think that they have never done this before, then you are sadly mistaken. How would you know whether or not they have been honest at all with you during the course of the whole relationship? Remember, people who lie usually always lie in relationships. It is second nature to them. They know that we will take them back, so making a promise they have no intentions of keeping is nothing more than simple words to them. And the worst part is that we already know this!

So let's get some wisdom today. Do not let your mind tell you it was just one mistake. Remember, your mind is not your friend. When you are being mindful you control your mind from fooling you and you look to your gut instead for the right answers. Your gut always tells you the truth. But do we ever listen to it?

Question: Do you listen to your inner voice that tells you negatives about life? Are you seduced by the outside world to always please others, thinking that there will be some reward for your attending to others even when you do not like some people?

DECEMBER 30

Part one of this season is over and now we all celebrate the coming new year together. Muslim, Jew, Christian, Hindu, or whatever your faith is or is not, ushering in the new year is truly the one common event that we all celebrate. Have you looked at this past year and seen who you have been and what your feelings and behaviors were? Was it a good year or a difficult year, or did you even bother to think about it? If you take your life as a journey, then it is so important to learn from this past year. Stop right now from making promises to yourself about this coming year until you look more closely at this past year.

Sure, you can tell yourself that you will go to the gym, lose weight, stop smoking and drinking, or cut off any addictive behaviors, but what is the real message of a new year? What kind of person have you really been this year? Are you someone who angers quickly and says hurtful things without realizing the consequence to another person? Are you someone who swallows their feelings and pretends not to be upset about something, while in reality you cannot let go of the stewing in your head? Are you a fair person, and one who has empathy and compassion? These are not part-time feelings or "once in a while" aspects of your life, but instead ones that are always there. The real resolve in our lives is truly not about stopping an action like smoking and drinking (although both worthwhile), but to better ourselves as a person.

Have you ever heard of the term "soul work"? Your "personality work" might include going to the gym, working harder at your job, or even promising yourself you will save more, but "soul work" is the deeper, *unconscious work* that we need to bring to the surface to help us on our journey to a richer life. And by "richer life" I do not a material one, but instead a "higher level" one. Now, this does not mean that if you do not believe in God that you have no work to do. What it means is that in all of us there is a higher self, and that it constantly needs our attention if we are to become better people.

If you have been faithfully following *Mirror, Mirror* for almost a full year now, then I can tell you right now that you have grown. And if you need further evidence, just simply go back and look at your writings,

LARRY ROBINSON

your notes, and your thought process and you will see the difference for yourself. And even for those of you who haven't been completely faithful (shame, shame), the fact that you keep coming back means that the growth that you have experienced is already leading you toward *becoming* a better person. You see, we are here together in this life, and therefore it is critical that we realize that we can grow together! So let's all join together in making this coming year a "soul year" in which we all enrich our souls!

Question: Do you see the growth that has occurred in your life? Describe it! Write about any changes that you see that you have made. Good for you!

_____

_____

_____

_____

_____

_____

_____

_____

_____

_____

_____

_____

_____

DECEMBER 31

Do you believe in *karma?* Do you really know what it is? There is a principle of cause and effect in nature that dictates that if you keep destroying what is natural and beautiful, soon there will be only ugliness left. *Karma* is not a religious word, but many religions and philosophies believe that it exists. Accepted science actually believes in the cause-and-effect law, in that it states that for every action there is an equal and opposite reaction. The Judeo-Christian Bible says, "Evildoers shall be punished and the good rewarded." Do you believe this? So many of us have been taught as children that if we are good then we will go to heaven, while if we are bad we'll go to hell. Do you believe that there are true consequences for deeds that we do, either good or bad?

The technical part is over, and now we can talk about the emotional/mental aspect of *karma*. Do you believe that we shape our own destinies, and that ultimately we are the creator of our own world? Let's assume that we do. I know that some of you will disagree, and you should if you do not believe in these words. But for those of you who do, do you know that thoughts can create karma also? You see, a thought has its own energy attached to it, and because we are human we allow ourselves to have the worst thoughts at times about our lives and even other people. We can appear to be agreeable, but inside we can become very angry and nasty. This has karma attached to it. Now, since we are always trying to be well-intentioned in life, we hardly ever think that our own actions are bad. But what if you, even unintentionally, create problems for others. Do you believe that it will cause you disharmony? Take a good look into your life. Find the action of "what goes around comes around" and you will begin to see the truth about karma.

Tomorrow is the start of a new year. You really are the creator of your own destiny. How do you want this year to be? Do you want it to be the same as last year, or are you now trying to be mindful about life? You are in the process now of acquiring the skills that will allow you to create a better life for yourself just by questioning your own actions. So when you think about resolutions, think in terms of karma, for "what

LARRY ROBINSON

you sow, so you shall reap!" May you have the best karma for the coming year; you deserve it.

Assignment: Set one goal for the coming year. Just one and begin to work on it.

_____

_____

_____

_____

_____

_____

_____

_____

_____

_____

_____

_____

_____

_____

_____

Stephanie Cavallo, Falmouth, Massachusetts, USA

Death clouds the thoughts
Sadness fills the mind, darkness
Encompasses the vision, sins
Obscure the judgment, faith fades
And love dies.
But God, God heals you and me
Forgiveness will be distributed to all
Who ask for it.
God loves you, you mustn't forget it!

Anakin Fleming, Peabody, Massachusetts, USA

Edwards Brothers Malloy
Oxnard, CA USA
November 7, 2014